Romantic Reformers
and the Antislavery Struggle
in the Civil War Era

On the cusp of the American Civil War, a new generation of reformers, including Theodore Parker, Frederick Douglass, Harriet Beecher Stowe, Martin Robison Delany, and Thomas Wentworth Higginson, took the lead in the antislavery struggle. Frustrated by political defeats, a more aggressive Slave Power, and the inability of early abolitionists such as William Lloyd Garrison to rid the nation of slavery, the New Romantics crafted fresh, often more combative approaches to the peculiar institution. Contrary to what many scholars have argued, however, they did not reject romantic reform in the process. Instead, the New Romantics roamed widely through romantic modes of thought, embracing not only the immediatism and perfectionism pioneered by Garrisonians but also new motifs and doctrines, including sentimentalism, self-culture, martial heroism, romantic racialism, and Manifest Destiny. This book tells the story of how antebellum America's most important intellectual current, romanticism, shaped the coming and course of the nation's bloodiest – and most revolutionary – conflict.

Ethan J. Kytle is Associate Professor of History at California State University, Fresno. He was a postdoctoral Fellow at the Avery Research Center for African American History and Culture in Charleston, South Carolina, and has been awarded the Mary Kelley Prize by the New England American Studies Association.

Romantic Reformers and the Antislavery Struggle in the Civil War Era

ETHAN J. KYTLE
California State University, Fresno

CAMBRIDGE UNIVERSITY PRESS

CAMBRIDGE
UNIVERSITY PRESS

32 Avenue of the Americas, New York NY 10013-2473, USA

Cambridge University Press is part of the University of Cambridge.

It furthers the University's mission by disseminating knowledge in the pursuit of education, learning and research at the highest international levels of excellence.

www.cambridge.org
Information on this title: www.cambridge.org/9781107426986

First published 2014
First paperback edition 2016

A catalogue record for this publication is available from the British Library

Library of Congress Cataloguing in Publication data
Kytle, Ethan J.
Romantic reformers and the antislavery struggle in the Civil War era / Ethan J. Kytle.
pages cm
Includes bibliographical references and index.
ISBN 978-1-107-07459-0 (hardback)
1. Antislavery movements – United States – History – 19th century.
2. Abolitionists – United States – Biography.   3. Social reformers – United States –
Biography.   4. Romanticism – Political aspects – United States – History – 19th century.
5. Romanticism – Social aspects – United States – History – 19th century.   6. Slavery
in literature.   7. Antislavery movements in literature   8. American literature – 19th
century – History and criticism.   9. United States – Intellectual life – 19th century.
10. United States – Politics and government – 1815–1861.   I. Title.
E449.K97   2014
326´.8097309034–dc23   2014010079

ISBN 978-1-107-07459-0 Hardback
ISBN 978-1-107-42698-6 Paperback

Contents

Illustrations

Acknowledgments

Although writing history often feels like a solitary venture, the truth is that this book was in many ways a team effort. I am happy to be able at last to thank my team.

The rough outline of this project emerged in my first few years of graduate school at the University of North Carolina at Chapel Hill. I am grateful to the faculty in the Department of History, especially Peter Coclanis and Judith Bennett, whose leadership made Chapel Hill a fantastic place for graduate study. Charlie Capper, who directed the doctoral dissertation that became this book even after he left UNC for Boston University, proved an ideal advisor for me, balancing patience, support, and constructive criticism. I also want to thank the rest of my dissertation committee – John Kasson, Don Mathews, Philip Gura, and Lloyd Kramer – for their incisive comments and the Dead Mule Writing Group – Matthew Brown, Joshua Guthman, Susan Pearson, and David Voelker – for their thoughtful feedback, good humor, and, most of all, flexible deadlines.

I am indebted to UNC's Department of History and Graduate School for early financial support of my work as well as the Avery Research Center for African American History and Culture at the College of Charleston for a postdoctoral fellowship that enabled me to begin to rethink this project. I completed my revisions – which proved more substantial than I ever imagined – at California State University, Fresno (CSUF), a teaching university that nonetheless provides ample support for faculty engaged in research. I am grateful to Dean Luz Gonzalez, the College of Social Sciences, and Provost William Covino for the research funding and course releases that allowed me to finish the book.

I must also thank Cambridge University Press and my editors Eric Crahan and Deborah Gershenowitz. Eric saw early promise in my work and was remarkably patient as I revised the manuscript, while Debbie enthusiastically embraced the project after she joined the Press. She and her colleagues at Cambridge, especially Jeanie Lee and Dana Bricken, guided my book to publication with the perfect blend of professionalism, advice, and encouragement. Bob Schwarz did a fantastic job with the index. I am also grateful to the anonymous reader who examined my unrevised dissertation many years ago as well as the two anonymous readers of the final manuscript. Their feedback improved my book markedly.

I would like to acknowledge the various venues where I first tested out many of my arguments as well. I have had the opportunity to present papers at the UNC Department of History Research Colloquium; the Triangle Intellectual History Seminar; the Annual Society for Utopian Studies Meeting; the Organization of American Historians Annual Conference; the Heroism, Nationalism, and Human Rights Conference at the University of Connecticut, Storrs; the Annual International Conference on Romanticism; the Interdisciplinary Nineteenth Century Studies Annual Conference; the Society for Historians of the Early American Republic Annual Meeting; and John Remembered: 150th Anniversary of the Raid on Harpers Ferry Conference at Harpers Ferry, Virginia. I appreciate the instructive feedback offered by my fellow panelists, the commentators, and other participants at these meetings.

Parts of this book have appeared as "From Body Reform to Reforming the Body Politic: Transcendentalism and the Militant Antislavery Career of Thomas Wentworth Higginson," *American Nineteenth Century History* 8 (Sept. 2007): 325–350 and "'A Transcendentalist Above All': Thomas Wentworth Higginson, John Brown, and the Raid at Harpers Ferry," *Journal of the Historical Society* 12 (Sept. 2012): 283–308, as well as on the *New York Times*'s "Disunion" blog. I am grateful to Taylor & Francis, Blackwell Publishing, and the *New York Times* for granting me permission to reuse this material.

Susan Pearson, Dan Malachuk, Dean Grodzins, Vernon Creviston, and Blain Roberts read portions of the revised manuscript and Kyle Behen and Jackson Kytle read the whole thing. All of them helped make the book better. So, too, did my CSUF students and colleagues, as well as the interlibrary loan staff of Henry Madden Library and archivists at more than a dozen libraries and special collections, from California to South

Carolina, Boston to New Orleans. Thanks to Amy Noel, Scott Hough, Neal Polhemus, and Christina Rae Butler for research assistance.

I am also grateful to my friends who have kept me going – even if that has meant distracting me from the book – over the past decade. From my Chapel Hill days: Matthew Brown, Leah Potter, Josh Nadel, Eva Canoutas, Susan Pearson, Mike Kramer, Joel Revill, Matt Andrews, Adam Tuchinsky, Jen Tuchinsky, Hans Muller, Jen Muller, David Sartorius, Mariola Espinosa, Marko Maunula, Spencer Downing, Steve Hall, Steve Wuhs, Peter Coclanis, Deborah Coclanis, Natalie Fousekis, Mike Ross, and Stacy Braukman. From Charleston: Jack Porter, Jason Solinger, Joelle Neulander, Kurt Boughan, Bo Moore, Don Wright, and Doris Wright. And from Fresno: Brad Jones, Flo Cheung, Dan Cady, Lisa Bennett, Kyle Behen, Alex Espinoza, Lori Clune, Maria Lopes, Alice Daniel, Ben Boone, Bill Skuban, Nora Chapman, John Farrell, Jeff Cummins, Frederick Vermote, and Gemma McLintock.

Most of all, however, I would like to thank my family. I could not ask for better in-laws than Ron and Martha Lou Roberts. They are bright, supportive, and fun – plus they have an apartment in the French Quarter! My sister Josi amazes me with her enthusiasm and creativity. She has a keen marketing mind, is the world's greatest aunt, and, much as I hate to admit it, the best skier in our family. I am also amazed by my parents, Tari Prinster and Jackson Kytle, whose immense talents and diverse interests are matched only by their love for their children. As for my own children, Eloise and Hazel, I must say that they slowed down this book significantly – and I wouldn't have had it any other way. Nothing picks me up after a frustrating day of writing like hearing them laugh or seeing them smile. Finally, I must thank Blain Roberts, who not only is my spouse, colleague, and frequent coauthor but also works in the office right next to mine! I often joke to my students that the classroom is my only place of refuge from my ever-present wife, but, truth be told, I never really need a break from her. And for that I am not only grateful but also truly lucky.

Abbreviations

Names

FD   Frederick Douglass
HBS   Harriet Beecher Stowe
MRD   Martin Robison Delany
TP   Theodore Parker
TWH   Thomas Wentworth Higginson

Sources

ASAOS   Theodore Parker, *Additional Speeches, Addresses, and Occasional Sermons*, 2 vols. (Boston: Little, Brown, 1855)

BAP   C. Peter Ripley et al., eds., *The Black Abolitionist Papers*, 5 vols. (Chapel Hill: University of North Carolina Press, 1985–1992)

BAPC   George E. Carter, C. Peter Ripley, and Jeffrey Rossbach, eds., *The Black Abolitionist Papers, 1830–1865* [microfilm collection] (Sanford, NC: Microfilming Corporation of America, 1981)

CWJ   *The Complete Civil War Journal and Selected Letters of Thomas Wentworth Higginson*, ed. Christopher Looby (Chicago: University of Chicago Press, 2000)

FDP   *The Frederick Douglass Papers, Series One: Speeches, Debates, and Interviews*, eds. John W. Blassingame and John R. McKivigan, 5 vols. (New Haven: Yale University Press, 1979–1992)

FDPAW   *The Frederick Douglass Papers, Series Two: Autobiographical Writings*, eds. John W. Blassingame, John R. McKivigan, and Peter P. Hinks, 2 vols. (New Haven: Yale University Press, 1999–2003)

FDPC   *The Frederick Douglass Papers, Series Three: Correspondence, Volume 1, 1842–1852*, ed. John R. McKigivan (New Haven: Yale University Press, 2009)

JMN   *The Journals and Miscellaneous Notebooks of Ralph Waldo Emerson*, eds. William H. Gilman et al., 16 vols. (Cambridge, MA: Harvard University Press, 1960–1982)

LBA   *Autobiography of Lyman Beecher*, ed. Barbara Cross, 2 vols. (Cambridge, MA: Harvard University Press, 1961)

LCTP   John Weiss, *The Life and Correspondence of Theodore Parker, Minister of the Twenty-Eighth Congregational Society*, 2 vols. (New York: D. Appleton, 1864)

LHBS   *Life of Harriet Beecher Stowe, Compiled from Her Letters and Journals*, ed. Charles Stowe (Boston: Houghton, Mifflin, 1890)

LTH   *The Letters and Journals of Thomas Wentworth Higginson, 1846–1906*, ed. Mary Thatcher Higginson (Boston: Houghton, Mifflin, 1921)

LWFD   *The Life and Writings of Frederick Douglass*, ed. Philip S. Foner, 5 vols. (New York: International Publishers, 1950–1975)

MDR   *Martin R. Delany: A Documentary Reader*, ed. Robert S. Levine (Chapel Hill: University of North Carolina Press, 2003)

OSR   *The Oxford Harriet Beecher Stowe Reader*, ed. Joan D. Hedrick (New York: Oxford University Press, 1999)

SAOS   Theodore Parker, *Speeches, Addresses, and Occasional Sermons*, 2 vols. (Boston: Crosby and Nichols, 1852)

SLL   Annie Fields, *Life and Letters of Harriet Beecher Stowe* (Boston: Houghton, Mifflin, 1898)

WGL   *The Letters of William Lloyd Garrison*, eds. Walter M. Merrill and Louis Ruchames, 4 vols. (Cambridge, MA: Harvard University Press, 1971–1975)

WTH   *The Magnificent Activist: The Writings of Thomas Wentworth Higginson (1823–1911)*, ed. Howard N. Meyer (New York: Da Capo Press, 2000)

WTP   *The Works of Theodore Parker* [Centenary Edition], 15 vols. (Boston: American Unitarian Association, 1907–1913)

Introduction

"We white Anglo-Saxon Abolitionists are too apt to assume the whole work as ours," announced Transcendentalist minister Thomas Wentworth Higginson to a packed house at New York City's Mozart Hall on a May evening in 1858. Having fought alongside African Americans in the increasingly violent antislavery struggles of the decade, he hoped to convince his fellow white abolitionists that blacks were more than capable of taking up the battle themselves. We must not "ignore the great force of the victims of tyranny," Higginson insisted, or overlook the plain fact that, in English Romantic poet George Gordon Byron's words, "to be free 'themselves must strike the blow.'"[1] During the next few years, Higginson sought to prove this point in both print and deed. He wrote a series of slave rebellion narratives in the *Atlantic Monthly*, aided John Brown as he plotted to spark a slave uprising at Harpers Ferry, and, eventually, served as colonel of the first Union regiment of former slaves to fight in the American Civil War.

Higginson was not the only abolitionist who employed Byron's verse to urge black resistance to subjugation. He was not, in other words, alone in interpreting the challenges posed by slavery in romantic terms. A decade earlier, black abolitionist Martin Robison Delany had chosen Byron's call to self-enacted emancipation – "HEREDITARY BONDSMAN! KNOW YE NOT WHO WOULD BE FREE, THEMSELVES MUST STRIKE THE BLOW!" – as the motto of his antislavery newspaper, the *Mystery*. Like Higginson, Delany had long argued that blacks themselves must resist

---

[1] *Liberator*, May 28, 1858; George Gordon Byron, *Childe Harold's Pilgrimage*, canto 2, st. 76.

I

their enslavers, at any cost. Just weeks before Higginson gave his Mozart Hall address, in fact, Delany had organized a meeting in the black community of Chatham, Canada, to consider John Brown's plans to invade the South and build an army of ex-slaves who would bring down slavery from within. Despite his support for Brown, by 1858, Delany settled on a different course of action. Having relocated to Canada a few years earlier, he had little hope for African Americans within the United States.[2] Instead, Delany began to organize an expedition to scout potential sites for an African colony comprising free black emigrants and their African-born brethren. While Higginson endorsed a biracial assault against slavery with people of African descent working alongside white supporters to bring down the institution in the United States, Delany envisioned – and worked to create – a black abolitionist enclave abroad.

Delany's former partner Frederick Douglass had little patience for this emigration scheme. He viewed slaves and free blacks as essential components of the American body politic. Since the early 1850s Douglass had dedicated himself to finding a way to use the nation's liberal ideals and institutions to destroy the chains that bound African Americans. Yet Douglass, too, was drawn to Byron's words, more so than even Higginson and Delany. In 1847 he quoted the same stanza at a meeting of the Eastern Pennsylvania Anti-Slavery Society, urging free blacks to resist state encroachments upon their citizenship rights. Douglass also punctuated his tale of physical confrontation with the slave-breaker Covey with Byron's verse in his 1855 and 1881 autobiographies.[3] Finally, five years after Higginson's appeal in Mozart Hall, the black abolitionist called on the newly recruited troops of the Fifty-fourth Massachusetts Regiment to put aside their personal hesitations about northern prejudice and go to war because "Action! Action! not criticism, is the plain duty of this hour." Douglass continued, "Liberty won by white men would lose half its luster. 'Who would be free themselves must strike the blow.'"[4]

[2] Victor Ullman, *Martin R. Delany: The Beginnings of Black Nationalism* (Boston: Beacon Press, 1971), 60–61; Dorothy Sterling, *The Making of an Afro-American: Martin Robison Delany, 1812–1885* (1971; repr., New York: Da Capo Press, 1996), 169–175; Robert S. Levine, *Martin Delany, Frederick Douglass, and the Politics of Representative Identity* (Chapel Hill: University of North Carolina Press, 1997), 182–183; David S. Reynolds, *John Brown, Abolitionist: The Man Who Killed Slavery, Sparked the Civil War, and Seeded Civil Rights* (New York: Knopf, 2005), 259–264.

[3] FD, "The Material and Moral Requirements of Antislavery Work: Addresses Delivered in Norristown, Pennsylvania, on 5, 6, August 1847," in *FDP*, 2: 89; FD, *My Bondage and My Freedom*, in *FDPAW*, 2: 142; FD, *The Life and Times of Frederick Douglass, Written by Himself* (Hartford, CT: Park Publishing, 1882), 178.

[4] FD, "Men of Color, To Arms!" in *LWFD*, 3: 318.

This militant catechism, echoed time and again by Higginson, Douglass, Delany, and countless other abolitionists, highlights the long shadow that Byron – and romanticism more generally – cast over the young republic. Lord Byron, wrote Boston publisher Samuel G. Goodrich, "could no more be kept at bay than the cholera." Harriet Beecher Stowe said that "Byronic fever" reached its greatest heights among young people who, like her, grew up in the early nineteenth century.[5] While the Romantic poet's life and work spoke to the nation's youth, his potent concoction of emotionalism, martial heroism, and calls for political and social liberation inspired reform-minded Americans in particular. Frederick Douglass, William Lloyd Garrison, Samuel Gridley Howe, and Abraham Lincoln, among others, pored over Byron's writings, imitated his hairstyle and dress, and hoped to live up to the heroic example he set by joining the Greek war for independence from Ottoman rule.[6] And Byron's influence was not singular. A handful of European Romantic poets and writers – including Walter Scott, William Wordsworth, and Thomas Carlyle – found a receptive audience in the nineteenth-century United States. Ultimately, European Romanticism merged with home-grown romantic currents to cut a wide path through the American cultural landscape – the nation's literary forms, artistic styles, and patterns of thought would never be the same.[7]

[5] Samuel G. Goodrich, quoted in Henry Mayer, *All on Fire: William Lloyd Garrison and the Abolition of Slavery* (New York: St. Martin's Press, 1998), 28; HBS, in *SLL*, 40; Peter X. Accardo, "Byron in America to 1830," *Harvard Library Bulletin* 9 (Summer 1998): 6.

[6] Booker T. Washington, *Frederick Douglass* (Philadelphia: George W. Jacobs, 1906), 303; John Stauffer, *Giants: The Parallel Lives of Frederick Douglass & Abraham Lincoln* (New York: Twelve, 2008), 125; John Stauffer, *The Black Hearts of Men: Radical Abolitionists and the Transformation of Race* (Cambridge, MA: Harvard University Press, 2002), 60; Mayer, *All on Fire*, 36; John T. Cumbler, *From Abolition to Rights for All: The Making of a Reform Community in the Nineteenth Century* (Philadelphia: University of Pennsylvania Press, 2008), 39–40; Stewart Winger, *Lincoln, Religion, and Romantic Cultural Politics* (DeKalb: Northern Illinois University Press, 2003), 180.

[7] In order to reinforce that romanticism had indigenous and popular sources as well as high European ones, I have elected not to capitalize "romanticism" and related terms except when they are used to refer specifically to European Romantics and their work. On indigenous forms of romanticism, see Henry F. May, "After the Enlightenment: A Prospectus," in his *The Divided Heart: Essays on Protestantism and the Enlightenment in America* (New York: Oxford University Press, 1991), 192; Perry Miller, "New England's Transcendentalism: Native or Imported?" in *Critical Essays on American Transcendentalism*, ed. Philip F. Gura and Joel Myerson (Boston: G. K. Hall & Co., 1982), 387–401; and Michael O'Brien, "The Lineaments of Antebellum Southern Romanticism," in his *Rethinking the South: Essays in Intellectual History* (Baltimore: Johns Hopkins University Press, 1988), esp. 42–45.

Nowhere were these changes more significant than in the antebellum campaign against slavery. As Byron's oft-repeated ode to self-emancipation suggests, romanticism provided a lexicon for militant abolitionists like Higginson, Delany, and Douglass. But it did more than that. Romanticism repeatedly transformed the antislavery movement. In the 1830s, romantic reformers such as William Lloyd Garrison combined moral perfectionism – the belief that individuals and society could be perfected – with demands for immediate emancipation to formulate a radical antislavery approach, which broke sharply from the gradualism of early abolitionists. Relying on direct, often emotional appeals to hearts and minds, Garrisonians hoped to convert the nation to the cause of the enslaved. Two decades later, a second generation of abolitionists also turned to romanticism as they crafted new – and often more militant – responses to solve the problem of slavery. Frustrated by political defeats, especially the Fugitive Slave Law of 1850, they embraced a wide range of romantic motifs and doctrines, from immediatism, perfectionism, and sentimentalism to self-culture, martial heroism, romantic racialism, and even Manifest Destiny. In the process, they reshaped American abolitionism yet again.

Historians have not fully appreciated these latter developments. Although we know a great deal about early types of romantic reform – particularly the immediatism and perfectionism associated with the birth of radical abolitionism in the 1830s – the connections between romanticism and the antislavery movement in the 1850s have not received sufficient attention. Some scholars have viewed the decade before the Civil War as a mature and settled period when it comes to ideas about social reform and as such, unworthy of study. Aileen Kraditor, for example, has argued that by 1850 "most of the major tactical problems that arose in the entire history of the abolitionist movement [had been] thrashed out," while Louis Ruchames has concluded that "the late 1840's and 50's saw no important changes in anti-slavery theory or practice."[8]

To other students of American culture, the period was not static but regressive. According to this line of thinking, the United States transitioned from a spirit of boundlessness – a limitless faith in the possibilities of the nation and its people – to a pattern of consolidation, which resulted

---

[8] Aileen Kraditor, *Means and Ends in American Abolitionism: Garrison and His Critics on Strategy and Tactics, 1834–1850* (New York: Pantheon Books, 1969), vii; Louis Ruchames, ed., *The Abolitionists: A Collection of Their Writing* (New York: G.P. Putnam's Sons, 1963), 24. See also Gilbert H. Barnes, *The Antislavery Impulse, 1830–1844* (1933; repr., Gloucester, MA: Peter Smith, 1957), 197.

in "the formation of a more stable, more disciplined, less adventurous culture," in the 1850s. For antebellum reformers, this meant that utopian attempts to transform the very building blocks of American society and culture gave way to "a more limited, if perhaps more realistic, vision of the possibilities of social change." One scholar has bluntly maintained that "the romantic phase of the antebellum reform movement came to an abrupt halt in 1850."[9]

Yet the 1850s were not simply a time of intellectual stasis or retrenchment, especially among romantic-minded Americans. Noting the remarkable number of American literary masterpieces that appeared in just the first half of the decade – including *The Scarlett Letter*, *Moby-Dick*, *Walden*, and *Leaves of Grass* – literary scholar F. O. Matthiessen long ago dubbed the period the "American Renaissance."[10] Although some of the artists associated with the American Renaissance (Poe, Whitman, Hawthorne, Melville) were indifferent, if not hostile, to abolitionism, recent scholarship has made it clear that others became outspoken opponents of slavery. We now know, for instance, that despite early skepticism about organized social reform Transcendentalists Ralph Waldo Emerson and Henry David Thoreau increasingly allied themselves with abolitionists over the course of the 1850s. In shoring up the antislavery credentials of these leading American romantics, however, scholars of Transcendentalism have undersold the breadth and impact of romantic reform in the decade before the Civil War. For, notwithstanding their eloquent pleas on behalf of the enslaved and encomiums to abolitionist martyrs like John Brown, Emerson and Thoreau remained aloof from

---

[9] John Higham, "From Boundlessness to Consolidation: The Transformation of American Culture, 1848–1860," in *Hanging Together: Unity and Diversity in American Culture*, ed. Carl J. Guarneri (New Haven, CT: Yale University Press, 2001), 158; Lori Ginzburg, "'Moral Suasion is Moral Balderdash': Women, Politics, and Social Activism in the 1850s," *Journal of American History* 73 (Dec. 1986): 604; Donald Yacovone, *Samuel Joseph May and the Dilemmas of the Liberal Persuasion, 1797–1871* (Philadelphia: Temple University Press, 1991), 155. See also Lori Ginzburg, *Women and the Work of Benevolence: Morality, Politics, and Class in the Nineteenth-Century United States* (New Haven, CT: Yale University Press, 1990) and John L. Thomas, "Romantic Reform in America, 1815–1865," *American Quarterly* 17 (Winter 1965): 656–681. For arguments that this shift away from romantic reform occurred during or after the Civil War, see George M. Frederickson, *The Inner Civil War: Northern Intellectuals and the Crisis of the Union* (New York: Harper & Row, 1965); Louis Menand, *The Metaphysical Club: A Story of Ideas in America* (New York: Farrar, Straus, and Giroux, 2001); and Drew Gilpin Faust, *This Republic of Suffering: Death and the American Civil War* (New York: Knopf, 2008).

[10] F. O. Matthiessen, *American Renaissance: Art and Expression in the Age of Emerson and Whitman* (New York: Oxford University Press, 1941), vii.

more formal parts of the antislavery struggle. They were fellow travelers, rather than the vanguard, of the movement.[11]

The same cannot be said of another set of romantics who came of age as abolitionists in the 1840s and 1850s. As the secession crisis intensified after the Mexican War, opponents of slavery were forced to revisit their fundamental beliefs, reimagine prevailing strategies, and reconsider their roles in the movement. Some flocked to the new Republican Party and its free labor ideology, which opposed the expansion of slavery into western territories. Others abandoned long-standing commitments to nonviolence, exploiting "intellectual loopholes" to accommodate more resistant approaches to abolitionism.[12] The rise of the Republican Party and the compromises of would-be pacifists, however, have long overshadowed the emergence of a new generation of romantic reformers in the 1850s. This group, whom I call the New Romantics, had close ties with many

[11] Len Gougeon, *Virtue's Hero: Emerson, Antislavery, and Reform* (Athens: University of Georgia Press, 1990); Richard F. Teichgraeber III, *Sublime Thoughts/Penny Wisdom: Situating Emerson and Thoreau in the American Market* (Baltimore: Johns Hopkins University Press, 1995); Albert J. Von Frank, *The Trials of Anthony Burns: Freedom and Slavery in Emerson's Boston* (Cambridge, MA: Harvard University Press, 1998); T. Gregory Garvey, ed., *The Emerson Dilemma: Essays on Emerson and Social Reform* (Athens: University of Georgia Press, 2001), Reynolds, *John Brown, Abolitionist*; Sandra Harbert Petrulionis, *To Set This World Right: The Antislavery Movement in Thoreau's Concord* (Ithaca, NY: Cornell University Press, 2006); Albert J. Von Frank, "On Transcendentalism: Its History and Uses," *Modern Intellectual History* 6 (Apr. 2009): 189–205; Alan M. Levine and Daniel S. Malachuk, eds., *A Political Companion to Ralph Waldo Emerson* (Lexington: University Press of Kentucky, 2011). For works that downplay the Transcendentalists' engagement with the slavery question, see Kraditor, *Means and Ends in American Abolitionism* and Anne C. Rose, *Transcendentalism as a Social Movement, 1830–1850* (New Haven, CT: Yale University Press, 1981).

[12] Eric Foner, *Free Soil, Free Labor, Free Men: The Ideology of the Republican Party* (1970; repr., New York: Oxford University Press, 1995); Lewis Perry, *Radical Abolitionism: Anarchy and the Government of God in Antislavery Thought* (Ithaca, NY: Cornell University Press, 1973), 239. On antislavery violence, see John Demos, "The Antislavery Movement and the Problem of Violent 'Means,'" *New England Quarterly* 37 (Dec. 1964): 501–526; Jane H. Pease and William H. Pease, "Confrontation and Abolition in the 1850s," *Journal of American History* 58 (Mar. 1972): 923–937; Lawrence J. Friedman, *Gregarious Saints: Self and Community in American Abolitionism, 1830–1870* (New York: Cambridge University Press, 1982), 196–222; John R. McKivigan and Stanley Harrold, eds., *Antislavery Violence: Sectional, Racial, and Cultural Conflict in Antebellum America* (Knoxville: University of Tennessee Press, 1999); Stauffer, *Black Hearts of Men*; Stanley Harrold, *The Rise of Aggressive Abolitionism: Addresses to the Slaves* (Lexington: University of Kentucky Press, 2004); Reynolds, *John Brown, Abolitionist*; Matthew J. Clavin, *Toussaint Louverture and the American Civil War: The Promise and Peril of a Second Haitian Revolution* (Philadelphia: University of Pennsylvania Press, 2009), 1–73; and Stanley Harrold, *Border War: Fighting over Slavery before the Civil War* (Chapel Hill: University of North Carolina Press, 2010).

early antislavery romantics, including Garrison, Lydia Maria Child, and Theodore Weld. Yet, as we shall see, the New Romantics broke decisively with their predecessors with regard to their tactics for fighting slavery and the ideas they used to justify those tactics.

Romantic Reformers is a study of the thought and action of five of these figures – Higginson, Delany, and Douglass as well as Theodore Parker and Harriet Beecher Stowe – all of whom became household names in the 1850s. Today, the fame of a few of these abolitionists remains as strong as ever, while the others tend to draw nods of recognition mainly from students of antebellum American culture. But in the years leading up to the Civil War, all five played a decisive role in the most important social movement of the era. They campaigned tirelessly across the country, decrying the institution of slavery from the pulpit and lectern, in novels and newspapers. By inspiring – and in some cases leading – violent conflict in the streets of Boston, plains of Kansas, and mountains of Virginia, they transformed the antislavery movement, pushing it toward increasing militancy. And, critically, they framed their objections and justified their actions chiefly on romantic grounds.[13]

Although many abolitionists abandoned romantic reform in the 1850s, thereby signifying that "the day of romantic dreams and visionary philanthropy had gone by," the New Romantics did the opposite.[14] They blended the immediatism and perfectionism of early reformers with new romantic points of emphasis, including martial heroism, romantic

---

[13] My interpretation builds on the recent efforts of a handful of historians and literary critics who have explored connections between romanticism and abolitionism in the 1850s. This includes studies of the Transcendentalists and the slavery question (see footnote 11) as well as works that focus on how romanticism proved an important set of ideas for abolitionists who theorized about, for instance, slave revolt. *Romantic Reformers* combines, and extends, these two lines of interpretation, pushing beyond the usual subjects – Emerson and Thoreau – to expose the ways in which a wide range of antislavery minds turned to romantic ideas as the sectional crisis intensified. For studies that explore romanticism and social reform in the 1850s, see Stauffer, *Black Hearts of Men*; Reynolds, *John Brown, Abolitionist*; Stanley Harrold, "Romanticizing Slave Revolt: Madison Washington, the *Creole* Mutiny, and Abolitionist Celebration of Violent Means," in *Antislavery Violence*, 89–107; Eric J. Sundquist, *To Wake the Nations: Race in the Making of American Literature* (Cambridge, MA: Harvard University Press, 1993); Levine, *Martin Delany, Frederick Douglass*; Winger, *Lincoln, Religion, and Romantic Cultural Politics*; Mathew J. Grow, *"Liberty to the Downtrodden": Thomas L. Kane, Romantic Reformer* (New Haven, CT: Yale University Press, 2009); David S. Reynolds, *Mightier than the Sword:* Uncle Tom's Cabin *and the Battle for America* (New York: Norton, 2011); and Larry J. Reynolds, *Righteous Violence: Revolution, Slavery, and the American Renaissance* (Athens: University of Georgia Press, 2011).

[14] Sarah Smith Martyn, quoted in Ginzburg, "'Moral Suasion is Moral Balderdash," 601.

racialism, sentimentalism, and self-culture. Historians have done much to expose the ways that evangelicalism, republicanism, and Free Soil ideology shaped the sectional crisis. At the same time, earlier studies have lost sight of another prominent intellectual tradition.[15] We cannot understand the final chapter in the antislavery struggle, or the coming of the Civil War, until we acknowledge the pivotal role that romanticism – arguably the most influential set of ideas in nineteenth-century America – played in the tumultuous events of the 1850s and 1860s.

Romantic America

Romanticism captured the antebellum American imagination like nothing else. At once a state of mind and a constellation of motifs and doctrines, romanticism was fed by both indigenous and imported sources, finding expression in varied forms. It seemed to speak directly to the young nation's citizenry, whether cultured Boston Brahmins or rough-hewn frontiersmen. Romanticism's emphasis on organic growth and the beauty and wildness of nature appealed to a people who, in just a half century, pushed from the Atlantic to the Pacific Ocean. The romantic commitment to individuality and self-expression likewise resonated in a liberal republic that was transitioning from classical republicanism to mass democracy.[16] Meanwhile, romanticism's dark and decadent elements tempted

[15] David Goldfield's *America Aflame* is a case in point. In emphasizing the role of evangelicalism in the coming of the Civil War, this otherwise masterful synthesis misidentifies Theodore Parker as an evangelical and claims that "most" of the "Secret Six" – the abolitionists who supported and advised John Brown as he planned his raid at Harpers Ferry – had "close ties to evangelical Protestantism." Yet four of the Secret Six – Parker, Thomas Wentworth Higginson, Samuel Gridley Howe, Franklin Sanborn – were Unitarians and Transcendentalists who shared romantic ideas with evangelical Protestants but were nonetheless theologically worlds apart. Goldfield is not wrong to point to evangelicalism's centrality in the Civil War period, but if we want a term that encompasses the antislavery theories emanating from both evangelicals and liberal Christians, then we would be better off choosing "romanticism." David Goldfield, *America Aflame: How the Civil War Created a Nation* (New York: Bloomsbury, 2011), 47, 158. On abolitionists' evangelicalism, see Barnes, *Antislavery Impulse*; Friedman, *Gregarious Saints*; and Robert H. Abzug, *Cosmos Crumbling: American Reform and the Religious Imagination* (New York: Oxford University Press, 1994). On the role of Free Soil and republican forms of antislavery thought in the sectional crisis, see Foner, *Free Soil, Free Labor*, Daniel J. McInerney, *The Fortunate Heirs of Freedom: Abolition and Republican Thought* (Lincoln: University of Nebraska Press, 1994), and Adam-Max Tuchinsky, *Horace Greeley's New-York Tribune: Civil War-Era Socialism and the Crisis of Free Labor* (Ithaca, NY: Cornell University Press, 2009).
[16] Stow Persons, *American Minds: A History of Ideas* (New York: Henry Holt, 1958), 201–208.

even the country's most stern moralists. Revivalist Lyman Beecher, for example, was a great Byron aficionado in spite of – and, perhaps at some level, because of – the poet's scandalous eroticism. Upon Byron's death, Beecher lamented, "What a harp he might have swept," had the English Romantic been converted to God's work.[17] By the middle of the nineteenth century, romanticism was all but inescapable. As historian Henry May has written, "Romanticism pervaded every aspect of American culture, from low to high, from politics and religion to literature" in the three decades before the Civil War, dominating the young republic more thoroughly than just about any European nation.[18]

Elite minds, from Boston to Charleston, devoured the works of Goethe, Samuel Taylor Coleridge, Wordsworth, and Madame Anne Louise Germaine de Staël. American intellectuals were fascinated by the challenges that European Romantics posed to the Enlightenment's stale, passionless world. While the latter stood for order, predictability, and universality, romanticism took the side of emotion, idiosyncrasy, and subjectivity.[19] Romantic writers intoxicated their readers with visions of medieval knighthood and brooding, valiant heroes. One summer, a young

[17] Lyman Beecher, quoted in *SLL*, 39; May, "After the Enlightenment," 188.

[18] May, "After the Enlightenment," 190–91, 195–96; O'Brien, "Lineaments of Antebellum Southern Romanticism," 45. For a fascinating discussion of the ways in which romanticism can be used to describe the cultural transition of middle-class Americans in the nineteenth century, see Anne C. Rose, *Victorian America and the Civil War* (New York: Cambridge University Press, 1992).

[19] These points of comparison fail to capture the breadth of romanticism in either its European or American context. To some minds, the word "romanticism" refers to a series of literary, artistic, and philosophical movements that emerged in Europe and spread elsewhere between the 1780s and 1830s. Yet others have used "romanticism" more broadly, describing it as a state of mind that has found subscribers in the ancient, medieval, and modern world. Indeed, as Arthur Lovejoy wrote seventy years ago, the term "has acquired so many – and such incongruous and opposed – meanings that no lexicographer has ever yet come near to enumerating them correctly and exhaustively." This wisdom applies as much today as it did when Lovejoy wrote it and, for the record, I have no interest in being the first to summit this lexicographic mountain. Arthur O. Lovejoy, "The Meaning of Romanticism for the Historian of Ideas," *Journal of the History of Ideas* 2 (June 1941): 257–278 (quotation 258); Russell B. Nye, *Society and Culture in America, 1830–1860* (New York: Harper and Row, 1974), 19–24; Persons, *American Minds*, 201–208; Norman Risjord, *Representative Americans: The Romantics* (Lanham, MD: Rowman & Littlefield, 2001), xi–xiii; Rollin G. Osterweis, "Romanticism Defined," in his *Romanticism and Nationalism in the Old South* (New Haven, CT: Yale University Press, 1949), 235–239; Isaiah Berlin, *The Roots of Romanticism* (Princeton, NJ: Princeton University Press, 2001), esp. 1–20; O'Brien, "Lineaments of Antebellum Southern Romanticism," 38–56; Lawrence Buell, *Literary Transcendentalism: Style and Vision in the American Renaissance* (Ithaca, NY: Cornell University Press, 1973), esp. 2–9.

Harriet Beecher Stowe plowed through Walter Scott's *Ivanhoe* seven times, memorizing a good portion of it. And, as popular as Scott was in antebellum America, Stowe believed that Lord Byron's reign "was, if possible, more universal, binding, and absolute. How many young men of tolerably respectable talents, began to tie their collars with black ribbon, to gaze with sullen gloom on everything general or particular, to drink gin and water, and write bad poetry, has never been accurately computed."[20]

New England Transcendentalists, too, consumed the verse of Byron and Scott with "feverish excitement."[21] Even so, these American romantics – who formed the most influential intellectual coterie in the young republic – devoted more time to plumbing the philosophical and epistemological depths of high European Romanticism. Dissatisfied with the Lockean sensationalist philosophy that then prevailed in Boston's Unitarian circles, Emerson, Parker, Margaret Fuller, and George Ripley found a far more satisfactory explanation of the world and its workings in a romantic emphasis on intuition and organicism. They read *Sartor Resartus*, in which Thomas Carlyle outlined what he called "natural supernaturalism": a quasi-religious strain of romanticism that invested the natural world and thus humankind with divine potential. Transcendentalists also embraced new theories of knowledge, largely derived from Immanuel Kant but disseminated by English and French Romantics, including Coleridge and de Staël.[22]

But romanticism was not simply an imported tradition, spreading from Europe to the United States "like ripples on a pond into which Immanuel Kant had thrown a stone."[23] Although the Transcendentalists crafted an epistemology that invoked Kant's authority and employed some of his terminology, they pushed beyond his philosophical position. Kant, for instance, made some room for sensory impressions in his epistemology;

[20] Charles Beecher, ed., *Autobiography, Correspondence, Etc. of Lyman Beecher, D.D.* (New York: Harper Brothers, 1864), 1: 526; Joan D. Hedrick, *Harriet Beecher Stowe: A Life* (New York: Oxford University Press, 1994), 20; *New-York Evangelist*, July 28, 1842.

[21] William Henry Channing, quoted in Barbara L. Packer, "Romanticism," in *The Oxford Handbook of Transcendentalism*, ed. Joel Myerson, Sandra Harbert Petrulionis, and Laura Dassow Walls (New York: Oxford University Press, 2010), 85.

[22] Stanley M. Elkins, *Slavery: A Problem in American Institutional and Intellectual Life* (Chicago: University of Chicago Press, 1959), 164; Charles Capper, *Margaret Fuller: An American Romantic Life, Vol. 1: The Private Years* (New York: Oxford University Press, 1992), 181; M. H. Abrams, *Natural Supernaturalism: Tradition and Revolution in Romantic Literature* (New York: Norton, 1971); Barbara L. Packer, *The Transcendentalists* (Athens: University of Georgia Press, 2007), 20–23.

[23] O'Brien, "Lineaments of Antebellum Southern Romanticism," 42.

he was not a pure idealist. Most Transcendentalists, in contrast, put no limits on the capacity of the human mind.[24]

It would be more accurate to say that European Romanticism stirred and stimulated what Perry Miller called the "latent propensities" of American romantics, without delimiting the scope of their ideas. Native sources and contexts – including the Revolutionary tradition, the Second Great Awakening, the rise of mass democracy, and the wide-open American frontier – also shaped high and popular forms of American romanticism.[25] Indeed, American romantics would not have had it any other way. Bemoaning the fact that native authors seemed to take their cues from their European counterparts, American intellectuals self-consciously sought to craft original, uniquely national forms of expression. And to a great extent they succeeded. While few early nineteenth-century American authors and poets could match their European counterparts, by the 1850s the artists associated with the American Renaissance more than held their own. So, too, did a second group of romantic writers: runaway slaves. Curiously, while the literary merits of fugitive slave narratives escaped critics for the better part of the twentieth century, they were not lost on antebellum romantics. Writing of books like the *Narrative of the Life of Frederick Douglass*, Theodore Parker mused that "all the original romance of Americans is in them, not in the white man's novel."[26]

Fugitive slaves were hardly the only non-elites who were drawn to romantic thought. Although the broader populace would struggle to elucidate the finer points of Transcendentalist metaphysics, they, too, found romantic language appealing. Samuel G. Goodrich, for example, lauded the accessibility of romantic poetry to Americans of all stripes. "Everybody could read and comprehend" Walter Scott's poems, wrote Goodrich. "Newspapers, magazines, and even volumes, teemed with

[24] Lawrence Buell, *Emerson* (Cambridge, MA: Harvard University Press, 2003), 61; Lawrence Buell, *Literary Transcendentalism: Style and Vision in the American Renaissance* (Ithaca, NY: Cornell University Press, 1973), 4–5; William R. Hutchinson, *The Transcendentalist Ministers: Church Reform in the New England Renaissance* (New Haven, CT: Yale University Press, 1959), 22–28.

[25] Miller, "New England's Transcendentalism," 393; May, "After the Enlightenment," 192; O'Brien, "Lineaments of Antebellum Southern Romanticism," 45; Ralph H. Gabriel, "Evangelical Religion and Popular Romanticism in Early Nineteenth-Century America," *Church History* **19** (Mar. 1950): 34–47.

[26] TP, "The American Scholar," in *WTP*, 8: 37; William L. Andrews, introduction to *My Bondage and My Freedom*, by FD (Urbana: University of Illinois Press, 1987), xv. On the literary merits of fugitive slave narratives, see William L. Andrews, *To Tell a Free Story: The First Century of Afro-American Autobiography, 1760–1865* (Urbana: University of Illinois Press, 1988).

imitations and variations inspired by the 'Wizard Harp of the North.'"[27] Some even found a new name in Scott's verse. When a young fugitive slave who called himself Fredrick Johnson arrived in New Bedford, Massachusetts, in the late 1830s, his host, who had been engrossed in *The Lady of the Lake*, suggested that Fredrick adopt the surname of one of the poem's heroic characters. Thus Fredrick Johnson became Fredrick Douglass.[28]

Romantic ideas and tropes also spilled out from the revivals of the Second Great Awakening and the pages of sentimental literature. Like the New England Transcendentalists and their European counterparts, evangelical preachers stressed individual regeneration and the power of emotional experience. Frontier revivalists used dramatic sermons to stir audiences to a frenzy. Converts could lose themselves in the ecstasy of camp meeting revivals like Cane Ridge in much the same way that Transcendentalists, communing in the wilds of Concord, sought to become one with nature. Meanwhile, middle-class evangelists preached a gospel of the heart that proved particularly appealing to their female congregants. Many of these women, in turn, became the producers and consumers of sentimental literature that, like high romantic writing, was rooted in appeals to emotion and feeling.[29]

American romantics also defined nineteenth-century social and political conversations. Romantic nationalists, from Andrew Jackson to James

---

[27] Samuel Griswold Goodrich, *The Story of Peter Parley's Own Life: From the Personal Narrative of the Late Samuel Goodrich ("Peter Parley")*, ed. Frank Freeman (London: Sampson Low, Son, & Co., 1863), 152–163; James D. Hart, *The Popular Book: A History of America's Literary Taste* (Berkeley and Los Angeles: University of California Press, 1950) 69.

[28] FD, *My Bondage and My Freedom*, in *FDPAW*, 2: 197; Waldo E. Martin, *The Mind of Frederick Douglass* (Chapel Hill: University of North Carolina Press, 1984), 15; and William S. McFeeley, *Frederick Douglass* (New York: Norton, 1991), 78. Scott's 1810 poem *The Lady of the Lake* chronicled the exploits of James Douglas, a Scottish chieftain, renowned for bravery.

[29] Timothy L. Smith, *Revivalism and Social Reform* (New York: Abingdon Press, 1957), 8; Ralph H. Gabriel, "Evangelical Religion and Popular Romanticism," 33–47; O'Brien, "Lineaments of Antebellum Southern Romanticism," 45; May, "After the Enlightenment," 190–191. Framing sentimentalism as a type of romanticism is not uncontroversial. After all, many literary critics contrast complex and sophisticated romantic literature with its sappy and melodramatic sentimental stepsister. Yet whatever the respective aesthetic merits of romantic and sentimental literature – a question that is beyond the scope of this book – both are deeply rooted in an appeal to sentiment and feeling. Osterweis, "Romanticism Defined," 238. For the classic critique of sentimentalism as an art form, see Ann Douglas, *The Feminization of American Culture* (1977; repr., New York: Doubleday, 1988).

Polk, mixed Anglo-Saxon chauvinism and divine providence together into a forceful formula they labeled "Manifest Destiny." The most articulate proponents of this program were the Young Americans, a loose network of political theorists and literati associated with John L. O'Sullivan's *United States Magazine and Democratic Review*. Dedicated to western expansionism, the creation of a more exciting, democratic, and indigenous literary tradition, and the success of the Democratic Party, Young Americans channeled romanticism in a partisan, nationalistic, and, frequently, anti-abolitionist direction. Their vision for America justified policies like the Indian Removal Act and conflicts such as the Mexican War, which extended U.S. boundaries to the Pacific Ocean. And when tens of thousands of Americans marched south to fight Mexico in the late 1840s with visions of martial glory dancing through their heads like so many sugar plums, they inspired romantic flights of fancy among their fellow Americans at home. Reared on Scott's historical romances, volunteers in the Mexican War appeared to Nathaniel Hawthorne "to have been animated by the spirit of young knights."[30]

Southern romantics, too, found visions of westward expansion seductive. But they put just as much stock in defending the past – both real or imagined – as in creating a new future in the West. Planters and yeomen alike cherished "rural simplicity," finding solace in the cultures and practices of ancient Greece and feudal England.[31] This was particularly true in Virginia, where the gentry combined long-standing local traditions with the visions of medieval Europe found in the works of such Romantics as Walter Scott. Believing that the social order of the Virginia plantation mirrored that of the feudal past, these self-styled lords of the manor idealized plantation life, courtly manners, codes of honor, military service, even romantic oratory. The most remarkable manifestation of romanticism in the South, of course, was the idea of an independent southern nation.

---

[30] Widmer, *Young America*, 39–40, 91, 205–206; Yonathan Eyal, *The Young American Movement and the Transformation of the Democratic Party, 1828–1861* (New York: Cambridge University Press, 2007), 185–186, 198–199; Daniel Walker Howe, *What Hath God Wrought: The Transformation of America, 1815–1848* (New York: Oxford University Press, 2007), 342–357, 702–708; Yonatan Eyal, "A Romantic Realist: George Nicholas Sanders and the Dilemmas of Southern International Engagement," *Journal of Southern History* 78 (Feb. 2012): 107–130; Nathaniel Hawthorne, "Life of Franklin Pierce," in his *Sketches and Studies* (Boston: Houghton, Mifflin, 1883), 76; Robert W. Johannsen, *To the Halls of the Montezumas: The Mexican War in the American Imagination* (New York: Oxford University Press, 1988), 68–71.

[31] Clement Eaton, *Freedom of Thought in the Old South* (New York: Peter Smith, 1951), 317–318; Osterweis, *Romanticism and Nationalism*, 14–17.

Dreamed up by proslavery theorists in the decades before the Civil War, brought to fruition with the creation of the Confederate States of America, and put on a pedestal by Lost Cause proponents after Appomattox, this provocative vision reflected the power of romantic ideas to unite and embolden a wide range of white southerners. With characteristic acumen and hyperbole, Mark Twain later blamed the Civil War on the spread of "Sir Walter disease" across the South.[32]

In contrast, northern romantics – notwithstanding the Young Americans – found in slavery little to admire and much to criticize. As historians John L. Thomas and David Brion Davis long ago made clear, the proliferation of two related romantic mindsets – immediatism and perfectionism – fueled the rise of the modern antislavery movement in the 1830s. That decade witnessed a transition from a gradual approach to the problem of slavery associated with the Enlightenment to a romantic sensibility that stressed "the innate moral capacities of the individual" and sought to destroy slavery in one fell swoop.[33]

Since the Revolutionary period, opponents of slavery had worked in a cautious, piecemeal fashion. Although many Americans were troubled by slavery, they nonetheless worried about the practical implications of attempts to limit, not to mention abolish, it. Even committed abolitionists warned that reform must be pursued in a sober fashion. "Be careful to join moderation to your zeal," advised the Pennsylvania Abolition Society in 1789.[34] As northern states moved toward emancipation, they often implemented gradual programs, which enabled slaveholders to retain control and earn profits from their bondsmen and women well into the nineteenth century. Gradualism was the hallmark

---

[32] Osterweis, *Romanticism and Nationalism*, 82–102, 132–154; Wilbur J. Cash, *The Mind of the South* (1941; repr., New York: Vintage, 1991), 59–99; Paul Quigley, *Shifting Grounds: Nationalism and the American South, 1848–1865* (New York: Oxford University Press, 2011), 30–49; Mark Twain, quoted in Wallace Hettle, *The Peculiar Democracy: Southern Democrats in Peace and Civil War* (Athens: University of Georgia Press, 2001), 122. On intellectual life in the antebellum South, see Michael O'Brien, *Conjectures of Order: Intellectual Life and the American South, 1810–1860*, 2 vols. (Chapel Hill: University of North Carolina Press, 2004).

[33] Thomas, "Romantic Reform in America," 656–681; David Brion Davis, "The Emergence of Immediatism in British and American Anti-Slavery Thought," *Mississippi Valley Historical Review* **49** (Sept. 1962): 228–230 (quotation 229). On early abolitionism, see Richard S. Newman, *The Transformation of American Abolitionism: Fighting Slavery in the Early Republic* (Chapel Hill: University of North Carolina Press, 2002) and David N. Gellman, *Emancipating New York: The Politics of Slavery and Freedom, 1777–1827* (Baton Rouge: Louisiana State University Press, 2006).

[34] Quoted in Newman, *Transformation of American Abolitionism*, 44.

of the most influential antislavery organization in the early Republic, the American Colonization Society (ACS), as well. Supported by leading political and religious figures, the ACS sought to free slaves little by little, while compensating masters and shipping as many blacks as possible to Africa.[35]

In the 1830s, however, a more radical approach to the problem of slavery gained a national following. The major figures in this movement were white reformers like Boston editor William Lloyd Garrison and New York merchant Lewis Tappan, both of whom had once counted themselves colonizationists. Early black opposition to colonization had convinced Garrison, Tappan, and many other white abolitionists that organizations such as the ACS were founded on the prejudicial notion that the United States was a white nation. By the 1830s, they were echoing calls for immediate abolitionism that had first been heard in black communities across the North. Emancipation, they argued, must commence without compensation or delay. More broadly, immediatists demonstrated a sense of moral absolutism on the question of slavery; they insisted that slavery was a sin, denounced it with unmeasured language, and dedicated their lives to bringing it to an end. Immediatism found national outlets in the 1830s, when Garrison and his radical abolitionist colleagues, both black and white, established newspapers such the *Liberator* and organizations such as the American Anti-Slavery Society (AASS).[36]

Garrisonians also tapped into a second romantic attitude – perfectionism – that spread rapidly across the North in the early nineteenth century. Perfectionism, or entire sanctification, was rooted in the biblical injunction, "Be ye perfect, even as your Father in Heaven is perfect."[37] Trumpeted first by Methodist founder John Wesley, here was a doctrine that in theological terms urged Christian believers to strive for a state of

---

[35] Arthur Ziversmit, *The First Emancipation: The Abolition of Slavery in the North* (Chicago: University of Chicago Press, 1967); Gellman, *Emancipating New York*; Newman, *Transformation of American Abolitionism*; Joanne Pope Melish, *Disowning Slavery: Gradual Emancipation and Race in New England* (Ithaca, NY: Cornell University Press, 2000); P. J. Staudenraus, *The African Colonization Movement, 1816–1865* (New York: Columbia University Press, 1961); Eric Burin, *Slavery and the Peculiar Solution: A History of the American Colonization Society* (Gainesville: University Press of Florida, 2005); Beverly C. Tomek, *Colonization and its Discontents: Emancipation, Emigration, and Antislavery in Antebellum Pennsylvania* (New York: New York University Press, 2011).

[36] Newman, *Transformation of American Abolitionism*, 68–130.

[37] Quoted in Wendell Phillips Garrison and Francis Jackson Garrison, *William Lloyd Garrison, 1805–1879: The Story of His Life Told By His Children, Vol. III: 1841–1860* (New York: Century Co., 1889), 13.

"perfect love" with God rather than absolute sinlessness. Perfectionism as an ideal extended far beyond Wesleyan circles, however; ultimately, it appealed to a wide range of antebellum Americans. Evangelicals like Charles G. Finney and Theodore Weld viewed perfectionism as Christian deliverance from sin, while liberal Christians understood it as the "realization of the divine potential in all human beings."[38] Some took the doctrine literally. John Humphrey Noyes, who converted Garrison to perfectionism in 1837 and later founded the utopian Oneida Community in upstate New York, believed that he had personally reached a state of total sanctification. He hoped Garrison would follow his example by setting, as Noyes put it, his "face toward *perfect* holiness." Few perfectionists were as self-assured as Noyes, but they all agreed that individuals should strive to live perfect lives and thereby help usher in a millennium of peace and justice.[39]

In the 1830s, perfectionism hit antebellum America like a tidal wave, sweeping up evangelicals, liberal Christians, and secular utopians, shattering conservative benevolent societies, and clearing a path for a new, far more radical program of reform. To perfectionists, social problems such as dueling, fornication, and the consumption of alcohol were not simply bad habits but signs of abject failure to live up to the standards of perfection to which all should aspire. And no sin loomed larger in antebellum America than slavery.[40]

By the end of the decade, Garrison and his allies had combined immediatism and perfectionism into a distinctive antislavery approach, one that reflected the temper of the age. They challenged traditional social barriers – even among reformers – by encouraging African Americans and women to actively participate in their campaign. They envisioned the creation of a racially blind America, in which both slavery and racial prejudice would be dusty relics.

---

[38] Paul E. Johnson and Sean Wilentz, *The Kingdom of Matthias: A Story of Sex and Salvation* (New York: Oxford University Press, 1994), 190n16; Douglas M. Strong, *Perfectionist Politics: Abolitionism and the Religious Tensions of American Democracy* (Syracuse, NY: Syracuse University Press, 1999), 32; Howe, *What Hath God Wrought*, 619.

[39] John Humphrey Noyes, quoted in John L. Thomas, *The Liberator: William Lloyd Garrison, A Biography* (Boston: Little, Brown, and Co., 1963), 231; Perry, *Radical Abolitionism*, 65–70; Thomas, *The Liberator*, 229–235; Mintz, *Moralists and Modernizers*, 16–17, 28–29; Howe, *What Hath God Wrought*, 284–289; Wallace Brown, "American Romantic Reform," *History Today* 25 (Aug. 1975): 552–560.

[40] Thomas, "Romantic Reform in America," 659–660; Mintz, *Moralists and Modernizers*, 26–29.

Even the tactics of radical abolitionists betrayed a romantic bent. Seeking to trade debased human institutions and practices for the perfect government of God, Garrisonians rejected political agitation as well as violent resistance to bondage. They preferred moral suasion – an emotional appeal to the American conscience. Garrisonians also embraced come-outerism, a practice in which individuals separated themselves from institutions that had been corrupted by slavery, ranging from individual churches to the American republic. Eventually, they denounced organized religion and publicly endorsed disunion, calling the Constitution "the most bloody and heaven-daring arrangement ever made by men."[41]

Radical positions such as these alienated Americans on both sides of the Mason-Dixon Line. A South Carolina vigilance association offered $1,500 for the capture of anyone who circulated the *Liberator*, while the Georgia legislature put up a $5,000 reward for Garrison's arrest on the charge of spreading seditious libel. In Charleston, South Carolina, an angry crowd broke into the post office, seizing sacks filled with antislavery letters and pamphlets to burn in a public bonfire. Up north, violent mobs disrupted antislavery rallies, chased abolitionists through the streets, and murdered antislavery editor Elijah Lovejoy.[42]

Some antislavery allies also bristled at Garrisonian radicalism, leading to the movement's factionalization. By the early 1840s, a host of moderate abolitionists, including James G. Birney, Theodore Weld, Elizur Wright Jr., and the Tappan brothers, left the AASS fold, founding new organizations such as the American and Foreign Anti-Slavery Society and the Liberty Party. Garrison's antislavery opponents objected to his critique of organized religion and his insistence that abolitionist organizations allow women to serve in positions of leadership. Most of all, they rallied around the use of the political system to bring an end to slavery. Still, Garrisonians – and their brand of romantic reform – set the emotional tone for the antislavery movement throughout the 1840s.[43]

---

[41] William Lloyd Garrison to the editor of the *London Patriot*, Aug. 6, 1833, in *WGL*, 1: 249.

[42] Mayer, *All on Fire*, 122–123; William W. Freehling, *The Road to Disunion, Volume 1: Secessionists at Bay, 1776–1854* (New York: Oxford University Press, 1990), 291; James Brewer Stewart, *Holy Warriors: The Abolitionists and American Slavery* (New York: Hill and Wang, 1976), 50–73. On antebellum mobs, see Leonard L. Richards, *"Gentlemen of Property and Standing": Anti-Abolition Mobs in Jacksonian America* (New York: Oxford University Press, 1970) and David Grimsted, *American Mobbing, 1828–1861* (New York: Oxford University Press, 1998).

[43] Stewart, *Holy Warriors*, 91–96.

The New Romantics of the 1850s

In the decade before the Civil War, a new generation of abolitionists changed the face of romantic reform in America yet again. They lived in towns and cities across the country, from Boston to Cincinnati, Chicago to Rochester. They were wealthy and poor, black and white, male and female. This book focuses on five New Romantics who reflect this diversity. Thomas Wentworth Higginson and Theodore Parker were born into Boston's rich cultural terrain, both from old New England stock. Higginson traced family members back to the Great Puritan Migration, while Parker's grandfather had fought in the Battle of Lexington. Both trained for the Unitarian ministry at Harvard Divinity School, became important figures in the Transcendentalist movement, and established congregations amenable to their radical social and religious message. Like Higginson and Parker, Harriet Beecher Stowe was a talented youngster who enjoyed a better education than most of her (female) contemporaries. She, too, was reared in a family with deep New England roots. But Stowe's father, evangelical/orthodox minister Lyman Beecher, despised liberal Christianity and moved his family to Boston to counter the spread of Unitarianism in the 1820s.

While Stowe came from a different wing of New England's Protestant culture than Higginson and Parker, Martin Robison Delany and Frederick Douglass came from another world entirely. Born a slave in Maryland, Douglass at a young age was separated from his mother and spent much of his life trying in vain to discover his father's identity. Largely self-educated, Douglass eventually ran away to the North, settling first in New England and later in Syracuse, New York. Delany, who like Douglass hailed from the mid-Atlantic, was the offspring of an enslaved father and a free black mother. Although born free – Virginia's slave code held that a newborn's status followed the mother's – Delany and his family faced steep racial barriers and, like Douglass, also fled north, to Pennsylvania. Delany came of age in the free black communities of Chambersburg and Pittsburgh.

Despite dissimilar origins, these New Romantics developed close connections. Parker was a mentor to Higginson, while Delany and Douglass were co-editors of the antislavery newspaper the *North Star* for several years. All five exchanged ideas with one another regularly, either through direct correspondence, through publications and public addresses, or at antislavery conventions. Still, few contemporaries would have recognized them as a close circle of friends or an intellectual clique.[44] This fact is telling. Romantic reform was a broadly shared mind-set, especially in the 1850s. The five central figures in this book were but a few of the countless antebellum Americans who turned to romantic ideas as the crisis over slavery intensified.

Why are these five of interest? Taken together, they provide a vivid picture of both the diversity and vitality of New Romanticism. They were, for one, among the most significant American minds to engage the problem of slavery in a serious and sustained fashion in the Civil War era. Second, their antislavery work reflected the creative combination of multiple strains of romanticism. They built upon early romantic approaches, which had been pioneered by abolitionists like Garrison, while also experimenting with romantic modes, including martial heroism and romantic racialism, which Garrisonians rejected. Third, the New Romantics took on leading roles in the abolitionist movement's final years. Their prominent position in a number of the most important antislavery battles of the 1850s and early 1860s – the fugitive slave cases in Boston, John Brown's raid at Harpers Ferry, the campaign to enlist African Americans in the Union army – highlights the impact of romantic reform on the burgeoning sectional crisis and the Civil War.

Fourth, the disparate backgrounds of the five figures examined here underscores the degree to which romantic reform penetrated all walks of American life, drawing together cultured Bostonians and runaway slaves. Historians over the last few decades have done much to shatter "the long-standing presumption…that the abolitionist movement was a white man's struggle to end slavery," but, as Timothy McCarthy and John Stauffer have recently noted, a "separate but equal" approach frequently characterizes abolitionist studies today. By juxtaposing the stories of Martin Delany and Theodore Parker, Frederick Douglass and Harriet Beecher Stowe, *Romantic Reformers*, in contrast, offers a desegregated picture of abolitionism in the 1850s, combining the often "discrete narratives" about reformers of different races, religions, sexes, and regions.[45]

---

[44] The New Romantics formed what intellectual historian David Hollinger calls a "discourse community": a group that "share[s] certain values, beliefs, perceptions, and concepts," and, most importantly, "*questions*." David A. Hollinger, *In the American Province: Studies in the History and Historiography of Ideas* (Bloomington: University of Indiana Press, 1985), 132.

[45] Timothy Patrick McCarthy and John Stauffer, eds., introduction to *Prophets of Protest: Reconsidering the History of American Abolitionism* (New York: New Press, 2006), xx; Graham Russell Gao Hodges, *David Ruggles: A Radical Black Abolitionist and the Underground Railroad in New York City* (Chapel Hill: University of North Carolina

Finally, the New Romantics' antislavery careers, like their backgrounds, were far from uniform. As a result, their stories shed light not only on the diverse appeal of romantic reform but also on the myriad ways the ideology played out in practice. Since romantic reform fostered different – at times even competing – approaches to slavery, I have selected figures whose thoughts and actions reflected the full spectrum of possible responses.

Notwithstanding their differences, the New Romantics found plenty of common ground not only with one another but also, to a lesser extent, with fellow romantics in the United States and abroad. Like most of the artists and authors associated with either high or popular romanticism, they stressed the boundless creative capacity of the individual mind. They shared an affinity for nature, too, regularly expressing awe and wonder at the world around them.

The New Romantics had even more in common with the romantic reformers who preceded them. Like abolitionists of Garrison's generation, they were immediatists. The New Romantics also demonstrated a strong sense of moral certitude; they viewed slavery as a sin, critiqued it without qualification, and brooked no compromise with its defenders. In addition, they agreed that the piecemeal tactics and dispassionate argumentation of early opponents of slavery were ill-suited to the challenges posed by the institution and its supporters.[46]

The New Romantics were perfectionists too. More so than many early romantic reformers, in fact, Higginson, Parker, Delany, and Douglass viewed all individuals as potentially divine. Finally, the New Romantics agreed with most early romantic reformers that appeals to emotion and feeling were central to the antislavery project. Parker, for example, insisted that moral sentiment was the fundamental building block of reform. "We

Press, 2010), 3. For other studies that emphasize the diversity of the antislavery movement, see Julie Roy Jeffrey, *The Great Silent Army of Abolitionism: Ordinary Women in the Antislavery Movement* (Chapel Hill: University of North Carolina Press, 1998); Newman, *Transformation of American Abolitionism*; Patrick Rael, *Black Identity and Black Protest in the Antebellum North* (Chapel Hill: University of North Carolina Press, 2002); Stauffer, *Black Hearts of Men*; Susan Zaeske, *Signatures of Citizenship: Petitioning, Antislavery, and Women's Political Identity* (Chapel Hill: University of North Carolina Press, 2003); James Oakes, *The Radical and the Republican: Frederick Douglass, Abraham Lincoln, and the Triumph of Antislavery Politics* (New York: Norton, 2007); Bruce Laurie, *Beyond Garrison: Antislavery and Social Reform* (New York: Cambridge University Press, 2007); and Stauffer, *Giants*.

[46] See, for example, FD, "What to the Slave is the Fourth of July? An Address Delivered at Rochester, New York, on 5 July 1852," in *FDP*, 2: 369 and TWH, *Cheerful Yesterdays* (Boston: Houghton, Mifflin, 1898), 121.

begin with a sentiment," he wrote, "that spreads to an idea; the idea grows to an act, to an institution; then it has done its work."[47] The New Romantics also proved willing to employ that tactic most associated with Garrisonianism: moral suasion. Indeed, Harriet Beecher Stowe's novel *Uncle Tom's Cabin* was the most influential moral suasionist tract produced by an American abolitionist.

Despite clear ties to early romantic reform, the New Romantics departed from Garrison and the AASS in important ways. They often interpreted – and applied – immediatism and perfectionism differently. Timing had something to do with this. The New Romantics became major players in the movement decades after Garrison had announced in the first edition of the *Liberator*, "I am in earnest – I will not equivocate – I will not excuse – I will not retreat a single inch – AND I WILL BE HEARD."[48] Garrison and his colleagues had been true to their words. They had not equivocated, excused, or retreated and no one in antebellum America doubted that they had been heard. Yet the institution of slavery not only survived this verbal assault, its power and influence seemed to expand in the 1850s. To a new generation of immediatists, more militant responses were needed.

This departure from Garrisonianism reflected more than just a pragmatic reaction to a new context. It also was rooted in their sense that perfectionism was not simply a one-way street to nonresistant moral suasion. Many early perfectionists had foresworn "all manifestations of force" in what Lewis Perry described as "the quest for perfect holiness."[49] The romantic reformers of the 1850s, in contrast, stressed the importance of following their inner moral compass, even if the needle pointed them toward forceful resistance. As did earlier generations of perfectionists, they rejected debased human statutes that made compromises with immoral institutions like slavery, insisting that they followed the higher law of God. Yet the New Romantics were willing to use higher law doctrine to justify not just pacifist disunion but also active resistance. As Parker argued in the wake of the Fugitive Slave Law of 1850, "an unjust statute is not only morally void; it is positively wicked to obey it, or allow it to be enforced to the injury of innocent men. It is my duty to resist a wicked law by all expedients that are naturally just."[50] What to

---

[47] TP, "The State of the Nation," in *WTP*, 12: 107.

[48] Garrison, quoted in *WGL*, 1: 76.

[49] Perry, *Radical Abolitionism*, 57, 63.

[50] TP to Samuel J. May, Sept. 25, 1852, Theodore Parker Papers (TPP), Massachusetts Historical Society (MHS), Boston, Massachusetts; *Liberator*, Oct. 22, 1852.

Garrisonians was beyond the pale – direct resistance to sin – became in the 1850s quite the opposite for many perfectionists.

This pronounced militant drift was reinforced by romantic ideas for which their predecessors had demonstrated less enthusiasm. First, many New Romantics viewed the antislavery movement as an opportunity both to protect and to pursue the romantic goal of self-culture. Proponents of self-culture stressed the importance of cultivating human potential, championing the gradual improvement of moral, intellectual, and imaginative faculties.[51] Naturally, then, slavery to them was an anathema. Romantic reformers such as Higginson, Douglass, and Delany, however, did not simply believe that slavery was a barrier to self-improvement; they also argued that active participation in the antislavery cause presented another avenue for self-help, for both the reformer and the enslaved. This interpretation dovetailed neatly with a second romantic ideal – martial heroism – that also proved influential in the 1850s and 1860s.

Thus, as the Civil War loomed, the New Romantics called for heroic resistance against the Slave Power. As we have seen, they turned repeatedly to Byron's ode to self-emancipation. They also wrote short stories and novels that cast slave rebels – whether real or imagined – as romantic heroes.[52] Eventually, most of the New Romantics joined their European counterparts in positing war not as a destructive force but rather "an elemental, cleansing, even redemptive experience."[53] Combining the twin goals of self-culture and martial heroism, Higginson, Douglass, and Delany began to see participation in the antislavery movement as an opportunity for opponents of slavery to reconstruct themselves as well as the world around them. Indeed, Higginson – who formulated the most thoroughgoing philosophy of antislavery violence – argued that by taking up arms against proslavery forces, abolitionists and slaves alike could

[51] Leslie Butler, *Critical Americans: Victorian Intellectuals and Transatlantic Liberal Reform* (Chapel Hill: University of North Carolina Press, 2007), 7. On self-culture, see David Robinson, *Apostle of Culture: Emerson as Preacher and Lecturer* (Philadelphia: University of Pennsylvania Press, 1982); Daniel Walker Howe, *Making the American Self: Jonathan Edwards to Abraham Lincoln* (Cambridge, MA: Harvard University Press, 1997); and Rael, *Black Identity and Black Protest in the Antebellum North*, esp. 118–156.

[52] On antebellum portrayals of slave rebels, see Sundquist, *To Wake Nations*, 27–225; Richard Yarborough, "Race, Violence, and Manhood: The Masculine Ideal in Frederick Douglass's 'The Heroic Slave," in *Frederick Douglass: New Literary and Historical Essays*, ed. Eric J. Sundquist (New York: Cambridge University Press, 1990), 166–188; and Stanley Harrold, "Romanticizing Slave Revolt," 89–107.

[53] David A. Bell, *The First Total War: Napoleon's Europe and the Birth of Warfare as We Know It* (New York: Houghton Mifflin, 2007), 6.

not only destroy slavery but also overcome the alienation that plagued modern America.

Still, the New Romantics could not be called warmongers. They had misgivings about the moral implications and practical effects of active resistance. Although all five flirted with antislavery violence to one degree or another, only Higginson translated his call to arms into a coherent program of armed resistance. This should not surprise us. The New Romantics were, after all, first and foremost men and women of the mind, not the body. As public intellectuals of the day, they were more inclined to verbal disputation than violent struggle.

Romanticism also pointed them toward nonviolent solutions. Romantic ideas about race, for instance, led Delany away from direct confrontation and toward the creation of a black colony abroad. African Americans, he insisted by the end of the 1850s, should embrace their racial identity and reunite with their brethren in Africa. More generally, all five New Romantics we examine in this book subscribed to their own version of what George Frederickson has labeled "romantic racialism." According to this line of thinking, humankind was divided into different races, each of which embodied a particular set of traits. For many romantic racialists, people of African descent were affectionate, religious, and feminine by nature, while Anglo-Saxons were aggressive, sinful, and masculine.[54] Although these stereotypes had some positive connotations for African Americans, they also left Parker and Stowe wondering whether the enslaved had what it took to seize their freedom. Higginson, Delany, and Douglass had fewer doubts about African Americans' martial capacities, yet they struggled to convince fellow abolitionists – and, at times, themselves – that armed resistance was the appropriate response to slavery.

A second – and far more important – check on antislavery militancy was the New Romantics' faith in liberal democracy. Here, again, our small group stood apart from most early romantic reformers. Garrisonian perfectionists were unwilling to work from within traditional political and religious institutions to achieve their goals. The New Romantics, in sharp contrast, decried the corruption of political systems and religious traditions without dismissing them as inherently flawed or unsalvageable. They did not accept the Garrisonian premise that political action was simply "a naive plunge into a smarmy world of compromise and

---

[54] George M. Fredrickson, *The Black Image in the White Mind: The Debate on Afro-American Character and Destiny, 1817–1914* (New York: Harper & Row, 1971), 97–107.

accommodation."[55] In fact, they often grounded their higher law arguments squarely within the nation's liberal tradition. Frederick Douglass, for example, rejected critiques of the Constitution as proslavery in favor of a romantic interpretation of it as a "GLORIOUS LIBERTY DOCUMENT."[56] Even Martin Delany, whose disillusionment with America's racial politics in the 1850s led him to embrace emigration out of the country, was not willing to throw out republican practices or values with the proverbial bathwater.[57]

All told, the New Romantics forged a new brand of abolitionism, moving back and forth between a range of antislavery strategies. Although they continued to work with Garrison and his colleagues at the AASS – the branch of abolitionism that has received the bulk of attention from historians over the last half century – they broke with them on two major fronts.[58] On the one hand, the New Romantics believed that the democratic system provided some openings for perfectionist reform. Although far from traditional political abolitionists – the contributions of whom scholars have done much to salvage in recent years – they urged active participation in antislavery parties and efforts to combat slavery through the political system.[59] On the other hand, as the 1850s wore on the New

---

[55] Laurie, *Beyond Garrison*, 4.

[56] FD, "What to the Slave," 385.

[57] The New Romantics' story thus challenges the long-standing interpretation that romantic reform was fundamentally anti-institutional. Although many Garrisonians rejected human institutions and structures as impediments to the establishment of a divine order, these second-generation romantic reformers insisted that America's political system should not be dismissed outright. They infused their antislavery efforts with a romantic fervor and flirted with violent resistance and revolution, while simultaneously trying to operate within – and reform – the liberal tradition. For romantic reformers as anti-institutionalism, see Elkins, *Slavery*; Fredrickson, *Inner Civil War*; Thomas, *The Liberator*; and Kraditor, *Means and Ends in American Abolitionism*. For a persuasive argument that the evangelical perfectionists of New York's burned-over district also did not fit this anti-institutionalist bill, see Strong, *Perfectionists Politics*.

[58] See Thomas, *The Liberator*; Kraditor, *Means and Ends in American Abolitionism*; James Brewer Stewart, *Wendell Phillip: Liberty's Hero* (Baton Rouge: Louisiana State University Press, 1986); Mayer, *All on Fire*; and James Brewer Stewart, ed., *William Lloyd Garrison at Two Hundred: History, Legacy, and Memory* (New Haven, CT: Yale University Press, 2008).

[59] See Laurie, *Beyond Garrison*; Frederick J. Blue, *No Taint of Compromise: Crusaders in Antislavery Politics* (Baton Rouge: Louisiana State University, 2005); Jonathan H. Earle, *Jacksonian Antislavery & the Politics of Free Soil, 1824–1854* (Chapel Hill: University of North Carolina Press, 2004); John Ashworth, *Slavery, Capitalism, and Politics in the Antebellum Republic, Volume 2: The Coming of the Civil War* (New York: Cambridge University Press, 2007); and Reinhard O. Johnson, *The Liberty Party, 1840–1848: Antislavery Third-Party Politics in the United States* (Baton Rouge: Louisiana State University Press, 2009).

Romantics became increasingly pessimistic about fighting slavery through moral suasion or political agitation, gravitating instead toward a forceful, even violent, response.

In a sense, the New Romantics' vacillation about how to best bring slavery to an end was – outside of their shared romanticism – the most obvious characteristic that united them. Although "ambivalence is not customarily associated with the American abolitionists," the New Romantics helped make it a defining feature of the antislavery movement in the 1850s.[60] Over the course of that decade, they struggled mightily with the question of how to solve the problem of slavery; on their own, with one another, and with fellow abolitionists more generally. At different times and to different degrees they embraced moral suasion, political agitation, and armed struggle against slavery.

This failure to settle on a clear program by which to translate, in Douglass's words, "antislavery sentiment into antislavery action" did not mean that romantic reformers of the 1850s were uncreative or incoherent.[61] Quite the contrary, their failure to fit neatly into traditional abolitionist categories reveals the depth of, and tensions between, the different strains of romanticism that permeated antebellum American culture. Faced with an emboldened enemy, the New Romantics roamed widely through romantic ideals and mindsets, from martial heroism to Manifest Destiny, self-culture to immersion in nature. In the process, they took center stage in the final chapter of the campaign against slavery in the United States, which culminated in the secession crisis and, ultimately, civil war.

The Civil War was the defining event in nineteenth-century America. In four short years, an institution that abolitionists had battled since the Revolution was destroyed and four million men, women, and children were emancipated. But, as Civil War scholars have highlighted in recent years, the conflict was not without its costs. Southern cities were burned to the ground, children starved, and widows mourned. According to a recent estimate, approximately 750,000 Union and Confederate soldiers died during the war as did countless emancipated slaves, who were ravaged by outbreaks of yellow fever, small pox, and cholera. In light of this suffering, death, and destruction, literary critic Andrew Delbanco suggests that we revisit the centrist critiques of the abolitionists by figures such as Hawthorne, Melville, and Henry James. Although no apologists

---

[60] Daniel Carpenter, forward to Andrew Delbanco, *The Abolitionist Imagination* (Cambridge, MA: Harvard University Press, 2012), x.
[61] *Douglass' Monthly*, June 1860, p. 274.

for slavery, these writers highlighted the destructive impact of romantic reform – "the high brutality of good intentions" in novelist William Gass's words.[62]

This Civil War revisionism is an important reminder that we must balance our appreciation for what was achieved during the conflict – the perpetuation of the Union, the destruction of slavery – with a frank assessment of its costs. At the same time, however, we should neither let those costs skew our understanding of what led up to the war in the first place, nor blindly accept (or echo) the caricatures of the abolitionists as frenzied fanatics, which have been served up by their critics for more than a century. Instead, a full reckoning with the American Civil War – and especially the role that romantic reformers played in it – demands that we consider the social and political crises of the 1850s, when increasingly vigilant proslavery forces sought not only to maintain the institution but also to expand its reach and power. Just as importantly, we must examine the ideas that animated the romantic reformers in the run-up to the conflict – ideas that prompted them to contemplate militant responses like insurrection and war.

Historians have long known that romantic nationalism was critical in both pushing secessionists out of the Union and motivating Confederate troops as they marched off to battle. Romantic modes and tropes drove slavery's most radical opponents as well. The decade before the Civil War did not witness a rejection of romanticism by northern reformers, but rather a reconfiguration of that tradition. *Romantic Reformers* tells the story of how antebellum America's most important intellectual current shaped the coming and course of the nation's bloodiest – and most revolutionary – conflict.

A word about the methodology and structure of this book is in order. Since the romantic reformers I examine were idiosyncratic figures who often operated on the margins of traditional antislavery organizations, it

---

[62] Harry S. Stout, *Upon the Altar of the Nation: A Moral History of the Civil War* (New York: Viking, 2006); Drew Gilpin Faust, *This Republic of Suffering: Death and the American Civil War* (New York: Knopf, 2008); Goldfield, *America Aflame*; J. David Hacker, "A Census-Based Count of the Civil War Dead," *Civil War History* 57 (Dec. 2011): 307–348; Jim Downs, *Sick from Freedom: African-American Illness and Suffering during the Civil War and Reconstruction* (New York: Oxford University Press, 2012); Megan Kate Nelson, *Ruin Nation: Destruction and the American Civil War* (Athens: University of Georgia Press, 2012); William Gass, quoted in Delbanco, *Abolitionist Imagination*, 36.

is tempting to view them as *sui generis*. After all, that is how they thought of themselves. Stowe once claimed that "no two persons of independent minds ever view a subject precisely alike," while Higginson boasted that he had "never yet found any one who thought just as [he] did."[63] These claims are fair, but only to a point.

In order to underscore the commonalities shared by the New Romantics without flattening the differences between them, I have organized this study biographically rather than topically. Nearly fifty years ago, David Brion Davis promoted collective biography as a particularly productive approach to cultural history. "By showing how cultural tensions and contradictions may be internalized, struggled with, and resolved within individuals," he argued, biography "offers the most promising key to the synthesis of culture and history."[64] Over the past few decades, scholars such as Daniel Walker Howe, Robert Abzug, John Stauffer, Leslie Butler, and Frederick Blue have borne out Davis's insight, producing collective biographies that profitably explore nineteenth-century American reform culture. *Romantic Reformers* follows in their footsteps, using group biography to capture not simply what my figures shared but also, in Christopher Lasch's words, "possibilities in a certain line of thought or action."[65] Separately, each of the first five chapters traces how romanticism functioned in the career of a leading New Romantic. As a whole, these portraits suggest the range of reactions to the challenges of slavery as well as the possibilities and limitations of romantic reform in America. My conclusion and epilogue draw together the experiences of the four *dramatis personae* who lived through the Civil War (all but Theodore Parker), focusing on how their brand of romantic reform played out during the conflict and beyond.

Our story begins decades earlier, however, when the Civil War was but distant thunder on the nation's horizon. In the spring of 1850, many Americans feared that the United States would be consumed by fires sparked by a different conflict: the recent war with Mexico.

---

[63] HBS to William Lloyd Garrison, Dec. 1853, Boston Public Library (BPL), Boston, Massachusetts; *Newburyport Daily Evening Union*, Dec. 19, 1850.

[64] David Brion Davis, "Some Recent Directions in American Cultural History," *American Historical Review* 73 (Feb. 1968): 705.

[65] Howe, *Making the American Self*; Abzug, *Cosmos Crumbling*; Stauffer, *Black Hearts of Men*; Leslie Butler, *Critical Americans*; Frederick Blue, *No Taint of Compromise*; Christopher Lasch, *The New Radicalism in America, 1889–1963: The Intellectual as a Social Type* (New York: Norton, 1965), 348.

Yet, as with the secession crisis a decade later, the match – slavery – was the same. So, too, were the deep divisions that the crisis opened up among Americans, north and south. While politicians scrambled to offer up concessions that might snuff out the fire, reformers like Theodore Parker refused to compromise their principles, regardless of the consequences.

I

The Transcendental Politics of Theodore Parker

Both the Senate floor and its gallery were overflowing on March 7, 1850. Washingtonians had risen early on a crisp morning, packing the small, stuffy chamber. Latecomers could do little more than linger outside, hoping that some space would materialize. Acknowledging the unusually large crowd, Wisconsin Senator Isaac Walker, who had not yet finished his remarks from the day before, stood and announced, "Mr. President, this vast audience has not assembled to hear me; and there is but one man, in my opinion, who can assemble such an audience." Walker then ceded the floor to his colleague from Massachusetts, Daniel Webster.[1]

Webster was a renowned orator. Ralph Waldo Emerson lauded "the perfection of his elocution," insisting that his "voice, accent, intonation, attitude, [and] manner are such as one cannot hope to see again in a century."[2] Yet soaring rhetoric alone did not account for the crowd that day in early March. People came to hear what the distinguished politician, widely known as the great expounder and defender of the Constitution, had to say about the compromise legislation that had gripped the public mind since its introduction by Henry Clay two months earlier. The Kentucky Whig's compromise bill sought to ease the sectional tensions that had been building since the annexation of Texas and the Mexican War. The bill would, among other measures, admit California as a free state, organize the rest of the Mexican territories without restricting or

---

[1] Allan Nevins, *Ordeal of the Union, Volume One: Fruits of Manifest Destiny, 1847–1852* (New York: Charles Scribner's Sons, 1947), 287; Isaac Walker, quoted in Daniel Webster, *Speech of Hon. Daniel Webster on Mr. Clay's Resolutions, in the Senate of the United States, March 7, 1850* (Washington, DC: Gideon & Co., 1850), 5.
[2] Ralph Waldo Emerson, Journal, Aug. 17, 1843, in *JMN*, 10: 393.

authorizing slavery, abolish the slave trade (but not slavery) in the District
of Columbia, and enact a stricter fugitive slave law. Clay was hoping to
transcend sectional divisions by appeasing pro- and antislavery constit-
uencies alike.

Americans were of two minds about Clay's proposal. Unionists across
the country had responded enthusiastically to the compromise plan. In
New York City in late February, twenty thousand people gathered at the
Battery, cheering Clay's name. Not everyone, however, was so ebullient.
Horace Greeley's *New-York Tribune*, typically a stalwart Whig paper,
equivocated on the issue, while militant voices (antislavery in the North
and proslavery in the South) found little to admire.[3]

Few in the South, of course, were more radical than South Carolina
Senator John C. Calhoun, the third member of the Great Triumvirate –
Webster and Clay were the other two – that had dominated American
politics for much of the century. Just three days before Webster's address,
Calhoun had dismissed Clay's compromise as beyond the pale. Once
again casting the North in the role of bully and the South as aggrieved
victim, the architect of nullification placed the burden of restoring sectional balance solely on northern shoulders. The South, he insisted, "has
no compromise to offer."[4] Many people wondered how Daniel Webster,
Calhoun's counterpart from the North, would respond.

Staking out the middle ground between northern agitators and southern firebrands, the senator chose national citizenship over sectional parti-
sanship. "Mr. President, – I wish to speak to-day, not as a Massachusetts
man, nor as a Northern man, but as an American," Webster announced. He
was unwilling to accept Calhoun's idea about northern political supremacy, arguing that the South had controlled the national government for
much of the country's history. But the Massachusetts senator saved his
sharpest blows for reformers from the North. Despite his personal dis-
taste for slavery, he dismissed the moral absolutism of antislavery forces
as naïve, maintaining that abolitionists have "produced nothing good

---

[3] *Congressional Globe*, 31 Cong., 1 sess., 244–247, 944–948; Holman Hamilton, *Prologue
to Conflict: The Crisis and Compromise of 1850* (Lexington: University of Kentucky
Press, 1964), 43–62; Freehling, *Road to Disunion, Vol. 1*, 487–498; Don E. Fehrenbacher,
*The Slaveholding Republic: An Account of the United States Government's Relations to
Slavery*, completed and edited by Ward M. McAfee (New York: Oxford University Press,
2001), 83–87; Michael F. Holt, *The Fate of Their Country: Politicians, Slavery Extension,
and the Coming of the Civil War* (New York: Hill and Wang, 2004), 68–72; David Potter,
The Impending Crisis, 1848–1861, completed and edited by Don E. Fehrenbacher (New
York: Harper and Row, 1976), 99–100.

[4] *Congressional Globe*, 31 Cong., 1 sess., 455.

or valuable" in twenty years of agitation. On the critical fugitive slave issue, he bluntly stated that "the South is right, and the North is wrong." All told, Webster's address was a ringing endorsement of unionism over sectionalism. Although he did not proffer explicit support for Clay's measures, Webster made it clear that he shared his colleague's overarching goal of avoiding the extremes of northern and southern radicalism. Compromise was the answer.[5]

Webster's speech elicited outrage among northern reformers. While the region's leading businessmen, politicians, and newspapers hoped it might forestall civil war, opponents of slavery charged him with treason. Once, said Emerson, he had counted the senator "the best head in Congress," but "on the 7th March, 1850, in opposition to his education, association, and to all his own most explicit language for thirty years, he crossed the line, and became the head of the slavery party in this country." Second-generation Transcendentalist Thomas Wentworth Higginson likewise felt betrayed by Webster. As a young man, he had decorated his Harvard dormitory room with a bust of the statesman. But Webster's Seventh of March address rendered his vast powers impotent in Higginson's mind. "Is greatness of intellect the greatest greatness?" he asked in 1852. "Can it cover the sudden change from a love of freedom, flickering indeed, but sincere, to a blind, servile concentration of all faculties in opposing the cause of freedom?"[6]

Emerson's friend and Higginson's mentor, Theodore Parker, was Webster's most fervent critic. "No speech ever delivered in America has excited such deep and righteous indignation," Parker declared two months after Webster's address.[7] Like Webster, he thought America was poised on a precipice. For the Transcendentalist minister, however, the choice was not between union or disunion but rather a future of slavery or a future of freedom. He maintained that the dominant political parties could not provide a remedy to the dilemma because "old party distinctions, once so sacred and rigidly observed, here vanish out of sight."

5 Daniel Webster, *Speech of Hon. Daniel Webster*, 5, 51, 47; Michael F. Holt, *The Rise and Fall of the American Whig Party: Jacksonian Politics and the Onset of the Civil War* (New York: Oxford University Press, 1999), 488.
6 Ralph Waldo Emerson, "Address to the Citizens of Concord," in *Emerson's Antislavery Writings*, ed. Len Gougeon and Joel Myerson (New Haven, CT: Yale University Press, 1995), 66; Tilden Edelstein, *Strange Enthusiasm: A Life of Thomas Wentworth Higginson* (New Haven, CT: Yale University Press, 1968), 1–2; TWH, *Elegy Without Fiction: A Sermon, Preached October 31st, 1852* (Worcester, MA, 1852), n.p.
7 TP, "A Speech at the New England Anti-Slavery Convention in Boston, May 29, 1850," in *SAOS*, 2: 188.

Issues such as tariffs and the national bank fell by the wayside as two new associations – the Party of Slavery and the Party of Freedom – stood poised "to swallow up all the other parties."

Parker was particularly disappointed by his fellow New Englander's failure to marshal his "great gifts of the understanding" for the side of freedom. "I know no deed in American history, done by a son of New England, to which I can compare this," he insisted, "but the act of Benedict Arnold!"[8] Two years later, he went further, saying Webster "drew his sword to sheathe it in the bowels of his brother-man." Even after the politician died of cirrhosis of the liver two years later, Parker refused to relent.[9]

This anger with Webster reflected more than simply personal disappointment with a fallen hero. The senator's speech struck at the heart of the minister's worldview. In the early 1840s, Parker had burst on to Boston's religious scene with his critique of Unitarian supernatural rationalism. Like most of his fellow Transcendentalists, he was a firm believer in romantic intuition. From his idealist perspective, universal truths were more effectively accessed by plumbing the depths of one's soul than by following external directives from a church, minister, or even the Bible. Although isolated from mainstream Unitarianism by the mid-1840s for distinguishing "transient" Christian beliefs and practices from God's "permanent" wisdom, Parker nonetheless developed a large following of liberal Bostonians.

Eventually he built a diverse, nondenominational church, the Twenty-Eighth Congregational Society, which had more than two thousand regular worshippers. When Wendell Phillips addressed the congregation in 1862, he claimed that the "diocese of Theodore Parker extended to the Pacific." Hyperbole, to be sure, but Bostonians of all stripes – from merchants and laborers to escaped slaves and prominent abolitionists such as William Lloyd Garrison – came to hear Parker in the 1850s. On occasion Daniel Webster may have even attended.[10]

---

[8] TP, "A Speech at a Meeting of the Citizens of Boston in Faneuil Hall, March 25, 1850, to consider the Speech of Mr. Webster," in *SAOS*, 2: 148, 170.

[9] TP, "The Boston Kidnapping. A Discourse to Commemorate the Rendition of Thomas Sims, Delivered on the Anniversary Thereof, April 12, 1852, Before the Committee of Vigilance, at the Melodeon, in Boston," in *ASAOS*, 1: 100; TP, "Discourse on the Death of Daniel Webster," in *WTP*, 7: 339, 346, 343.

[10] Dean Grodzins, "Theodore Parker and the Twenty-Eighth Congregational Society: The Reform Church and the Spirituality of Reformers in Boston, 1845–1859," in *Transient and Permanent: The Transcendentalist Movement and Its Contexts*, ed. Charles Capper and Conrad E. Wright (Boston: Massachusetts Historical Society, 1999), 73–117;

Although Parker's participation in the struggle against slavery was limited in the early 1840s, as the decade wore on he became increasingly involved. By the 1850s, he was among the most influential and aggressive abolitionists in America. An early biographer wrote, "to trace the life of Mr. Parker through the great agitation for anti-slavery principles ... would be almost equivalent to writing the history of the antislavery movement since 1845."[11] From debates over the Mexican War to the fugitive slave cases in Boston to John Brown's raid at Harpers Ferry, Parker left his stamp on the political struggles of this tumultuous era, especially when it came to the development of higher law doctrine, a set of arguments embraced by many antebellum abolitionists. All individuals, insisted Parker, were invested with the capacity to tap into the universal moral law through intuition. Human law, in turn, had to bear constant comparison to the higher law. If the former is found wanting, then it must be rejected. Although each of the New Romantics considered in these pages had a basic commitment to higher law doctrine, Parker was its most forceful proponent.[12]

Nonetheless, fundamental tensions informed his approach to reform. Parker was, on the one hand, devoted to universal notions of individual perfectibility, a transcendent higher law, and the progressive thrust of history. On the other hand, he often cast these ideals in particularist terms, whether national or racial. Indeed, his antislavery addresses and private correspondence were peppered with appeals to racial essentialism. Thus, Parker has frustrated modern readers, who have trouble reconciling his

Liberator, July 11, 1862; TP to [Daniel?] Webster, Dec. 12, 1850, Theodore Parker Papers (TPP), Andover-Harvard Theological Library (AHTL), Harvard Divinity School, Cambridge, MA; TP to Millard Fillmore, Nov. 21, 1850, TPP, AHTL. While scholars have long believed that Webster heard Parker preach at the Melodeon, the minister's best modern biographer, Dean Grodzins, doubts that this was, in fact, the case. Von Frank, *Trials of Anthony Burns,* 100; *LCTP,* 2: 99; Charles Wiltse and Michael J. Birkner, eds., *The Papers of Daniel Webster* (Hanover, NH: University Press of New England, 1986), 7: 189–190; Robert V. Remini, *Daniel Webster: The Man and His Time* (New York: Norton, 1997), 144, 696n43; Peter Harvey, *Reminiscences and Anecdotes of Daniel Webster* (Boston: Little, Brown, and Co., 1877), 396; Grodzins, e-mail message to author, Nov. 10, 2011.

[11] *LCTP,* 2: 68.

[12] Von Frank, *Trials of Anthony Burns,* 100; David Reynolds, *John Brown, Abolitionist,* 482; Len Gougeon, "Fortune of the Republic: Emerson, Lincoln, and Transcendental Warfare," *ESQ: A Journal of the American Renaissance* 45 (3rd and 4th qt. 1999): 266; Henry Steele Commager, *Theodore Parker: Yankee Crusader* (Boston: Little, Brown, and Co., 1936), 197–213; and George E. Carter, "The Use of the Doctrine of Higher Law in the American Anti-Slavery Crusade, 1830–1860" (PhD diss., University of Oregon, 1970), 288–313.

deep opposition to slavery with his romantic racialist ideas.[13] Parker's intellectual methods have likewise appeared inconsistent to some scholars. Despite his romantic epistemology, Parker was the preeminent bookworm, boasting a massive library, an encyclopedic memory, and a working knowledge of nearly two dozen languages. Relentlessly, he sought out any and all empirical evidence by which to verify ideas accessed through intuition.[14]

This intellectual ambivalence dovetailed with Parker's open-minded approach to abolitionist tactics. As a minister he was predisposed to moral suasion, the antislavery strategy endorsed by many romantic reformers. Parker, however, insisted that political agitation was a necessary accommodation to life's exigencies. Unlike most Garrisonians, he believed that America's democratic institutions and practices were salvageable. Although Parker lambasted Webster for his willingness to compromise, he acknowledged the role conventional democratic politics could play in the antislavery struggle. And, as the encroachment of what he dubbed the "Party of Slavery" seemed to grow over the course of the 1850s, he made the case for still more extreme methods, despite his misgivings. Physical self-defense, he argued as a leader of the Boston Vigilance Committee, was the right response of a fugitive slave – or his supporters – when confronted by slave catchers. In the face of an increasingly belligerent Party of Slavery, the higher law even seemed to justify the violation of both the rule of law and the sanctity of private property, at least in human form.

Parker's antislavery career, in short, was forged through the dynamic interplay between his intellectual and tactical ambivalence and his firm commitment to the higher law. Unwilling either to ignore the corruption of politics or to abandon politics altogether, he formulated a distinctive democratic vision, one founded on an uncompromising defense of higher law doctrine. Ultimately, Parker's most famous trope – the transient and permanent – provides a key by which to unlock his romantic mind-set. His was a philosophy that, in the end, demanded that any and every resource, regardless of how flawed or transient, be marshaled in the name of the permanent truth – the higher law.

---

[13] Fredrickson, *The Black Image in the White Mind*, 119–120n47; Michael Fellman, "Theodore Parker and the Abolitionist Role in the 1850s," *Journal of American History* 61 (Dec. 1974): 666–684; and Paul Teed, "Romantic Nationalism and Its Challengers: Theodore Parker, John Rock, and the Antislavery Movement," *Civil War History* 41 (June 1995): 142–160.

[14] Henry Steele Commager, "The Dilemma of Theodore Parker," *New England Quarterly* 6 (June 1933): 257–277.

The Transient and Permanent

Theodore Parker was from liberal Christian stock. Born in 1810 to John and Hannah Stearns Parker in Lexington, Massachusetts, he grew up as Unitarians battled with evangelical and orthodox Christians for Boston-area supremacy. His father, who earned a modest living building cider presses and pumps, owned a pew at the Lexington Congregational Church, which displayed sure signs of liberalism. Although as a young man Parker flirted with the fires of evangelicalism that were spreading across the country, he was uncomfortable with the drama and immediacy of the conversion experience and the stern Calvinist deity of the Old Testament. Early on, he was a mainstream Unitarian.[15]

New England Unitarianism developed in the late eighteenth and early nineteenth centuries. Given their name by orthodox opponent Jedidiah Morse – who accused liberal Christians in Boston of doubting Jesus's divinity and thus the Holy Trinity – Unitarians tended not to be unitarian in a strict sense. They rejected the Trinitarian view of God as Father, Son, and Holy Spirit, but believed that Jesus, although not one and the same with God, was nonetheless divine. In any case, Unitarians were more concerned with the fallacy of the doctrine of original sin than the Trinity question. They renounced the Calvinist notion of a vengeful God, insisting that, in historian Paul Conkin's words, "they were good Christians in spite of, not because of, such doctrines as depravity and election."[16]

Parker entered the epicenter of Unitarianism, Harvard Divinity School, in 1834. Although he did not begin his studies until midway through the year, he finished the three-year curriculum in just over two years. This speedy progress was even more impressive in light of the many detours he took from the traditional curriculum. "His great, omnivorous, hungry intellect must have constant food, – new languages, new statistics, new historical investigations, new scientific discoveries, new systems of scriptural exegesis," fellow New Romantic Higginson explained years later.[17] Parker graduated from the Divinity School with a basic grasp of perhaps twenty languages and a thorough grounding in traditional English, Greek, and Roman literature as well as recent British and French philosophy.

---

[15] Dean Grodzins, *American Heretic: Theodore Parker and Transcendentalism* (Chapel Hill: University of North Carolina Press, 2002), 8–18; TP, "An Autobiographical Fragment," in *WTP*, 13: 11; TP, "Experience as a Minister," in *WTP*, 13: 296.

[16] Paul K. Conkin, *American Originals: Homemade Varieties of Christianity* (Chapel Hill: University of North Carolina Press, 1997), 58, 70–71 (quotation 71).

[17] TWH, *Contemporaries* (Boston: Houghton, Mifflin, 1899), 39.

While in Cambridge, he also explored German idealism and biblical criticism, beginning his journey away from Unitarian orthodoxy.[18]

Romantic ideas that emanated from Germany had a profound impact on Parker and a number of his young Unitarian colleagues. In the early nineteenth century, German philosophers and theologians had formulated appealing epistemological alternatives to the Lockean sensationalism and Scottish commonsense philosophy that predominated at Harvard. "It is hard to imagine a study more dry, more repulsive, more perplexing, and more totally unsatisfactory to a scientific mind" than Unitarian theology, complained fellow Transcendentalist George Ripley. It "pulverized" the heart and sapped vitality from life.[19]

German Romantic theology and philosophy was like a beacon of light by which to revive the faith. Parker, who had dabbled in Coleridge, Goethe, and Victor Cousin before he enrolled at the Divinity School, warmed to European Romanticism over the course of his Harvard career. He read Madame de Staël, Thomas Carlyle, and Johann Gottfried von Herder. Parker was impressed by the intellectual rigor of German biblical criticism, which his German proficiency allowed him to read unmediated by French or English translations. More compelling still were the ideas of Friedrich Schleiermacher, who put emotion and intuition at the center of his religious theories. By the end of his time at Cambridge, Parker's exploration of German Romanticism left the young divinity student questioning his faith's core tenet – that biblical miracles provided definitive proof of Christianity. The traditional distinction between natural and revealed religion began to blur for him as he moved toward a more intuitive approach to religious truth. In sum, Parker entered Harvard a conventional Unitarian but left a Transcendentalist.[20]

Parker graduated in 1836, a year that Perry Miller has called the *annus mirabilis* of Transcendentalism because it saw Emerson publish his essay *Nature*, Bronson Alcott produce his *Conversations with Children on the Gospels*, and George Ripley complete his *Discourses on the Philosophy of Religion*, as well as the first Transcendental Club meeting. Drawn to the new movement from the start, Parker began attending club meetings in late 1836 or early 1837. He was also taken with the work of his fellow Harvard graduate and Unitarian minister Emerson, who he counted

[18] Grodzins, *American Heretic*, 31–62.
[19] George Ripley, "Martineau's Rationale," in *The Transcendentalists, An Anthology*, ed. Perry Miller (Cambridge, MA: Harvard University Press, 1950), 131.
[20] Grodzins, *American Heretic*, 62–74.

as an important early influence.[21] Like so many romantics in Europe and the United States, however, Parker found even greater inspiration in the natural world around him. "You know I lamented the missing of Mr. Emerson's lectures," he once admitted, "but a single walk along the banks of the Connecticut, or among the hills ... have taught me more than Mr. Emerson and all the Boston Association of Ministers."[22]

Parker's first ministry was a small Unitarian church in West Roxbury, Massachusetts, not far from Boston. Although largely within the Unitarian mainstream upon graduation from divinity school, he wrote privately about the increasingly radical nature of his sermons soon after he was ordained in 1837. "I preach abundant heresies, and they all go down – for the listeners do not know how heretical they are," confessed the young minister. "Nay I preach the worst of all things[,] Transcendentalism, the grand heresy itself."[23]

Parker's militant message dovetailed with his striking style in the pulpit. Five feet, eight inches tall, he had a massive forehead and powerful physique that "made him a riveting and seemingly uncompromising presence."[24] When Parker addressed his congregation, noted one observer, "his lead-like eyes begin to glow with genius, and his bald head seems to shine transparently with thought" (Figure 1.1). Caroline Healy Dall described the minister's rhetoric in equally visceral terms: "Every word falling from Mr Parker's lip is a battle ax – it cleaves a skull."[25]

Soon Parker's ax took aim at the heart of Unitarian orthodoxy. In May 1841, at the ordination of new Unitarian minister Charles C. Shackford, Parker delivered the sermon that first earned him widespread attention and scorn: "A Discourse on the Transient and Permanent in Christianity." Since a handful of orthodox and evangelical ministers attended

[21] Miller, ed., *The Transcendentalists*, 106–107; Joel Myerson, "A Calendar of Transcendentalist Club Meetings," *American Literature* 44 (May 1972): 197–207; TP, notes, July 15, 1838, in *LCTP*, 1: 113; TP to Martha M. Parker, Oct. 9, 1851, TPP, MHS; Daniel Aaron, *Men of Good Hope: A Story of American Progressives* (New York: Oxford University Press, 1951), 21.

[22] TP to Lydia Dodge Cabot, Feb. 13, 1837, in *LCTP*, 1: 96.

[23] TP to William Silsbee, Sept. 22, 1837, TPP, MHS.

[24] John White Chadwick, *Theodore Parker: Preacher and Reformer* (Boston: Houghton, Mifflin, 1901), 211; Grodzins, "Theodore Parker and the Twenty-Eighth Congregational Society," 74; Philip F. Gura, *American Transcendentalism: A History* (New York: Hill and Wang, 2007), 117.

[25] George W. Bungay, *Off-Hand Takings or, Crayon Sketches of the Noticeable Men of Our Age* (New York: Robert M. De Witt, 1854), 254; Caroline Dall, Diary, Jan. 20, 1851, in *Daughter of Boston: The Extraordinary Diary of a Nineteenth-Century Woman*, ed. Helen R. Deese (Boston: Beacon Press, 2005), 138.

Theodore Parker
From the lithograph by Grozelier.

FIGURE 1.1. Theodore Parker, n.d.
Source: Photomechanical of a lithograph by Leopold Grozelier, n.d. Courtesy of
the Massachusetts Historical Society, Portraits of American Abolitionists, photograph number 81.497a.

Shackford's ordination at Hawes Place Church in South Boston, the sermon exposed what was heretofore a family squabble within Unitarian
circles to Boston's broader religious community.[26]

For several years, Transcendentalist ministers such as Parker and
George Ripley had been ruffling Unitarian feathers over their embrace of
German biblical criticism. As supernatural rationalists, Unitarians did not
object to biblical criticism per se; combining Locke's sensationalist philosophy with religious faith, they agreed that the Bible should be inves-
tigated diligently. Yet most Unitarian theologians would not go so far as
to question the validity of scripture, particularly the miracles of the New
Testament. In contrast, Parker and company argued that the foundations
of Christianity should be religious feeling, an intuitive sense of the divine,
thereby sparking the so-called miracles controversy.[27]

---

[26] Grodzins, *American Heretic*, 246; Gura, *American Transcendentalism*, 145–146.
[27] Conkin, *American Originals*, 85; Grodzins, *American Heretic*, 157–171, 180–199;
Ripley, "Martineau's Rationale," 132.

Parker's ordination sermon placed most of Christian doctrine and practice in the category of transient, in contrast to God's innate moral truths, which alone merited the label permanent. He argued that Christianity "has never been the same thing in any two centuries or lands, except only in name." Christians should cast off the transient manifestations of religion that claim to be the truth based "on the personal authority of Jesus," leaving just the "immutable truth of the doctrines themselves." What is more, Parker placed a premium on the role that the individual played in interpreting God's message, whether manifested in the Old Testament, New Testament, or through inner inspiration. This provocative sermon, in short, questioned the authenticity of core Christian belief and practice, substituting a personal faith in which the individual looked inward for divine inspiration.[28]

It was therefore no surprise that Christians across Boston responded quickly. Three weeks after the ordination sermon, the orthodox and evangelical ministers in attendance published an abstract of Parker's views, sharply questioning whether his ideas represented mainstream Unitarianism. What to Parker seemed an innocuous statement of his devout faith in God's universal truths sounded to them like a direct assault on the solemn authority of Jesus and the Bible. Meanwhile, the Unitarian establishment moved swiftly to distance itself from the upstart. Although Unitarianism's liberal foundations and congregational structure gave its ministers few weapons with which to put down a doctrinal revolt, they made the best with what they had. Within the year, most Boston Unitarians refused to exchange pulpits with Parker, depriving the Transcendentalist of the wider audience that he sought, while also isolating him from friends and colleagues.[29]

Soon new opportunities, both secular and sacred, opened for the young minister and his provocations, however. Parker found appreciative audiences at local lyceums. In the 1850s, he regularly traveled to lyceums across the country, speaking before more than sixty thousand people a year by his own estimate.[30] By this point, Parker was also preaching to a much larger congregation than he had in West Roxbury. In early 1846, he had become the minister at the deliberately nondenominational Twenty-Eighth Congregational Society of Boston. A heterogeneous lot, regular

[28] TP, "The Transient and Permanent in Christianity," in *WTP*, 4: 5, 18, 6, 17.

[29] Grodzins, *American Heretic*, 248–292; TP to Convers Francis, June 24, 1842, in *LCTP*, 1: 184; TP to Chandler Robbins, Feb. 28, 1845, in *LCTP*, 1: 251.

[30] Grodzins, "Theodore Parker," in *The American Renaissance in New England: Third Series*, ed. Wesley T. Mott (Detroit, MI: Gale, 2001): 313.

worshippers at the new church ranged from prosperous merchants and prominent politicians to working-class laborers. It was one of the few unsegregated churches in Boston, a place where white abolitionists such as Garrison and Francis Jackson sat alongside African American counterparts such as William Nell and Lewis Hayden. In 1850, Parker described his new church as a "large religious society composed of 'all sorts and conditions of men,'" including both "fugitive slaves who do not legally own the nails on their fingers" and "also men & women of wealth & fine cultivation."[31] Parker's audiences were huge: up to a thousand people came to hear his 1840s sermons in the Boston Melodeon, whereas more than twice that number turned up once he moved to the Boston Music Hall in the 1850s. By then, his was the city's largest congregation. "Criticism took Theodore Parker from a village pulpit and gave him the whole country for a platform and the whole nation for an audience," wrote Frederick Douglass a half-century later.[32]

Week in and week out, Parker captivated liberal audiences with his scriptural erudition, unorthodox theology, and his increasingly radical social message. While the minister still counted himself a Unitarian and refused to "come out" of Unitarianism, he nonetheless was unwilling to keep silent about the errors maintained by the purported liberal Christian faith. Repeatedly Parker insisted from his pulpit that the Bible was a useful, but flawed, spiritual guide. "No doubt the Bible contained the imperfection of the men and ages concerned in writing it," he reasoned. "The hay tastes of the meadow where it grew, of the weather when it was made, and smells of the barn wherein it has been kept."[33] Parker allowed that Jesus was "the greatest person of the ages," but he had no doubt "that God has yet greater men in store."[34] Left unsaid was what this argument spelled for mankind. For, by making Jesus a mortal, Parker could give humanity no higher compliment. This humanist vision was, in the end, the core principle of Parker's theology. "In becoming Christians,"

[31] Grodzins, "Theodore Parker and the Twenty-Eighth Congregational Society," 90; TP to Fillmore, Nov. 21, 1850.

[32] Grodzins, *American Heretic*, ix; Packer, *Transcendentalists*, 169; FD, "Self-Made Men: An Address Delivered in Carlisle, Pennsylvania, in March 1893," in *FDP*, 5: 575.

[33] TP, "The Nebraska Question. Some Thoughts on the New Assault upon Freedom in America, and the General State of the Country in Relation Thereunto, Set Forth in a Discourse Preached at the Music Hall, in Boston, on Sunday, February 12, 1854," in *ASAOS*, 1: 306.

[34] TP, "The Relation of Jesus to His Age and the Ages. A Sermon preached at the Thursday Lecture, in Boston, December 26, 1844," in *SAOS*, 1: 15.

he warned, "let us not cease to be men," for it is "unchristian to love Christianity better than the truth, or Christ better than man."[35]

As did many of his fellow Transcendentalist ministers, Parker urged his parishioners to strive for moral perfection rather than to adhere strictly to religious doctrine. "What is man here on earth to accomplish?" he asked in an 1851 sermon. "He is to unfold and perfect himself, as far as possible, in body and spirit; to attain the full measure of his corporeal and spiritual powers, his intellectual, moral, affectional, and religious powers; to develop the individual into a complete man."[36] In addition, Parker often applied his millennial optimism not just to individual Americans but to the United States as a whole. He looked to "a future to be made ... a society full of industry and abundance, full of wisdom, virtue, and the poetry of life; a state with unity among all, with freedom for each; ... a society without ignorance, want, or crime, a state without oppression."[37] History may doubt that such a millennium was possible, but Parker believed that both America and its citizenry could be perfected.

Antislavery and the Higher Law

Two years after his trenchant sermon on the transient and permanent in Christianity enraged Boston Unitarians, Parker published a short, rather facile piece that pointed to his next provocation. "Socrates in Boston: A Dialogue between the Philosopher and a Yankee," which appeared in the antislavery journal the *Liberty Bell* in 1843, mimicked the form of a Socratic dialogue. Recounting a short conversation between Socrates and a Yankee deacon named Jonathan, the story explored an issue to which the New Romantic would devote himself a decade later: the capture of a fugitive slave in Boston.

Most of the story depicts Socrates, in typical fashion, questioning his counterpart about how Americans square their commitment to liberty, justice, and Christianity with the institution of slavery, in general, and the capture of runaways, in particular. As one might expect, Jonathan proved no match for Socrates, admitting at the end of the didactic dialogue that slavery violates both democratic and Christian principles. Still, Jonathan insists that the institution is lawful, if unjust. Rushing off at the sound of

---

[35] TP, "The True Idea of a Christian Church," in *WTP*, 13: 20.
[36] TP, "The Three Chief Safeguards of Society, Considered in a Sermon at the Melodeon, on Sunday, July 6, 1851," in *SAOS*, 2: 360.
[37] TP, "Transcendentalism," in *WTP*, 6: 38.

the church bell to listen to appropriately named Dr. Smothertext preach on *"the danger of being righteous over much,"* he remains unconverted. The reader, in contrast, is left to hear Socrates' final words. "Slavery in a free land; defended in a Christian land; by men who do not *own* slaves!" he cries. "This must be all a dream!"[38]

Parker's Socratic dialogue illustrated the means by which he would apply his romantic beliefs to the nightmare of slavery in the coming years. By asking how the law could make anything right that Christianity deemed wrong, he highlighted the enormous gap between transient rules such as the 1793 fugitive slave law and permanent truths such as the incompatibility of Christian morality and slavery. Just as historical Christianity had contaminated God's truth, so too had proslavery forces perverted a young nation's moral foundations. Increasingly, the institution of slavery seemed to him the most prevalent violation of God's law in America. Although largely disengaged from both everyday politics and social reform as a young man, Parker became, by the late 1840s, America's higher law prophet.[39]

According to higher law doctrine, human statutes were only valid insofar as they conformed to natural or divine law. Although this concept had roots dating back to antiquity, it gained particular currency among antebellum opponents of slavery. In the Missouri Compromise debates, for instance, New York Senator Rufus King declared all proslavery laws "absolutely void, because [they are] contrary to the laws of nature, which is the law of God, by which he makes his way known to man and is paramount to all human control." Thirty years later, the New England Anti-Slavery Convention resolved that "any theory which bids one man [to] submit his moral convictions, and square his actions by the votes of a majority, is anti-republican, tyrannical, unchristian, and atheistical." Democratic might, in other words, does not make moral right.[40]

---

[38] TP, "Socrates in Boston: A Dialogue between the Philosopher and a Yankee," *Liberty Bell* (1843): 117–144 (quotations 144); Grodzins, *American Heretic*, 335–336.

[39] *Liberator*, Nov. 2, 1855; Grodzins, *American Heretic*, 328–333; Grodzins, "Theodore Parker," 310.

[40] Carter, "Use of the Doctrine of Higher Law," 18–52; Gregg D. Crane, *Race, Citizenship, and Law in American Literature* (New York: Cambridge University Press, 2002), 12–19; Ferenc M. Szasz, "Antebellum Appeals to the 'Higher Law,'" 1830–1860," *Essex Institute Historical Collections* 110 (January 1974): 33–48; Edward S. Corwin, *The "Higher Law" Background of American Constitutional Law* (1928; reprint, Ithaca, NY: Great Seal Books, 1959), 5; Rufus King, quoted in David Brion Davis, *Inhuman Bondage: The Rise and Fall of Slavery in the New World* (New York: Oxford University Press, 2006), 276; *Liberator*, June 6, 1851.

William Henry Seward made the most famous invocation of higher law doctrine in antebellum America in the wake of Webster's Seventh of March address. Believing Clay's "scheme" to be a "magnificent humbug," the New York senator framed the debate along the lines of Parker's most infamous sermon. "Slavery is only a temporary, accidental, partial, and incongruous" institution, he held, while "freedom, on the contrary, is a perpetual, organic, universal one, in harmony with the Constitution of the United States." Unlike Webster, who pledged himself to the Constitution, Seward suggested that a different law took precedence. "There is a higher law than the Constitution, which regulates our authority over the domain, and devotes it to the same noble purposes," he maintained.[41]

Seward's insistence that there was a law higher than the Constitution of the United States – a point he made from the Senate floor, no less – fed flames across the North and South. The *New Orleans Weekly Picayune* called him an "unscrupulous demagogue." Edward Bates, a Whig lawyer and politician from Missouri, privately concluded that "he [who] would set himself above [the Constitution and statute law] claiming some transcendental authority for his disobedience, must be ... either a Canting hypocrite, a presumptuous fool, or an arbitrary designing knave."[42] Northern opponents of slavery, no surprise, championed Seward's stand. Horace Greeley put out a special edition of the *New-York Tribune* to circulate the senator's ideas throughout the Middle West and the American and Foreign Anti-Slavery Society distributed ten thousand copies of the speech across the North. Years later, an antislavery ally marveled at Seward's ability to "compress into a single sentence, a single word, the whole issue of a controversy."[43]

[41] William H. Seward, quoted in Hamilton, *Prologue to Conflict*, 68; William H. Seward, "Freedom in the New Territories," in *The Works of William H. Seward*, ed. George E. Baker (New York: Redfield, 1853), 1: 84, 74–75; Hamilton, *Prologue to Conflict*, 84–86. As numerous historians have pointed out, Seward was more moderate on the question of slavery than this speech made him appear. Holt, *Rise and Fall of the American Whig Party*, 490; Van Deusen, *William Henry Seward*, 128; Foner, *Free Soil, Free Labor*, 140; James Oakes, *Freedom National: The Destruction of Slavery in the United States, 1861–1865* (New York: Norton, 2013), 30.

[42] *New Orleans Weekly Picayune*, quoted in Hamilton, *Prologue to Conflict*, 85; Elizabeth Fox-Genovese and Eugene Genovese, *The Mind of the Master Class: History and Faith in the Southern Slaveholders' Worldview* (New York: Cambridge University Press, 2005), 624–635; Edward Bates, quoted in Doris Kearns Goodwin, *Team of Rivals: The Political Genius of Abraham Lincoln* (New York: Simon & Schuster, 2005), 159.

[43] Adam-Max Tuchinsky, "Horace Greeley's Lost Book: The *New-York Tribune* and the Origins of Social-Democratic Liberalism in America" (PhD diss., University of North Carolina, 2001), 391; John M. Taylor, *William Henry Seward: Lincoln's Right Hand* (New York: HarperCollins, 1991), 85; Carl Schurz, *The Reminiscences of Carl Schurz*,

If Seward's address provided the verbal ammunition of the moment, it was romantic reformers like Parker who put the new weapon into full effect. They launched an all-out barrage. By September 1850, Clay's original proposal had been successfully repackaged and passed as a series of smaller bills, which included a new fugitive slave law, one far more stringent than its 1793 predecessor. The Fugitive Slave Law of 1850 was odious and heavy-handed, stacking the deck against accused runaways. It rode roughshod over northern personal liberty laws by putting "the burden of proof on captured blacks," while denying them a trial by jury and the right to testify on their own behalf. The law also created a new office – the federal commissioner – which could issue warrants for arrest and hold quasi-judicial hearings to determine whether the accused should be returned to the South. Those who provided assistance to alleged runaways were subject to stiff fines, even jail time, while federal marshals were given the authority to enlist citizens to execute the law. Commissioners were even given a monetary incentive to side with claimants. They would collect ten dollars for each fugitive who was remanded to the claimant and only five dollars when the accused was set free.[44]

The new measure, in other words, subjected all northern blacks – whether born enslaved or not – to possible capture and rendition to the South and compelled northern whites to assist in the process. The law of the land now contradicted the law of God and, unlike Seward, the New Romantics readily endorsed the violation of the former in the name of the higher law. Higginson made this case in a series of articles written for the *Newburyport Daily Evening Union* in the fall of 1850. In general, he believed that Americans intuitively acted from higher law principles. Few people, reasoned the Transcendentalist minister, would countenance committing abhorrent actions such as murder, even if compelled to by law. When it came to the new fugitive slave law, however, Americans too often ignored their moral compass. The only way the vile measure would be defeated, Higginson concluded, was if "the higher law triumphs in men's souls." Thus, he counseled his fellow citizens to "DISOBEY" the

---

Volume Two: 1852–1863 (New York: McClure Company, 1907), 174; Goodwin, *Team of Rivals*, 14. Schurz referred here not only to Seward's "higher law" phrase but also his famous reference to "an irrepressible conflict" between the North and the South.

[44] James M. McPherson, *Battle Cry of Freedom: The Civil War Era* (New York: Oxford University Press, 1988), 80; Orville Vernon Burton, *The Age of Lincoln* (New York: Hill and Wang, 2007), 62; Steven Lubet, *Fugitive Justice: Runaways, Rescuers, and Slavery on Trial* (Cambridge, MA: Harvard University Press, 2010), 42–45; Potter, *Impending Crisis*, 130–131.

law, "when needful, and show our good citizenship by taking the legal penalties!"[45]

Harriet Beecher Stowe also embraced higher law doctrine in response to the fugitive slave law. In the summer of 1850 she published a short story about a northern farmer who refuses to aid a family of runaways being pursued by slave catchers. Not long after, the farmer is tormented by a dream in which God accuses him of betrayal, insisting that anything he does to his brethren he does also to Him. "Of late, there have seemed to be many in this nation, who seem to think that there is no standard of right and wrong higher than an act of Congress, or an interpretation of the United States Constitution," opined Stowe. Like her New Romantic colleagues, she sided with God's higher law over the law of the land. Two years later Stowe wrote *Uncle Tom's Cabin*, a novel that, according to a review in *Frederick Douglass' Paper*, offered unparalleled "arguments ... in favor of the '*Higher Law*' theory."[46]

Douglass likewise turned repeatedly to higher law doctrine in the years after the new fugitive slave law was passed. In early 1851, the black abolitionist served as the president of an abolitionist meeting in Syracuse, which pledged not to adhere to the new fugitive slave law on higher law grounds. "When the Civil Government tramples on the Divine authority," they insisted, "it is the Civil Government, which is the rebel – and not the citizen, who refuses to follow it." Even after Douglass broke with Garrison, declared the Constitution an antislavery document, and pledged himself to work within the American political system, he remained a devotee of the higher law. "The Supreme Court of the United States is high," he maintained in 1857, "but the Supreme Court of God is higher."[47] Douglass's short-lived partner Martin Delany also believed that higher law doctrine provided ample support for antislavery resistance. Two years before the new fugitive slave law was passed, in fact, he told Douglass that if a "ruthless slaveholder" seized his "wife, mother, or sister," Delany would follow "the laws of Nature's God" and stop at nothing "to arrest his outrageous grasp."[48]

---

[45] *Newburyport Daily Evening Union*, Nov. 5, 1850; *Newburyport Daily Evening Union*, Oct. 14, 1850; TWH, *Mr. Higginson's Address to the Voters of the Third Congressional District of Massachusetts* (Lowell, MA: C. L. Knapp, 1850), 5.

[46] HBS, "The Freeman's Dream: A Parable," in *OSR*, 58; *Frederick Douglass' Paper*, Apr. 8, 1852; Reynolds, *Mightier Than the Sword*, 118–123.

[47] *North Star*, Jan. 23, 1851; FD, "Colored Men's Rights in This Republic: An Address Delivered in New York, New York, on 14 May 1857," in *FDP*, 3: 147.

[48] MRD to FD, Feb. 6, 1848, in the *North Star*, Feb. 18, 1848, reprinted in *MDR*, 81.

Theodore Parker took this higher law rhetoric to a new and still more provocative level. Three days after President Fillmore signed the fugitive slave law, the minister insisted that the first duty of any individual was to God's law, not the laws of the country. "The natural duty to keep the law of God overrides the obligation to observe any human statute, and continually commands us to love a man and not hate him, to do him justice, and not injustice, to allow him his natural rights not alienated by himself; yes, to defend him in them, not only by all means legal, but by all means moral," he held. The Constitution had to live up to the higher law as much as the Bible, not vice versa. "Can any piece of parchment make right wrong, and wrong right?" asked Parker.⁴⁹

At times, the minister advanced practical arguments against the new law. Why, he wondered, must this new law be followed when Massachusetts citizens so readily disobey countless usury, gambling, and prohibition statutes? More often, though, Parker urged violation of the fugitive slave law for deeper reasons. "I owe it to God to obey His law," he concluded, "or what I deem his law; that is my duty."⁵⁰ He rejected gratuitous lawbreaking but also rained invective down upon clergymen, politicians, and businessmen who supported the apprehension of runaway slaves. Even if he could only tap into the higher law, however imperfectly, Parker thought he had no less of an obligation to act. "Having determined what is absolutely right, by the conscience of God, or at least relatively right, according to my conscience to-day," he wrote, "then it becomes my duty to keep it." To do otherwise, Parker said, would be to shrink before man's law while sneering at God's. "What grasshoppers we are before the statute of men; what Goliaths against the law of God!" he admonished.⁵¹

Using such powerful images, Parker appeared to challenge not only the new fugitive slave law but also the rule of law itself. Many Americans believed that casting off positive law in the name of inner moral conscience amounted to anarchy. The *Richmond Enquirer*, for example, complained that higher law arguments against slavery were rooted in the notion "that the persons who fancy themselves aggrieved by the operation of a law ...

---

⁴⁹ TP, "The Function and Place of Conscience, in Relation to the Laws of Men; A Sermon for the Times. Preached at the Melodeon, on Sunday, September 22, 1850," in *SAOS*, 2: 256; Dean Grodzins, "Why Theodore Parker Backed John Brown," in *Terrible Swift Sword: The Legacy of John Brown*, ed. Peggy A. Russo and Paul Finkleman (Athens: Ohio University Press, 2005), 8–9.

⁵⁰ TP, "The Chief Sins of the People. A Sermon delivered at the Melodeon, on Fast Day, April 10, 1851," in *SAOS*, 2: 338–339; TP, "Function and Place of Conscience," 247.

⁵¹ TP, "Boston Kidnapping," in *ASAOS*, 1: 49; *Frederick Douglass' Paper*, Apr. 8, 1852; TP, "Function and Place of Conscience," 247, 258.

can at any moment relieve themselves from the duty of obedience."[52] Parker had little time for this line of reasoning because to him it represented the debasement of politics. He even argued that the conception of government as founded on a social compact – an idea that he linked to Hobbes, Filmer, Locke, and Rousseau – served to undermine any moral obligation among individuals, suggesting that "Natural Rights are only certain conveniences agreed upon amongst men."[53]

This did not mean that Parker rejected liberal democracy wholesale, however. He was, to be sure, a strong critic of canonical liberal thinkers. He denounced the philosophy of Hobbes and the first principles of Locke for the flawed notion that laws were the product of a social compact. And Parker dismissed Whig and Democratic objections to higher law theory as rooted in the "selfish materialism" of Hobbes, David Hume, and Helvétius.[54] But the Transcendentalist embraced other components of liberalism. For instance, he had little patience for "socialistic Proudhon," asserting that "property is not the mere creature of compact, or the child of robbery; it is founded in the nature of man." Parker believed in the sanctity of private property, but was troubled that the only type of property that the United States government seemed concerned with protecting was "purely the creature of violence and law" – "Property in Men."[55]

Moreover, Parker staked his claim for the higher law on fundamentally liberal grounds: the intuitive powers of the individual. External sources, whether secular or sacred, were unreliable. As the New Romantic maintained during the miracles controversy, the Bible could be as beguiling as common law, providing contradictory wisdom and seemingly endorsing, in some passages, immoral practices such as slavery. Therefore, Parker urged people to look within their own hearts. According to his romantic conception of the self – indebted as it was to the German idealist tradition – every individual was endowed not only with "intellectual powers" but also the faculty of conscience "whose special function it is to discover the rules for a man's moral conduct." He admitted in an early sermon that, "All men do not stand on the same level in respect to a knowledge of the laws of nature." Nevertheless, "the *first man* knew this *moral* law,

[52] *Richmond Enquirer*, quoted in Crane, *Race, Citizenship, and, Law*, 14.
[53] TP, "A Sermon of the Dangers Which Threaten the Rights of Man in America, Preached at the Music Hall, on Sunday, July 2, 1854," in *ASAOS*, 2: 247–248.
[54] TP, "The Consequences of an Immoral Principle and False Idea of Life," in *WTP*, 14: 180.
[55] TP, "Sermon of the Dangers," 264–265.

as well as the last shall know it. Here at least all men are equal."[56] The higher law, to put the matter simply, provided the democratic foundations for a young nation and its conflicted citizenry.

The (American) Idea of Freedom versus the Idea of Slavery

Despite his abiding commitment to higher law universalism, Parker found ethnic and nationalist essentialism appealing. "Every nation has a peculiar character," he began in an 1848 lecture he delivered to a number of literary societies and subsequently published in the *Massachusetts Quarterly Review*. Distinct characteristics have defined all nations, from ancient civilizations, such as the Hebrews, Greeks, and Romans, to modern societies like his own. "We have a genius for liberty," the minister insisted, "the American idea is freedom, natural rights."[57] This tendency to give liberal values a distinctly American cast emerged in many of Parker's addresses in the late 1840s and 1850s, as he interchangeably used two phrases "the Idea of Freedom" and "the American Idea."

The American Idea, insisted Parker on July 5, 1852, was "that all men have natural rights to life, liberty, and the pursuit of happiness; that all men are equal in natural rights; that these rights can only be alienated by the possessor thereof; and that it is the undeniable function of government to preserve their rights to each and all." In other discussions of the American Idea, he pushed beyond the rights articulated in the Declaration of Independence, adding that it was also dedicated to the creation of "a government of all the people, by all the people, for all the people."[58] To the New Romantic, this triptych – which Lincoln later made famous in his Gettysburg Address – encapsulated the perfectionist potential of the United States.[59] If governed by the "Idea of Freedom," America could

---

[56] TP, "Function and Place of Conscience," 245; TP, "Conscience and the Moral Law," TPP, AHTL. For a recent biography of Parker that emphasizes the centrality of the concept of conscience to the minister, see Paul E. Teed, *A Revolutionary Conscience: Theodore Parker and Antebellum America* (Lanham, MD: University Press of America, 2012).

[57] TP, "The Political Destination of America, and the Sign of the Times. An Address delivered before several literary Societies in 1848," in *SAOS*, 2: 1, 6.

[58] TP, "The Aspect of Freedom in America. A Speech at the Mass Anti-Slavery Celebration at Abington, July 5, 1852," in *ASAOS*, 1: 110; TP, "Speech at the New England Anti-Slavery Convention," 176.

[59] Garry Wills, *Lincoln at Gettysburg: The Words That Remade America* (New York: Simon & Schuster, 1992), 90–120; TP, "A Sermon of Merchants. Preached at the Melodeon, on Sunday, November 22, 1846," in *SAOS*, 1: 186; TP, "The Position and Duty of a Minister," in *WTP*, 13: 104; Chadwick, *Theodore Parker*, 322–323.

"become a harmonious whole, a Unit of Freedom... reënacting the laws of God, and pursuing its way, continually attaining greater degrees of freedom and prosperity." It would become, in other words, the sort of place in which all Americans enjoyed not only equal rights and a political voice but also the opportunity to work toward spiritual perfection.

Yet corrosive forces, which he dubbed the Money Power and the Slave Power, put this future in jeopardy. The Money Power made trade a veritable religion in antebellum America, while the Slave Power, which promoted the Idea of Slavery, was even more destructive. A photonegative of the American Idea, the Idea of Slavery maintains that "there are no natural, unalienable, and equal rights," that the strong are entitled to "oppress, enslave and ruin the weak," and that there is no higher law of God that outlaws such abuses. If allowed to prevail, this idea would wreak havoc on the nation and its people.[60]

Like most abolitionists, Parker worried about the impact of slavery on the enslaved themselves. But he insisted that the destruction did not stop there; slavery also had a deleterious effect on all free men, white and black. While free blacks in the South were tainted by their association with "degrade[d]" slaves, Parker also thought that the rest of the country suffered economically and culturally. Slavery undermined land values and the value of labor, he added, while undercutting progress in literary, scientific, and religious realms. Drawn to the free labor critique popularized by the Free Soil and Republican parties, he held that manual labor is viewed as natural and dignified in the North, while in the South it "is considered menial and degrading; it is the business of slaves." Though hardly a free market shill, Parker argued that the social ills of the free labor North paled in comparison to the damage wrought by slavery. "There is no State in the Union but is poorer for slavery," he concluded. "Compare the North and the South, and see what a difference in riches, comfort, education. See the superiority of the North. But the South started with every advantage of nature – soil, climate, everything."[61]

Parker's vision of America as the battlefield between the Idea of Freedom and the Idea of Slavery resonated with his experience as a Transcendentalist minister struggling against Unitarian orthodoxy in Boston. It also drew on an intellectual tradition with deeper roots in

---

[60] TP, "Sermon of the Dangers," 258, 253; Grodzins, "Theodore Parker," 315–316.
[61] TP, "The Effect of Slavery on the American People," in *WTP*, 14: 327; TP, "Letter on Slavery," in *WTP*, 11: 116; TP, "An Address on the Condition of America, Before the New York City Anti-Slavery Society, at its First Anniversary, Held at the Broadway Tabernacle, May 12, 1854," in *ASAOS*, 1: 408.

Anglo-American culture: the Whig interpretation of history. Concerned with locating the origins and legitimacy of parliamentary authority in ancient Anglo-Saxon traditions, eighteenth-century Whig historians argued that English citizens enjoyed political rights that were undermined by the feudalism introduced after the Norman invasion in 1066. According to this logic, the Magna Carta was a restoration of ancient rights, historical figures were presented as heroes or villains depending on their particular stance regarding liberty, and modern English history was distinguished by its progressive march.[62]

In a number of ways, Parker's ideas fit squarely within the Whig tradition. First, he adopted wholesale its Manichean division of the world into a struggle between liberty and tyranny. Parker also subscribed to the Whig notion that history was a march toward greater freedom. Although the Slave Power and the Money Power were formidable obstacles, he believed that the moral character of parts of the nation – particularly his native New England – was steadily improving. In a phrase that Martin Luther King Jr. would borrow a century later, the Transcendentalist minister preached, "I do not pretend to understand the moral universe; the arc is a long one," but "from what I see I am sure it bends towards justice." Even after passage of the new fugitive slave law, Parker evinced an unwavering faith in history's progressive course.[63]

Moreover, like Whig historians, Parker posited the love of liberty as a distinctly Anglo-Saxon characteristic. But this point of emphasis reflected another important influence: nineteenth-century romantic racial theory. The Transcendentalist was well versed in the ethnological theories of German Romantics like Schleiermacher and Herder, who rejected Enlightenment universalism in favor of a worldview premised on fundamental racial or national difference. "Every nation is destined through its peculiar organization and its place in the world to represent a certain side of the divine image," held Schleiermacher.[64] Herder likewise maintained

[62] Trevor Colbourn, *The Lamp of Experience: Whig History and the Intellectual Origins of the American Revolution* (Chapel Hill: University of North Carolina Press, 1965); Daniel Walker Howe, *The Political Culture of the American Whigs* (Chicago: University of Chicago Press, 1979), 69–95; McInerney, *Fortunate Heirs of Freedom*, 27–57.

[63] TP, "A Sermon of the Moral Conditions of Boston. Preached at the Melodeon, on Sunday, February 11, 1849," in *SAOS*, 1: 283–284; TP, "Of Justice and the Conscience," in *WTP*, 3: 64; Joshua Cohen, *The Arc of the Moral Universe and Other Essays* (Cambridge, MA: Harvard University Press, 2010), 17; TP, "Effect of Slavery," 336.

[64] Friedrich Schleiermacher, quoted in Wilson Jeremiah Moses, *The Golden Age of Black Nationalism, 1850–1925* (New York: Oxford University Press, 1978), 49.

that humankind was divided into different races, or *Volk*, each of which had a distinctive spiritual genius, which would be brought into fruition over the course of time. By giving the study of race and culture a spiritual veneer, Herder's theory was particularly appealing to Parker, who, as we have seen, was predisposed to viewing the course of world history in an idealist, as opposed to materialist, fashion. At the same time, the German Romantic provided a seemingly scientific, if unenlightened, vocabulary by which to talk about the spiritual gifts of each *Volk*.[65]

Employing German naturalist Johann Friedrich Blumenbach's division of the human species into five races, Parker saw deep differences that sharply defined social groups. Like many romantic racialists, he believed people of Anglo-Saxon descent had an instinctual love for liberty, which they pursued with unmatched vigor. Yet Parker broke with romantic racialist orthodoxy – which did not necessarily translate racial difference into a defined hierarchy – by outlining a clear pecking order, with Anglo-Saxons at the top of the ladder and Africans near the bottom. His brand of romantic racialism thus resembled the American school of ethnology's theory of polygenesis, which insisted that the human species was divided into separate races that originated in different geographic centers of creation. In contrast to the proponents of polygenesis, however, Parker rejected ethnographic justifications for slavery and ridiculed attempts to draw close links between people of African descent and apes.[66]

Parker could also be critical of the Anglo-Saxon spirit, noting that the race often trampled the rights of others to secure their own. The Mexican War was a prime example. Although he was fond neither of Mexico nor its "wretched people," as he called them, the minister opposed the war, which he saw as a crass attempt to extend slavery. In addition, in terms of territorial expansion, Parker thought the war entirely unnecessary. The Anglo-Saxon people "will possess the whole of the continent before many years; perhaps before the century ends," he concluded. "But this may be had fairly; with no injustice to any one; by the steady advance of a superior race, with superior ideas and a better civilization;

[65] Frederickson, *Black Image in the White Mind*, 97–98; Grodzins, "Theodore Parker," 314. On nineteenth-century racial beliefs and theories, see Fredrickson, *Black Image in the White Mind*; Mia Bay, *The White Image in the Black Mind: African-American Ideas about White People, 1830–1925* (New York: Oxford University Press, 2000); and Bruce Dain: *A Hideous Monster of the Mind: American Race Theory in the Early Republic* (Cambridge, MA: Harvard University Press, 2002).

[66] Fredrickson, *Black Image in the White Mind*, 107; TP to Edward Desor, Apr. 30, 1854, TPP, AHTL; TP, "An Anti-slavery Address," in *WTP*, 12: 162–163.

by commerce, trade, arts, by being better than Mexico, humaner [*sic*], more free and manly."[67]

Yet even as Parker frowned upon the Mexican War, he did not reject the cultural chauvinism that animated groups like the Young Americans and other proponents of Manifest Destiny.[68] For him, the Anglo-Saxon exemplified the best of the human race, one that would inevitably come to dominate the continent. "It has many faults," Parker wrote of the Anglo-Saxon, "but I think it is the best specimen of mankind which has ever attained great power in the world." Occasional belligerence was but a minor flaw when considered alongside the values and achievements of the Anglo-Saxon people, including "the old love of liberty, the love also of law; the best institutions of the present age – ecclesiastical, political, social, domestic." Distinguished by vast wealth and political power worldwide, Anglo-Saxon character, maintained Parker, demonstrated the firmest devotion to liberty of any culture in the world. "Ours is the only tongue in which Liberty can speak," he concluded. All told, Parker's critique of Anglo-Saxon behavior was overshadowed by his broader faith in Anglo-Saxon superiority.[69]

This association of Anglo-Saxon character with liberty, in turn, helps explain his description of the universal goal of freedom (Idea of Freedom) as specifically rooted in the national destiny of America (the American Idea). "Liberty and equality," Parker insisted in 1848, "have long been American ideas." Building on Whig visions of the Anglo-Saxon march to progress, he framed the United States as the next site for the triumph of liberty. "The Anglo-Saxon tribe," he insisted, is "divided into two great political branches": the British and the American.[70]

---

[67] TP, "A Sermon of War. Preached at the Melodeon, on Sunday, June 7, 1846," in *SAOS*, 1: 71–72. See also TP, "Some Thoughts on the Progress of America, and the Influence of Her Diverse Institutions. An Address Prepared for the Anti-Slavery Convention, in Boston, May 31, 1854," in *ASAOS*, 2: 7.

[68] On the Young American movement, see Widmer, *Young America*; Eyal, *Young America Movement*; and William T. Kerrigan, "'Young America!' Romantic Nationalism in Literature and Politics, 1843–1861" (PhD diss., University of Michigan at Ann Arbor, 1997).

[69] TP to Frances Cobbe, Dec. 4, 1857, in *LCTP*, 1: 463; TP, "Address on the Condition of America," 434; TP, "Some Thoughts on the Progress of America," 5; Lewis Perry, *Boats Against the Current: American Culture Between Revolution and Modernity, 1820–1860* (New York: Oxford University Press, 1993), 250.

[70] TP, "A Speech at a Meeting of the American Anti-Slavery Society, to celebrate the Abolition of Slavery by the French Republic, April 6, 1848," in *SAOS*, 2: 101; TP, "Some Thoughts on the Progress of America," 3–4.

But the American experience, to Parker, was not Anglo-Saxon alone. Like many romantics, he lamented the lack of a distinctive American literary tradition that captured what was unique about the nation's culture. Yet Parker believed there was one exception to this rule, "one portion of permanent literature ... which is wholly indigenous and original": slave narratives like Douglass's. He also counted non-white Americans – eight-and-a-half million total by his estimate – a positive addition to the American body politic, for they tempered "the Anglo-Saxon blood, to furnish a new composite tribe, far better, I trust, than the old." In addition, Parker emphasized the egalitarian foundation of American democracy, which "rests on the idea that the substance of manhood, the human nature in which we are all alike, is superior to any human accident wherein all must differ."[71]

Still, the fact that Parker used the phrase "the American Idea" interchangeably with "the Idea of Freedom," underscores his ambivalence about whether freedom was a universal characteristic accessible by all or a trait that could never be entirely divorced from ethnicity or nationality. As much as he was committed to the idea of a universal higher law, he found nationalist and racialist visions of the struggle for liberty seductive.

Did Parker understand this tension in his thinking? On one level, the answers seems to be no. In fact, he consciously distinguished his own ideas from the Whig tradition on this very score. Although Whig historians often looked at the original charters of liberty – from the Declaration of Independence, to the Magna Carta, to ancient Anglo-Saxon traditions – Parker located the Idea of Freedom *outside* of history. "The transcendental politician does not merely interpret history, and look back to [the] Magna Charta and the Constitution," he wrote, "but into human nature, through to divine nature; and so anticipates history, and in man and God finds the origin a primary source of all just policy, all right legislation. So looking he transcends history." While the sensational school of politics cares nothing for ideas and leads naturally to either Humean skepticism or "there is no right but might" sloganeering, transcendental politics "appeals to a natural justice, natural right; absolute justice, absolute right."[72]

---

[71] TP, "The American Scholar," in *WTP*, 8: 37; TP, "Address on the Condition of America," 384; TP, "The Consequences of an Immoral Principle," in *WTP*, 14: 169.
[72] TP, "Transcendentalism," 26, 10, 25.

On another level, however, Parker did not think that intuition and empirical induction – the universal and the particular – were incompatible. He gave precedence to intuition, but extolled the scientific method as a critical tool that, when combined with intuition, might help man know the truth and act accordingly. Transcendental philosophy, he insisted, "in human history . . . finds confirmations, illustrations, of the ideas of human nature, for history represents the attempt of mankind to develop human nature."[73] And, as his contemporaries recognized, Parker's own intellectual practices reflected an artful integration of intuition and experience. Although universal appeals invariably formed the meat of his antislavery arguments, the New Romantic seasoned them with facts, citing statistic upon statistic to illustrate slavery's social and economic shortcomings.[74]

In sum, Parker's vision of the battle between the Idea of Slavery and the American Idea revealed deep and fundamental fissures in his thinking – and romanticism more generally. Despite a commitment to a transcendent higher law that every individual could access, he associated the love of liberty with the American nation and Anglo-Saxon people. Similarly, while he believed that romantic intuition was the lone method by which to tap directly into God's absolute laws, Parker looked to empirical facts for verification.

The Philosophical Party and Political Antislavery

"Several persons of late," confessed Parker in his journal in the spring of 1848, "have talked to me about going to Congress, as Representative or Senator." He did not think much of this idea for two reasons. First, no one would send him. And second, he admitted, "Politics are not my vocation, nor yet my desire. I am to labour for ideas – to set men a-thinking. I feel as if born for the pulpit, if for anything."[75] Parker's perfectionism made him skeptical of political parties and their organs. How many political newspapers "have ever advanced a great idea, or been constantly true to a great principle of natural justice?" he asked one year later. Yet, like his fellow New Romantics, Parker did not reject politics as inherently debased by its reliance on force. Instead, he saw great value in democratic

---

[73] TP, "Experience as a Minister," 301; TP, "Transcendentalism," 32.

[74] TWH, *Part of a Man's Life* (Boston: Houghton, Mifflin, 1905), 276; Commager, "The Dilemma of Theodore Parker," 268; Hutchison, *Transcendentalist Ministers*, 102–04; Perry, *Boats Against the Current*, 258–263.

[75] TP, Journal, 1848, quoted in *LCTP*, 1: 56; Octavius B. Frothingham, *Theodore Parker: A Biography* (Boston: James R. Osgood and Co., 1874), 377.

institutions and practices. Imagining a Transcendental politics, he concluded, "We can leave nothing to the next generation worth so much as ideas of truth, justice, and religion, organized into fitting institutions."[76] Higher law principles must be infused into the American republic.

Just as he walked a careful line between empiricism and romantic intuitionism, between a universal and a national vision of liberty, then, Parker balanced moral commitments and political methods. While giving precedence to the former, he thought that both were necessary to bring slavery down. "Slavery is a moral wrong and an economic blunder; but it is also a great political institution," he insisted in an 1858 speech at the Massachusetts Anti-Slavery Convention in Boston. "It cannot be put down by political economy, nor by ethical preaching; men have not only pecuniary interests and moral feelings, but also political passions. Slavery must be put down politically, or else militarily." As such, Parker sought to take a position both within and above politics, in order to steer political conversations (and politicians) without being corrupted by party politics. He acted as America's political conscience or, as he once put it, the nation's "top eye."[77]

Unlike a traditional politician, Parker spent little time thinking about short-term victories. He was concerned with the long-term "development of the people." And Parker did not reserve this role for himself alone. "There is a philosophical party in politics," he insisted, "a very small party it may be, but an actual one. They aim to get everlasting ideas and universal laws, not made by man, but by God, and for man, who only finds them."[78] Philosophical party members could be found in a variety of religious settings, from Quaker meetings to Catholic masses.

Parker also readily acknowledged the contributions of abolitionists who worked through traditional political channels, while taking note of the substantial dilemmas antislavery politicians faced. "It is easy for Mr. Garrison and Mr. Phillips or me to say all of our thought," he wrote. "I am responsible to nobody, and nobody to me. But it is not easy for Mr. Sumner, Mr. Seward, and Mr. Chase to say all of their thought;

---

[76] TP, "Sermon of the Moral Condition of Boston," 270, 297. This statement, like the New Romantic's approach to antislavery politics more generally, is at odds with the characterization of Transcendentalists as uniformly anti-institutional. See, for example, Elkins, *Slavery* and Frederickson, *Inner Civil War*.

[77] TP, "The Aspect of Slavery in America," in *WTP*, 14: 313–314; Frothingham, *Theodore Parker*, 377–78; *Liberator*, Feb. 25, 1853.

[78] TP, "Political Destination," 14.

because they have a position to maintain, and they must keep that position."[79]

More generally, Parker expressed an abiding confidence in liberal democracy. As his sermons about the corruptive influence of the Slave Power attest, he was well aware that the nation's political system could be easily abused. Some Americans, he claimed, follow the motto "You are as good as I, and let us help another," whereas many others adhere to an altogether different motto: "I am as good as you, so get out of my way." Such boorish individualism is the democracy of "the barroom of a tavern – dirty, offensive, stained with tobacco, and full of drunken, noisy, quarrelsome 'rowdies,' just returned from the Mexican war," concluded the New Romantic, displaying his gift for dramatic language and vivid imagery.[80]

Still, Parker did not give up on the liberal tradition, even after such political defeats as the Fugitive Slave Law of 1850. "I do not believe that American democracy is always to be Satanic, and never celestial," he wrote three years later. Parker's confidence in the liberal tradition – and in America itself – was rooted in two sources: God and man. Intertwining his faith in God with his faith in humanity, Parker proclaimed his confidence that "He knew what He did when He made the world, and made human nature sufficient for human history and its own salvation."[81] While Garrisonian perfectionists might worry that the crass nature of democratic deal making and party politics would taint the antislavery struggle, Parker had no such fears. Confident in the limitlessness of human potential, this Transcendentalist saw no reason to reject political action outright. Helping people "found Institutions which shall promote the welfare and the Progress of mankind for 1000 years," he wrote abolitionist Francis Jackson, "is the noblest aim of noblest men. I should like to see much more in American Politics."[82]

Little wonder, then, that Parker kept close watch on antislavery politicians. When Charles Sumner was first elected to the Senate, for instance, Parker celebrated privately in his journal. "This is the great triumph of the season," he wrote, "Dear old Massachusetts! Money has not quite eaten the heart out of thee, only out of Boston and its vassal towns!"[83]

[79] TP, "The Present Aspect of the Anti-slavery Enterprise," in *WTP*, 12: 426. See also *Liberator*, Feb. 25, 1853.
[80] TP, "Political Destination," 21.
[81] TP, "Position and Duty of a Minister," 104–105.
[82] TP to Francis Jackson, Aug. 22, 1859, in TPP, MHS.
[83] TP, Journal, Apr. 24, 1851, in *LCTP*, 2: 109.

Two days after the election, Parker wrote to congratulate Sumner, urging him to be a new sort of senator – one *"with a conscience."* "You told me once that you were in morals, not in politics," he wrote. "Now I hope you will show that you are still in morals although in politics."[84]

At first Parker was disappointed by the newly minted senator, who in his first months in Washington avoided the issue of slavery entirely. By the summer of 1852, however, pressure from Parker and others prompted Sumner to demand the repeal of the new fugitive slave law. His "Freedom National" address thrilled Parker. "You have made a grand speech, well researched, well arranged, well written, and, I doubt not, as well delivered," he told Sumner in September. "You have now done what I all along said you would do, though I lamented you did not do it long ago." In the years that followed, the minister's faith in Sumner would only grow. [85]

Parker's political contacts were not limited to those, like Sumner, with whom he had a personal relationship. On the contrary, he wrote far and wide to politicians of all stripes, complaining about the inhumanity of slavery and legislation that reinforced the institution. When the Compromise of 1850 left this one-time Whig supporter sure that both major political parties in the United States were in bed with the Slave Power, he looked more and more to politicians who operated outside the Democratic and Whig parties, such as Sumner, John P. Hale, and Horace Mann. In the early 1850s, he supported the Free Soil Party and tried to forge alliances between its leaders and non-voting Garrisonians based on their shared goals: the end of slavery. Later that decade, Parker cautiously embraced the Republican Party, calling it "a direct force for anti-Slavery."[86]

By the end of the decade, however, the New Romantic grew pessimistic that traditional means could successfully overcome the aggressive Party of Slavery. "We don't follow the lessons set us by the South," he wrote in 1859, "the Slaveholders stand to their Guns no matter who is

---

[84] TP to Charles Sumner, Apr. 26, 1851, in *LCTP*, 2: 111.

[85] TP to Samuel Gridley Howe, n.d., in *LCTP*, 2: 213; Charles Sumner to TP, Aug. 11, 1852, in *LCTP*, 2: 214; TP to Charles Sumner, Sept. 6, 1852, Theodore Parker Papers (TPP), Houghton Library (HL), Harvard University, Cambridge, MA; TP to Charles Sumner, Feb. 27, 1857, in *LCTP*, 2: 218.

[86] TP to Fillmore, Nov. 21, 1850; TP to William H. Seward, May 19, 1854, TPP, AHTL; TP, "Speech at the New England Anti-Slavery Convention," 186; Grodzins, *American Heretic*, 208, 471; TP to [Samuel Gridley Howe], Apr. 17, 1853, Moorland-Spingarn Research Center Manuscripts Division (MSRC), Howard University, Washington, DC; Grodzins, "Why Theodore Parker Backed John Brown," 6–7; TP, "Present Aspect of the Anti-slavery Enterprise," 412–413.

before them – a schoolmarm at Norfolk or the Supreme Court of the
U.S." Meanwhile, Republicans pursued a "course of timid crouching to
its masters at the South." Perhaps a new sort of action was necessary. As
Parker had forewarned three years earlier, "We may now end this crime
against humanity by ballots; wait a little, and only with swords and with
blood can this deep and widening blot of shame be scoured out from the
continent."[87] Violent conflict appeared on the horizon.

The Boston Vigilance Committee
and the Question of Violence

That Parker anticipated the bloodshed of the Civil War five years
before the firing on Fort Sumter would have surprised few antebellum
Bostonians. Over the course of the 1850s, he had been on the front-
lines of the rehearsal for that great conflict that emerged in their city's
streets. Responding to attempts to enforce the new fugitive slave law,
the Transcendentalist gravitated toward a militant antislavery response –
matching fugitive slave catchers blow for blow – that portended the violence to come.

The Fugitive Slave Law of 1850 not only made the city's perhaps 400
runaways vulnerable to re-enslavement but also undermined the rights
and liberties of the rest of Boston's 1,600 African American residents
(Figure 1.2). Not a few of these black Bostonians were members of
Parker's Twenty-Eighth Congregational Society. Thus the minister's outrage over the law was reinforced by his own sense of pastoral – if not
paternalistic – obligation. "I have many fugitive slaves in my parish," he
wrote in 1855, "they look to me for protection." Others sought out his
aid because he was one of the leaders of the Boston Vigilance Committee
(BVC), which had organized less than a month after the law was passed
in the fall of 1850.[88]

The BVC, which was created to assist black Bostonians made vulnerable
by the new legislation, was not the first organization of its kind. Beginning
in the 1830s, opponents of slavery in cities across the North – from
New York City to Detroit, Pittsburgh to Worcester, Massachusetts – had

---

[87] TP to Charles Wesley Slack, July 20, 1859, in Michael Stoneham, *John Brown and the
Era of Literary Confrontation* (New York: Routledge, 2009), Appendix B, 168; TP, "The
Present Crisis in American Affairs," in *WTP*, 12: 488.
[88] Von Frank, *Trials of Anthony Burns*, 37; James O. Horton and Lois E. Horton, *Black
Bostonians: Family Life and Community Struggle in the Antebellum North* (New York:
Holmes & Meier, 1999), 2; TP to James Brown Jr., Oct. 27, 1855, TPP, AHTL.

Effects of the Fugitive-Slave-Law.

FIGURE 1.2. "Effects of the Fugitive-Slave-Law," 1850. This lithograph critiques the new fugitive slave law, which undermined the liberties of all African Americans living in the North. It portrays six armed white men attacking four black men as they flee from a cornfield. Theodore Parker worried that the fugitive slaves who attended his church faced similar treatment.
Source: Theodor Kaufmann, 1850. Courtesy of the Library of Congress, Prints and Photographs Division, LC-USZC4–4550.d.

formed vigilance committees. Boston reformers founded at least three such organizations before 1850. In 1846, for instance, a group of black and white abolitionists, including Sumner, Wendell Phillips, and Parker met in Faneuil Hall to form a "Committee of Vigilance" in response to the recent rendition of a fugitive slave from New Orleans. This committee produced a short pamphlet declaring its willingness "to take all needed measures to secure the protection of the laws to all persons who may hereafter be in danger of abduction from this Commonwealth." It also raised one thousand dollars to assist runaways and, over the next six months, provided food, shelter, and job opportunities for nineteen fugitives in the city.[89]

[89] Jane H. Pease and William H. Pease, *They Who Would Be Free: Blacks' Search for Freedom, 1830–1861* (New York: Atheneum, 1974), 207–212; James O. Horton and

When Parker addressed the crowd at Faneuil Hall – the first of many addresses he would deliver in the hallowed space – he flirted with a more militant response than the legal methods the Committee of Vigilance as a whole was willing to endorse. You are *"citizens of Massachusetts,* citizens of the United States," he told the crowd, and if you violate state and federal laws you must "expect their penalty." Then the minister provocatively added, "you are also *citizens of the Universe,* born subject to God's eternal law," and allegiance to the higher law "transcends and over-rides all statutes of men."[90]

The 1850 BVC, which was officially known as the "Committee of Vigilance and Safety," was a larger and more militant operation than its predecessors. Within a month of the fugitive slave law's passage, it counted eighty members; eventually the BVC grew to 200 strong. Operating for nearly a decade, the new committee lasted longer than previous incarnations, and, as a result, it was able to assist far more runaways. BVC agent Austin Bearse estimated that the committee helped more than 100 fugitives escape capture; Parker, for his part, put the number much higher. Indeed, the Transcendentalist claimed that the BVC had "saved the liberties of not less than 400 citizens" in its first two years.[91]

It is hard to overstate Parker's influence on the new organization. One in four members of the BVC and five of the eight members of its executive committee attended services at his church. Chairman of the BVC's executive committee, Parker was also named "spiritual counselor" of all imperiled fugitive slaves in Massachusetts. When he died in Italy a decade later, black reformers in Boston paid tribute to the minister's "Herculean" efforts in this regard. "Wherever his voice or hand could assist those who would escape, or foil the attempt of those who would betray, there was he

---

Lois E. Horton, *In Hope of Liberty: Culture, Community, and Protest among Northern Free Blacks, 1700–1860* (New York: Oxford University Press, 1997), 229–235; Stephen Kantrowitz, *More Than Freedom: Fighting for Black Citizenship in a White Republic, 1829–1889* (New York: Penguin Press, 2012), 66–68; Irving H. Bartlett, "Abolitionists, Fugitives, and Imposters in Boston, 1846–1847" *New England Quarterly* 55 (Mar. 1982): 97–110; *Boston Courier,* Sept. 28, 1846; *Liberator,* Oct. 2, 1846; *Address of the Committee Appointed by a Public Meeting, Held at Faneuil Hall, Sept. 24, 1846 for the Purpose of Considering the Secret Case of Kidnapping from Our Soil, and of Taking Measures to Prevent the Recurrence of Similar Outrages* (Boston: White & Potter, Printers, 1846), 4, Appendix, 2–4.

[90] TP, in *Address of the Committee Appointed by a Public Meeting,* Appendix, 19–20.
[91] Austin Bearse, *Reminiscences of Fugitive-Slave Law Days in Boston* (Boston: Warren Richardson, 1880), 14; *Liberator,* Apr. 16, 1852; Kantrowitz, *More Than Freedom,* 183, 197–198, 466n21.

sure to be found, abundant in resources, and ready for any emergency," they proclaimed.[92]

Parker hoped that the BVC, in contrast to its predecessors, would not limit itself to legal assistance alone. The committee's official resolutions, which the New Romantic drafted, pledged "to endeavor by all just means to secure the fugitives and colored inhabitants of Boston and vicinity from any invasion of their rights by persons acting under this law." Illustrating the lengths to which the BVC would carry resistance, Parker wrote to President Fillmore, "We will suffer any penalties you may put upon us, *but we must keep the Law of God.*"[93] If both moral suasion and traditional political means failed to rebuff the encroachments of the Slave Power, the minister suggested, perhaps forceful resistance was the answer.

Yet Parker's thinking was nuanced and, when it came to violence, he had reservations. Like many abolitionists, he associated physical force with the institution of slavery. "The relation of master and slave begins in violence; it must be sustained by violence – the systematic violence of general laws, or the irregular violence of individual caprice," he wrote in 1847. Parker called nonresistance "the stoutest kind of combat," adding that "it requires very little courage to fight with sword and musket, and that of a cheap kind." The Transcendentalist minister hated war with "each particular fiber of [his] heart."[94]

But he hated slavery, too. The new fugitive slave law brought these two commitments – to peace, on the one hand, and the abolition of slavery, on the other – into direct conflict. So, for much of the early 1850s, the minister equivocated on the merits of resisting slavery. When Charles K. Whipple asked him to preach on the right of any individual or nation to take the life of an enemy just after the new law was passed, Parker responded that he was not sure such a sermon was necessary since most people assumed this right all too quickly.[95] The following day, however, Parker endorsed self-defense wholeheartedly. "I will do all in my power to rescue any fugitive slave from the hands of any officer who attempts

[92] Dean Grodzins, "Unitarianism," in *The Oxford Handbook of Transcendentalism*, ed. Joel Myerson, et. al. (New York: Oxford University Press, 2010), 60; Grodzins, "'Slave Law' versus 'Lynch Law' in Boston: Benjamin Robbins Curtis, Theodore Parker, and the Fugitive Slave Crisis, 1850–1855," *Massachusetts Historical Review* 12 (2010): 4; TP to Convers Francis, 1851, TPP, AHTL; *Liberator*, June 29, 1860.

[93] BVC Resolutions, in *LCTP*, 2: 94; TP to Fillmore, Nov. 21, 1850.

[94] TP, "Letter on Slavery," 50; TP, "Sermon of War," 49; TP, "True Idea of a Christian Church," in *WTP*, 13: 34.

[95] TP to Charles K. Whipple, Sept. 21, 1850, Theodore Parker Papers (TPP), BPL.

to return him to bondage," he pledged, insisting "that the fugitive has the same natural right to defend himself against the slave-catcher, or his constitutional tool, that he has against a murderer or a wolf."[96]

A year later, in response to a riot in Christiana, Pennsylvania, in which a Maryland farmer seeking to recapture his runaways was killed, Parker went still further, writing, "I am deeply rejoiced that the Negroes shot down the kidnappers at Christiana, and wish they had done so in Boston and every where else." Eight months later he urged caution, however. "Violence is resorted to nine times when it is needless, to every one instance when it is needed," the Transcendentalist opined.[97]

The American Revolution, however, was one of those rare moments when resistance was necessary in his mind. Parker deeply admired the patriots' willingness to defy Great Britain, even if that meant armed combat. As was the case with many abolitionists, he thought that the looming conflict over slavery evoked the colonial struggle against Britain. By 1854, Parker insisted that America had not been on such precarious ground since the Revolution, ground made all the more dangerous by the North's woeful state of military preparedness as compared to the eighteenth century. "Once, New England had more firelocks than householders," he wrote. "Now, the people have lost their taste for military discipline, and neither keep nor bear arms."[98] Moreover, Parker cast his own participation in the struggle against slavery in the brave light of colonial patriots such as his grandfather, Captain John Parker, who was a leader in the Battle of Lexington. In an 1858 letter to historian George Bancroft, Parker lauded his grandfather's martial heroism: "At the battle of Lexington, when Capt. P. drew up his men as the British were nearing, he ordered 'every man to load' his piece with powder and ball. 'Don't fire unless fired upon; but if they mean to have a war, let it begin here!'" he declared.[99]

[96] TP, "Function and Place of Conscience," 257, 258.

[97] TP to Samuel J. May, Oct. 2, 1851, TPP, MHS; TP to Robert White, June 8, 1852, in *LCTP*, 1: 393. On the Christiana Riot, see Thomas P. Slaughter, *Bloody Dawn: The Christiana Riot and Racial Violence in the Antebellum North* (New York: Oxford University Press, 1994).

[98] TP, "Sermon of the Dangers," 237.

[99] TP to George Bancroft, Sept. 10, 1858, in *LCTP*, 2: 11. On Parker and other abolitionists' approach to the revolutionary generation, see McInerney, *Fortunate Heirs of Freedom*, 27–57; Margot Minardi, *Making Slavery History: Abolitionism and the Politics of Memory in Massachusetts* (New York: Oxford University Press, 2010); and Paul Teed, "'A Brave Man's Child': Theodore Parker and the Memory of the Revolution," *Historical Journal of Massachusetts*, 22 (2001): 171–191.

Parker believed his connection to the American revolutionaries was more than merely one of national or regional identity. It was a tie, he thought, that was based on heredity – on blood. "My grandfather drew the first sword in the Revolution; my fathers fired the first shot; the blood which flowed there was kindred to this which courses in my veins today," he told a crowd in 1851.[100] In curious fashion, Parker's romantic racialist faith in Anglo-Saxon vigor reinforced his turn toward antislavery violence. He hoped that white abolitionists would follow in the heroic footsteps of the revolutionary generation, their Anglo-Saxon forefathers. More personally, he hoped to live up to his family legacy.

Yet Parker was not so sure whether black opponents of slavery – whether enslaved or free – would do the same. After all, the corollary to Anglo-Saxon vigor for romantic racialists was black passivity. At a meeting of the Massachusetts Anti-Slavery Convention in late January 1858, he declared that "the African is the most docile and pliant of all the races of men; none has so little ferocity: vengeance, instantial with the Caucasian, is exceptional in his history." While black slaves patiently await justice in the afterlife, insisted Parker, Anglo-Saxon men – even a dyed-in-the-wool pacifist like William Lloyd Garrison – would not hesitate to fight for his freedom. "I think his Saxon blood would move swift enough to sweep off his non-resistant creed," concluded the minister. "The stroke of an ax would have settled the matter long ago. But the black man would not strike."[101] Black abolitionists, no surprise, took issue with this characterization.

Just weeks later, John S. Rock, an African American lawyer, physician, and reformer, objected to Parker's characterization of black martial potential at the city's first Crispus Attucks Day commemoration. The meeting was held at Faneuil Hall on March 5, 1858, the eighty-eighth anniversary of the Boston Massacre and first anniversary of the infamous Dred Scott decision. Commemoration organizers hoped that a ceremony marking the role of an early black patriot like Attucks would be a fitting refutation to the Supreme Court's determination that black Americans could not be citizens.[102] Rock argued that the Dred Scott decision was the

---

[100] TP, "Speech at the Ministerial Conference," 14.

[101] TP, "Aspect of Slavery in America," 273, 275.

[102] Stephen Kantrowitz, "A Place for 'Colored Patriots': Crispus Attucks among the Abolitionists, 1842–1863," *Massachusetts Historical Review* 11 (Spring 2009): 108–109; Mitch Katchun, "From Forgotten Founder to Indispensable Icon: Crispus Attucks, Black Citizenship, and Collective Memory" *Journal of the Early Republic* 29 (Summer 2009): 277–278; Minardi, *Making Slavery History*, 162–163. For more on Rock, see Kantrowitz, *More Than Freedom*.

culmination of a series of slights made by white Americans, even allies like
Parker. Referring to the minister's recent speech, he quipped, "Mr. Parker
makes a very low estimate of the courage of his race, if he means that one,
two or three millions of these ignorant and cowardly black slaves could,
without means, have brought to their knees, five, ten, or twenty millions
of intelligent brave white men, backed up by a rich oligarchy." How, in
other words, could anyone who believed in Anglo-Saxon vigor expect the
vastly outnumbered and unsupported slaves to free themselves?

Parker followed Rock on stage and responded directly to his accusations. The New Romantic said that he still believed African Americans
to be "the most pacific race of men on the face of the earth," but Parker
nonetheless acknowledged the claims Rock had made about a black tradition of resistance. He even added an example of his own, recounting
the story of three fugitive slaves whose bravery matched that of any person with "white skin." "I hope the day will come when these exceptional
instances of valor will be brought forwards as a proof that valor is likewise instantial in the African race," concluded Parker.[103]

In the months that followed this confrontation, he seemed more convinced than ever that such episodes were more than exceptions to the rule
of black passivity. Parker told George Bancroft about the admirable performance of a number of black Americans who fought in the Revolution,
noting "Negroes get few honors." And, in an 1858 address, he implied
that American slaves were a smoldering fire that could engulf the nation
at any moment. "Unless we amend, one day there will be a San Domingo
in America," he warned, "and worse wrongs will requited worse." By that
point, we should note, Parker had begun working behind closed doors
to assist John Brown as he plotted to invade the South and spark a slave
insurrection. Whatever doubts Parker still had about black militancy he
kept to himself.[104]

Toward the end of the decade, Parker started keeping his doubts about
antislavery violence to himself as well. "I am more than ever of the opinion that we must settle this question in the old Anglo-Saxon way[,] with
the *sword*," he wrote in 1856.[105] Increasingly, pacifist approaches to the

[103] *Liberator*, Mar. 12, 1858; *Boston Daily Advertiser*, Mar. 6, 1858; Paul Teed, "Romantic
Nationalism," 142–160; Dean Grodzins, "Theodore Parker vs. John S. Rock on the
Anglo-Saxon and the African," in *A House Divided: The Antebellum Slavery Debates
in America, 1776–1865*, ed. Mason I. Lowance Jr. (Princeton, NJ: Princeton University
Press, 2003), 299–310.
[104] TP to George Bancroft, Mar. 16, 1858, in *LCTP*, 2: 234; TP, "Effect of Slavery," 334. For
more on Parker's support of Brown, see Chapter 5.
[105] TP to Sarah Hunt, Nov. 17, 1856, TPP, AHTL.

problem of slavery seemed to be little more than "passive obedience" to the minister. He also worried that northerners devoted too much of their energy to commerce and manufacturing, thereby neglecting the fact that "in American politics, the great battle of Ideas and Principles, yea of Measures, is to be fought." Where, he wondered, would this next American Revolution find its Washington or Lafayette? In a lengthy 1859 letter that Parker sent his congregation after leaving the country for health reasons, he laid bare his evolving ideas on nonresistance:

I have not preached the doctrine of the non-resistants, who never allow an individual to repel wrong by material violence; nor that of the ultra-peace man, who deny a nation's right to stave off an invader's wickedness with the people's bloody hand. The wrathful emotions are also an integral part of humanity, and with both nations and individuals have an indispensable function to perform, that of self-defense, which, in the present state of civilization, must sometimes be with violence, even with shedding aggressive blood.

At once integral to human nature – thus, potentially divine – and central to the progressive course of history, violence, on the eve of the Civil War, no longer seemed debased by its association with slavery. Although far from a universal good, the sword could be a necessary remedy. By this logic, just as Jesus's nonresistance was appropriate to his stage of civilization, forceful resistance might be the right response in antebellum America – as it had been during the Revolution. Antislavery violence, Parker determined, functioned much like the Bible. Though imperfect, it could be a moral tool. "God knew what he was about when he put the *instinct of vengeance* in the Heart of Man," Parker wrote two days before John Brown descended upon Harpers Ferry. "It is the first form of *Social Conscience.*"[106]

Parker's actions as the leader of the BVC also testify to this transition from his initial ambivalence about extralegal means to an increasing willingness to endorse them, at least in theory. The first major test of the 1850 Fugitive Slave Law took place in Boston just a couple of months after the new law was passed. On October 19, several slave hunters arrived in Boston intent on seizing runaways Ellen and William Craft, both members of Parker's church. A few years earlier, the Crafts had escaped from Macon, Georgia, with light-skinned Ellen posing as a white gentlemen and William as "his" body servant. The couple eventually settled in Boston,

[106] TP, "Boston Kidnapping," 1: 49; TP, "The New Crime against Humanity," in *WTP*, 12: 253; TP, "Sermon of the Dangers," 238; TP, "Experience as a Minister," 376; TP to J. Lyman, Oct. 14, 1859, TPP, MHS.

though they spent the better part of the next two years recounting this remarkable story to antislavery audiences across the United States and Great Britain.

Alerted to their whereabouts by the publicity, the Crafts' owner dispatched two agents, Willis Hughes and John Knight, to capture his property according to the provisions of the new law. Quickly, Boston's black community and the BVC went to work to make sure that would not happen. The BVC harassed the Georgians as they searched for the couple, shadowing their every move. On several occasions they managed to get the slave hunters thrown in jail for charges ranging from smoking and swearing in public to slander.[107]

In the meantime, Ellen was shuttled between the homes of sympathetic abolitionists in Boston and Brookline. She spent about a week in Parker's townhouse, sleeping just down the hall from where the minister sketched out his sermons, pistol and sword close at hand. William Craft initially refused to hide. Instead, the runaway transformed his carpentry shop into a citadel of sorts. "Mr. Craft is armed and resolved to stand his ground, and in less than an hour blood may flow in the streets of Boston," reported Douglass in the *North Star*.[108]

Whatever misgivings he harbored about the martial capacities of people of African descent, Parker believed that Craft was up to the task. The former bondsman, he wrote a few years later, was a "tall, brave man," who had "armed himself, pretty well too." After personally inspecting Craft's arsenal, Parker concluded, "His powder had a good kernel, and he kept it dry; his pistols were of excellent proof; the barrels true and clean; the trigger went easy; the caps would not hang fire at the snap. I tested his poniard; the blade had a good temper, stiff enough, yet springy withal; the point was sharp."[109] In spite of these preparations, Craft decided to trade his personal fortress for the heavily guarded Beacon Hill home of Lewis Hayden, who pledged to explode two kegs of dynamite if Hughes and Knight dared set foot inside.[110]

The outmatched Georgians were not much safer on Boston's streets. They were jeered, harassed, and, at one point, even chased through town

[107] *LCTP*, 2: 96; Gary Collison, *Shadrach Minkins: From Fugitive Slave to Citizen* (Cambridge, MA: Harvard University Press, 1997), 91–98; Horton and Horton, *Black Bostonians*, 113; Chadwick, *Theodore Parker*, 250–251.

[108] *North Star*, Oct. 24, 1850.

[109] TP, "Boston Kidnapping," 55.

[110] Collison, *Shadrach Minkins*, 98; Petrulionis, *To Set This World Right*, 78; Kantrowitz, *More Than Freedom*, 185–186.

by a large crowd. Eventually, Hughes and Knight sequestered themselves in the United States Hotel, fearful of what the angry Bostonians might do if they resumed their hunt. On October 30, Parker and other BVC members called on the Georgians in their hotel rooms, convincing the agents to leave Boston immediately for their own safety. "They both complained that they were ill-treated," Parker wrote in his journal, "that they could not step into the street but that they were surrounded and followed by men who called out, 'Slave-hunters, slave-hunters! there goes the slave-hunters!'" In this instance, the minister appeared the ally of caution, seeking to defuse the situation before mob violence prevailed. Still, his advice carried an implicit threat: He had done all he could, and, if they failed to cooperate, he would not take responsibility for the result.[111]

Parker's advice to William Craft told a different story. After marrying the Crafts – the runaways were not legally wed – the following week, the minister advised William that he had every right to resist re-enslavement. Even if Craft did not wish to put up a fight, Parker maintained after the wedding, he now had a moral obligation to do so on his new wife's behalf. "So I charged him," Parker wrote the following month, "if the worst came to the worst, to defend the life & liberty of his wife against any Slavehunter at all hazards, tho' in doing so, he dug his own grave & the grave of a thousand men." Then he gave Craft a sword and a Bible. "As a *Minister of Religion*," he concluded, "I put into his hands these two dissimilar instruments, one for the body if need were, the other for his *Soul* at all events."[112]

In the next fugitive slave case in which he was involved, Parker's commitment to antislavery violence seemed less sure. Runaway Thomas Sims was captured by slave hunters in Boston in April 1851. Stymied legally, the BVC debated a variety of rescue strategies. At first they hoped to rescue Sims by placing mattresses below his window on to which he could jump. When this plan was foiled, a few members of the BVC met at Parker's home to discuss other options, including a daring sea rescue. Ultimately, however, no efforts to free Sims were made, and he was returned to Georgia in chains. Some blamed Parker for this outcome. "My private opinion was that Theodore Parker shrunk in the *wetting*," Deborah Weston wrote. "At a time when everything practicable was advising for a rescue ... it was no time for Parker to preach peace."

---

[111] TP, quoted in *LCTP*, 2: 97. Later, one of the slave hunters refuted the claim that they easily acceded to Parker's request. *Liberator*, Dec. 6, 1850.
[112] TP to Webster, Dec. 12, 1850.

Parker, for his part, said a year later that although "the country has never forgiven the Committee" for failing to rescue Sims, they "did all they could."[113]

The New Romantic is perhaps best known for his participation in the effort to free Anthony Burns, an escaped slave captured in Boston in 1854. On the evening following Burns's capture, a large group of abolitionists gathered in Faneuil Hall to measure the popular sentiment regarding the case and, more specifically, to see if they could organize a party the following morning to seize the prisoner from the Boston courthouse.[114]

Wendell Phillips spoke first. "The question is to be settled to-morrow," he said, "whether we shall adhere to the case of Shadrach or the case of Sims." The choice for Phillips was between submission to the rendition of Burns (the course that was pursued with Sims) or resistance (as had happened with a slave named Shadrach in early 1851). Parker followed Phillips on stage and from the start it appeared that the audience needed little encouragement. "*Fellow-subjects of Virginia,*" he began. The crowd cried back, "no, no," and "you must take that back!" Quickly he launched into his standard litany of complaints: the Party of Slavery is an expanding force that "tramples on the Constitution" and "treads down States rights," and is so confident that Boston is no more than "a northern suburb of Alexandria" that "they do not even put chains round the Court House" to prevent an assault by Burns's allies. Marshaled against the slave law, continued Parker, "is another law, it is in your hands and arms." As a minister, he pledged himself to peace, but still maintained "that there is a means, and there is an end; liberty is the end, and sometimes peace is not the means towards it."

Parker asked the crowd what they planned to do. "Shoot, shoot," a voice replied. Swiftly, his ambivalence about antislavery violence resurfaced. "There are ways of managing this matter without shooting anybody," he implored. If they confronted the "cowards" who had kidnapped Burns the following morning, he was sure that they could free him, "*without shooting a gun.*" When he proposed to adjourn the meeting for the evening and reconvene the following morning at nine, the crowd objected. Some shouted, "Let's go to-night!" Others yelled, "Let's pay a visit to the

---

[113] TWH, *Cheerful Yesterdays*, 144; Deborah Weston to Anne Warren Weston, Apr. 15, 1851, TPP, BPL; TP, "Boston Kidnapping," 76.

[114] Von Frank, *Trials of Anthony Burns*, 56. Von Frank's account is the best reconstruction of the Burns case.

slave-catchers at the Revere House."[115] Parker, wrote one of the audience members, was by then drowned out by the "the billows of sound, and he stood gesticulating like one in a dumb show." Having worked the crowd into a lather, he could do little more than watch it overflow. When a man shouted from the back of the hall that there was "a mob of negroes in Court Square attempting to rescue Burns," the crowd of more than 500 people rushed out of the hall and headed toward the courthouse.[116]

Although Parker's caution that evening suggests a reluctance to initiate violence, we cannot know precisely why. Perhaps he preferred a more coherent plan to a disorganized attack that, in fact, proved easily repelled. After all, the minister was not preaching peace in Faneuil Hall, as he was accused of during the Sims case three years earlier. And, according to Higginson, in the days after the failed attempt to free Burns, Parker had "wrung his hands" in dismay when he heard that black abolitionist Lewis Hayden had shot at – but failed to hit – one of the marshals guarding the accused. Such tough talk, of course, was nothing new for the minister. Militant rhetoric energized his antislavery addresses just as his rifle and sword seemed to inspire his Sunday sermons. "I have written my sermons with a pistol in my desk, – loaded, a cap on the nipple, and ready for action," he wrote of the week in which Ellen Craft hid in his home. "Yea, with a drawn sword within reach of my right hand."[117]

Still, in the heat of the moment Parker had difficulty translating his theoretical support for violence, such as it was, into concrete action. Just as he preferred to act as a conscience for antislavery politicians – exhorting and inspiring them – he supported active resistance to the institution of slavery, while remaining aloof from attempts to put it into practice. Despite his desire to live up to his revolutionary forefathers' heroic example and his association of the fight for liberty with the militant Anglo-Saxon spirit, violence remained an imperfect strategy that Parker supported, but looked to others to carry out. Whether, in the end, this inability to see violence through reflected an unwillingness to reject the rule of law entirely, a personal reluctance to push beyond words into the realm of action, or even doubts about blacks' capacity to participate in

---

[115] TP, "Speech of Theodore Parker at the Faneuil Hall Meeting," in Charles Emery Stevens, *Anthony Burns: A History* (Boston: John P. Jewett, 1856), Appendix M, 289, 291, 292, 294, 295.

[116] Quoted in Stevens, *Anthony Burns*, 40–41; Von Frank, *Trials of Anthony Burns*, 61. For more on the attempt to free Anthony Burns, see Chapter 5.

[117] TWH, *Cheerful Yesterdays*, 155; TP, "Speech at the Ministerial Conference in Boston, May 29, 1851," in *ASAOS*, 1: 13.

their own liberation, is difficult to know for certain. By the time the Civil War severed America into two warring factions, the New Romantic had died while seeking relief from tuberculosis in Italy.[118]

Not long after he delivered his Seventh of March address, Daniel Webster wrote to a group of citizens in Newburyport, Massachusetts, of the need to rebuke "the spirit of faction and disunion, that spirit of discord and of crimination and recrimination" that was tearing the country in two. The Massachusetts senator insisted that the philosophy associated with the New Romantics was the major cause of northern intransigence on the key issues of the day. "Borne away, by the puffs of a transcendental philosophy, into an atmosphere flickering between light and darkness," insisted Webster, the minority of Americans who rejected compromise represented an enormous threat to the majority who sought it.[119]

Webster likely had Parker in mind when he wrote this passage. Less than two months earlier, the most popular minister in Webster's home-town of Boston had publicly denounced the senator's Seventh of March address in a meeting at Faneuil Hall. The speech, which worked against "the permanent good of a great nation," was a crass bid for the presi-dency, maintained Parker.[120] Over the course of the next decade, the Transcendentalist led the charge in denouncing not just Webster, but everything for which he stood. Traditional commitments – to private property, to the rule of law, even to democratic solutions to the nation's political problems – seemed to fall away in the face of the dictates of the higher law. It permitted no compromise. It justified any response.

But Parker too had his limits. He had trouble separating his universal claims about liberty from his national and racial assumptions and biases. And while he flirted with resistance during the fugitive slave cases in Boston, he had difficulty proffering an unqualified endorsement of violent means, not to mention taking up arms himself. His ambivalence about violence dovetailed with the mediatory role that he played in the aboli-tionist movement as a whole. Parker tried to draw together Garrisonian nonresistants, antislavery politicians, and the new breed of militants

---

[118] On Parker's inability to follow through on abstract commitments to violence, see Jeffrey Rossbach, *Ambivalent Conspirators: John Brown, the Secret Six, and a Theory of Slave Violence* (Philadelphia: University of Pennsylvania Press, 1982).

[119] Daniel Webster to Edward Sprague Rand, et al. [citizens of Newburyport], May 15, 1850, in *Papers of Daniel Webster*, 7: 94.

[120] TP, "Speech at a Meeting of the Citizens of Boston," 166.

that included his protégé and fellow New Romantic Thomas Wentworth Higginson, whom we will consider shortly. Although the minister could never bring himself to abandon his study and pulpit for the antislavery trench, he crafted a romantic approach to politics whose vivid and emotional terms inspired many fellow abolitionists to do precisely that.

Perhaps the most famous member of that group was Frederick Douglass. Although born a slave and alienated from the United States for much of his life, by the 1850s, Douglass began to rethink what the nation and its citizenry might achieve. Ultimately, he challenged America to live up to ideals for which Parker had argued so eloquently.

2

Frederick Douglass, Perfectionist Self-Help, and a Constitution for the Ages

Resisting the temptations of a beautiful summer day, some six hundred people crowded into Rochester's Corinthian Hall on July 5, 1852. Paying about a dime each, the largely white audience gathered to hear what prominent black abolitionist Frederick Douglass had to say about the nation's birthday. Invited to give an Independence Day lecture by the Rochester Ladies' Anti-Slavery Society, Douglass chose to speak on July 5 because that year the fourth had fallen on a Sunday. This fortuitous postponement allowed him to follow in the footsteps of reformers in the antebellum North, who frequently waited until July 5 to recognize the holiday, in order to highlight the gap between the high promises of the Fourth of July and low realities of life for African Americans, while also avoiding confrontations with drunken white revelers.[1]

Douglass's Fifth of July address, as it has come to be known, echoed the critiques of previous Independence Day orations. "What, to the American slave, is your 4th of July?" he asked the crowd in Rochester. Douglass's answer underscored the nation's dissimulation. It is "a day that reveals to

[1] *Frederick Douglass' Paper*, July 1, 1852; *Frederick Douglass' Paper*, July 9, 1852; James A. Colaiaco, *Frederick Douglass and the Fourth of July* (New York: Palgrave Macmillan, 2006), 1–31; John Ernest, *Liberation Historiography: African American Writers and the Challenges of History, 1794–1861* (Chapel Hill: University of North Carolina Press, 2004), 236–237; Leonard Sweet, "The Fourth of July and Black Americans in the Nineteenth Century: Northern Leadership Options within the Context of the Black Experience," *Journal of Negro History* 61 (July 1976): 256–275; Shane White, "'It Was a Proud Day': African Americans, Festivals, and Parades in the North, 1741–1834," *Journal of American History* 81 (June 1994): 38–40; Edward Bartlett Rugemer, *The Problem of Emancipation: The Caribbean Roots of the American Civil War* (Baton Rouge: Louisiana State University Press, 2008), 228–232.

him, more than all other days in the year, the gross injustice and cruelty to which he is the constant victim." To the slave, he said, America's purported commitment to liberty, equality, and morality was "mere bombast, fraud, deception, impiety, and hypocrisy." You could scour the globe and not find a nation that rivaled the United States in terms of "revolting barbarity and shameless hypocrisy." The Fourth of July "is the birthday of your National Independence," he told his audience "of your political freedom." The same could not be said, however, for Douglass or his fellow African Americans, enslaved or free. Even though he was an honored guest who had been asked to speak publicly on the nation's birthday, by the laws of the land Douglass remained little more than a slave. Highlighting the wide gulf that separated him from his white listeners, he held, "I am not included within the pale of this glorious anniversary! ... This Fourth [of] July is *yours*, not *mine*." It is difficult to find a more incendiary jeremiad in American letters.[2]

Yet Douglass – in word and symbol – sounded more than this negative note. Standing before the hundreds that had gathered the black editor must have seemed living testimony to the potential that the United States offered at least a few African Americans. He was the most famous abolitionist in Rochester, perhaps the nation's most recognizable reformer (Figure 2.1). Despite being born in bondage, Douglass had seized his freedom as a young man, thereafter earning a reputation as an inspiring, tireless antislavery lecturer. For the past five years, he had published his own antislavery weekly newspaper in Rochester. By 1852, Douglass was a leading figure in the struggle against slavery in upstate New York and, as a result, he was invited to speak to the Rochester Ladies' Anti-Slavery Society.

Douglass's Fifth of July address, like the orator himself, spoke as much to hope and possibility as to the disheartening realities of antebellum America. For all his vitriol, Douglass refused to dismiss the nation's founders, notwithstanding their many compromises with slavery. "They were statesmen, patriots and heroes," he announced, "I can not contemplate their great deeds with less than admiration."

The foundational documents they wrote, the black abolitionist added, also deserved high praise. The Declaration of Independence announced "saving principles" that should be followed "on all occasions, in all places, against all foes, and at whatever cost." It was the "RING-BOLT" of American destiny. The United States Constitution, insisted Douglass,

---

[2] FD, "What to the Slave," 371, 360, 363, 368.

FIGURE 2.1. Frederick Douglass, n.d.
Source: Unknown. Courtesy of the Library of Congress, Prints and Photographs Division, LC-USZ62–15887.

when interpreted correctly, was a "GLORIOUS LIBERTY DOCUMENT." His spirits were buoyed not only by the principles articulated in the Declaration of Independence and the Constitution but also by what he termed "the genius" of American institutions and the revolutions in commerce, communication, education, and travel that seemed to be simultaneously uniting and transforming every nation on the planet. Despite America's failings, Douglass concluded his address on a note of millennial optimism, citing a poem by his former mentor William Lloyd Garrison, titled, "The Triumph of Freedom." The large crowd in Corinthian Hall showered him with applause, having just heard what historian David Blight calls "the rhetorical masterpiece of abolitionism."[3]

Two years later, almost to the day, it was Garrison who took the stage to consider the meaning of the Fourth of July in a nation that continued to condone slavery. Standing before hundreds at a picnic on a hot afternoon in Framingham, Massachusetts, America's leading abolitionist delivered a speech reminiscent of Douglass's Fifth of July address in many ways. "To-day, we are called to celebrate the seventy-eighth anniversary of American Independence. In what spirit? with what purpose? to what

[3] FD, "What to the Slave," 364, 363, 385, 387–388, 359; David W. Blight, *American Oracle: The Civil War in the Civil Rights Era* (Cambridge, MA: Belknap Press of Harvard University Press, 2011), 167.

end?" he wondered. Like his protégé, Garrison had great esteem for the document that was produced on Independence Day. Also like Douglass, Garrison contrasted the Declaration's high idealism with the sad facts of life in antebellum America. "Alas!" he lamented, "our greed is insatiable, our rapacity boundless, our disregard of justice profligate to the last degree."

Yet whereas Douglass found solace in the Constitution's ideals and the "genius" of American institutions and practices, his mentor Garrison demonstrated no such faith. The Slave Power, he insisted, dominates the federal government, rejects the antislavery views of the Founding Fathers, and proposes to annex "foreign territory for slaveholding purposes." Then the abolitionist editor reinforced his fiery message with a series of gestures that would be remembered long after his words that day were forgotten. Pulling out a copy of the fugitive slave law, Garrison lit a match and set the document on fire. The crowd erupted in cheers. Not content, he proceeded to burn two more proslavery documents before Garrison got to his primary target: the U.S. Constitution. Lifting the nation's foundational compact high in the air, "he branded it as the source and parent of all the other atrocities," and then burned it to ashes, too, crying, "And let all the people say, Amen!" Most of them did.[4]

These two defining moments in American abolitionism expose the critical divide – at once personal and ideological – that was emerging in the early 1850s between Douglass and his one-time mentor. The preeminent romantic reformer in the country since the 1830s, Garrison had pioneered an immediate, uncompromising approach to ending slavery in the United States. As nonresistants, Garrison and many of his American Anti-Slavery Society (AASS) colleagues rejected both traditional political methods and the more forceful assaults on the forces of slavery prophesized by black militants like David Walker. While never an orthodox Garrisonian, Douglass had embraced and publicly defended many of Garrison's positions since the early 1840s. By decade's end, however, he began moving away from the famous editor of the *Liberator*, reconsidering his controversial stances on antislavery politics and the nature of the Constitution. A troubling rift opened between the two men.

How do we explain this divide? Scholars often frame Douglass's split from Garrison as rooted in their different reform temperaments. Whereas Douglass sought to work for change within the political system, Garrison rejected not only slavery and prejudice but also the democratic institutions

---

[4] *Liberator*, July 7, 1854; Mayer, *All on Fire*, 443–445.

and practices upon which the country was founded. According to this line of thinking, Douglass played the practical reformer to Garrison's idealistic revolutionary. At times, Douglass seemed to agree with this characterization. On the eve of the Civil War, for example, he wrote that in comparison to Garrison, his position was "one of reform, not of revolution."[5]

True enough, the label reformer captures some of the contours of Douglass's thinking quite well. He did have a strong pragmatic streak. Yet to conclude that the black abolitionist played the reformer to Garrison's revolutionary is to neglect other aspects of his personality, philosophy, and reform agenda. Such a distinction misses his proclivity to idealize American values and institutions, so evident in his Fifth of July speech. Douglass's devotion to the principles of both the Declaration of Independence and the Constitution was not founded solely on a practical commitment to democratic procedures and principles – to piecemeal reform and compromise. He appealed, instead, to the militant spirit of American revolutionaries and the egalitarian rhetoric of the Declaration of Independence. Rejecting the Garrisonian interpretation of the Constitution, Douglass urged Americans to look past contemporary interpretations of the nation's foundational compact to the higher goals it espoused. The Constitution, he concluded, "contain[s] principles and purposes, entirely hostile to the existence of slavery." Interpreted in light of the ideals articulated in its preamble and the Declaration of Independence, as well as "the sentiments of the founders of the Republic," the Constitution was an abolitionist instrument. Douglass, in short, reimagined America's liberal tradition, urging a romantic interpretation of its key principles and core compact.[6]

Just as Douglass called on the United States to live up to the ideals on which it was founded, he pushed individuals – particularly black

---

[5] Benjamin Quarles, "The Breach between Douglass and Garrison," *Journal of Negro History* 23 (Apr. 1938): 152; Tyrone Tillery, "The Inevitability of the Douglass-Garrison Conflict," *Phylon* 37 (June 1976): 137–49; FD, "The Constitution of the United States: Is it Pro-slavery or Anti-slavery?," in *LWFD*, 2: 480.

[6] FD, "What to the Slave," 386; FD, "The Dred Scott Decision: An Address Delivered, in Part, in New York, New York, in May 1857," in *FDP*, 3: 171. Recent scholarship, which has tended to focus on the relationship between Douglass and Abraham Lincoln, highlights Douglass's other facets. When compared to Lincoln, rather than Garrison, Douglass appears more like a radical. I believe that the label New Romantic captures both sides of Douglass, helping to reconcile interpretations of Douglass as pragmatic reformer with those of him as revolutionary. Oakes, *Radical and the Republican*; Stauffer, *Giants*; and Stephen Kendrick and Paul Kendrick, *Douglass and Lincoln: How a Revolutionary Black Leader and a Reluctant Liberator Struggled to End Slavery and Save the Union* (New York: Walker and Co., 2008).

Americans – to take an active hand in their liberation and uplift. In this way, he closely linked the romantic project of reconceiving the Constitution with a second romantic strain so crucial to his thinking: perfectionist self-help. Turning frequently to Byron's words of self-enacted liberation, Douglass stressed the moral and psychological effects of working for one's own elevation. His autobiographies were odes to the pursuit of individual uplift. So, too, were his antislavery newspapers, which he believed were the sort of enterprises that would enable African Americans to emancipate themselves. True elevation, he held, would only come to those who took an active hand in their own improvement. Even slave insurrection, Douglass eventually insisted, could be justified because of the transformative power of individual action.[7]

Of course, this embrace of antislavery violence was not that easy to reconcile with his devotion to the United States Constitution, in particular, or liberal democracy more generally. Like most of his fellow New Romantics, Douglass vacillated for much of the 1850s between working for abolition through traditional channels and extralegal, violent ones. In the end, the Civil War enabled Douglass to resolve his romantic dilemma. As the United States government committed itself not simply to preserving the Union but also to ending slavery and allowing African American men to play a key role in that effort, he found a way to harmonize his faith in perfectionist self-help with his devotion to a Constitution that was, as he put it, "for ages."[8]

Antislavery Argument or Antislavery Exemplar?

William Lloyd Garrison first heard Frederick Douglass at an antislavery convention on Nantucket Island in the summer of 1841. He was mesmerized. "I shall never forget his first speech at the convention," Garrison later wrote, "the extraordinary emotion it excited in my own mind – the powerful impression it created upon a crowded auditory."[9]

---

[7] My interpretation builds on the work of several scholars who have noted the romantic elements in Douglass's thinking. See Martin, *Mind of Frederick Douglass*; David W. Blight, *Frederick Douglass' Civil War: Keeping Faith in Jubilee* (Baton Rouge: Louisiana State University Press, 1989); and Bill E. Lawson, "Douglass among the Romantics," in *The Cambridge Companion to Frederick Douglass*, ed. Maurice S. Lee (New York: Cambridge University Press, 2009), 118–131.

[8] FD, "The American Constitution and the Slave: An Address Delivered in Glasgow, Scotland, on 26 March 1860," *FDP*, 3: 348.

[9] William Lloyd Garrison, preface to *Narrative of the Life of Frederick Douglass, An American Slave*, in *FDPAW*, 1: 3.

Within months, the former bondsman began appearing regularly on the antislavery circuit. He was a natural. Years later, Harriet Beecher Stowe insisted that few college graduates "could compete successfully with Frederick Douglass as an orator," while Thomas Wentworth Higginson observed that "Mr. Douglass always commands attention.... His dramatic power is always ... great."[10] And, of course, he had a personal familiarity with slavery that few abolitionist orators – college graduates or not – could match. An agent for the Massachusetts Anti-Slavery Society (MASS) introduced Douglass to audiences as a "graduate from the peculiar institution," whose "*diploma*" was "*written on* [his] *back!*"[11]

This characterization was true, but only to a point. It would be a mistake to overlook the gulf between Douglass's experiences and those of most people who suffered under slavery. After all, Douglass managed not only to seize his freedom but also to become a prominent member of northern society. He was, in other words, much closer to what Emerson called an "anti-slave" – someone who manages to mold his own destiny – than a typical bondsman.[12]

Douglass had been born Frederick Augustus Washington Bailey in 1818 in Talbot County, on Maryland's Eastern Shore. He was the son of Harriet Bailey, an enslaved woman who was the property of Aaron Anthony, the plantation manager for one of the state's wealthiest planters, Colonel Edward Lloyd. Douglass never knew the identity of his father, though he later confessed that "it was sometimes whispered that my master was my father." Not only did he grow up fatherless, Douglass also was separated from his mother, who lived and worked on another plantation for the majority of his childhood. Like so many slaves, he was denied the chance to develop a close relationship with his parents.[13]

Still, Douglass had a relatively benign childhood for a person in bondage. As the most comprehensive biographer of his early years explains, Douglass was "recognized by his white masters as an unusually gifted boy and, within the limits of their conditioned attitudes as slaveholders, he was treated as such." Chosen to be the playmate of Colonel Lloyd's son Daniel, he enjoyed protection from abuse at the hands of older boys,

[10] HBS, *The Lives and Deeds of Our Self-Made Men* (Hartford, CT: Worthington, Dustin, 1872), 382; *Newburyport Daily Evening Union*, Nov. 4, 1850.
[11] John A. Collins, quoted in FD, *My Bondage and My Freedom*, in *FDPAW*, 2: 206.
[12] Ralph Waldo Emerson, "Emancipation in the West Indies," in *Emerson's Antislavery Writings*, ed. Len Gougeon and Joel Myerson (New Haven, CT: Yale University Press, 1995), 31.
[13] FD, *My Bondage and My Freedom*, 31–36 (quotation 31).

which was one of the painful rites of boyhood passage in antebellum America. Early on, Douglass also largely escaped the violence that followed chattel slavery.[14]

Douglass had atypical educational opportunities as well. At the age of ten, he was sent to live in Baltimore where he was to work for Hugh and Sophia Auld, relatives of his master's son-in-law. His new mistress, Sophia, was a deeply pious woman, who began to teach Douglass to read. When a confrontation with her husband led Sophia to abandon the lessons, however, the young slave was forced to find new sources of learning. Convincing – and sometimes bribing – white boys to give him spelling lessons, Douglass spent many hours in Baltimore pursuing a clandestine course of study. He also obtained copies of *Webster's Spelling-Book* and *The Columbia Orator*. The latter proved to be an essential primer in the political power of oratory, exposing Douglass to the speeches of Cato, William Pitt, and George Washington.[15]

Soon Douglass broadened his studies. Influenced by a white Methodist preacher and a black lay minister, he "saw the world in a new light." Thereafter, he collected portions of the Bible wherever he could find them, even gathering scraps of it from the gutter. A third figure – a black drayman named Charles Lawson – had perhaps the biggest impact of all on Douglass's emerging spiritual life. Lawson and Douglass spent hour after hour together in the former's home in Happy Alley, which was close to the Auld household. They were a good team, the abolitionist later recalled, "I could teach him '*the letter*,' but he could teach me '*the spirit*.'" Douglass also joined white Methodist congregations in Baltimore and later in St. Michael's, Maryland, where he moved in the spring of 1833 to live with a new master, who had inherited Douglass after Aaron Anthony died.[16]

For all the inspiration he found in his newfound faith, Douglass learned early that Christianity, in the wrong hands, could serve as cover for repugnant behavior. Sent by his new owner to live for a year with a slave-breaker named Covey, Douglass faced the brutality from which he

---

[14] Dickson J. Preston, *Young Frederick Douglass: The Maryland Years* (Baltimore, MD: Johns Hopkins University Press, 1980), xv, 53–55; FD, *My Bondage and My Freedom*, 74, 49–52.

[15] McFeeley, *Frederick Douglass*, 23–25; FD, *My Bondage and My Freedom*, 90–91. On early black education, see Heather Andrea Williams, *Self Taught: African American Education in Slavery and Freedom* (Chapel Hill: University of North Carolina Press, 2005), esp. 7–44.

[16] FD, *My Bondage and My Freedom*, 95–105 (quotations 95); Martin, *Mind of Frederick Douglass*, 9.

had largely escaped during his childhood. "A professor of religion – a pious soul – a member and a class-leader in the Methodist church," he explained sarcastically, Covey also had a well-deserved reputation as a "nigger-breaker."

After enduring near constant abuse at the hands of Covey for six months, Douglass decided that he had had enough. He went to see his owner, who, to his dismay, did nothing. Upon returning to Covey's home, Douglass, for the first time, resisted. A long struggle ensued. Eventually Covey, who came out on the worse end of the fight, gave up, never laying a finger on Douglass again. Like his exposure to reading and his conversion to Christianity, Douglass counted his fight with Covey as among the most important elements of his adolescence.[17]

Three years later, Douglass escaped to the North. Armed with a protection pass he had borrowed from a free black sailor, he fled to New York City before settling in New Bedford, Massachusetts. There, Douglass adopted a new surname. In New York City, he had started calling himself Frederick Johnson, but upon arriving in Massachusetts, Douglass learned that the last name "Johnson" was common among runaways in the area. After his New Bedford host suggested he instead assume the last name of a Scottish chieftain from Walter Scott's *Lady of the Lake*, which he had been reading, the newcomer started calling himself Frederick Douglass.[18]

Not long after Douglass moved to New Bedford, he began subscribing to Garrison's *Liberator*. The young runaway quickly became a devoted student of Garrisonian abolitionism. A half-century later, he told members of Boston's Wendell Phillips Club, "I have often been asked where I got my education. I have answered, from Massachusetts Abolition University, Mr. Garrison, President."[19]

Garrison first outlined his brand of romantic reform a decade before he met Douglass. Building on the efforts of pioneering black activists, the antislavery editor challenged the gradualism of earlier reformers. He was especially unhappy with organizations like the American Colonization Society, which sought to emancipate slaves and "return" them to Africa.

---

[17] FD, *Narrative*, 45–55 (quotation 45).
[18] FD, *My Bondage and My Freedom*, 200–203.
[19] FD, quoted in Frederic May Holland, *Frederick Douglass: The Colored Orator* (New York: Funk & Wagnalls, 1891), 363; Martin, *Mind of Frederick Douglass*, 22. See also FD, *Life and Times*, 263 and FD, "Recollections of the Anti-Slavery Conflict," n.d., Frederick Douglass Papers (FDP), Library of Congress (LOC), microfilm reel 18, no. 66.

FIGURE 2.2. William Lloyd Garrison, n.d. Editor of the *Liberator* and pioneering romantic reformer, Garrison was an early mentor to Douglass before the two split in the early 1850s.
Source: Unknown. Courtesy of the Library of Congress, Prints and Photographs Division, LC-USZ62–10320.

Through his newspaper, the *Liberator*, which he published weekly from 1831 until 1865, Garrison came to be the most famous abolitionist in America: a man celebrated by opponents of slavery but vilified by its supporters (Figure 2.2). He fumed about the inhumanity of slavery, demanded immediate emancipation, and ridiculed the idea of compensating slaveholders. Despite these militant positions, Garrison did not advocate direct physical confrontation with the proponents of slavery. Instead, he adhered to nonresistance, a doctrine that was "derived from Christ's injunction to individuals not to resist evil." Like many romantic reformers, nonresistants were pacifists. They went beyond nonviolence, however, to embrace "no-governmentism" – the complete renunciation of "all manifestations of force, including human government."[20]

Garrison and most of his colleagues in the AASS denounced all forms of antislavery coercion – political or extralegal – in favor of moral suasion.

---

[20] Perry, *Radical Abolitionism*, 56–57. On occasions in which Garrison equivocated on nonresistance, see Harold, *Rise of Aggressive Abolitionism*, 17–29.

The AASS's Declaration of Sentiments, for instance, pledged the organization to "the destruction of error by the potency of truth – the overthrow of prejudice by the power of love – and the abolition of slavery by the spirit of repentance."[21] To thoroughly rid America of the sin of slavery, Garrisonians believed that the American people had to be convinced of the institution's immorality. They sought to convert the nation to their holy cause. "Genuine abolitionism is not a hobby, got up for personal or associated aggrandizement; it is not a political ruse," said Garrison. "It is of heaven, not of men.... In short[,] it is a life, not an impulse – a quenchless flame of philanthropy, not a transient spark of sentimentalism."[22]

Early on, the AASS had experimented with one important form of political action – petitioning. By 1837, it had gathered perhaps 1 million signatures on antislavery petitions that the AASS forwarded to Congress. Yet the response of proslavery congressmen left many Garrisonians frustrated. Through diverse procedures that were collectively known as the gag rule, Congress ensured that antislavery petitions would not be heard in either the House or the Senate for the better part of a decade.[23]

By the end of the 1830s, the gag rule had helped to split AASS stalwarts. While Amos Phelps, Lewis Tappan, and James Birney determined that abolitionists could make good use of political parties or organized churches, Garrison and his followers concluded, on the contrary, that such institutions were impotent when it came to effecting social change. Instead, Garrisonians aimed "to subvert the relation of master and slave – not by machinery political or ecclesiastical, but by establishing in the hearts of men a deep and wide-spreading conviction of the brotherhood of the human race."[24] Inspired by the perfectionist notion that Christians must sever all ties to sinful institutions and practices, they urged reformers to "come out" of northern churches that tolerated

---

[21] Quoted in Stewart, *Holy Warriors*, 54–55.

[22] *Liberator*, July 19, 1839.

[23] Newman, *Transformation of American Abolitionism*, 137–149; Stewart, *Holy Warriors*, 81–86; Howe, *What Hath God Wrought*, 512–515, 609–611; Daniel Wirls, "'The Only Mode of Avoiding Everlasting Debate': The Overlooked Senate Gag Rule for Antislavery Politicians," *Journal of the Early Republic* 27 (Spring 2007): 115–138; William Lee Miller, *Arguing About Slavery: John Quincy Adams and the Great Battle in the United States Congress* (New York: Vintage, 1995); Freehling, *Road to Disunion, Vol. 1*, 308–352; Russel B. Nye, *Fettered Freedom: Civil Liberties and the Slavery Controversy, 1830–1860* (East Lansing: Michigan State University Press, 1963), 45–46; and George C. Rable, "Slavery, Politics, and the South: The Gag Rule as a Case Study," *Capitol Studies* 3 (Fall 1975): 69–87.

[24] "Fourth Annual Report of the American Anti-Slavery Society," *Quarterly Anti-Slavery Magazine* 2 (July 1837): 421.

slavery. In the early 1840s, Garrison started advocating coming out of the American republic altogether, making "the repeal of the Union" a new motto for the *Liberator*. He denounced the U.S. Constitution and called for the dissolution of a Union founded on such a corrupt compact.[25]

A number of Garrison's ideas immediately appealed to Douglass. Just after he arrived in New Bedford, Douglass had briefly attended a nominally integrated Methodist church. He was frustrated, however, by the fact that its African American congregants were required to take the sacrament after the white congregants and eventually severed all ties with the church.[26] More generally, Douglass shared the Garrisonians' misgivings about the prejudicial tendencies of organized religion, a topic he pursued vigorously as he began lecturing for the AASS. He contrasted true Christianity, which was designed to establish peace on earth and good will toward man, with "the whining, canting, psalm-singing, nasal, [and] hypocritical system of the present day in America." Most Americans, Douglass believed, were "too reverential God-ward to be honest man-ward," he concluded.[27]

As an antislavery tactician, Douglass was persuaded by several Garrisonian positions. He embraced moral suasion rather than political agitation as the most effective means to combat slavery. "Was it political action that removed your prejudices, and raised in your minds a holy zeal for human rights?" he asked a Boston crowd in 1842.[28] No, changing the hearts and minds of Americans appeared the only answer to him. At this point, Douglass also agreed with Garrisonians that the Constitution was "radically and essentially slaveholding." As he declared in 1847, it gave slaveholders "the physical and numerical power of the nation," keeping "the slave in his chains, by promising that that power shall in any emergency be brought to bear upon the slave, to crush him in obedience to his master." Not just flawed in its origins, the Constitution also had troubling consequences for the present day. Without the protection it afforded

---

[25] *Liberator*, Dec. 29, 1832; Perry, *Radical Abolitionism*, 57, 92–128, 159–166; Mayer, *All on Fire*, 313–316. For a smart reappraisal of Garrisonian disunionism in a transatlantic context, see W. Caleb McDaniel, "Repealing Unions: American Abolitionism, Irish Repeal, and the Origins of Garrisonian Disunionism," *Journal of the Early Republic* 28 (Summer 2008): 243–269.

[26] FD, *My Bondage and My Freedom*, 203.

[27] FD, "Suppose You Yourselves Were Black: An Address Delivered in New York, New York, on 10 May 1848," in *FDP*, 2: 129, 128.

[28] FD, "Abolitionists and Third Parties: An Address Delivered in Boston, Massachusetts, on 26 January 1842," in *FDP*, 1: 14.

slavery, implied Douglass, those in bondage would be more likely to rise up and seize their own liberty.[29]

It was on the critical question of slave rebellion that the black abolitionist did not see eye to eye with Garrisonians. His new colleagues had convinced him of the merits of pacifism. "I would suffer rather than do any act of violence – rather than that the glorious day of liberty might be postponed," held Douglass. But unlike many first-generation romantic reformers, he tended to express pragmatic rather than ideological misgivings about violence. Douglass worried more about would-be slave rebels' chances of success than the morality of forceful resistance. It would, of course, be difficult to imagine otherwise, for Douglass counted his fight with slave-breaker Covey as among the most important moments in his life.[30]

Douglass, in sum, constructed his own antislavery platform during the 1840s, sifting through Garrisonian ideas for what he found efficacious. Although dedicated to most of his new mentor's positions – immediate abolition, disunionism, moral suasion, the proslavery character of the Constitution, the corruption of American churches – the black abolitionist did not leave the thinking to his AASS colleagues as some had wanted. Douglass's suggestion that he had attended Massachusetts Abolition University was apt. Like any good student, he tested the lessons he learned against his own experiences, accepting some, rejecting others. By 1847, Douglass was ready to graduate.

From Agent to Principal

Two years earlier Douglass had left for an extended tour of the British Isles. There he spent his time speaking to overflowing lecture halls and making innumerable contacts with reformers across the British Isles. The trip transformed Douglass. "I go back to the United States not as I landed

---

[29] FD, "Love of God, Love of Man, Love of Country: An Address Delivered in Syracuse, New York, on 24 September 1847," in *FDP*, 2: 101; FD, "My Slave Experience in Maryland: An Address Delivered in New York, New York, on 6 May 1845," in *FDP*, 1: 33.

[30] FD, "Love of God, Love of Man, Love of Country," 104; Leslie Freidman Goldstein, "Violence as an Instrument for Social Change: The Views of Frederick Douglass (1817–1895)," *Journal of Negro History* 61 (Jan. 1976): 65–66; "Minutes of the National Convention of Colored Citizens Held at Buffalo," in *Minutes of the Proceedings of the National Negro Conventions, 1830–1864*, ed. Howard H. Bell (New York: Arno Press, 1969), 13; "Proceedings of the National Convention of Colored People and their Friends, in Troy, N.Y.," in *Minutes of the Proceedings*, 31.

here," he declared in his farewell speech in London. "I came a slave; I go back a free man. I came here a thing – I go back a human being." With this profound statement, Douglass simultaneously flagged not only his newfound sense of belonging but also his new legal status. While he was abroad, the runaway slave had been purchased by several of his American friends and legally freed.[31]

This was not the first time that Douglass described himself as making a transition from thing to human being. A couple of years earlier, he had highlighted the transformative impact of his fight with Covey in his first autobiography, *Narrative of the Life of Frederick Douglass*. "You have seen how a man was made a slave," he wrote of the slave-breaker's abuse, now "you shall see how a slave was made a man." Indeed, Douglass characterized his battle with Covey as "the turning-point" in his life as a slave in all three of his autobiographies. In the 1854 edition, he added, "I was a changed being after that fight. I was *nothing* before; I WAS A MAN NOW. It recalled to my life my crushed self-respect and my self-confidence, and inspired me with a renewed determination to be A FREEMAN."[32]

Examined apart from other episodes in his life, Douglass's fight with Covey appears to have been a conversion experience. Yet the New Romantic eschewed the evangelical schema of immediate awakening, preferring a vision that fit more closely with the liberal Christian notion of gradual self-culture. "Men talk much of a new birth," he announced in Boston's Tremont Temple in 1861. "The fact is fundamental. But the mistake is in treating it as an incident which can only happen to a man once in a life time; whereas, the whole journey of life is a succession of them."[33] As Daniel Walker Howe has argued, Douglass's autobiographies are replete with turning points. Howe highlights several moments of self-discovery that Douglass emphasized in his autobiographies: his religious awakening, his struggle with Covey, and the surge of empowerment he felt when he delivered his first antislavery speech in Nantucket in 1841.[34] Douglass would likely have added to this list other episodes, including his initial exposure to reading by Sophia Auld and his first meeting with Garrison.

---

[31] FD, "Farewell to the British People: An Address Delivered in London, England, on 30 March 1847," in *FDP*, 2: 50; McFeely, *Frederick Douglass*, 143–144.

[32] FD, *Narrative*, 50, 54; FD, *My Bondage and My Freedom*, 140–141; FD, *Life and Times*, 177.

[33] FD, "Pictures and Progress: An Address Delivered in Boston, Massachusetts, on 3 December 1861," in *FDP*, 3: 460.

[34] Howe, *Making the American Self*, 151.

The turning points to which Douglass attached the most importance, however, were those in which he had been the active agent. Although he was grateful for those moments when he benefited from the assistance of others, during the late 1840s and early 1850s, he stressed that improvement had to come from oneself. And more than any other New Romantic, Douglass turned to Lord Byron's words, both in print and on the stump, to make this point. In an August 1847 meeting in Norristown, Pennsylvania, he urged black men in that state not to passively accept political disfranchisement, concluding, "Who would be free, themselves must strike the blow." Less than a year later, Douglass noted in his antislavery newspaper, the *North Star*, that while African Americans' "white friends" were "removing the barriers to our improvement ... the main work must be commenced, carried on, and concluded by ourselves." Again, he used Byron's call to underscore his argument, quoting the stanza in full.[35] Two of his three autobiographies – *My Bondage and My Freedom* (1855) and *The Life and Times of Frederick Douglass* (1881) – likewise drew on this call to action to justify his fight against the slave-breaker Covey. Even his 1845 autobiography seems to owe a debt to the British Romantic. In describing his struggle with Covey in his *Narrative*, Douglass employed similar syntax to Byron's famous call, while also expressing virtually the same sentiment. "He only can understand the deep satisfaction which I experienced, who has himself repelled by force the bloody arm of slavery," wrote the black abolitionist.[36]

Douglass's faith in the power of self-enacted emancipation doubtless informed what he would later count as another of his life's turning points: starting his own antislavery newspaper, the *North Star*, in 1847. Without preparation or experience, the consummate autodidact would have to spend days and nights toiling to produce his four-page weekly paper. Yet "it was the best school possible for me," he later concluded. Not only did

[35] FD, "Material and Moral Requirements of Antislavery Work, Addresses Delivered in Norristown, Pennsylvania, on 5, 6 August 1847," in *FDP*, 2: 89; *North Star*, July 14, 1848; Wolfgang Mieder, *"No Struggle, No Progress": Frederick Douglass and His Proverbial Rhetorical Civil Rights* (New York: P. Lang, 2001), 229–230.

[36] FD, *My Bondage and My Freedom*, 142; FD, *Life and Times*, 178; FD, *Narrative*, 54. For other examples of Douglass's use of Byron's ode to self-emancipation, see *Frederick Douglass' Paper*, Sept. 28, 1855; FD, "The Significance of Emancipation in the West Indies," An Address Delivered in Canadaigua, New York, on 3 August 1857, in *FDP*, 3: 202; FD, "The Proclamation and a Negro Army: An Address Delivered in New York, New York, on 6 February 1863," in *FDP* 1: 566; FD, "Parties Were Made for Men, Not Men for Parties: An Address Delivered in Louisville, Kentucky, on 25 September 1883," in *FDP*, 5: 95; and FD, "The Greatest Revolution the World Has Yet Seen: An Address Delivered in Providence, Rhode Island, on 3 December 1884," in *FDP*, 5: 166–167.

publishing the *North Star* force Douglass to think, read, and write more carefully, it made him self-reliant. "It made it necessary for me to lean upon myself," he wrote, "and not upon the heads of our Anti-Slavery church, to be a principal, and not an agent."[37]

Douglass's decision to produce his own newspaper was rooted in a philosophy of self-help that predominated in antebellum black communities. African American reformers had long stressed self-improvement as an essential component of racial progress. "Our oppressors have divested us of many valuable blessings and facilities for improvement and elevation," wrote Douglass in an early issue of the *North Star*, "but, thank heaven, they have not yet been able to take from us the privilege of being honest, industrious, sober and intelligent." His co-editor and fellow New Romantic Martin Robison Delany agreed. Championing what he styled "the glorious cause of self-elevation," he urged Pittsburgh blacks to establish institutions and organizations, which would empower them to improve themselves.[38]

Although this call for black self-help was born in African American communities that had few direct ties to Boston's elite Unitarian circles, it resembled the romantic vision of gradual self-culture embraced in the latter. The leading exponent of self-culture in the mid-nineteenth century was Unitarian minister William Ellery Channing, whose 1838 lecture, "Self-Culture," became the foundation of a widely read tract by the same name. "Self-culture," insisted Channing, is "the care which every man owes to himself, to the unfolding and perfecting of his nature." He believed individual improvement was a gradual process, akin to the cultivation of a garden. By his logic, people need to pay the same sort of daily attention to their own growth as gardeners do to the plants they tend. "To cultivate anything, be it a plant, an animal, a mind, is to make [it] grow," maintained Channing. "Nothing admits culture, but that which has a principle of life capable of being expanded." Taking the Unitarian idea of self-culture to the logical extreme, Emerson maintained that to pursue self-reliance was to recognize the divine nature of every individual: "There are in each of us all the elements of moral and intellectual

---

[37] FD to Charles Francis Adams, June 27, 1847, in *FDPC*, 1: 221; FD, *Life and Times*, 327.

[38] Frederick Cooper, "Elevating the Race: The Social Thought of Black Leaders, 1827–1850," *American Quarterly* 24 (Dec. 1972): 604–625; Rael, *Black Identity and Black Protest*, 126; *North Star*, July 14, 1848; MRD to FD, June 13, 1850, in the *North Star*, June 27, 1850, reprinted in *MDR*, 176; MRD, "Self-Elevation Tract Society," *Mystery*, Dec. 16, 1846, reprinted in *MDR*, 36.

excellence, that is to say, if you act out yourself, you will attain and exhibit a perfect character." A program of gradual self-culture, in short, could lead to moral perfection.[39]

While Douglass never acknowledged that his emphasis on black self-help mirrored romantic self-culture, he was an admirer of the ideas of the New England Transcendentalists and their European counterparts. In his early days in the North, he pored over the works of Emerson, Byron, and Carlyle, while later counting Walter Scott as among his favorite writers. Betraying his great esteem for Margaret Fuller three decades after she died off the coast of Fire Island, Douglass wrote in 1884 of his good fortune in having married a woman "who can as Margaret Fuller says cover one in all his range."[40]

It is easy to see the influence of leading romantics on the black abolitionist's lectures and editorials. Douglass, for one, celebrated the beauty and dynamism of the natural world as if he were a Lake Poet. "How glorious is nature in action," he pronounced in 1861. "On goes the great mystery of mysteries – Creating, unfolding, expanding, renewing, changing perpetually, putting on new forms, new colours, issuing new sounds, filling the world with new perfumes, and spreading out to the eye and heart, unending scenes of freshness and beauty."[41]

Douglass imagined the ocean in particular as a sublime place of unfettered dynamism. Take the famous apostrophe "to the moving multitudes of ships" of the Chesapeake Bay in his first autobiography. "You are loosed from your moorings, and are free; I am fast in my chains, and am a slave!" lamented Douglass. "You move merrily before the gentle gale, and I sadly before the bloody whip!" Or, consider his 1853 novella *The Heroic Slave*, in which a white sailor contrasts slaveholding at land and sea: "It is one thing to manage a company of slaves on a Virginia plantation, and quite another thing to quell an insurrection on the lonely billows of the Atlantic, where every breeze speaks of courage and liberty." Higginson likewise used nautical symbolism to capture humanity's innate vitality. "The human soul, like any other noble vessel, was not built to be

[39] Howe, *Making the American Self*, 130–135; Rael, *Black Identity and Black Protest*, 124–135; William Ellery Channing, *Self-Culture. An Address Introductory to the Franklin Lectures, Delivered at Boston, United States, September, 1838* (London: Palmer and Clayton, 1839), 6, 8; Ralph Waldo Emerson, quoted in Robinson, *Apostle of Culture*, 55.

[40] Stauffer, *Giants*, 90; Paul C. Jones, *Unwelcome Voices: Subversive Fiction in the Antebellum South* (Knoxville: University of Tennessee Press, 2005), 61; FD to Elizabeth Cady Stanton, May 30, 1884, in *LWFD*, 4: 411.

[41] FD, "Pictures and Progress," 472.

anchored, but to sail," wrote the second-generation Transcendentalist. "Men forget the eternity through which they have yet to sail, when they talk of anchoring here upon this bank and shoal of time."[42]

Like many romantics, Douglass also stressed the progressive course of history and the possibility of human perfection. In 1841 Emerson famously urged, "what is a man born for but to be a Reformer, a Re-maker of what man had made."[43] Twenty years later Douglass echoed these sentiments, holding that "life is agitation and agitation progress" in a talk given as a part of the Parker Fraternity Lectures, a lecture series sponsored by the Twenty-Eighth Congregational Society. In a similar fashion, Douglass employed Parker's famous distinction between the transient and permanent in his third autobiography, writing, "The forces against us are passion and prejudice, which are transient, and those for us are principles, self-acting, self-sustaining, and permanent."[44]

Douglass, in fact, had been drawn to the humanistic theology preached by Boston's most popular and infamous preacher since the early 1850s. "My heart goes out only toward a practical religion," Douglass proclaimed at an 1852 antislavery convention in Cincinnati.[45] Less than two years later, the Rochester editor published a letter in his newspaper that framed a recent sermon by Parker in precisely these terms. "I heard Theodore Parker last Sabbath," wrote his associate editor William J. Watkins from Boston in late 1853. "No man preaches more truth than this eloquent man, this astute philosopher.... Though denounced and held up to the world as an infidel, he is a practical Christian."[46] Six years later Douglass echoed his colleague's admiration for Parker in response to an invitation to deliver a Parker Fraternity Lecture in November 1859. "To speak in Boston is a large undertaking, but to speak in the pulpit of Mr. Parker is a huge undertaking," he told Charles Wesley Slack, the chairman of the

---

[42] FD, *Narrative*, 49; FD, *The Heroic Slave*, in *Autographs for Freedom*, ed. Julia Griffiths (Boston: John P. Jewett and Co., 1853), 228; Gesa Mackenthun, *Fictions of the Black Atlantic in American Foundational Literature* (New York: Routledge, 2004), 98–102; TWH, "The Sympathy of Religions," in *WTH*, 354.

[43] Ralph Waldo Emerson, "Man the Reformer," in *The Collected Works of Ralph Waldo Emerson, Volume 1: Nature, Addresses, and Lectures*, ed. Robert E. Spiller and Alfred R. Ferguson (Cambridge, MA: Harvard University Press, 1971), 156.

[44] FD, "Life Pictures," quoted in Blight, *Frederick Douglass' Civil War*, 13; Commager, *Theodore Parker*, 268; *FDP*, 3: 452–453n1; FD, *Life and Times*, 618.

[45] FD, "Antislavery Principles and Antislavery Acts: Addresses Delivered in Cincinnati, Ohio, on 27, 28, 29, April 1852," in *FDP*, 2: 345.

[46] *North Star*, Jan. 6, 1854. Following J. R. Balme, Waldo Martin misattributes these words to Douglass himself. J. R. Balme, *American States, Churches, and Slavery* (London: Hamilton, Adams, & Co., 1863), 221; Martin, *Mind of Frederick Douglass*, 178.

lecture series. "I shall come to the work with fear and trembling, but shall come nevertheless."[47]

The following year, in the wake of the minister's untimely death, Douglass wrote, "Ten thousand times over would we prefer the religion of Theodore Parker, with its downright honesty, its sympathy for the poor, its honor to man as man ... than that miserable trash passing as Evangelical Religion."[48] When Douglass toured Europe several decades later, the first place he visited upon arriving in Florence, Italy, was Parker's grave. "It did not seem well that the remains of the great American preacher should rest thus in a foreign soil," the black reformer noted in the second edition of his third autobiography, "far away from the hearts and hands which would gladly linger about it and keep it well adorned with flowers."[49]

What is more, Douglass joined Parker in putting man, rather than God, at the center of his cosmos. At the final meeting of the AASS, which had decided to disband after the passage of the Fifteenth Amendment in 1870, Douglass wondered aloud why so many people felt the need to thank a higher deity for antislavery successes. "I want to express my love and gratitude to God, by thanking those faithful men and women, who have devoted the great energies of their souls to the welfare of mankind," he countered. "It is only through such men and women that I can get any glimpses of God anywhere."[50] Despite early evangelical influences, Douglass came to embrace the liberal theology that to so many Bostonians made Theodore Parker a heretic.

Not surprisingly, then, Douglass's program of black self-help closely correlated with the vision of self-culture articulated by Parker, Emerson, and their fellow romantics in America and abroad. Although most proponents of black uplift paid more attention to social and economic improvement than to moral and intellectual nourishment, Douglass thought these

---

[47] FD to Charles Wesley Slack, Aug. 26, 1859, in Stoneham, *John Brown and the Era of Literary Confrontation*, Appendix C, 169. Douglass canceled this lecture after John Brown's raid at Harpers Ferry forced him to flee the country. Stoneham, *John Brown and the Era of Literary Confrontation*, 76–77.

[48] *Douglass' Monthly*, July 1860, p. 289; Booker T. Washington, *Frederick Douglass* (1906; repr., New York: Greenwood Press, 1969), 321; William L. Van Deburg, "Frederick Douglass: Maryland Slave to Religious Liberal," *Maryland Historical Magazine* **69** (Spring 1974): 36; Martin, *Mind of Frederick Douglass*, 178.

[49] FD, *The Life and Times of Frederick Douglass* [second edition] (1892; repr., Mineola, NY: Dover Publications, 2003), 432.

[50] FD, "A Reform Absolutely Complete: An Address Delivered in New York, New York, on 9 April 1870," in *FDP*, 4: 264.

different types of advancement went hand in hand. Once the demands for food, clothing, and shelter were met, he maintained in 1861, "it is natural" for man to turn to deeper concerns: "By the cultivation of his intellect, by the development of his natural resources, by under standing the science of his own relations to the world, man has the marvellous [*sic*] power of enlarging the boundaries of his own existence." And like most reform-minded romantics, he believed human progress was a gradual, organic process as inevitable as the tides: "Conceive of life without progress and sun[,] moon and stars instantly halt in their courses. The restless ocean no longer heaves on high his proud dashing billows. The lightening hides itself in sombre [*sic*] sky."[51] Douglass best outlined his philosophy of perfectionist self-help in his popular lecture, "Self-Made Men," which he delivered more than fifty times between 1859 and 1893. The black editor had a democratic conception of self-improvement, insisting that every person, even the most humble, had the potential to "buil[d] the ladder on which they climbed and buil[d] as they climbed."[52]

This emphasis on individual uplift did not make Douglass an apologist for unfettered individualism, however. On the contrary, he stressed the organic connection that united all of humankind. "I believe in individuality," the New Romantic announced in an 1893 incarnation of the lecture, "but individuals are, to the mass, like waves to the ocean. The highest order of genius is as dependent as is the lowest."[53] Here again, Douglass's ideas dovetailed neatly with Transcendentalist theories about human greatness. Emerson, in a lecture series that he published in 1850 as *Representative Men*, had suggested that representative individuals simply demonstrate the potential shared by every person. Napoleon Bonaparte, concluded Emerson, was "the idol of common men, because he had in transcendent degree the qualities and powers of common men." Parker said something similar in his widely read eulogy of John Quincy Adams: "The great man has more of human nature than other men, organized in him. So far as that goes, therefore, he is more me than I am myself.... In kind we are the same; different in degree."[54] Parker's vision of the

[51] FD, "Pictures and Progress," 472.
[52] Blight, *Frederick Douglass' Civil War*, 6; Martin, *Mind of Frederick Douglass*, 172; Howe, *Making the American Self*, 153; FD "The Trials and Triumphs of Self-Made Men: An Address Delivered in Halifax, England, on 4 January 1860," in *FDP*, 3: 293.
[53] FD, "Self-Made Men: An Address Delivered in Carlisle, Pennsylvania, in March 1893," in *FDP*, 5: 439.
[54] Ralph Waldo Emerson, "Napoleon, or the Man of the World," in *The Collected Works of Ralph Waldo Emerson, Volume 4: Representative Men*, ed. Wallace E. Williams and Douglas Emory Wilson (Cambridge, MA: Belknap Press of Harvard University Press,

connection between great men and common men had a profound impact on Douglass, who regularly referenced them decades after the minister first delivered his eulogy. Like the Transcendentalists, he praised the self-made man as "our best representative," one who "reflects, on a colossal scale, the scale to which we would aspire, our highest aims, objects, powers and possibilities." As such, Douglass's standard list of self-made men was not filled with Ragged Dicks. Although they often overcame similar, if not greater, barriers than Horatio Alger's rags-to-riches exemplar, Douglass's heroes were scholars and writers, political and revolutionary leaders.[55]

So as not to be mistaken on this score, he concluded an early version of his address with the stipulation that perfectionist self-help was valuable only if coupled with an unselfish purpose. "Patriotism, religion, philanthropy – some grand motive power other than the simple hope of personal reward must be present," insisted Douglass.[56] Stowe identified similar factors when outlining the selection criteria for her 1872 book, *The Lives and Deeds of Our Self-Made Men.* Her self-made men – comprising leading abolitionists, Republicans, and Union veterans – distinguished themselves through "frugality, strict temperance, self-reliance and indomitable industry," but, most of all, through their "moral nature." "They were men of good and honest hearts – men who have set their faces as a flint to know and do the RIGHT," she concluded. From a group that included Lincoln, Garrison, and Ulysses S. Grant, Stowe singled out Douglass as having done more than any other self-made man to improve himself.[57]

Douglass, however, did not do it alone. When he returned from Great Britain in 1847, the black abolitionist came armed not only with his freedom but also with a printing press, which Douglass's British supporters had purchased. By helping him start the *North Star*, they believed

---

1987), 131; Lawrence Buell, *Emerson* (Cambridge, MA: Belknap Press of Harvard University Press, 2003), 83–86; TP, "John Quincy Adams," in *WTP*, 7: 204.

[55] FD, "Self-Made Men," 549, 548. For Douglass's references to Parker's theories of human greatness, see FD, "The Lessons of Emancipation to the New Generation: An Address Delivered in Elmira, New York, on 3 August 1880," in *FDP*, 4: 572; FD, "Give Women Fair Play: An Address Delivered in Washington, D.C., on 31 March 1888," in *FDP*, 5: 355–356; FD, "Haiti Among the Foremost Civilized Nations of the Earth: An Address Delivered in Chicago, Illinois, on 2 January 1893," in *FDP*, 5: 531; and FD, "This Is Not a Layman's Day, But a Bishop's Day: An Address Delivered in Baltimore, Maryland, on 21 May 1894," in *FDP*, 5: 615.

[56] FD, "Trials and Triumphs of Self-Made Men," 300.

[57] Howe, *Making the American Self*, 137; HBS, *Lives and Deeds of Our Self-Made Men*, vii-viii, 380–383 (quotations vii, viii).

that they were providing him an essential tool for self-improvement: "the most powerful lever for the attainment of emancipation."[58]

His Garrisonian associates, however, were not nearly as supportive of this new project. There were already plenty of African American anti-slavery papers, held the *Liberator* in mid-1847, and Douglass lacked the necessary experience to succeed in publishing. His old friends also worried that the endeavor would distract him from his important role as an antislavery lecturer, where "his extraordinary powers can be the most successfully employed for the promotion of the anti-slavery cause."[59]

Although these objections were petty and paternalistic, they were not entirely unfounded. Indeed, if anyone understood the precarious nature of producing a viable antislavery newspaper it was Garrison and his associates, who worked hard merely to keep the *Liberator* afloat. Garrison, for his part, was hurt by the fact that on this matter Douglass never sought out his mentor's advice on the matter. Others speculated that the leading abolitionist was threatened by his protégé's move. Parker wrote of his fellow Bostonian, "I think Garrison has been so long in the habit of ruling that he 'takes not an equal to the throne.'" Douglass tried to keep up a diplomatic front in public, but behind closed doors, it was clear to all that the new editor had deeply disappointed his former colleagues, who viewed him as little more than a subordinate.[60]

Douglass chose the growing city of Rochester as the home for his newspaper. Located in what has come to be called the burned-over district of western New York, Rochester was home to waves of revivalism in the early nineteenth century and thus fertile ground for a range of reform movements, from communitarianism to abolitionism. Douglass, who had toured through western New York extensively as an antislavery agent, was well acquainted with the region's merits. He also thought that by establishing his paper there he could build an audience without undercutting the circulation of other antislavery papers.[61]

[58] *Liberator*, June 18, 1847.
[59] *Liberator*, June 25, 1847. See also *Liberator*, July 23, 1847.
[60] McFeeley, *Frederick Douglass*, 147; TP to Increase Smith, Apr. 3, 1848, TPP Papers, MHS; *Liberator*, Dec. 17, 1847. On paternalism that Garrisonians displayed toward Douglass, see Jane H. Pease and William H. Pease, "Boston Garrisonians and the Problem of Frederick Douglass," *Canadian Journal of History* 2 (Sept. 1967): 29–48 and John Sekora, "'Mr. Editor, If You Please': Fredrick Douglass, *My Bondage and My Freedom* and the End of the Abolitionist Imprint," *Callaloo* 17 (Spring 1994): 608–624.
[61] Whitney R. Cross, *The Burned-over District: The Social and Intellectual History of Enthusiastic Religion in Western New York, 1800–1850* (Ithaca, NY: Cornell University Press, 1950); Milton C. Sernett, *North Star Country: Upstate New York and the Crusade*

The new editor hoped his paper would not only open the door to more active African American participation in the antislavery struggle but also undermine the racial ideas that plagued the nation. "The general contempt with which my people are regarded," wrote Douglass in 1849, "the low estimate entertained of the negro's mental and moral qualities among the white people of this land – and the absences of any very striking confutation of the ... depressing theories ... led me to establish this paper." If he and his partners were able to establish a successful black antislavery paper, they could strike a blow against racist assumptions about black Americans.[62]

Douglass was not immune to his own brand of racial stereotyping, however. Like Parker, he denounced polygenesis yet subscribed to the notion that every race of humanity was endowed with a unique set of traits that distinguished it from other races. In addition, he agreed that Anglo-Saxon people were more inclined toward democracy, although he was quicker than the Transcendentalist minister to highlight the aggressive nature of Anglo-Saxon culture. "The love of power is one of the strongest traits in the Anglo-Saxon race," concluded Douglass.[63]

When it came to people of African descent, however, the black editor departed from conventional wisdom. Unlike most romantic racialists – who emphasized submissive nature or inherent religiosity of Africans – Douglass pointed to the "tenacity of life" and "malleable toughness" that has allowed the race to thrive despite harrowing trials like the Middle Passage. He contrasted Africans' resilient spirit with the vulnerability of Native Americans, who die "under the flashing glance of the Anglo-Saxon." Douglass also put greater emphasis on environmental factors than many romantic racialists. The Anglo-Saxon "love of power" had been bolstered, he said, by the absolute authority whites had commanded in the American South under the institution of slavery: "Strong by nature it has become stronger by habit."[64]

for *African American Freedom* (Syracuse, NY: Syracuse University Press, 2002); FD, *Life and Times*, 322.

[62] FD to Elizabeth Pease, Nov. 8, 1849, BPL; McFeeley, *Frederick Douglass*, 152.

[63] FD, "The Claims of the Negro Ethnologically Considered: An Address Delivered in Hudson, Ohio, on 12 July 1854," in *FDP*, 2: 497–525; Bay, *White Image in the Black Mind*, 66–71; Dain, *A Hideous Monster of the Mind*, 249–256; FD, "In Law Free, In Fact, A Slave: An Address Delivered in Washington, D.C., on 16 April 1888," in *FDP*, 5: 360.

[64] FD, "The Claims of the Negro Ethnologically Considered," in *FDP*, 2: 524; FD, "In Law Free, In Fact, A Slave," in *FDP*, 5: 360.

Douglass never fully reconciled the tension between his theories about human equality and the role of the environment, on the one hand, and the special gifts of each race, on the other. The former predominated in his thinking, nonetheless, especially when it came to his newspaper. Black Americans, he insisted, were just as capable as their white counterparts in succeeding in such an enterprise; they simply needed the opportunity. The *North Star* was just such a chance.

The New Romantic had spent much of the 1840s working as an agent for the AASS. At the same time, however, he formulated a romantic philosophy of self-help that compelled him to seek out a new role. The *North Star* seemed an ideal way to him to take an active hand in the antislavery struggle – to be a principal, not just an agent. To some critics, this move was a departure from an integrated vision of America. Yet viewed in terms of political ideology, it had quite the opposite effect on Douglass. As the crisis over slavery intensified over the decade to come, Douglass began drawing directly on America's liberal tradition, calling the nation's institutions to live up to the values on which the country was founded. Perfectionist self-help ultimately brought Douglass back to the nation from which he felt so alienated.

A Constitution for the Ages

When Douglass moved to Rochester to start the *North Star*, his Garrisonian allies in New England feared he would fail. They were also concerned that he could fall under the sway of the political abolitionists who predominated in the region. Although this paternalistic perspective overlooked a key characteristic about the black abolitionist – Douglass had never been the passive narrator of the wrongs that some of his white allies envisioned – they nonetheless had some reason to worry. For, over the next few years, he forged close ties with reformers such as Gerrit Smith.[65]

A wealthy New York abolitionist and one of the founders of the Liberty Party, Smith befriended Douglass immediately. He also provided financial support that allowed the black reformer to keep his newspaper afloat. In 1851, Douglass decided to merge his paper with the *Liberty Party Paper*, which was bankrolled by Smith. The two abolitionists agreed that by combining their financial and intellectual resources they could set at least

---

[65] FD, *My Bondage and My Freedom*, 208. On Smith's abolitionist clique, see Friedman, *Gregarious Saints*, 96–126.

one western New York antislavery paper, which they called *Frederick Douglass' Paper*, on sure ground for the future. But the fact that the merger coincided with Douglass's break with Garrisonianism on several fronts sparked rumors that Douglass and his paper had been bought. "They accuse me now, openly, of having sold myself to one Gerrit Smith Esq. and to have changed my views – more in consequence of your purse than your arguments!" steamed the editor in a letter he wrote Smith in early 1852.[66]

Truth be told, however, Douglass's stance on key issues like the Constitution had been softening for years. In 1849, for instance, he had admitted in the *North Star* that a strict reading of the Constitution suggested that it was not "a pro-slavery instrument." "Had the Constitution dropped down from the blue overhanging sky, upon a land uncursed by slavery, and without an interpreter," he ventured, "no one would have imagined that it recognized or sanctioned slavery." Interpreted literally, the Constitution did not reinforce slavery in any way. The words "slave" and "slavery" did not even appear in the document, Douglass noted. But the proslavery intentions of many of its Framers told a different story:

Having a terrestrial, and not a celestial origin, we find no difficulty in ascertaining its meaning in all the parts which we allege to relate to slavery. Slavery existed before the Constitution, in the very States by whom it was made and adopted. – Slaveholders took a large share in making it. It was made in view of the existence of slavery, and in a manner well calculated to aid and strengthen that heaven-daring crime.

In theory, the Constitution might not be proslavery, but understood in light of those who wrote it – not to mention the way it had been interpreted since ratification – the document bolstered the peculiar institution.[67]

Two years later, at a meeting of the AASS in Syracuse, Douglass went further than this. Angered by a proposal that the Garrisonian society should only endorse newspapers that explicitly rejected the Constitution as a proslavery document, Douglass publicly broke ranks. The black editor not only rejected the proposed exclusionary position but also explained that after extensive study he had revised his position on the

[66] John R. McKivigan, "The Frederick Douglass-Gerrit Smith Friendship and Political Abolitionism in the 1850s," in *Frederick Douglass: New Literary and Historical Essays*, 211; Stauffer, *Black Hearts of Man*, 134–181; FD to Gerrit Smith, Mar. 24, 1852, in *FDPC*, 1: 526.
[67] *North Star*, Mar. 16, 1849.

nation's founding compact. Douglass now deemed the Constitution an antislavery weapon.[68]

Surrounded by Garrisonians, the New Romantic must have appeared an apostate. When Garrison himself heard Douglass argue that the Constitution could work against slavery, he could not believe his ears, saying, "There is roguery somewhere!" The relationship between leading Garrisonians and their former colleague swiftly went from bad to worse. At an 1852 AASS meeting, Douglass felt like an outcast. When he asked why he was being "treated as an alien," his former colleagues and mentors had plenty to say. Ranging from substantive objections to his new views on the Constitution to petty problems, such as his choice to inform Gerrit Smith of his change of opinion before the AASS, the grievances they voiced were the opening salvo in what came to be a vituperative war of words between Douglass and the Garrisonians.[69]

Personal slights and petty squabbles aside, the two parties were now worlds apart on a major question to antebellum abolitionists. Wendell Phillips was the most forceful proponent of the Garrisonian interpretation of the Constitution, laying out in the 1840s the arguments that justified Garrison's dramatic incineration of the Constitution a decade later. Phillips maintained that the Constitution was, at its most basic level, a compromise with slavery. This, he insisted, was abundantly clear in both the text of the document itself and the debates that had raged as it was written. Phillips cited numerous parts of the Constitution that demonstrated its proslavery character: (1) the three-fifths clause; (2) the provision to use force to suppress insurrections; (3) the foreign slave trade clause; (4) the clause guaranteeing the return of persons held in service or labor; and (5) the stipulation of federal government protection for states against domestic insurrection.

The Framers' intentions, Phillips continued, likewise provide a clear sense of the founding document's support for slavery. Drawing on the recently published "Madison Papers," the Garrisonian compiled a lengthy series of excerpts to demonstrate that the Constitution was a compromise that granted "to the slaveholder distinct privileges and protection

---

[68] FD, "Change of Opinion Now," in *LWFD*, 2, 155–56; McFeeley, *Frederick Douglass*, 169.

[69] *Liberator*, May 23, 1851; FD to Gerrit Smith, May 21, 1851, in *FDPC*, 1: 447; FD to Gerrit Smith, May 15, 1852, in *FDPC*, 1: 536–537; Quarles, "Breach Between Douglass and Garrison," 144–154; Pease and Pease, "Boston Garrisonians and the Problem of Frederick Douglass," 29–47; Tillery, "Inevitability of the Douglass-Garrison Conflict," 137–149.

for his slave property, in return for certain commercial concessions on his part toward the North." Finally, Phillips held that the interpretations and actions of federal officials over the last half century, as well as the general assent of the American people in the same period, point to an obvious conclusion: the Constitution is a proslavery document. "What the Constitution may become a century hence, we know not; we speak of it *as it is* and repudiate it *as it is*," he concluded.[70]

Like the New Romantics, Garrisonians were committed to higher law doctrine. But they drew a sharper distinction between higher and positive law, refusing to acknowledge that the latter could be anything more than, in Noah Webster's words, "a rule of civil conduct prescribed by the Supreme power of a State, commanding what its subjects are to do, and prohibiting what they are to forbear."[71] To swear allegiance to the Constitution, vote, or otherwise participate in American democratic practices amounted to choosing government over morality. This Garrisonians would not do. They argued that the only solution to the problem of slavery – the only path to justice – "is *over* the Constitution, trampling it under foot; not *under* it, trying to evade its fair meaning."[72]

Political abolitionists were less willing to walk over the document. Moderates like Sumner, Salmon P. Chase, and William Seward emphasized the antislavery leanings of many of the Framers. The Constitution, argued Chase, omitted direct reference to slavery and "left it a State institution – the creature and dependent of State law – wholly local in its existence and character." According to this reading, it permitted abolition in federally controlled areas such as the District of Columbia and western territories. At the state level, moderates hoped that in time the combined force of federal patronage and judicial appointments might enable local opponents of slavery to bring an end to the institution. This view that "freedom is national; slavery only is local and sectional" became by the mid-1850s a basic tenet of the Republican Party.[73]

---

[70] Wendell Phillips, *The Constitution a Pro-Slavery Compact: Or, Extracts from the Madison Papers* (1844; repr., New York: American Anti-Slavery Society, 1856), 6, 5, 8; William M. Wiecek, *The Sources of Antislavery Constitutionalism in America, 1760–1848* (Ithaca, NY: Cornell University Press, 1977), 239.

[71] Noah Webster, quoted in Wendell Phillips, *Review of Lysander Spooner's Essay on the Unconstitutionality of Slavery* (Boston: Andrews & Prentiss, 1847), 7.

[72] *Liberator*, July 26, 1844; Phillips, *Review of Lysander Spooner's Essay*, 35.

[73] Chase, quoted in Foner, *Free Soil, Free Labor*, 76, 83. On Chase's view of the Constitution, see Foner, *Free Soil, Free Labor*, 73–102. On the Republicans' antislavery constitutionalism, see James Oakes, *Freedom National*, esp. 1–48.

More radical political abolitionists, like William Goodell and Douglass's new partner Smith, argued that the Constitution did not support slavery anywhere or in any fashion. They also thought that the document granted the federal government the authority to abolish the institution, pointing to the principles articulated in the Constitution's preamble. Goodell could not square the goal of promoting "the general welfare" with "crushing the laboring, the producing class, in half the States of the Republic."[74]

Perhaps the most prominent proponent of this line of constitutional interpretation in the 1840s and 1850s was Lysander Spooner. A lawyer from Massachusetts, Spooner grounded his seminal 1845 treatise, *The Unconstitutionality of Slavery*, in two fundamental commitments: to the supremacy of natural, rather than positive, law and a strict adherence to the text of the Constitution alone. Rejecting the Garrisonian tendency to look to external documents, such as Madison's notes on the debates of the Convention, he wondered, "why are words used in writing a law, unless it is to be taken for granted that when written they contain the law?" Spooner blended natural-rights arguments with strict, textualist hermeneutics to produce a complicated set of rules by which to interpret the Constitution. These rules of interpretation set different standards for laws that comported with "natural right" and those that "authorize or sanction anything contrary to the natural right." While the former "may be sanctioned by natural implication and inference," when it came to provisions that are at odds with natural laws, "no terms, except those that are plenary, express, explicit, distinct, unequivocal, *and to which no other meaning can be given, are legally competent.*" Put another way, when in doubt the Constitution should be read in order to favor natural right.[75]

Armed with this set of rules, Spooner then refuted the Garrisonian reading of the Constitution, clause by clause. The three-fifths clause, for example, makes a distinction between "free persons" and "all others." Yet the term "free persons," he insisted, does not necessarily mean the opposite of the word "slave." Instead, Spooner held that "free persons" was meant to signal citizens of the United States and "all other persons" was a reference to aliens. And since he found it perfectly reasonable and just to count aliens partially in terms of representation and taxation, he deemed

74 William Goodell, quoted in Crane, *Race, Citizenship, and the Law*, 110.
75 Spooner, *Unconstitutionality of Slavery*, 16, 161–162, 59; Diane J. Schaub, "Frederick Douglass's Constitution," in *The American Experiment: Essays on Theory and Practice of Liberty*, ed. Peter A. Lawler and Robert M. Schaefer (Lanham, MD: Rowman & Littlefield, 1994), 468.

this interpretation preferable to the traditional reading of the clause as a compromise with slavery.[76]

Douglass credited Smith, Goodell, and others for influencing his change of heart on the Constitution. Nonetheless, he owed his greatest debt to Spooner, who, he believed, had laid out "the ablest argument ever written in favor of" an antislavery Constitution. Like Spooner, Douglass embraced a rule of legal interpretation rooted in higher law doctrine. "The very idea of law," he insisted, "carries with it ideas of right, justice and humanity." Indeed, many of his 1850s speeches on the Constitution drew on Spooner's reasoning.[77]

This is not to say, however, that Douglass followed Spooner on all fronts. He disagreed with Spooner's reading of the three-fifths clause, for instance. Unlike Spooner, the New Romantic was willing, at least for the sake of argument, to admit that the clause meant to contrast "free persons" with slaves. Even so, Douglass insisted that the three-fifths clause should not be understood "*to guarantee, in any shape or form, the right of property in man in the United States.*" Instead, by counting the entire free population, white or black, but just "three-fifths" of the slave population, the clause, in fact, worked against the institution of slavery. By imposing "a downright disability" on slaveholding states, it encouraged them to abandon slavery for freedom.[78]

Moreover, Douglass did not limit his interpretation of the Constitution to its text alone, putting stock in the intentions of the Framers as well. Although Douglass admitted that some of them supported slavery, he maintained that the best minds in all corners of the republic viewed "slavery … as a great evil," and believed it to be on the road to extinction in the United States. Douglass argued in 1851 that the explicit endorsement of liberty and justice in the preamble of the Constitution, on the one hand, and the lack of any specific reference to slavery, on the other, were "proof of the intention to make the Constitution a permanent liberty document." As he would later put the matter in his Fifth of July address: "What would be thought of an instrument, drawn up, *legally* drawn up,

---

[76] Spooner, *Unconstitutionality of Slavery*, 242; Kraditor, *Means and Ends in American Abolitionism*, 193–195.

[77] *Douglass' Monthly*, Nov. 1860, p. 354; *Liberator*, May 25, 1851; FD, "Antislavery Principles and Antislavery Acts," 350; FD, "The U.S. Constitution Anti-Slavery," in *LWFD*, 5: 285: Peter C. Myers, *Frederick Douglass: Race and the Rebirth of American Liberalism* (Lawrence: University Press of Kansas, 2008), 226–227n24; FD, "The Inaugural Address," in *LWFD*, 3: 76.

[78] FD, "American Constitution and the Slave," 352; Schaub, "Frederick Douglass's Constitution," 471.

for the purpose of entitling the city of Rochester to a track of land, in which no mention of land was made?"[79]

Douglass also broke with Spooner by stressing the practical benefits of interpreting the Constitution in an antislavery fashion. Garrisonians, he believed, undercut attempts to combat the institution by arguing that the foundational document of the United States sanctioned, and worked for, slavery. Even if their position was theoretically valid – a point that Douglass was no longer willing to concede – the implications of this admission undercut any real effort to effect change. "What I contend," he concluded, "is that if the Constitution shall be *presumed* to favor liberty, and to be consistent with its noble preamble, its language will inevitably secure the extinction of human slavery, and forever, in this Republic." Here Douglass found common ground with Higginson, Parker, and Stowe. Although agnostics on the question of whether the Constitution was ultimately pro- or antislavery, these romantic reformers insisted that the critical point was what could be done with the document.[80]

Parker approached the Constitution much as he approached the Bible: as a flawed, but useful instrument. "Men talk a great deal about the Compromises of the Constitution, but forget the GUARANTEES of the Constitution," he wrote Higginson in early 1857. While the Constitution offered ambiguous support for slavery with such measures as the rendition clause, it declared a commitment to ensuring a republican form of government – and thus to the abolition of the despotic institution of slavery – in "plain words." Four months later, Higginson elaborated on the Constitution's antislavery potential suggested by Parker. In the hands of a "Supreme Court that is favorable to liberty," the younger minister held at an AASS meeting in New York City, any "opportunity" the Constitution offered – any ambiguity or "loophole," no matter how small – would turn it into "an anti-slavery document tomorrow."[81]

---

[79] *Frederick Douglass' Paper*, July 24, 1851; FD, "What to the Slave," 385.

[80] FD, "Antislavery Principles and Antislavery Acts," 349. Delany thought that the Constitution was "an ambiguous document, susceptible of almost any construction concerning human rights," but he was less sanguine about its antislavery potential, at least in the hands of antebellum statesmen. MRD, *University Pamphlets. A Series of Four Tracts on National Polity: To the Students of Wilberforce University; Being Adapted to the Capacity of the Newly-Enfranchised Citizens, The Freedmen* [Charleston, SC: Republican Book and Job Office, 1870], in *MDR*, 422.

[81] TP to TWH, Jan. 18, 1857, in *Proceedings of the State Disunion Convention, held at Worcester, Massachusetts, January 15, 1857* (Boston: Massachusetts Committee for Disunion, 1857), Appendix, 5; TP, "The Anti-Slavery Convention," in *WTP*, 11: 185; Grodzins, "Why Theodore Parker Backed John Brown," 8–9; TWH, *The New*

Stowe, for her part, did not explicate her theories of constitutional interpretation as fully as did her male counterparts. Yet in an 1862 *Atlantic Monthly* essay, she endorsed a similar approach. Lincoln and congressional Republicans, Stowe suggested, have made considerable antislavery strides – including the abolition of slavery in the District of Columbia and western territories and the preliminary Emancipation Proclamation – by assuming that the "anti-slavery framers" of the Constitution made room for slavery to "be peaceably abolished" through "the exercise of normal Constitutional powers." Stowe willingly admitted that "this theory of the Constitution has been disputed by certain Abolitionists," but that did not really mean much to the novelist. What mattered to her were the revolutionary changes that Republicans were making with the Constitution's assistance. Three years earlier, Douglass had predicted precisely this course of events in a speech he delivered in Glasgow, Scotland. "If the South had made the Constitution bend to the purposes of slavery," he held, "let the North now make that instrument bend to the cause of freedom and justice."[82]

Such pragmatic arguments for using the Constitution as a weapon in the abolitionist struggle, however, were overshadowed by Douglass's core contention that it was *prima facie* an antislavery document. Paying particular attention to the general goals of establishing justice and promoting the general good articulated in the preamble, he argued that a proslavery interpretation of the document was simply disingenuous. Although the editor was willing to engage in complicated legal debates about the precise meaning of specific clauses or the possible intentions of the Framers, he thought such measures superfluous. One did not need extensive legal training to read the Constitution. "I hold that every American citizen has a right to form an opinion of the constitution, and to propagate that opinion, and to use all honorable means to make his opinion the prevailing one," announced Douglass in his Fifth of July address. "Read its preamble, consider its purposes," he urged the crowd. "Is slavery among them? Is it at the gateway? or is it in the temple? It is neither." Quite the contrary, Douglass, like Parker, concluded that a "plain reading" of the Constitution will find it "to contain principles and purposes, entirely hostile to the existence of slavery." In the end, his antislavery interpretation

---

Revolution: A Speech Before the American Anti-Slavery Society at their Annual Meeting in New York, May 12, 1857 (Boston: R.F. Wallcut, 1857), 7.

[82] HBS, "A Reply to 'the Affectionate and Christian Address of Many Thousands of Women of Great Britain and Ireland to Their Sisters the Women of the United States of America,'" *Atlantic Monthly* 11 (Jan. 1863): 125; FD, "Constitution of the United States," 480.

of the Constitution rested on a democratic faith that the document's core meaning could be intuitively grasped by all.[83]

A decade later Douglass deployed a telling metaphor for this romantic reading of America's foundational compact. Speaking in Philadelphia just months after Abraham Lincoln had issued his Emancipation Proclamation and the U.S. army had begun actively recruiting black troops, Douglass compared any compromises the Constitution made with slavery to scaffolding that is used to erect a great building and then discarded. "If in its origin slavery had any relation to the government, it was only as the scaffolding to the magnificent structure, to be removed as soon as the building was completed." Unwilling to acknowledge a fact upon which most scholars today agree – that the Framers were, at the very least, divided about slavery – Douglass nonetheless underscored a critical point: "abolish slavery tomorrow, and not a sentence or syllable of the Constitution need be altered." And for this very reason Douglass, more than any of his fellow New Romantics, refused to give up on the Constitution. Just as Parker saw past Christianity's "transient" elements to the "permanent" core, his black counterpart highlighted the Constitution's potential to transcend its historical freight. As he asked a Scottish audience just months before South Carolina voted to secede in 1860, "What will the people of America, a hundred years hence, care about the intentions of the men who framed the constitution of the United States? These men were for a day – for a generation, but the constitution is for ages."[84]

Making the Fugitive Slave Law Dead Letter

As Douglass began to rethink his position on the Constitution, he also started to reevaluate his opposition to ending slavery through the political system. In the spring of 1852, he told Gerrit Smith of an upcoming trip to Cincinnati for an antislavery convention where he anticipated debating C. C. Burleigh, a staunch advocate of the non-voting theory. "Men should not, under the guidance of a false philosophy – be led to

---

[83] FD, "Antislavery Principles and Antislavery Acts," 347; FD, "What to the Slave," 385–386.

[84] FD, "Address for the Promotion of Colored Enlistments, Delivered at a Mass Meeting in Philadelphia, July 6, 1863," in *LWFD*, 3: 365; FD, "American Constitution and the Slave," 348; Myers, *Frederick Douglass*, 101–106; Schaub, "Frederick Douglass's Constitution," 473. On the Framers and slavery, see Fehrenbacher, *Slaveholding Republic*; David Waldstreicher, *Slavery's Constitution: From Revolution to Ratification* (New York: Hill and Wang, 2009); and Richard Beeman, *Plain, Honest Men: The Making of the American Constitution* (New York: Random House, 2010).

fling from them such powerful instrumentalities against slavery as the Constitution and the ballot," Douglass wrote.[85] By 1854, Douglass was arguing that "political Abolition is now the most powerful agency at work for the overthrow of Slavery. The political anti-slavery press and the political anti-slavery men, in Congress and out of Congress, are doing more to abolitionize the North and to abolish slavery, than any other earthly influence now in operation."[86]

Which antislavery party Douglass would cast his lot with remained unsettled, however. For most of the decade, the New Romantic jumped back and forth between parties, often within a single election cycle. At one time or another, he voiced his support for candidates from the Liberty Party, the Free Soil Party, the Free Democrats, the Radical Abolitionist Party, and the Republican Party. On first glance, such "waffling" can appear evidence of the black reformer's "lingering Garrisonian dogmatism." Yet the chief concern of Garrison and his AASS colleagues was not the watered-down politics of organizations such as the Free Soil Party but rather the "impurity" of the political process in general. Douglass's failure to locate "stable political allegiances," in contrast, bespoke a more nuanced understanding of the benefits and drawbacks of the American liberal tradition and all that went with it.[87]

Douglass had little time for the negotiations and concessions that seemed to go hand in hand with party politics. During the debates about the Kansas-Nebraska Act in early 1854, he worried that reformers were too willing to whitewash the Missouri Compromise simply because it was less odious than the new legislation Stephen Douglas had proposed. This was a mistake, Douglass held, for the Missouri Compromise was still "a demoralized bargain," which "in the face of the universality of the principles of justice, humanity and religion ... would localize and legalize a crime against humanity."[88] He was also well aware of the limits of mainstream politicians and the parties they represented. Shortly after Abraham Lincoln earned the Republican nomination for president in 1860, the black editor insisted that even if the Illinois candidate were elected, antislavery newspapers like his would still be needed. "The Republican party is ... only negatively anti-slavery," wrote Douglass. "It

---

[85] FD to Gerrit Smith, Apr. 15, 1852, in *FDPC*, 1: 530.
[86] FD, "We Are in the Midst of a Moral Revolution, An Address Delivered in New York, New York, on 10 May 1854," in *FDP*, 2: 489.
[87] Blight, *Frederick Douglass' Civil War*, 35–58; Oakes, *Radical and the Republican*, 22, 28.
[88] *Frederick Douglass' Paper*, Feb. 24, 1854.

is opposed to the *political power* of slavery, rather than to slavery itself." He hoped that one day a true antislavery party – one "fully committed to the doctrine of 'All rights, to all men'" – would emerge, but in the meantime, he would keep up the abolitionist fight while also wishing Republican candidates success. Like Parker, Douglass strove to be simultaneously a part of, and above, the political debates of the 1850s and 1860s. He balanced his absolute opposition to slavery – an issue about which he remained unrelenting – with a keen sense of what could, and could not, be accomplished through the democratic process. As he told a Boston crowd in 1869, "perfection is an object to be aimed at by all, but is not an attribute of any form of government." Americans should not reject their political system, but rather engage it and try to improve it, while understanding that it would always be flawed and imperfect.[89]

This romantic approach to antislavery politics led Douglass, along with Smith and a handful of other abolitionists, to form a new organization – the Radical Abolition Party – in 1855. At the inaugural meeting in Syracuse, the Radical Abolitionists debated and approved a series of documents that laid out the new party's tenets and objectives. The Constitution, they held, was an antislavery document, the U.S. government had an obligation to promote human rights, and the party itself was dedicated to abolishing slavery immediately. Although a few people who attended the convention rejected violent resistance, the majority believed that it might be warranted in places like the Kansas territory. Douglass was at the forefront of this later group, helping to raise money – and perhaps acquire weapons – to support John Brown's antislavery efforts in Kansas. After Border Ruffians attacked the Free Soil outpost at Lawrence the following year, Douglass proclaimed at a second Radical Abolitionist Party convention that "liberty must either cut the throat of Slavery, or have its own cut by slavery."[90]

No sooner had Douglass helped to form a political party then he started talking about solutions that lay far beyond the ballot box. This militant shift, to the New Romantic's mind, simply reflected the rising tide of proslavery repression. "South Carolina can as little endure freedom of speech, as Russia, France, or Austria," he told the Rochester Ladies

---

[89] *Douglass' Monthly*, June 1860, p. 277; Oakes, *Radical and the Republican*, 33–38; FD, "Our Composite Nationality: An Address Delivered in Boston, Massachusetts, on 7 December 1869," in *FDP*, 4: 244.

[90] Stauffer, *Black Hearts of Men*, 12–14; FD, "The Danger of the Republican Movement: Speech Before the First National Nominating Convention of the Radical Abolition Party, Market Hall, Syracuse, New York, May 28, 1856," in *LWFD*, 5: 389.

Anti-Slavery Society on May 22, 1856. "You have only to drop a word against slavery, to set a whole community in a blaze, and bring down upon you the violence of the mob." Southern politicians are "foaming with rage" at the antislavery addresses of John Patrick Hale and Charles Sumner, he complained, and political negotiation increasingly appears impotent. "It seems that the time for words is passed and the time for blows has come," concluded Douglass. Little did he know that earlier that day South Carolina Congressman Preston Brooks had brutally attacked Sumner on the Senate floor.[91]

In the face of such assaults, Douglass began advocating forceful resistance to the institution of slavery. Although he had never counted himself a nonresistant, this move was a significant departure from the pacifist stance he had taken as a Garrisonian in the 1840s. At a meeting of the London Peace Society in 1846, for instance, Douglass had denounced war, even if it meant the liberation of 3 million enslaved people.[92]

The New Romantic's conversations with militant abolitionist John Brown had something to do with his willingness to consider violent means. The two reformers had first met in the winter of 1847–1848 in Brown's home in Springfield, Massachusetts. There, after a hearty meal of beef soup, cabbage, and potatoes, Brown gave Douglass an early glimpse of the plan that he would put into effect at Harpers Ferry a decade later. Brown had no confidence in non-violent solutions to the problem of slavery. So, according to a lecture Douglass delivered three decades later, the fiery Calvinist outlined a scheme in which armed abolitionists would travel down the Alleghany Mountains into the South, eventually destroying the peculiar institution from within. Brown believed that this mountain range, which had "thousands of strongholds where ten men could withstand a hundred," was God's predetermined key to the eradication of slavery. More positively, he articulated a justification for slave

---

[91] FD, "Aggressions of the Slave Power: An Address Delivered in Rochester, New York, on 22 May 1856," in *FDP*, 3: 131–132, 114–115; David Donald, *Charles Sumer and the Coming of the Civil War* (New York: Knopf, 1961), 293–297. Although Douglass spoke several hours after Brooks's attack on Sumner, his speech – in which he referred specifically to threats against the senator but said nothing of the recent caning in Washington – suggests that the Rochester abolitionist had not yet heard about the assault. For more on the caning of Charles Sumner, see Chapter 5.

[92] FD, "My Opposition to War: An Address Delivered in London, England, on 19 May 1846," in *FDP*, 1: 262; Maurice O. Wallace, "Violence, Manhood, and War in Douglass," in the *Cambridge Companion to Frederick Douglass*, 75–79. On Douglass's early thoughts on violence, see FD to Richard J. Hinton, Jan. 17, 1893, John Brown Manuscripts (JBM), Rare Book and Manuscript Library (RBML), Columbia University (CU), New York, New York; McFeely, *Frederick Douglass*, 108–112.

rebellion that dovetailed with Douglass's romantic vision of self-enacted emancipation. "No people," said Brown, "could have self-respect, or be respected, who would not fight for their freedom." Although Douglass never enlisted in John Brown's war against slavery, the black abolitionist later recalled that this discussion had raised early doubts in his mind that slavery could be solved peacefully.[93]

Signs of this change of heart trickled out slowly in the late 1840s. Before a crowd of twelve hundred black New Yorkers in 1849, Douglass called himself "a peace man," but, echoing John Brown, he said that he "recognize[d] in the Southern States ... a *state of war*." Although Douglass did not endorse slave rebellion overtly, he told listeners – including the reporters who would convey his sentiments to the rest of the nation – that if an insurrection should break out in the South, he "would greet with joy the glad news." A couple weeks later, Douglass announced that while the "elevation of the colored people" in the North could be effected through pacifist self-help, "the sword might be required at the South."[94]

After the passage of the Fugitive Slave Law of 1850, Douglass began to wonder whether violent resistance in the North might also be necessary. At a Faneuil Hall rally in October to protest the new law in Boston, he sounded a familiar theme. Five hundred thousand free African Americans, intoned Douglass in front of a large audience that included Parker and Wendell Phillips, were no match for 18 million whites. Thus, he concluded, we "proclaim no united resistance to this law." Still, Douglass swiftly added, "we one and all – without the slightest hope of making successful resistance, – are resolved rather to die than go back." When the crowd of abolitionists erupted with cheers, the New Romantic continued, "If you are ... prepared to see the streets of Boston flowing with innocent blood, if you are prepared to see sufferings such as perhaps no

---

[93] *Boston Daily Globe*, Dec. 17, 1873; FD, *Life and Times*, 340, 342; Goldstein, "Violence as an Instrument for Social Change," 66–70; James H. Cook, "Fighting with Breath, Not Blows: Frederick Douglass and Antislavery Violence," in *Antislavery Violence*, 138–139, 156–157n32. It is not clear whether the first meeting between Douglass and Brown took place in late 1847 or early 1848. In an 1873 lecture and then in his 1881 autobiography, Douglass recalled that the meeting had taken place in 1847. Yet a letter Douglass wrote from Lynn, Massachusetts, on February 5, 1848 suggests that he may have met Brown for the first time on a visit to Springfield a few days earlier. *Boston Daily Globe*, Dec. 17, 1873; FD, *Life and Times*, 342, 383; FD to William C. Nell, Feb. 5, 1848, in the *North Star*, Feb. 11, 1848.

[94] FD, "Slavery, the Slumbering Volcano: An Address Delivered in New York, New York, on 23 April 1849," in *FDP*, 2:153; *Liberator*, May 11, 1849; FD, *Life and Times*, 341; FD, "Self-Help: An Address Delivered in New York, New York, on 7 May 1849," in *FDP*, 2: 170.

country ever before witnessed, just give in your adhesion to the fugitive slave bill – you, who live on the street where the blood first spouted in defence of freedom; and the slave-hunter will be here to bear the chained slave back, or he will be murdered in his streets."[95] Wary of the violence Douglass had long associated with slavery, he nonetheless invoked a more positive vision of forceful resistance by casting it in the heroic light of Boston's revolutionary past.

By late 1851, Douglass had come to believe that nonresistance was, in fact, harming the antislavery cause by encouraging slave-catcher aggression. In the wake of the bloodshed that followed the September attempt to capture runaways in Christiana, Douglass blamed pacifists such as Garrison for "the lamb-like submission with which men of color have allowed themselves to be dragged away from liberty, from family and all that is dear to the hearts of man." A few months later, Douglass publicly defended Parker after he praised the black citizens who had fought off the slave catchers at Christiana. When a pacifist abolitionist denounced the Transcendentalist's "approval of violent resistance to the Fugitive Slave Law," Douglass responded that Parker was "consistent and right" on the matter. The following summer, he concluded that resistance was the logical response – perhaps the only response – to the encroachments of the Slave Power. "The only way to make a Fugitive Slave Law a dead letter is to make half a dozen or more dead kidnappers," Douglass proclaimed to cheers in Pittsburgh.[96]

Two years later, in a seminal editorial, the black reformer laid out his theoretical defense for violent resistance. Just as a man can be deprived of his liberty if he abuses it, he argued, so too can a man be deprived of his life if he lives in direct violation of God's higher law. "Life," Douglass wrote, "is but a means to an end, and must be held in reason to be not superior to the purposes for which it was designed by the All-wise Creator."[97]

What on the surface appears a surprisingly utilitarian view of human existence was, at its core, evidence of Douglass's romantic heart. To him the purpose of life was not simply to act as one freely chose, but instead to be in accord with God's plan. By this logic, gross violations of the higher law might well justify killing other human beings. One week later – not

---

[95] FD, "Do Not Send Back the Fugitive: An Address Delivered in Boston, Massachusetts, on 14 October 1850," in *FDP*, 2: 247–248.

[96] *Frederick Douglass' Paper*, Sept. 25, 1851; *Frederick Douglass' Paper*, Nov. 27, 1851, quoted in Teed, *A Revolutionary Conscience*, 158; FD, "Let All Soil Be Free Soil: An Address Delivered in Pittsburgh, Pennsylvania, on 11 August 1852," in *FDP*, 2, 390.

[97] *Frederick Douglass' Paper*, June 2, 1854.

long after runaway Anthony Burns's capture in Boston – Douglass urged "every colored man" to have "*a good revolver, a steady hand, and a determination to shoot down any man attempting to kidnap.*"[98]

Douglass, like Parker, bolstered this justification of antislavery violence with appeals to martial heroism and the legacy of the American Revolution. In his didactic 1853 novella, *The Heroic Slave*, the editor offered a fictionalized portrayal of the slave rebel Madison Washington, both evocative names. Certainly, Douglass's titular protagonist fit the part: "Tall, symmetrical, round, and strong.... His whole appearance betokened Herculean strength." Literary scholar Eric Sundquist has argued that Douglass portrayed Washington "as a conventional Byronic hero," but this is not quite right. The fictive Washington was not the dark, brooding outcast typically associated with Byronic heroism. Despite his extraordinary physical prowess, Douglass's slave rebel had a gentle side. "There was nothing savage or forbidding in his aspect," noted the Rochester abolitionist. "His broad mouth and nose spoke only of good nature and kindness.... He was just the man you would chose when hardships were to be endured, or danger to be encountered, – intelligent and brave."[99]

Likewise, Douglass jettisoned the heroic type around which Walter Scott constructed several of his historical romances. Heroes such as Edward Waverley and Francis Osbaldistone are middling, indecisive figures, who are drawn into – yet fail to take a clear ideological stand upon – the great struggles of the day. In sharp contrast, Madison Washington acts from well-defined principles, shaping, rather than being shaped by, his historical circumstances. But if Washington lacked Childe Harold's pathos or Waverly's wavering ordinariness, he was still a heroic figure. Intuitive, rebellious, and naturally charismatic, Washington was blessed with, in Douglass's words, "that mesmeric power which is the invariable accompaniment of genius." He won the confidence and allegiance of others easily, trusting his own moral compass completely.[100]

---

[98] *Frederick Douglass' Paper*, June 9, 1854.

[99] FD, *Heroic Slave*, 179; Sundquist, *To Wake the Nations*, 118; Harrold, "Romanticizing Slave Revolt," 96–98; Mackenthun, *Fictions of the Black Atlantic*, 98–102; Peter L. Thorslev, Jr., *The Byronic Hero: Types and Prototypes* (Minneapolis: University of Minnesota Press, 1962); Atara Stein, *The Byronic Hero in Film, Fiction, and Television* (Carbondale: Southern Illinois University Press, 2004), 1–34. Stowe sketched a more classically Byronic slave rebel with the titular character in her second antislavery novel, *Dred*. See Chapter 3.

[100] Jones, *Unwelcome Voices*, 11–13, 68–69; FD, *Heroic Slave*, 217.

Madison Washington, in other words, was closer to a conventional romantic hero than the Byronic type. Inspiring imitation, if not worship, he was cut from the same cloth as Scott's medieval knights – including the very character that inspired Douglass's surname. His antislavery protagonist also resembled the idols Thomas Carlyle touted in a popular series of lectures on heroism he offered in the 1840s. "The Great Man," wrote Carlyle, "is a Force of Nature; whatsoever is truly great in him springs up from the *in*articulate deeps." The English Romantic's good friend Emerson also found individual greatness inexorable. "It is natural to believe in great men," he insisted. Douglass agreed with Emerson on this score. He counted himself "something of a hero-worshiper by nature," insisting that most Americans not only believe in great men, we "worship them."[101]

It will come as no surprise, then, that Douglass went to some lengths to associate Madison Washington with "the great men" of the American past. Born in Virginia, like so many of the nation's "statesmen and heroes," Douglass's slave rebel displayed the same lust for liberty as more famous sons of the Commonwealth such as Washington, Jefferson, and Patrick Henry. When the "heroic slave" justifies his uprising, he invokes the precedent of his fellow Virginia heroes. "We have struck for our freedom, and if a true man's heart be in you, you will honor us for the deed," announces the rebel. "We have done that which you applaud your fathers for doing, and if we are murderers, *so were they*." In the same spirit, Douglass compared his own exploits to the celebrated actions of the Founding Fathers. "In coming to a fixed determination to run away," he wrote in his 1845 *Narrative*, "we did more than Patrick Henry, when he resolved upon liberty or death." For runaway slaves, Douglass insisted, liberty was doubtful, while failure meant "almost certain death."[102]

Although Douglass cast slave rebellion in the heroic – and forgiving – light of the American Revolution, he also took pains to minimize Madison Washington's proclivity for violence. Before settling on armed resistance, he imagined a range of methods to escape bondage. Washington rejects the label "*black murderer*," repeatedly reminding Tom Grant, an injured white sailor who narrates part of the story, that he would not kill him in cold blood. Eventually, Washington's bravery and restraint convinces

---

[101] Thomas Carlyle, *On Heroes, Hero-Worship, & the Heroic in History: Six Lectures* (London: James Fraser, 1841), 182; FD, *Life and Times*, 264; FD, "Self-Made Men," 548; Martin, *Mind of Frederick Douglass*, 264–265.
[102] FD, *Heroic Slave*, 174, 235; Jones, *Unwelcome Voices*, 80–81; FD, *Narrative*, 62.

his white captive that the "heroic slave" is, in Grant's words, "a superior man; one who, had he been a white man, I would have followed willingly and gladly in any honorable enterprise." Washington's judicious use of violence underscores a critical fact about the evolving place of violence in Douglass's antislavery arsenal. Reluctant to embrace a pattern of behavior that he associated so closely with the institution of slavery, Douglass was uncomfortable with the notion that slaveholders deserved death. The New Romantic's burgeoning faith in the Constitution and the American liberal tradition likewise acted as ballast against such militancy. The ballot, he wrote in 1859, remained the first line of defense, but when it failed to work, the bullet was entirely justified. Both politics and violence had their time and place.[103]

By the late 1850s, Douglass had departed from first-generation romantic reformers on two major fronts. He was devoted simultaneously to an antislavery reading of the Constitution and political abolitionism as well as to antislavery violence. These inconsistent, even paradoxical commitments, to some extent simply reflected Douglass's pragmatism. Unlike many other radical abolitionists, he was willing to work through the political system – and in accordance with the Constitution – when he deemed it appropriate. And, when that no longer seemed to work, he was not above promoting armed combat in the defense of freedom.

Yet Douglass's faith in forceful resistance, on the one hand, and the potential of the American political system to right the wrong of slavery, on the other, also reflected his romantic bent. Antislavery violence, he believed, was both a righteous response to the Slave Power's "merciless war on the natural and inalienable rights of Humanity" and a means by which black Americans could work for their own uplift. Resistance to slavery, in other words, might enable the enslaved to enjoy the moral and psychological as well as literal rewards of striking a blow for freedom. It might allow bondspeople to become heroes, even "great men."[104]

Douglass's newfound vision of the Constitution also highlighted the millennial potential that lay dormant in the document. He looked beyond the contemporary application of America's foundational compact to the higher ideals articulated in its preamble. If individual growth relied on the

---

[103] FD, *Heroic Slave*, 234, 237; Yarborough, "Race, Violence, and Manhood," 174–175; Ronald T. Takaki, *Violence in the Black Imagination: Essays and Documents* (New York: Putnam's, 1972), 18–33; *Douglass' Monthly*, Oct. 1859, p. 149.

[104] FD, "Antislavery Principles and Antislavery Acts," 347.

persistent pursuit of self-culture, then the progress of the nation necessitated consistent appeals to the principles upon which it was founded. It required romantic jeremiads such as his Fifth of July address.

The Civil War, in the end, enabled Douglass to reconcile these disparate romantic impulses. Since the mid-1850s, he had drawn on the arguments of John Quincy Adams that the president or Congress could, in the case of insurrection or war, use constitutionally derived war powers to end slavery. The Confederate assault on Fort Sumter made that hypothetical situation a reality. Once the war commenced, Douglass, like many abolitionists, pushed Lincoln and Congress to make the war a fight not just to preserve the Union but also to end slavery. And black men, he insisted, had to do some of the fighting.[105]

Initially, Lincoln was not persuaded. Hoping to keep the fight a limited conflict and worried about alienating border state whites, he resisted such entreaties for more than a year. By the middle of 1862, however, the war was becoming more destructive by the week and the enslaved were running away by the thousands. Facing a critical shortage of white troops, a war that was dragging on much longer than anticipated, and contraband camps that teemed with runaways, Lincoln began to change course. That fall, he quietly authorized the War Department to begin to recruit black soldiers. A few months later the president issued the final Emancipation Proclamation, which drew on the very war power arguments Adams and Douglass had made years earlier. By these momentous decisions, Lincoln transformed the meaning of the war and the role played in it by African Americans.[106]

In March 1863, Douglass, who became a Union army recruiter, announced that the Civil War now allowed slaves and free blacks alike to unite self-emancipation and constitutional action. "I now for the first time during this war feel at liberty to call and counsel you to arms," he admitted. "I urge you to fly to arms, and smite with death the power that would bury the government and your liberty in the same hopeless grave." At long last, the African American fight for freedom was a part of, not counter to, the aims and actions of the federal government. The Civil War had become a war to end slavery.[107]

---

[105] FD, "Hope and Despair in These Cowardly Times: An Address Delivered in Rochester, New York, on 28 April 1861," in *FDP*, 3: 428; Stauffer, *Black Hearts of Men*, 26; Blight, *Frederick Douglass' Civil War*, 148–149.

[106] Eric Foner, *The Fiery Trial: Abraham Lincoln and American Slavery* (New York: Norton, 2010), 166–247.

[107] FD, "Men of Color, To Arms!" in *LWFD*, 3: 318; Blight, *Frederick Douglass' Civil War*, 156–158.

Like so many former slaves, Frederick Douglass played no small role in these remarkable developments. But if one could poll nineteenth-century Americans about which abolitionist was most responsible for the coming of the Civil War – and the revolutionary changes that followed with it – a different New Romantic would have likely topped the list. In 1852, Harriet Beecher Stowe wrote a novel that many believed had changed the nation. Years later, Douglass concluded that *Uncle Tom's Cabin* was "a work of marvelous depth and power.... No book on the subject of slavery had so generally and favorably touched the American heart."[108]

[108] FD, *Life and Times*, 351.

3

Harriet Beecher Stowe and the Divided Heart of *Uncle Tom's Cabin*

No one had ever seen anything like it. Five thousand copies flew off the shelves the week it was published. Three hundred thousand more had sold in the United States before a year was up, easily eclipsing previous sales records. The novel was translated into French, German, Spanish, Polish, and Magyar – and soon global sales exceeded one million. Popular demand for the book proved so strong, in fact, that the production staff in the United States worked around the clock. "Three paper mills are constantly at work, manufacturing the paper, and three power presses are working twenty-four hours per day, in printing it, and more than one hundred bookbinders are incessantly plying their trade to bind them, and still it has been impossible as yet to supply demand," announced its publisher John P. Jewitt breathlessly. Harriet Beecher Stowe's *Uncle Tom's Cabin: or, Life among the Lowly* was the publishing phenomenon of the nineteenth century.[1]

Remarkable as these numbers are for the time, they fail to capture the full impact of Stowe's first book. Novel reading, after all, was often a social event in the antebellum period, as whole families would sit down before a roaring fire to listen to stories read aloud. Contemporaries reasoned, therefore, that the true size of *Uncle Tom's Cabin*'s audience

---

[1] Sarah Meer, *Uncle Tom Mania: Slavery, Minstrelsy, and Transatlantic Culture in the 1850s* (Athens: University of Georgia Press, 2005), 4; Reynolds, *Mightier than the Sword*, 126–128; *National Era*, Apr. 15, 1852. On *Uncle Tom's Cabin*'s sales, see Claire Parfait, *Publishing History of 'Uncle Tom's Cabin,' 1852–2002* (Abingdon, UK: Ashgate, 2008), esp. 91–112 and Michael Winship, "'The Greatest Book of Its Kind': A Publishing History of 'Uncle Tom's Cabin,'" *Proceedings of the American Antiquarian Society* 109 (1999): 309–332.

greatly exceeded the number of copies sold. "Uncle Tom has probably ten readers to every purchaser," hazarded the *Literary World*.[2] Well before the advent of modern mass marketing campaigns, the book gained a level of cultural prominence that would make even a twenty-first century Madison Avenue advertising executive jealous. One London newspaper reported that the United States and Great Britain were gripped by "Tom-Mania" in the years after its 1852 publication. Stowe's characters and plotlines surfaced in songs, plays, and unauthorized novels as well as merchandise ranging from paintings, puzzles, and cards to ornaments, board games, and dolls. Dry goods shops and creameries in London were named "Uncle Tom's Cabin," while one could buy Uncle Tom's Candy in Parisian stores.[3]

Abolitionists, no surprise, were thrilled by the spotlight Stowe shined on slavery's human costs. At an 1853 Massachusetts Anti-Slavery Society meeting, Theodore Parker announced that *Uncle Tom's Cabin* "has excited more attention than any book since the invention of printing." Wendell Philips went a step further, calling it "rather an event than a book."[4] Estimations of the novel's influence eventually reached dizzying heights. Poet Henry Wadsworth Longfellow judged it "one of the greatest triumphs recorded in literary history, to say nothing of the higher triumph of its moral effect," while Higginson maintained that "of all the blows which slavery received, none was so great as that delivered by this tale of 'life among the lowly.'"[5]

Countless Americans attributed the coming of the Civil War to Stowe's work. Basking in the glory of victory, Northern voices tended to celebrate the novel's role in galvanizing antislavery forces. Uncle Tom marched "all through the conflict, up and down," declared Oliver Wendell Holmes Sr. in a poem he wrote for Stowe's seventy-first birthday celebration. Some southerners also viewed the war as the logical outcome of *Uncle Tom's Cabin*, but, in the wake of defeat, they heaped scorn upon Stowe. An editorial in the *Montgomery Advertiser* called her "an unchristian, an unfeminine creature," who "so fatally contributed to all the dire consequences of civil war in this country." More positively and famously, Abraham Lincoln, on meeting Stowe in 1862, was supposed to have said,

[2] *Literary World*, Dec. 4, 1852, quoted in Reynolds, *Mightier than the Sword*, 128.
[3] Meer, *Uncle Tom Mania*, 1–2; Reynolds, *Mightier than the Sword*, 136.
[4] *Liberator*, Feb. 25, 1853; *Liberator*, Feb. 18, 1853.
[5] Henry Wadsworth Longfellow, quoted in *LHBS*, 161; TWH and William MacDonald, *History of the United States from 986 to 1905* (New York: Harper & Brothers, 1905), 489.

"So you're the little woman who wrote the book that started this great war!" Whether Lincoln ever used these words – and recent research suggests that the anecdote merits a hefty grain of salt – they nonetheless reflect a broadly shared sentiment in the nineteenth century: Stowe's book changed the young nation.[6]

But why? What accounts for the unprecedented popularity and impact of *Uncle Tom's Cabin*? Stowe believed that it was the novel's divine inspiration; scholars offer secular explanations. David Reynolds explicates how *Uncle Tom's Cabin* drew on the diverse forms of popular culture that prevailed in antebellum America, including "visionary fiction, biblical narratives, pro- and anti-Catholicism, gender issues, temperance, moral reform, [and] minstrelsy." Meanwhile, Ronald Walters highlights the ease with which Stowe's "vivid characters, comic interludes, and melodramatic storytelling" could be divorced from her antislavery message, thereby enabling people who cared little for the cause of the slave to appreciate the book and its many imitations. Finally, James Brewer Stewart focuses on the ways in which the novel "satisfied every antislavery taste." Nonresistants gravitated toward the pious, pacifist Uncle Tom, just as militants found the armed George Harris attractive. And racist Free Soilers, for their part, simultaneously laughed at Stowe's racial stereotypes and nodded approvingly at her free labor critiques of plantation life and gestures toward colonization.[7]

Like most popular works of art, then, *Uncle Tom's Cabin* was influenced by the cultural modes and tropes that were fashionable in its day. Nowhere is this more evident than in Stowe's imaginative combination and reconfiguration of different types of high and popular romanticism. The major romantic chord struck by Stowe was her sentimental appeal. As Parker insisted in 1853, the "triumph" of *Uncle Tom's Cabin* "is not due alone to the intellectual genius and culture of the writer; it is due to a quality far higher and nobler than mere intellect.... She has won this audience because she has appealed to their Conscience, because she

---

[6] Oliver Wendell Holmes Sr., quoted in *LHBS*, 504; *Montgomery Advertiser*, quoted in *Moulton* [Alabama] *Advertiser*, Oct. 15, 1869, http://utc.iath.virginia.edu/proslav/prar181at.html; HBS, quoted in Hedrick, *Harriet Beecher Stowe*, vii; Daniel R. Vollaro, "Lincoln, Stowe, and the 'Little Woman/Great War' Story: The Making, and Breaking, of a Great American Anecdote," *Journal of the Abraham Lincoln Association* 30 (Winter 2009): 18–34; Reynolds, *Mightier than the Sword*, x.

[7] Reynolds, *Mightier than the Sword*, 87–88; Ronald Walters, "Stowe and the American Reform Tradition, " in *The Cambridge Companion to Harriet Beecher Stowe*, ed. Cindy Weinstein (New York: Cambridge University Press, 2004), 177; Stewart, *Holy Warriors*, 161.

has touched their Hearts, because she has awakened their Souls. She has brought justice, love and piety to bear the burden which her genius imposed upon them."[8] Stowe artfully repackaged the antislavery tactic most associated with early romantic reform (moral suasion) into what had become, by the 1850s, a wildly popular form of expression in the United States: the sentimental novel.

Like Garrisonians, Stowe aimed to convert her readers to the cause of the enslaved. But Stowe's appeal to the hearts and minds of America discarded much of the vitriol that characterized the writing of first-generation romantic reformers. Emphasizing the shared humanity of white and black Americans rather than the wickedness of slaveholding, Stowe wove a stirring moral drama about slavery out of the familiar threads of a sentimental literature. Even more, by placing pious and suffering Uncle Tom and Eva at the center of her novel, Stowe hitched pacifist moral suasion to other romantic points of emphasis, including sentimental identification, romantic racialism, and the idealization of childhood.

Stowe counterbalanced Tom and Eva's tragic stories with the daring and more traditionally heroic exploits of George and Eliza Harris. These resistant rebels prove themselves unwilling to submit to bondage, even in the face of death. Their stories, in turn, prove Stowe's unwillingness to settle on a single answer to the problem of slavery. Tom and Eva's suffering lights an antislavery fire in the hearts of several of the characters, a response Stowe hoped to provoke in her readers, helping them, as she put it, "*feel right.*"[9] The failure of these conversions to topple the institution of slavery within the novel, however, highlights the fact that Stowe herself was uncertain about whether moral suasion could bring slavery to a close. In contrast, George and Eliza Harris – who not only escape to the North but also forcefully resist those who would return them to bondage – suggest that the novelist had an open mind when it came to what to do about slavery. Reluctant to sacrifice themselves, the Harrises force Stowe's readers to wrestle with the question of whether opponents of slavery should concentrate on moral suasion or take the fight more directly to the institution's supporters. Taken together, these heroic archetypes – the sentimental martyr and the resistant rebel – reveal Stowe's ambivalent, multilayered, antislavery thinking.

---

[8] *Liberator*, Feb. 25, 1853.
[9] HBS, *Uncle Tom's Cabin: Or, Life Among the Lowly* (1852; repr., New York: Viking, 1981), 624.

Ambivalence, to be sure, was not unreasonable in a tumultuous age. But Stowe had a particularly acute case. The daughter of Lyman Beecher, perhaps the most influential preacher of the early nineteenth century, she was, on the one hand, the product of her father's modified Calvinism. Quick to minimize her own agency, Stowe gave credit to a higher source for *Uncle Tom's Cabin*. On the other hand, her novel stressed not the awesome power of God but rather the ways in which Christians who opened their hearts to Jesus Christ could almost become divine themselves. This message reflected an altogether different context – what Emerson called "the age of the first person singular" – in which somber Calvinist notions of original sin and a limited elect seemed anachronistic holdovers from a bygone era.[10] Viewed this way, *Uncle Tom's Cabin* spoke directly to perfectionist America.

Unlike her fellow New Romantics, however, Stowe had doubts about the demands of perfectionist striving as well as the likelihood of achieving a state of spiritual perfection. She had misgivings as well about her lifelong interest in popular and elite romantic currents. As a young girl, Stowe had plowed through the works of Byron and Scott, which both tantalized and disturbed her. After befriending Byron's widow, she wrote a scathing essay to excoriate the English poet for his incestuous infidelity.[11] In similar fashion, Stowe was drawn to – and repelled by – the religious theories of German Romantics such as Schleiermacher and Schelling and their Transcendentalist counterparts. She appreciated the weight that romantic theology attached to intuition and feeling, though she had significant reservations about the liberal hermeneutics of ministers like Parker. As was the case with so much in her life, Stowe wrestled with romantic modes and ideas, accepting parts, rejecting others. In these struggles, she proved herself to be, if anything, a representative New Romantic.

Growing Up Calvinist in the Age of Byron

Born on June 14, 1811 in Litchfield, Connecticut, Harriet Beecher Stowe was the seventh child of Lyman and Roxana Beecher. Stowe's

---

[10] HBS, in *SLL*, 377; HBS, in *LHBS*, 156; Emerson, Journal, Jan.-Feb. 1827, in *JMN*, 3: 70.

[11] HBS, "The True Story of Lady Byron's Life," *Atlantic Monthly* 24 (Sept. 1869): 295–313. See also HBS, *Lady Byron Vindicated: A History of the Byron Controversy* (Boston: Fields, Osgood, 1870).

mother died from tuberculosis when she was just five years old, leaving her imposing father Lyman the central influence in the novelist's early life.[12]

Among the nation's most influential clergymen, Beecher preached a modified version of New England Calvinism. As a young minister, he clung tightly to the doctrine of original sin, telling his parishioners and family that unless touched by God they were doomed to damnation. Beecher dispensed similarly stern sentiments at home. "Henry, do you know that every breath you breathe *is sin*?" he asked Stowe's younger brother when he was just a toddler. "Well, it is – every breath."[13]

Yet Beecher also softened Calvinism's sharpest edges. His alteration of the catechism, "No mere man since the fall is able perfectly to keep the commandments of God" to "No man since the fall is willing to keep the commandments of God," demonstrates the distance between John Edwards's austere Calvinism and Beecher's more hopeful stance. While Edwards thought all men shared Adam's original sin, Beecher stressed humankind's vast, if largely unrealized, potential.[14]

Although Beecher's theology tacitly undermined the absolute sovereignty of God, he did not go as far along this line as liberal Christians, who were gaining a foothold in New England, not to mention radicals like Parker. Indeed, in the mid-1820s he moved his family from Litchfield to Boston in hope of saving a city that he believed was under siege from within. "Calvinism or orthodoxy was the despised and persecuted form of faith" in Boston, Stowe explained decades later. "All the literary men of Massachusetts were Unitarian. All the trustees and professors of Harvard College were Unitarians. All the élite of wealth and fashion crowded Unitarian churches. The judges on the bench were Unitarians." Her father hoped to prevent this liberal tide from engulfing the symbolic seat of New England Puritanism.[15]

---

[12] *LHBS*, 2; Hedrick, *Harriet Beecher Stowe*, 7–9; HBS, *SSL*, 9.

[13] Caskey, *Chariot of Fire*, 38–42; Samuel A. Schreiner Jr., *The Passionate Beechers: A Family Saga of Sanctity and Scandal That Changed America* (New York: Wiley and Sons, 2003), 23; Lyman Beecher, quoted in Debby Applegate, *The Most Famous Man in America: The Biography of Henry Ward Beecher* (New York: Random House, 2006), 37.

[14] Lyman Beecher, quoted in Applegate, *Most Famous Man in America*, 122; Lyman Beecher, in *LBA*, 1: 259.

[15] Mark G. Vásquez, *Authority and Reform: Religious and Educational Discourses in Nineteenth-Century New England Literature* (Knoxville: University of Tennessee Press, 2003); Howe, *What Hath God Wrought*, 170; Caskey, *Chariot of Fire*, 46; Abzug, *Cosmos Crumbling*, 51; HBS, in *SLL*, 57.

The following decade Beecher opened a western front in his holy war, taking the presidency of Lane Theological Seminary in Cincinnati. There, he battled with the city's Catholic population and later had a falling out with – and effectively drove off – evangelical abolitionists led by Theodore Weld. Beecher reveled in this fight over the spiritual future of America. "I was built for war," he boasted.[16]

Beecher's heroic self-posturing had as profound an impact on his family as did his modified version of Calvinism. Facing the daunting Unitarian establishment in Boston, he alone seemed to hold up the orthodox mantle. "It was the high noon of my father's manhood," Stowe wrote, "the flood-tide of his powers."[17] Her father also described his decision to leave Boston for Cincinnati in epic terms. "If we gain the West, all is safe," he told his daughter Catharine, "if we lose it, all is lost." Harriet displayed this sort of romantic affectation too. "The heroic element was strong in me," she once noted, "having come down by ordinary generation from a long line of Puritan ancestry, and just now it made me to do something, I knew not what: to fight for my country, or to make some declaration on my own account" (Figure 3.1).[18]

European Romantic currents fed the Beechers' proclivity for heroic self-posturing. Although poetry and prose were forbidden fruit in many Calvinist households, Beecher and his children were well versed in the popular English Romantics. Later in life, Stowe recalled her father telling her brother George, "You may read Scott's novels. I have always disapproved of novels as trash, but in these is real genius and real culture, and you may read them."[19] While the more philosophical Romantics, such as Schelling and Coleridge, held little appeal for the Beecher family, they reveled in the work of accessible Romantic writers and poets, especially Scott and Lord Byron.

Stowe discovered Byron's work in the home of her Aunt Esther, who lived but a half-minute walk from the Beecher home in Litchfield. Eventually the English Romantic would become, in the words of literary critic Alice Crozier, "the single greatest literary and imaginative influence on the writings of Harriet Beecher Stowe." Lyman was also smitten with Byron. "My dear, Byron's dead – *gone*," he said when he learned of the

---

[16] Lyman Beecher, quoted in Applegate, *Most Famous Man in America*, 25.

[17] HBS, in *SLL*, 56.

[18] Lyman Beecher to Catharine Beecher, July 8, 1830, in *LBA*, 2: 167; HBS, quoted in *LHBS*, 11.

[19] HBS, "Early Remembrances," in *LBA*, 1: 391.

FIGURE 3.1. Harriet Beecher Stowe, ca. 1880.
Source: Unknown. Courtesy of the Library of Congress, Prints and Photographs Division, LC-USZ62–11212.

poet's passing. "Oh, I'm sorry that Byron is dead. I did hope he would live to do something for Christ."[20]

The Beecher family's exposure to European Romanticism was due in large part to Roxana's brother Samuel Foote, a worldly sea captain who returned from his journeys with the latest continental poetry and prose. Stowe and her brothers and sisters devoured these exotic morsels. Catharine Beecher mimicked Sir Walter Scott's ballads, while her more famous sister had an entire "Walter Scott bookcase" as an adult. Stowe was also drawn to Madame de Staël's *Corrine*, which she used to plumb the depths of her dissatisfaction in more despondent moments. She even ascribed an innate moral sensibility to European Romantics, despite their ethical failings. "Moore, Byron, Goethe, often speak words more wisely descriptive of the true religious sentiment, than another man, whose whole life is governed by it," she maintained in *Uncle Tom's Cabin*.[21]

Popular Romantic poetry and prose were but one part of the uncommon education the novelist enjoyed as girl. From an early age the Beecher

[20] HBS, in *SLL*, 38; Alice C. Crozier, "Harriet Beecher Stowe and Byron," in *Critical Essays on Harriet Beecher Stowe*, ed. Elizabeth Ammons (Boston: G.K. Hall, 1980), 195–196; Lyman Beecher, quoted in *SLL*, 38–39.
[21] Hedrick, *Harriet Beecher Stowe*, 20, 75; Joan D. Hedrick, Introduction to *OSR*, 2; HBS to Georgiana May, May 1833, quoted in *LHBS*, 67; HBS, *Uncle Tom's Cabin*, 440.

family recognized her sharp mind and sought to hone it. She studied mathematics, geography, moral philosophy, and logic at Litchfield Female Academy. Later, she mastered rhetoric, oratory, history, Latin, and Greek at her sister's Hartford Female Seminary, where she spent eight years as a student, teacher's assistant, and, finally, an instructor of rhetoric and composition.[22]

During these years, Stowe struggled with the implications of a second romantic impulse – moral perfectionism – which had roots closer to home. In the decades before the Civil War, Americans across the country, from the polished parlors of Boston to frontier towns of the Wisconsin Territory, sought to make themselves perfect. Perfectionism had a profound impact on social reform in America, fueling the temperance and abolitionist movements, among many reform efforts, and leading to the creation of utopian communes like the Oneida Community and Brook Farm. While Emerson's essays and Parker's sermons set a perfectionist tone for liberal Christian circles, its most famous exponent among evangelicals was Charles Grandison Finney, a Second Great Awakening preacher who fanned the flames of evangelical revival in the United States and Great Britain like no other. Finney and his followers embraced the doctrine of sanctification, or Christian perfection, which held that human beings had the ability – and the duty – to try to purify themselves and live sin-free lives.[23]

Lyman Beecher rejected perfectionism outright. Nevertheless, as Joan Hedrick has written, "his brand of Calvinism, by opening the door for the exercise of free will, let perfectionism sweep in behind." And this exacting ideal, for all its social utility, could wreak havoc on individuals, especially sensitive souls like Stowe and her brother George, who were already burdened with the demands of Calvinist introspection. Decades after waging what he called "interminable warfare" with himself in search of "complete and perfect sanctification," in fact, George shot himself in the head with a shotgun in his Ohio garden. Although the local coroner concluded that this 1843 death was an accident, most modern scholars believe that it was more likely the result of a manic-depressive mind, exacerbated by the personal toll of the culture's perfectionist impulse.[24]

---

[22] HBS, "Early Remembrances," 398; Hedrick, *Harriet Beecher Stowe*, 24–54.
[23] Howe, *What Hath God Wrought*, 172–176; Mintz, *Moralists and Modernizers*, 28–29.
[24] Hedrick, *Harriet Beecher Stowe*, 145–152 (quotation 145); George Beecher, *The Biographical Remains of Rev. George Beecher* (New York: Leavitt, Trow, and Co., 1844), 85; George Beecher, "Essay on Christian Perfection," in *Biographic Remains of Rev. George Beecher*, 167–201; *LHBS*, 108; Schreiner, *Passionate Beechers*, 122–127;

Like her brother George, Stowe strove to make herself perfect while doubting whether she – or anyone else – could live up to such a standard. She had difficulty, for one, living up to the demands of the Victorian middle-class household, in which a woman was expected to provide a haven for her family from the stresses of the modern world. After marrying Calvin Stowe, a biblical scholar she met in her father's Cincinnati seminary, she complained regularly of the toll of trying to be the ideal wife and mother. "The arranging of the whole house ... the cleaning etc., the childrens['] clothes & the baby often have seemed to press on my mind all at once," she wrote Calvin in 1844. "Sometimes it seems as if anxious thoughts has [*sic*] become a disease with me from which I could not be free."[25]

Stowe felt this perfectionist angst more acutely when it came to spiritual matters. Her letters to friends and family from the 1820s through the 1840s testify to an abiding desire to find spiritual quiescence. "Religious feeling ... and social affection seem all to be smothered in the same – murky vapours," she wrote George at one point. Stowe admitted that she felt "no sympathy for others – no desire[,] no wish except to lie down & lie still forever more." As an adolescent, she had experienced a spiritual conversion that she hoped would put to rest her anxiety, but a local pastor convinced the would-be convert that she had deceived herself. Stowe's torment returned swiftly. "My whole life is one continual struggle," Stowe lamented, "I do nothing right."[26]

Two decades later, Stowe experienced a second conversion. Having recently lost George and facing an ill child whom she was unable to comfort, she felt helpless. Just as Stowe seemed to hit bottom, however, "when self-despair was final ... then came the long-expected and wished help," she wrote in March 1844. "My *all* changed – Whereas once my heart ran with a strong current to the world it now runs with a current the other way.... The will of Christ seems to me the steady pulse of my being & I go because I cannot help it. Skeptical doubt cannot exist ... I am *calm*, but *full* – everywhere & in all things instructed & find I can do all things thro Christ." Reduced to a state of despair, Stowe lost herself in Christ and, in the process, she finally found spiritual solace. Although her

Barbara A. White, *The Beecher Sisters* (New Haven, CT: Yale University Press, 2003), 41–42.

[25] HBS to Calvin E. Stowe, [May–June, 1844], #1, folder 68, Beecher-Stowe Papers (BSP), Arthur E. and Eliza Schlesinger Library on the History of Women in America (SCH), Radcliffe College, Cambridge, MA.

[26] HBS to George Beecher, February 20, [1830?], Harriet Beecher Stowe Center Library (HBSCL), Hartford, CT; SLL, 50–51; *LHBS*, 36; HBS, in *LHBS*, 36–37.

religious doubts did not fade entirely after this conversion, Stowe found a bedrock of faith in a Christ-centered vision of suffering and salvation.[27]

Submit to divine guidance, she urged her husband in the months after the experience, "learn to know Christ & be transformed by him."[28] Jesus was universal and immanent, she believed, enabling individuals to do his work if only they opened their hearts to him. Stowe developed this Christocentric theology further in the pages of the *New-York Evangelist*, for which she had begun to write after relocating to Cincinnati with her family. Christians, she held, should resist the temptation to judge others by their own standards for there are too many different "style[s] of living" to isolate a clear set of spiritual guidelines. "We know of but one safe rule: read the life of Jesus with attention – *study* it ... live in constant sympathy and communion with him – and there will be within a kind of instinctive rule by which to try all things," she concluded.[29]

Stowe emerged from despair following George's suicide by becoming one with the martyred Christ, whom she styled, "a captain whom suffering made perfect." Five years later, she once again found divine strength through pain when she lost her young son Charley to cholera. "Poor Charley's dying cries and sufferings rent my heart," lamented Stowe. Yet through "the baptism of sorrow we come to a full knowledge of the sufferings of God – who has borne for us all that we bear." To Stowe, Charley's death, like George's suicide, had been "one more great lesson of humanity which must needs be learned to attain perfection."[30]

Stowe turned repeatedly to the phrase, "the baptism of sorrow," to describe the experience of divine grace in the years after Charley's death.[31] At the same time, she believed that Christians attached too much weight to dramatic moments of conversion. Do not look for God merely in times of despair, she advised readers of the *New-York Evangelist*. Instead, she counseled them to seek celestial fellowship in everyday events. "To the Christian that really believes in the agency of God in the smallest events of life," Stowe wrote, "the thousand minute cares and perplexities of life

[27] HBS to Thomas K. Beecher, Mar. 16, 1844, copy in HBSCL, original in Park Church Archive, Elmira, NY; Hedrick, *Harriet Beecher Stowe*, 155; HBS to Calvin E. Stowe, [May-June, 1844], #1, BSP, SCH.

[28] HBS to Calvin E. Stowe, [May–June, 1844], #2, folder 68, BSP, SCH.

[29] *New-York Evangelist*, Sept. 11, 1845.

[30] HBS to Charles Stowe, Oct. 8, 1877, quoted in Hedrick, *Harriet Beecher Stowe*, 157; HBS to Delia Bacon, after July 29, 1849, quoted in Reynolds, *Mightier than the Sword*, 29.

[31] See HBS to Calvin E. Stowe, 1853, in *SLL*, 170 and HBS, *Betty's Bright Idea. Also, Deacon Pitkin's Farm, and First Christmas of New England* (New York: J.B. Ford, 1876), 76.

become each one a fine affiliating bond between the soul and its God." Nearly a decade later, Stowe expanded on this vision in her 1859 novel *The Minister's Wooing.* "There is a ladder to heaven," she wrote, "whose base God has placed in human affections, tender instincts, symbolic feelings, sacraments of love, through which the soul rises higher and higher, refining as she goes, till she outgrows the human, changes as she rises, into the image of the divine." In this passage, Stowe seems to break with her father's brand of Calvinism and mainstream evangelical thinking, both of which put great stock in the conversion experience. Her conception of salvation as the steady growth of the soul toward the divine, in fact, sounds like something that Parker or Douglass might have said.[32]

By the mid-1840s, Stowe had begun to find common ground with these New Romantics on a variety of fronts. Her husband Calvin had exposed her to the same German Romantic theology that helped to ignite the miracles controversy in Boston. The couple sat up late at night discussing the religious theories of Schleiermacher and Schelling. Like Parker, Ripley, and their Transcendentalist colleagues, Harriet and her husband believed that intuition and feeling were the foundation of religious truth. And these ideas, as the Stowes well knew, were far more heretical in their conservative circles than they were in liberal Boston. "There is not a soul that I can say a word to about any of these matters," Calvin confessed to his wife in 1842.[33]

Stowe also shared the Transcendentalists' vision of a loving deity, whose divine spirit was immanent in nature. "Do not think of God as a strict severe Being," she once told a student at her sister Catharine's academy. "Think of him as a Being who means to make you perfect ... who looks on all you say and do with interest."[34] When Stowe visited Niagara Falls, she was moved by its natural splendor and cascading power. "Oh, it is lovelier than it is great; it is like the Mind that made it: great, but so veiled in beauty that we gaze without terror," she wrote. "I felt as if I could have *gone over* with the waters; it would be so beautiful a death; there would be no fear in it. I felt the rock tremble under me with a sort

[32] *New-York Evangelist,* Aug. 1, 1850; HBS, *The Minister's Wooing* (1859; repr., Boston: Ticknor and Fields, 1866), 88; Carolyn A. Haynes, *Divine Destiny: Gender and Race in Nineteenth-Century Protestantism* (Jackson: University Press of Mississippi, 1998), 59–60.

[33] Calvin E. Stowe to HBS, May 11, 1842, quoted in Patricia R. Hill, "*Uncle Tom's Cabin* as a Religious Text," Interpretative Exhibits, Uncle Tom's Cabin and American Culture: A Multi-Media Archive, http://utc.iath.virginia.edu/interpret/exhibits/hill/hill.html.

[34] HBS to Elizabeth Phoenix, Dec. 23, 1828, quoted in Reynolds, *Mightier than the Sword,* 10.

of joy."[35] This conception of a benevolent deity, in turn, led Stowe to question the fire-and-brimstone sermons of orthodox ministers, which she called the "refined poetry of torture." Why, she wrote Edward, should we tell sinners that God hates them? She endorsed an altogether different message: "Is it right to say to those who are in deep distress, 'God is interested in you; He feels for and loves you?'"[36]

Stowe even turned orthodox Calvinist ideas about original sin and infant damnation on their head, contrasting the pristine virtue of the newborn with the wrongs perpetrated by adults. Children, she insisted, were born pure; it is "*the world*" that defiles them. Here she seemed to echo a position outlined by Parker just a few years earlier. In a controversial series of lectures on religion delivered across New England and later published as *A Discourse of Matters Pertaining to Religion*, the Transcendentalist worried that the divine inspiration of youth fades with time. Too many adults, he maintained, "cease to believe in inspiration," counting "it a phantom of their inexperience; the vision of a child's fancy, raw and unused to the world." Age, Parker lamented, does not always beget wisdom when it comes to spiritual matters.[37]

Despite these many affinities, Stowe was no Transcendentalist. She preferred, for one, a literal interpretation of the Bible to the liberal hermeneutics of Parker or George Ripley. After carefully reading Parker's sermons, Stowe admitted that her "respect & esteem" for the minister increased. She could not stomach, however, his doubts about the inerrancy of the Bible or professions that Jesus Christ was human rather than divine.[38] Stowe also had reservations about the perfectionist impulse. While Parker and Douglass held that all people had divine potential, she believed that "saintly elevation" was possible for only the "few selectest spirits ever on earth." As such, the quest to make oneself perfect spelled an endless cycle of spiritual torment for the rest of humanity, leaving some "to long for death as the end alike of their struggles and their sins!"[39]

It took years, but Stowe made her peace with perfectionism, though only by moving away from the humanist version espoused by liberal perfectionists. Christians, she concluded, should put aside their paralyzing

---

[35] HBS, 1834, in *SLL*, 90.

[36] HBS, *Minister's Wooing*, 337; HBS to Edward Beecher, 1827, in *SLL*, 62.

[37] *New-York Evangelist*, Jan. 15, 1846; Grodzins, *American Heretic*, 262–294; TP, *A Discourse of Matters Pertaining to Religion* (Boston: Little and Brown, 1842), 232.

[38] HBS to William Lloyd Garrison, Nov. 1853, BPL; HBS to Garrison, Dec. 1853, BPL.

[39] HBS, *Minister's Wooing*, 88; Haynes, *Divine Destiny*, 59–60; *New-York Evangelist*, Apr. 17, 1845; *New-York Evangelist*, June 19, 1845.

questions about whether "entire perfection" was attainable and rest assured that, as the New Testament illustrates, a "state of feelings … high enough" has – and thus can – be achieved. The solution to the perfectionist dilemma was simple: Make yourself one with Jesus, be absorbed by his love, "say, I am crucified with Christ, yet I live; yet *not* I, but *Christ* liveth in me."[40] Whereas Parker counseled his parishioners not to love "Christ better than man," Stowe believed that the path to personal sanctification was to surrender to Jesus Christ. Whereas Emerson touted self-reliance, Stowe put greater weight on the assistance that God could provide to would-be perfect souls. "God's existence, his love and care," she argued, "seem to us more real than any other source of reliance."[41] Although a perfectionist, Stowe refused to collapse the distinction between humanity and the divine.

Nevertheless, it is telling that Stowe could be confused, if only for a moment, for an Emerson or a Parker. Reared in an orthodox household, she had broken with her father on a number of fronts by the 1840s. Stowe formulated a Christocentric religion of the heart, which bore little resemblance to Beecher's theology, not to mention that of his Puritan forebearers. And her early interest in Byron and Scott – the seeds of which Lyman himself had helped to plant – had matured into an exploration of new modes and concepts, ranging from evangelical perfectionism to German Romantic theology to Transcendentalist theories of childhood. The Calvinist's daughter became a romantic. Soon she would break with Lyman Beecher on yet another front: What to do about the problem of slavery.

Moral Suasion, Recast

Stowe believed that her son Charley's death was a pathway to heaven, bringing her closer to Christ through "the baptism of sorrow." This distraught mother was also convinced that she needed to use the trying experience to effect changes on earth. "There were circumstances about his death of such peculiar bitterness, of what might seem almost cruel suffering, that I felt I could never be consoled for it, unless it should appear that this crushing of my own heart might enable me to work out some great good to others," Stowe confessed. That "great good," of course, was

---

[40] *New-York Evangelist*, June 19, 1845.
[41] TP, "True Idea of a Christian Church," in *WTP*, 13: 20; *New-York Evangelist*, Aug. 1, 1850.

Uncle Tom's Cabin. Between her son's death in 1849 and late 1852, the novelist wrote the nineteenth century's most socially impactful novel. As her book steadily captured the imagination of the Western world, Stowe insisted that it "had its root in the awful scenes & bitter sorrows of that summer." The loss of a child exposed Stowe to what she determined was the most tragic component of slavery. "It was at *his* dying bed, and at *his* grave," she wrote of Charley, "that I learned what a poor slave-mother may feel when *her* child is torn away from her."[42] Soon Stowe would help millions of readers get a glimpse of such loss and pain.

While Charley's passing helped Stowe forge a common emotional bond with slave mothers separated from their children, the Fugitive Slave Law of 1850 provided the political context that compelled her to explore those emotions on paper. Like her fellow New Romantics, Stowe was transformed by the measure that put thousands of northern blacks' freedom at risk, while punishing those who assisted them. Despite the new law's obvious moral failings, she lamented, ministers – men of God – flocked to support it. "To me it is incredible, amazing, mournful!!," wrote Stowe in December 1850. "I feel as if I should be willing to sink with it, were all this sin and misery to sink in the sea."[43]

Stowe had not always been willing to sacrifice her life if she could take down slavery with it. Early on, she had followed her father's more moderate cues. A member of the American Colonization Society (ACS), Lyman Beecher believed that immediate abolitionists like Garrison went too far. His refusal to support Theodore Weld and a group of Lane seminarians who wanted to debate the merits of colonization and immediatism, in fact, had sparked an exodus from the school in the mid-1830s. By that point, however, Stowe had begun to drift away from her father on the slavery question. In the decade that followed, she advocated the creation of an "*intermediate* society" between abolitionists and colonizationists and started writing antislavery essays for periodicals such as the *New-York Evangelist.*[44]

---

[42] HBS to [Eliza Cabot Follen], Dec. 16, 1852, HL. For a slightly different version of this letter from a London library, see HBS to Eliza Cabot Follen, Dec. 16, 1852, in *OSR*, 71–76.

[43] HBS, Dec. 1850, quoted in *SLL*, 131.

[44] HBS to Wendell Phillips, Feb. 23, 1853, HL; Abzug, *Cosmos Crumbling*, 30–56, 129–130, 137–140; Mintz, *Moralists and Modernizers*, 50–60; HBS to Calvin E. Stowe, [1836], Beecher Family Papers (BFP), Sterling Memorial Library (SML), Yale University, New Haven, CT; HBS to Calvin E. Stowe, 1837, in *LHBS*, 87–88; *New-York Evangelist*, Jan. 2, 1845.

The new fugitive slave law solidified her commitment to the antislavery cause, a point she made clear in a letter to her sister Catharine. "Dear Sister," she wrote, "Your last letter was a real good one, it did my heart good to find somebody in as indignant a state as I am about this miserable wicked fugitive slave business." Overwhelmed by "pent up wrath" toward northern apologists for the law, Stowe scoffed at the grounds on which politicians such as Daniel Webster and Henry Clay made their famous appeals for compromise, writing, "The Union! – Some unions I think are better broken than kept." Then Stowe relayed the details of a recent encounter with Thomas Upham, a professor of mental and moral philosophy at Bowdoin College and long-time member of the ACS. After Calvin accepted a faculty appointment at Bowdoin in early 1850, the Stowe family had moved to Brunswick, Maine. Harriet had befriended the professor and his wife only to find the relationship strained over the issue of slavery. Upham, she seethed to her sister Catharine, believes that the United States "ought to buy [all the slaves] with the public money & send them off – & until that is done he is for bearing every thing in silence – stroking & saying 'pussy pussy' so as to allay all prejudice & avoid all agitation!" On one visit to the Upham household, Stowe confronted her host. Would you obey the fugitive slave law, she asked, if a runaway came knocking on your door? Upham "laughed & ... hemmed & hawed" without offering a clear response, but his young daughter Mary announced, "I wouldnt I know.'"

As fate – or, more likely, the dictates of a good yarn – would have it, a fugitive slave headed for Canada was directed to Upham's doorstep the very next day. Despite his prior equivocation, the professor promptly brought the runaway to his study, listened to his story, and gave him a dollar. After his wife Phebe provided the fugitive with provisions, the runaway was shuttled off to the Stowe household to spend the night before moving on to Canada. This story, which not only validates Stowe's abiding faith in the innate moral compass of children but also provides an all-too-timely life lesson for Professor Upham, seems too good to be true. Apocryphal or not, it highlights a critical theme that Stowe would shortly develop at length: that individuals' "hearts are better on this point than their heads."[45]

On March 9, 1851, Stowe contacted Gamaliel Bailey, editor of the Washington-based antislavery weekly the *National Era*, about a story she had in mind. "Up to this year I have always felt that I had no particular

---

[45] HBS to Catharine Beecher, [1850 or 1851], in *OSR*, 61–62.

call to meddle with this subject," she wrote, "and I dreaded to expose even my own mind to the full force of its exciting power." But the Fugitive Slave Law of 1850 had compelled her to act. "I feel now that the time is come when even a woman or a child who can speak a word for freedom and humanity is bound to speak," she held. According to family legend, Stowe's decision to write *Uncle Tom's Cabin* was provoked by a letter she received from her sister-in-law Isabella. "Hattie," Isabella wrote, "if I could use a pen as you can, I would write something to make this whole nation feel what an accursed thing slavery is." Stowe, her children later remembered, read this letter to her family in the parlor of their home in Brunswick. When Stowe came to the passage urging her to take up her pen, the matriarch announced, "I would write something that would make this whole nation feel what an accursed thing slavery is.... I will write something. I will if I live." [46]

From June 1851 to April 1852, *Uncle Tom's Cabin* appeared weekly in the *National Era*, earning a book contract before the serialization was even completed. Stowe attributed the novel's extraordinary success not to her own literary efforts and talent but to divine inspiration. In late 1852, as the novel was breaking global sales records, she wrote a public letter to a Scottish fan, which was printed in the *New York Times*. "For myself, I can claim no merit in that work which has been the cause of this," she insisted. "It was an instinctive, irresistible outburst.... I can only say that this bubble of my mind has risen on the mighty stream of a *divine purpose*, and even a bubble can go far on such a tide." In her later years, she told a neighbor, "I did not write it.... God wrote it.... I merely did his dictation." [47] Whether such gestures reflect her humility or a genuine feeling that God had worked through her is impossible to know, although the latter seems likely. Regardless, her stance as a writer reflects the distance between Stowe and many of her New Romantic counterparts, who preferred to attribute accomplishments like *Uncle Tom's Cabin* to human potential for greatness rather than God's grace.

Notwithstanding her appeals to divine inspiration, Stowe had plenty of worldly sources from which to craft her tale. While living in Cincinnati, she had direct exposure to plantation life in the neighboring state of Kentucky. In 1834, Stowe had visited a nearby plantation, providing her

[46] HBS to Gamaliel Bailey, Mar. 9, 1851, BPL; Isabella Beecher, in *SLL*, 130; HBS, in *SLL*, 130.

[47] HBS to Dr. Wardlaw, Dec. 4, 1852, reprinted as "Letter from Mrs. Stowe," *New York Times*, Feb. 17, 1853; HBS, quoted in *SLL*, 377. See also HBS, quoted in *LHBS*, 156.

a model for her portrait of slave life in *Uncle Tom's Cabin*. Escaped slaves, who found shelter in her Cincinnati and Brunswick homes, proved a rich resource too. In addition, Stowe solicited the assistance of prominent runaways like Frederick Douglass. "I am very desirous here to gain information from one who has been an actual labourer on one," she wrote the black editor, "& it occurs to me that in the circle of your acquaintance there might be one who would be able to communicate to me some such information as I desire." True to her desire to present as unbiased a picture as possible, she also gathered evidence from slave owners. "I have before me an able paper written by a southern planter in which the details & modus operandi are given from *his* point of sight," she admitted to Douglass, "I am anxious to have some now from another stand point – I wish to be able to make a picture that shall be graphic & true to nature in its details."⁴⁸ In this way, Stowe hoped to both build on – and transcend – previous efforts to illustrate slavery's horrors.

More so than most of her fellow New Romantics, Stowe had faith that the solution to the problem of slavery lay in converting the nation to the cause of the enslaved. In her 1845 short story, "Immediate Emancipation," she implied that slaveholders need only to be exposed to the destructive potential of human bondage to be convinced of its immorality. Fifteen years later, on the cusp of the Civil War, Stowe wrote that slavery in New England "fell before the force of conscience and moral appeal." And if moral suasion was, in historian Ronald Walters's words, Stowe's "weapon of choice," then *Uncle Tom's Cabin* was the most powerful round that she ever fired.⁴⁹

Stowe's novel worked from the arsenal of ideas assembled by a previous generation of romantic reformers. Garrisonians had pledged themselves to non-coercive tactics two decades earlier, while many evangelical abolitionists likewise embraced moral suasion despite their misgivings about nonresistance. Consider, for example, the popular 1839 compendium, *American Slavery as It Is: Testimony of a Thousand Witnesses*, which Theodore Weld produced along with wife Angelina Grimké and her sister Sarah. By coupling runaway slave advertisements and other materials from southern newspapers with excerpts from fugitive slave narratives and first-hand testimonials about the institution, Weld and the

---

⁴⁸ *SLL*, 84–85; HBS to Mr. [Edward] and Mrs. Baines, May 24, 1856, HBSCL; HBS to Henry Ward Beecher, Feb. 1, 1851, in *OSR*, 63; HBS to Frederick Douglass, July 9, 1851, in *OSR*, 59.

⁴⁹ *New-York Evangelist*, Jan. 2, 1845; HBS, *Minister's Wooing*, 568; Walters, "Stowe and the American Reform Tradition," 175.

Grimkés exposed the American public to the brutality of slavery. They let slaveholders and their former property speak for themselves. Despite the falling out between Weld and Lyman Beecher at Lane Seminary, the evangelical abolitionist's moral-suasionist text appears to have had a strong influence on Stowe. Her 1853 *A Key to Uncle Tom's Cabin*, in which she sought to defend her novel against accusations that it misrepresented slavery, included a good deal of material found in *American Slavery as It Is*. The romantic novelist even kept Weld's compendium "in her work basket by day, and slept with it under her pillow at night, till its facts crystallized into Uncle Tom," according to Angelina Grimké.[50]

Even so, Stowe was not entirely comfortable with the brand of moral suasion practiced by nonresistants such as Garrison or evangelicals like Weld. "With all credit to my good brother Theodore," she wrote of Weld in 1853, "I must say that prudence is not his forte.... It seems to me that it is not necessary always to present a disagreeable subject in the most disagreeable way possible, and needlessly to shock prejudices which we must combat at any rate." Stowe made similar comments about Garrison, whose confrontational stances and harsh invective put Weld to shame. The nation's sins, the impassioned editor believed, merited "an avalanche of wrath, hurled from the Throne of God, to crush us into annihilation." Although Stowe sympathized with Garrison's positions and admired the *Liberator*'s "frankness, fearlessness – truthfulness & independence," she worried about the zeal with which he critiqued all who disagreed with him, whether friend or foe. In an 1853 letter to Garrison, Stowe playfully called him "the celebrated Wolf of all wolves," confessing that she "was exceedingly afraid of being devoured" by the radical abolitionist.[51]

In *Uncle Tom's Cabin*, Stowe set out to recast moral suasion in a less confrontational fashion. Like many abolitionists, she was frustrated by the degree to which the South had closed itself off to any discussion of slavery. "The sensitiveness of the south on this subject is so great that they have enclosed themselves with a 'cordon sanitaire' to keep out all sentiments or opinions in favor of freedom," she observed. Stowe wanted to write a book that, by presenting the institution of slavery in all its guises, would attract southern as well as northern readers. "I shall show the

---

[50] Robert H. Abzug, *Passionate Liberator: Theodore Dwight Weld and the Dilemma of Reform* (New York: Oxford University Press, 1980), 210–219; Angelina Grimké, quoted in Barnes, *Antislavery Impulse*, 231; Hedrick, *Harriet Beecher Stowe*, 230–231.

[51] HBS to Wendell Phillips, Feb. 23, 1853, HL; William Lloyd Garrison, quoted in Stewart, *Holy Warriors*, 91; HBS to Garrison, Nov. 1853, BPL; HBS to Garrison, [after Feb. 18, 1853], HBSCL.

best side of the thing, and something *faintly approaching the worst*," she wrote in early 1851.[52] In *A Key to Uncle Tom's Cabin*, published in 1853, Stowe maintained that the novel was "a very inadequate representation of slavery" for the institution, "in some of its workings, is too dreadful for the purposes of art." In this way, she broke with the pattern set by Garrisonians, who were infamous for their blanket denunciations of slavery and its proponents. At one point, Garrison called slaveholders "murderers of fathers, and murderers of mothers, and murderers of liberty, and traffickers in human flesh, and blasphemers against the Almighty."[53]

Uncle Tom's Cabin's slave owners, in contrast, run the gamut from sympathetic yet feckless Augustine St. Clare to cruel and abusive Simon Legree. While Garrison alienated friend and foe alike, Stowe hoped that her balanced portrait would open doors to individuals who might otherwise feel no obligation to the enslaved. "Even earnest and tender-hearted Christian people seemed to feel it a duty to close their eyes, ears, and hearts to the harrowing details of slavery," she wrote in the introduction that she added to an illustrated version of *Uncle Tom's Cabin*. "These people cannot know what slavery is," she reasoned.[54]

Stowe saw herself as an artist, not an agitator. "My vocation is simply that of *painter*," she insisted, "There is no arguing with *pictures*, and everybody is impressed by them, whether they mean to be or not."[55] Certainly her deeply held belief in the inhumanity of slavery informed this position; slavery was so awful that even a tempered picture of it was enough to sway the public against the institution. So, too, did prevailing gender norms, which advised against women taking too strident a public stance. This is not to say, however, that Stowe lacked the acid tongue of a Garrison or a Douglass. Indeed, as biographer Joan Hedrick has argued, "a highly refined and pointed anger" rears its head from time to time in *Uncle Tom's Cabin*. After painstakingly highlighting the horrors of slave trading, for instance, the New Romantic laid blame not at the feet of slave traders, like Haley, but rather at those of leading Americans – particularly politicians – who have created a culture in which human

[52] HBS to Sir Arthur Helps, Aug. 22, 1852, HBSCL; HBS to Bailey, Mar. 9, 1851.

[53] HBS, *A Key to Uncle Tom's Cabin; Presenting the Original Facts and Documents upon Which the Story is Founded, Together with Corroborative Statements Verifying the Truth of the Work* (1853; repr., Bedford, MA: Applewood Books, 1998), 2; Garrison to G.W. Benson, Mar. 22, 1842, quoted in Garrison and Garrison, *William Lloyd Garrison*, III, 50.

[54] HBS, quoted in *SLL*, 146.

[55] HBS to Bailey, Mar. 9, 1851.

trafficking thrives. "Who is most to blame?" Stowe asked. "The enlightened, cultivated, intelligent man, who supports the system of which the
trader is the inevitable result, or the poor trader himself?" When the day
of judgment comes, she warned, the elite may pay a greater price than the
coarse and ignorant.[56]

On the whole, though, Stowe's indictment of slavery tempered the
immediatist critique of the South by spreading blame for the institution across the nation. White southern characters, like Emily Shelby and
Augustine St. Clare, express doubts about slavery, while the true villain
of the novel – Simon Legree – is the product of Stowe's cherished New
England. And even Legree, for all his malevolence, seems almost capable
of salvation when exposed to the saintly Tom. "Legree," wrote Stowe,
"had had the slumbering moral elements in him roused by his encounters
with Tom."[57]

This lenient treatment drew criticism from some abolitionists. Although
Higginson admired "the extraordinary book," he initially thought Stowe
sold slavery's sinfulness short. "I charge upon Mrs. Stowe that she has
softened down the actual evil – that her woman's fear shrank from it," he
declared. In later years, however, Higginson put a positive spin on Stowe's
restraint. Despite his deep admiration for Garrison and his followers, the
Transcendentalist had come to believe that the intolerance they had for
slaveholders was excessive. Garrisonians, Higginson complained, rarely
let the practical barriers that some slaveholders faced – such as state
laws limiting manumission – get in the way of fierce invective. Stowe,
in contrast, "was more discriminating." Her depiction of St. Clare as a
Byronic figure – tragically stuck between his personal misgivings about
slavery and the reality that he could not do anything about it "because his
slaves belonged really to his wife, who had no such feeling" – rang true to
Higginson in the twilight of the nineteenth century.[58]

Still, Stowe faced daunting challenges trying to turn fiction toward
effective social critique. For one, fiction that aimed at social reform had
failed to garner much attention in the United States. Sentimental novels

[56] Hedrick, *Harriet Beecher Stowe*, 216; HBS, *Uncle Tom's Cabin*, 212.
[57] Reynolds, *Mightier than the Sword*, 114; HBS, *Uncle Tom's Cabin*, 567.
[58] TWH to Louisa Higginson, 1852, quoted in *LTH*, 54; TWH, "Lecture on Romance
   of Slavery or American Feudalism" (Oct. 9, 1853), 7, HL; TWH "Anti-Slavery Days,"
   Outlook 60 (Sept. 3, 1898): 50; Caroline Franklin, "Stowe and the Byronic Heroine,"
   in *Transatlantic Stowe: Harriet Beecher Stowe and European Culture*, ed. Denise Kohn,
   Sarah Meer, and Emily B. Todd (Iowa City: University of Iowa Press, 2006), 10.

such as Susan Warner's *The Wide, Wide World* had begun to sell well by the middle of the century, but antislavery fiction had, to this point, found readers only among the converted. What is more, many Americans harbored doubts about the implications of reading and writing imaginative literary works. Before Scott's historical fiction gained popularity in the United States, nary a novel could be found in the Beecher household. As an adult, she remembered that in her youth "most serious-minded people regarded novel reading as an evil." Although Stowe was convinced that fiction was "not merely a matter of amusement, but a high intellectual exercise," she admitted as late as 1849 that the "doubtful hue of romance" that attends all imaginative literature was difficult to shake. Novel readers do not enjoy having "their sympathies enlisted and their feelings carried away by what, after all, may never have happened."[59]

To make matters worse, although the great authors of her childhood had produced works of beauty and sophistication, too often they wrote without "any express moral design." Stowe saved her sharpest barbs for Lord Byron. "The evil influence … exerted by Byron on the minds of the young and sensitive, is not to be lightly estimated," she wrote in the *New-York Evangelist* in 1842.[60] Stowe expanded this critique of Byron in an essay she published the following year. Contrasting Romantics like Byron with "*moral*" writers like Dickens, she placed a premium on the social consciousness stimulated by imaginative literature. Writers such as Byron, she lamented, tend "to withdraw interest from the common sympathies, wants, and sufferings of every day human nature, and to concentrate them on high wrought and unnatural combinations in the ideal world."

Dickens was different. He did not dismiss "the joys and sorrows of ordinary life as decidedly coarse and vulgar," but rather used "the warmth of poetic coloring" to illuminate "the every day walks and ways of men." Stowe believed that Dickens, unlike Byron or Scott, had performed a

---

[59] Walters, "Stowe and the Reform Tradition," 177; HBS, "Early Remembrances," 391; Mary Kelley, *Learning to Stand and Speak: Women, Education, and Public Life in America's Republic* (Chapel Hill: University of North Carolina Press, 2006), 182; *New-York Evangelist*, July 28, 1842; Barbara Hochman, *Uncle Tom's Cabin and the Reading Revolution: Race, Literacy, Childhood, and Fiction, 1851–1911* (Amherst: University of Massachusetts Press, 2011), 28–31; HBS, "Introductory Essay" to Charles Beecher, *The Incarnation; or, Pictures of the Virgin and Her Son*, reproduced with introduction by Barbara Hochman in *PMLA* 118 (Oct. 2003): 1323; HBS to the Ladies New Anti-Slavery Society of Glasgow, in the *Liberator*, Jan. 6, 1854.

[60] *New-York Evangelist*, July 28, 1842.

great service to "the cause of humanity" by depicting "the whole class
of the oppressed, the neglected, and forgotten, the sinning and suffering,
within the pale of sympathy and interest." Indeed, Stowe made precisely
this point in a letter she wrote to Dickens just as *Uncle Tom's Cabin* was
becoming an international sensation. "There is a moral bearing" in your
work, confided Stowe, "that far outweighs the amusement of a passing
hour. If I may hope to do only something like the same, for a class equally
ignored and despised by the fastidious and refined of my country, I shall
be happy."[61]

The New Romantic, in fact, aimed to do more than Dickens because
the British novelist had one glaring flaw in the eyes of his American counterpart: he did not provide positive representations of the Christian faith.
Stowe, in contrast, would attend to both social and spiritual concerns.
She imagined a literary concoction that combined Dickens's gritty realism, Byron's soaring prose, and her own deep piety – all in equal parts.
She would serve this drink in the reassuring glass of antebellum sentimental literature. *Uncle Tom's Cabin*'s domestic setting, its keepsake imagery,
and Eva's deathbed scene no doubt proved familiar to millions of consumers weaned on sentimental fiction.[62]

Stowe was richly rewarded for these efforts as people across the
Western world rushed like never before to buy her book. Abolitionists
toasted it, while white southerners and not a few northerners vilified it.
Nonetheless, everyone was talking about *Uncle Tom's Cabin* after its
publication in early 1852. This singular achievement was not lost on her
fellow New Romantics. "To have written at once the most powerful of
contemporary fictions and the most efficient of anti-slavery tracts," wrote
Higginson, "is a double triumph in literature and philanthropy, to which
this country has heretofore seen no parallel." Stowe had repackaged
moral suasion in a less confrontational and more approachable narrative,
a fact that she herself highlighted. Responding to a letter from an admir-
ing English lord, she counted among the book's most important effects
the conversion "to abolitionist views many whom" had been alienated by
antislavery "bitterness."[63]

[61] *New-York Evangelist*, July 13, 1843; HBS to Charles Dickens, n.d., in introduction to
   Uncle Tom's Cabin; or, Life Among the Lowly (Boston: Houghton, Osgood and Co.,
   1879), xvii.
[62] *New-York Evangelist*, July 13, 1843; Hedrick, *Harriet Beecher Stowe*, 156–157.
[63] *Frederick Douglass' Paper*, Jan. 21, 1853; Unsigned, *Southern Press Review*, 1852, http://
   utc.iath.virginia.edu/reviews/rere27at.html; *Frederick Douglass' Paper*, Mar. 4, 1853;
   TWH, in *LHBS*, 162; HBS to Lord Carlisle, n.d., in *LHBS*, 169.

Tom and Eva as Sentimental Martyrs

Frederick Douglass visited Stowe at her home in Andover, Massachusetts, in early 1853, not long after she and Calvin had relocated there. He came away thinking how easily the five-foot tall author – who had been an early *North Star* subscriber – could get lost in a crowd. "Sitting at the window of a milliner's shop, no one would ever suspect her of being the splendid genius that she is! She would be passed and repassed, attracting no more attention than ordinary ladies," observed the editor in his newspaper. But, he continued, once one engaged Stowe in conversation, she revealed herself to have "that deep insight into human character, that melting pathos, keen and quiet wit, powers of argumentation, exalted sense of justice, and enlightened and comprehensive philosophy, so eminently exemplified in the *master book* of the nineteenth century."[64]

His former partner Delany begged to differ. In a series of letters that he sent Douglass not long after the editor had visited Stowe in Andover, this New Romantic laid his misgivings bare. White abolitionists like Stowe, insisted Delany, knew nothing about blacks and must not be allowed to take the lead in their liberation. He also objected to Stowe's seeming advocacy of colonization toward the end of *Uncle Tom's Cabin*. Finally, the black abolitionist took issue with Stowe's positive portrayal of Tom as a pacifist martyr.[65]

Delany was not alone in this final critique. Indeed, the passivity of Stowe's titular character has been denounced time and again by critics of the novel in the century and a half since it was published. To many readers – white and black, radical and conservative, old and young – the figure of Uncle Tom epitomizes meek submission. Although this characterization's durability has something to do with stage adaptations of *Uncle Tom's Cabin*, which often depicted Tom as little more than a passive, happy-go-lucky figure, the fact remains that even careful readers of the novel have interpreted Stowe's titular hero as an "Uncle Tom."[66]

---

[64] FD, "A Day and A Night in 'Uncle Tom's Cabin,'" *Frederick Douglass' Paper*, Mar. 4, 1853, in *DLW*, 2: 227; Reynolds, *Mightier than the Sword*, x.

[65] MRD to FD, Mar. 20, Apr. 13, 15, 18, 1863 in *Frederick Douglass' Paper*, Apr. 1, 22, 29, May 6, 1853. These letters, along with brief responses by Douglass, are republished in *MDR*, 224–238.

[66] James M. McPherson, "Tom on the Cross," in his *Drawn with the Sword: Reflections on the American Civil War* (New York: Oxford University Press, 1996), 34; Meer, *Uncle Tom Mania*, 253–256; Reynolds, *Mightier than the Sword*, 255–260.

This representation, however, simultaneously elides Tom's moral resolution and the purpose for which Stowe sought to use it in her novel. Instead of centering her story on a martial hero like Madison Washington, Stowe focused, first and foremost, on the experiences of a different type of romantic hero: the sentimental martyr. Tom's myriad personal sacrifices, especially his tragic demise (as well as that of his symbolic soul mate Eva), rather than the more conventionally heroic escapades of runaways George and Eliza, provide the emotional foundation of *Uncle Tom's Cabin*. In making Tom a sentimental martyr, in other words, Stowe did not craft a timid character. Instead, from start to finish, she paints Tom using bold colors. "The hero of our story," she writes, "was a large, broad-chested, powerfully-made man." Though gentle, pious, and unwilling to escape his bondage, he is strong, courageous, and principled. While barely literate, Tom has an admirable work ethic and sharp business acumen, qualities recognized by all of his masters. Moreover, while Tom ultimately accepts death at the hands of his master and his henchmen, all of his decisions are guided by his conscience rather than his owners' orders. In the novel's early stages, he agrees to be sold down the river in order to save the rest of the Shelby slaves from the same fate. Likewise, he refuses to whip Lucy, despite Legree's threats, explaining, "I'm willin' to work, night and day, and work while there's life and breath in me; but this yer thing I can't feel it right to do' – and Mas'r, I *never* shall do it, *never!*"[67]

Thus, Tom follows his own moral compass, a fact that angers Legree enough to kill him. And when Tom refuses to beg his master's forgiveness and take up the whip against his fellow slaves, Stowe suggests that his forbearance trumps the brutal master's physical might: "Tom stood perfectly submissive; and yet, Legree could not hide from himself that his power over his bond thrall was somehow gone." Tom's refusal to reveal Cassy and Emmeline's hideout ultimately provokes Legree to beat him savagely and then to turn him over to Sambo and Quimbo to finish the job. Even in death, Tom acts of his own volition, if not in his own best interests. Feeling "strong in God to meet death," Tom admits to Legree that he knows Cassy and Emmeline's whereabouts, but he refuses to betray them. "I can't tell anything," insists the martyr, "*I can die*." Although rooted in his deep Christian faith, this self-sacrifice was not motivated simply by his desire for salvation in heaven but also his concern for fellow bondspeople

---

[67] Beatrice A. Anderson, "Uncle Tom: A Hero at Last," *American Transcendental Quarterly* 5 (June 1991): 95–108; Elizabeth Ammons, "Heroines in *Uncle Tom's Cabin*," *American Literature* 49 (May 1977): 161–179; HBS, *Uncle Tom's Cabin*, 68, 507.

on earth. "Tom in various ways manifested a tenderness of feeling, a commiseration for his fellow-sufferers," writes Stowe. Epitomizing the religion of the heart that the New Romantic had come to embrace a decade earlier, Tom was, to Stowe, a hero in the mold of Jesus Christ. Or, to put the matter in another way, he was anything but an "Uncle Tom."[68]

Some scholars argue that it would be more accurate, if oddly put, to call Tom "the supreme heroine of the book." After all, Stowe's central character embodied the qualities that nineteenth-century Americans associated with true womanhood – submission, piety, and self-sacrifice – qualities that Stowe put at the core of the Christocentric theology she developed in the 1840s. The novelist, in fact, viewed Jesus Christ as the natural offspring of God and Mary, whose miraculous conception "was the union of the divine nature with the nature of a pure woman," concluding that "there was in Jesus more of the pure feminine element than in any other man."[69]

If no living man could rival Jesus in his feminine characteristics, she created a fictional character who seemed equal to the task. Like any true woman, Uncle Tom is dutiful, pious, and altruistic. He puts the interests of family and hearth and home ahead of all else. After accepting his fate of being sold down the river rather than jeopardizing his family, Tom sobs uncontrollably over his sleeping children. He then urges young George Shelby – his owner's son – to respect his parents in what Stowe describes as "a voice as tender as a woman's."[70] Later, as Eva lies dying, Tom becomes a surrogate mother of sorts. As her own mother Marie spends Eva's final days absorbed in her own suffering – a model of what a true woman would not do – Tom dutifully dotes on the young girl. In the meantime, Eva plays the role of good mother herself, reaching out and inspiring the abused and motherless Topsy.

Exemplars of feminine and maternal values, Uncle Tom and Evangeline St. Clare were Christ-like figures for Stowe. After describing Legree's brutal beating of Tom, she writes, "But, of old, there was on One who suffering changed an instrument of torture, degradation and shame, into a

---

[68] HBS, *Uncle Tom's Cabin*, 558, 581–582, 500–501; Anderson, "Uncle Tom," 99; Paul F. Boller, *Not So! Popular Myths About America from Columbus to Clinton* (New York: Oxford University Press, 1995), 66.

[69] Ammons, "Heroines," 173; Isabelle White, "Sentimentality and the Uses of Death," in *The Stowe Debate: Rhetorical Strategies in Uncle Tom's Cabin*, ed. Mason I. Lowance Jr., Ellen E. Westbrook, and R. C. De Prospo (Amherst: The University of Massachusetts Press, 1994), 108; HBS, *Religious Studies*, in *The Writings of Harriet Beecher Stowe* (Boston: Houghton, Mifflin, 1896), 15: 36.

[70] HBS, *Uncle Tom's Cabin*, 172.

symbol of glory, honor, and immortal life; and, where His spirit is, neither degrading stripes, nor blood, nor insults, can make the Christian's last struggle less than glorious." Tom, like Christ, sacrifices his life not only to save Cassy and Emmeline but, more generally, as a moral lesson – and a path to salvation – for others. The same can be said of Eva. "She's no more than Christ-like," admits Miss Ophelia once she sees Eva's effect on Topsy. "I wish I were like her. She might teach me a lesson."[71]

Tom's martyrdom, of course, follows the pattern that Stowe had set earlier in the book with Eva, who seems to be physically and emotionally consumed by exposure to slavery. In a conversation she has with Tom not long before her death, Eva foreshadows her fate as well as its purpose. "I can understand why Jesus *wanted* to die for us," she said to Tom, acknowledging that she had "felt so, too." When Tom expresses confusion, Eva explains that watching slaves who have been separated from their mother and fathers, wives and husbands, got her thinking about what she could do. "I would be glad to die, if my dying could stop all this misery," she concluded. "I *would* die for them, Tom, if I could."[72]

Stowe's saintly portrait of Tom and Eva amounts to a creative combination of her Christocentric theology with three other romantic currents: romantic racialism, the idealization of childhood, and sentimentalism. Like so many of her contemporaries, she embraced the romantic racialist assumption that African Americans were inherently meek, pious, and emotional. Stowe's racial imagination was most likely shaped by the work of Alexander Kinmont, a Swedenborgian educator who offered a series of influential ethnographical lectures in Cincinnati in 1837 and 1838. Born in Scotland, Kinmont had converted to Swedenborgianism – a Christian sect that followed the teachings of eighteenth-century Swedish mystic Emmanuel Swedenborg – after moving to the United States in the 1820s. He settled in Cincinnati, where he founded Kinmont's Boys Academy, a school that offered students a classical and scientific education as well as a thorough grounding in Swedenborgianism. Although Swedenborgian converts were few and far between, his "doctrine of correspondence," which posited a direct connection between the objects of the physical world and truths of the spiritual world, influenced Transcendentalists like Emerson and Higginson.[73]

---

[71] HBS, *Uncle Tom's Cabin*, 583, 411; McPherson, "Tom on the Cross," 32–36.
[72] Ammons, "Heroines," 156–157; HBS, *Uncle Tom's Cabin*, 400–401.
[73] *History of Cincinnati and Hamilton County, Ohio; Their Past and Present....* (Cincinnati: S. B. Nelson & Co., 1894), 101–102; Gura, *American Transcendentalism*, 59–64; Packer, *Transcendentalists*, 48; Frederickson, *Black Image in the White Mind*, 104n13.

Kinmont, in turn, popularized Swedenborg's more obscure racial theories. In several minor works, the Swedish visionary had insisted that Africans have the innate ability to communicate with God in a more direct, unmediated fashion than other races. Hence, he concluded, they "are more receptive of the Heavenly Doctrines than most others on this earth, because they readily accept the Doctrine." Kinmont expanded upon this idea in his *Twelve Lectures on the Natural History of Man*, which depicted Africans as inherently spiritual, feminine, and childlike. He insisted that Caucasians were, in contrast, naturally rational, masculine, and aggressive, so much so that "all the sweeter graces of the Christian religion appear almost too tropical, and tender plants, to grow in the soil of the Caucasian mind."[74]

No conclusive evidence has been found confirming that Stowe, in fact, heard Kinmont deliver these lectures. We do know, however, that she too was an educator, lived in Cincinnati in the years in which he gave his lectures, and followed cultural happenings closely. Stowe even took note of Kinmont's death in late 1838. We can imagine that the well-read author was at least exposed to Kinmont's ideas after his lectures were published to much fanfare in Cincinnati the following year.[75]

In any case, one thing is certain: the romantic racialist vision that emerged in the budding abolitionist's public and private writing in the early 1850s aligned precisely with the theories Kinmont had laid out a decade earlier in Cincinnati. Stowe, too, judged people of African descent as inferior to whites in terms of their intellectual capacity and fighting spirit, but superior in terms of religious and emotional capacities. As she wrote of African Americans in 1851: "I have seen the strength of their instinctive and domestic attachments in which *as a race* they excel the anglo saxon."[76] In *Uncle Tom's Cabin* she repeatedly associated simplicity, religiosity, and meekness with African ancestry. Tom, wrote Stowe, had "the soft, impressible nature of his kindly race, ever yearning toward the simple and child-like." Lacking in the "daring and enterprising" qualities that both Stowe and Kinmont associated with whites, African Americans, she insisted, were domestic, affectionate, and pious by nature.

---

[74] Emmanuel Swedenborg, quoted in Josephine Donovan, "A Source for Stowe's Ideas on Race," *NWSA Journal* 78 (Autumn 1995): 29; Alexander Kinmont, *Twelve Lectures on the Natural History of Man, and the Rise and Progress of Philosophy* (Cincinnati: U.P. James, 1839), 218; Fredrickson, *Black Image in the White Mind*, 103–111.

[75] Hedrick, *Harriet Beecher Stowe*, 209–210, 437n31; Donovan, "A Source for Stowe's Ideas on Race," 26–28.

[76] HBS to Henry Ward Beecher, Feb. 1, 1851, in *OSR*, 65.

She concluded in *A Key to Uncle Tom's Cabin* that "the divine graces of love and faith, when in-breathed by the Holy Spirit, find in their natural temperament a more congenial atmosphere" among blacks "than any other races." Uncle Tom, of course, epitomized this innate black spirituality.[77]

If, in Stowe's mind, Tom derived his Christ-like qualities from his black ancestry, then Eva's divine nature was similarly conditioned by her youth. Like many romantics across the Western world, Stowe thought children were oracles of divine wisdom who could teach as much as they could learn. Transcendentalist Bronson Alcott called the child "a Type of Divinity," who revealed the "nature" of man, "despoiled of none of its glory." Emerson opined that "infancy is the perpetual Messiah, which comes into the arms of fallen men, and pleads with them to return to paradise" in his widely read essay, "Nature." Closer to nature, children seemed closer to God. Stowe likewise believed that children had much to "teach us," especially insofar as morality and spirituality were concerned. "Wouldst thou know, O parent, what is that *faith* which unlocks heaven?" she asked in an 1846 essay. "Go not to wrangling polemics, or creeds and forms of theology, but draw to thy bosom thy little one, and read in that clear, trusting eye, the lesson of eternal life."[78]

No character in American literature better exemplifies the divine interpretation of childhood than Little Eva. Stowe renders her as a romantic, otherworldly figure. When Tom first catches a glimpse of her aboard a Mississippi steamboat, Eva "seemed something almost divine." Blonde-haired, blue-eyed, and "always dressed in white," she has "an undulating and aërial grace, such as one might dream of for some mythic and allegorical being." In her purity, selflessness, and deep piety, Eva reflected Stowe's faith that children were the spiritual foundation of the nation (Figure 3.2).[79]

<hr/>

[77] HBS, *Uncle Tom's Cabin*, 231, 164; HBS, *Key to Uncle Tom's Cabin*, 25; Donovan, "A Source for Stowe's Ideas on Race," 28.

[78] Susan J. Pearson, *The Rights of the Defenseless: Protecting Animals and Children in Gilded Age America* (Chicago: University of Chicago Press, 2011), 30–32; Packer, *The Transcendentalists*, 43, 55–58; Reynolds, *Mightier than the Sword*, 26–28; Gura, *American Transcendentalism*, 85–90; Bronson Alcott, quoted in Steven Mintz, *Huck's Raft: A History of American Childhood* (Cambridge, MA: Belknap Press of Harvard University Press, 2004), 76; Ralph Waldo Emerson, *Nature: Addresses and Lectures*, in *The Complete Works of Ralph Waldo Emerson*, ed. Edward Waldo Emerson (Boston: Houghton, Mifflin, 1903), 1: 71; *New-York Evangelist*, Jan. 15, 1846.

[79] HBS, *Uncle Tom's Cabin*, 231, 230; Ammons, "Heroines," 156–158; White, "Sentimentality and the Uses of Death," 108–109.

FIGURE 3.2. Lithograph of Eva ascending to heaven (1899) captures Stowe's romanticized portrayal of her sentimental martyr.
Source: Courier Litho. Co, Buffalo, NY, 1899. Courtesy of the Library of Congress, Prints and Photographs Division, LC-USZ62–50215.

Stowe's saintly characterization of Eva, especially her overwrought
death scene, has provoked almost as much critical opprobrium as the
image of Uncle Tom. "Little Eva gains her force not through what she
does, not even through what she is, but through what she does and is
to us, the readers," Ann Douglas argued in the most forceful critique
of the scene. Eva is little more than a "decorative" character, she wrote,
whose "sainthood is there to precipitate our nostalgia and our narcissism." Her death typifies the larger problem that Douglas identified in
works of Victorian sentimentalism like *Uncle Tom's Cabin*: the betrayal
of the seriousness and artistry of elite culture in favor of "sentimental
peddling of Christian belief for its nostalgic value." Contrasting sentimental literature with the work of such European Romantics as Goethe,
Keats, Shelley, and Coleridge, Douglas insisted that the former lacks
the latter's "political and historical sense," its "spirit of critical protest."
Instead, sentimentalism encourages "self-absorption, a commercializa-
tion of the inner life." Yet Douglas's test for whether a work of literature
is romantic or sentimental has more to do with aesthetics than its social
or political import. Romanticism, she held, "no matter how strained or
foreign to modern ears, has not – to use Hemingway's phrase – 'gone
bad.'" Sentimental literature, in contrast, sounds sappy and dated. The
eminent black novelist James Baldwin agreed. As he wrote in a scathing
1949 essay, "*Uncle Tom's Cabin* is a very bad novel, having, in its self-
righteous, virtuous sentimentality, much in common with *Little Women*."
Baldwin called "sentimentality ... the ostentatious parading of excessive
and spurious emotion" – "the mark of dishonesty."[80]

While Douglas's and Baldwin's interpretations of *Uncle Tom's Cabin's*
aesthetic shortcomings are on target, they miss the mark in other ways.
First of all, as scholars like Jane Tompkins have ably demonstrated, senti-
mentalists like Stowe did not retreat "from the world into self-absorption
and idle reverie." Quite the contrary, by positing the transformation of
America into a more just republic at the hands of "Christian women,"
they put the seemingly conservative values of sentimentalism and domesticity to work in the service of radical social reform. Secondly, sentimentalism was far from a dishonest or intellectually bankrupt body of ideas.
Instead, it had deep philosophical roots, some of which could be found in
the romantic soil that Douglas valued so highly.[81]

---

[80] Douglas, *The Feminization of American*, 3, 4, 6, 255; James Baldwin, "Everybody's
Protest Novel," in *Critical Essays on Harriet Beecher Stowe*, 92.

[81] Jane Tompkins, *Sensational Designs: The Cultural Work of American Fiction, 1790–1860*
(New York: Oxford University Press, 1985), 143–144; Carolyn Haynes, "Domesticity and

Sentimental literature reached its apogee in the nineteenth century, but arguments for the centrality of emotion and feeling date back to the early modern period. Responding to the perceived ethical shortcomings of Lockean empiricism, Scottish Common Sense philosophers like Francis Hutcheson and Adam Smith posited an internal moral sense by which to guide all individual action. In his influential 1759 *The Theory of Moral Sentiments*, Smith stressed the use of imagination in the process of identification with another. "By the imagination we place ourselves in his situation," he wrote, "we conceive ourselves enduring all the same torments, we enter as it were into his body, and become in some measure the same person with him."[82]

Stowe was likely exposed to Common Sense theories by such writers as Hugh Blair and Archibald Alison, whom she read as a young girl. Her sister Catharine, who developed an education theory based on awakening "affection in the human mind" at the Hartford Seminary, reinforced this early interest in Common Sense philosophy. Drawing directly on Smith's theories, Catharine wrote that instructors could help students develop their faculty of "*Sympathy*" – "the power the mind possesses of experiencing such emotions as ... exist in another mind."[83]

Stowe also found intellectual support for sentimentalism in the contemporary arguments of romantics in the United States and Europe. Since the 1840s, Stowe and her husband had been reading the work of Schleiermacher, who maintained that "religion's essence is neither thinking

Sentimentalism," in the *Encyclopedia of American Cultural and Intellectual History*, ed. Mary Kupiec Cayton and Peter W. Williams (New York: Charles Scribner's Sons, 2001), 1: 450–451. In the preface to the 1988 edition of *Feminization of American Culture*, Douglas admitted that she "underrated" the "long-term efficacy" of the "social goals and methods" of sentimental authors like Stowe. Douglas, *Feminization of American Culture*, xii–xiii.

[82] Adam Smith, *The Theory of Moral Sentiments* (1759; repr., Indianapolis: Liberty Fund, 1984), 9; R.S. Crane, "Suggestions Toward a Genealogy of the 'Man of Feeling,'" *English Literary History* 1 (Dec. 1934): 205–230; Norman Fiering, "Irresistible Compassion: An Aspect of Eighteenth-Century Sympathy and Humanitarianism," *Journal of the History of Ideas* 37 (Apr.-June 1976): 195–218; Gregg Camfield, The Moral Aesthetics of Sentimentality: A Missing Key to *Uncle Tom's Cabin*," *Nineteenth-Century Literature* 43 (Dec. 1988): 319–345; Karen Halttunen, "Humanitarianism and the Pornography of Pain in Anglo-American Culture," *American Historical Review* 100 (Apr. 1995): 303–334; Elizabeth B. Clark, "'The Sacred Rights of the Weak': Pain, Sympathy, and the Culture of Individual Rights in Antebellum America," *Journal of American History* 82 (Sept. 1995): 478–79.

[83] Catharine Beecher, quoted in Maurice S. Lee, *Slavery, Philosophy, and American Literature, 1830–1860* (New York: Cambridge University Press, 2005), 73; Camfield, "The Moral Aesthetics of Sentimentality," 328–332.

nor acting, but intuition and feeling." Her fellow New Romantics likewise identified sentiment as the wellspring of humanity. "A man without
large power of feeling is not good for much as a man," wrote Parker.
"He may be a good mathematician, a very respectable lawyer, or a doctor of divinity, but he is not capable of the high and beautiful and holy
things of manhood."[84] Douglass believed that mankind's "affinities" were
so powerful that even the institution of slavery could not sunder them.
On the anniversary celebration of West Indian emancipation in 1848,
he confidently announced that "the magic power of human sympathy is
rapidly healing national divisions, and bringing mankind into the harmonious bonds of a common brotherhood." Fourteen years later, while
serving in South Carolina as a commander of a regiment of ex-slaves,
Higginson also invoked the bonds of sympathy that unite all people. In
a journal passage in which he explored the elements that set his African
American soldiers apart from their white counterparts, he wrote, "As for
sugar, no white man can drink coffee after they have sweetened it – perhaps I could, I never tried it – & perhaps this sympathy of sweetness is
the real bond between us." Even the simple act of tasting his soldiers'
coffee, Higginson implied in Smithian fashion, had the potential to foster
sympathetic identification with another.[85]

   As Stowe formulated her unique brand of reform fiction, she drew
on both romantic and Common Sense theories of sentimentalism. Like
Smith, Parker, Schleiermacher, and countless others, she highlighted
the extraordinary power of "the faculty of the imagination," which,
she insisted in 1849, exists "burning and God-given, in many a youth-
ful soul."[86] As she would later illustrate with her evocative "ladder to
heaven" metaphor, Stowe believed the foundation of society and individual salvation lay "in human affections, tender instincts, symbolic
feelings, [and] sacraments of love," which transcended all races and
cultures. Indeed, at one point in *Uncle Tom's Cabin,* Stowe posited

---

[84] Friedrich Schleiermacher, quoted in Richard Crouter, *Friedrich Schleiermacher: Between
   Enlightenment and Romanticism* (New York: Cambridge University Press, 2008), 54n68;
   TP, "Traits and Illustrations of Human Character and Conduct," in *WTP,* 5: 136.
[85] FD, "The Anti-Slavery Movement: An Address Delivered in Rochester, New York, on
   19 March 1855," in *FDP,* 3: 49; FD, "A Day, A Deed, an Event, Glorious in the Annals
   of Philanthropy: An Address Delivered in Rochester, New York, on 1 August 1848,"
   in *FDP,* 2: 136; Dan McKanan, *Identifying the Image of God: Radical Christians and
   Nonviolent Power in the Antebellum United States* (New York: Oxford University Press,
   2002), 6–7; TWH, Journal, Dec. 2, 1862, in *CWJ,* 26; Looby, introduction to *CWJ,*
   26–27.
[86] HBS, "Introductory Essay," 1324.

sentimental identification as nothing less than the *sine qua non* of the human condition. The moment in question takes place on the northern Quaker settlement to which Eliza and her son flee. When Eliza's host Rachel Halliday learns that George has, unbeknownst to Eliza, also found his way to the settlement, she asks her friend Ruth whether she should tell the runaway immediately. "Now! to be sure, – this very minute," replies Ruth. "Why, now, suppose 't was my John, how should I feel?" After Rachel's husband Simeon applauds her neighborly love, Ruth asks, "Isn't it what we are made for?"[87]

The same could be said of *Uncle Tom's Cabin*, which Stowe deliberately crafted to help her audience feel the suffering of the enslaved. As she wrote in her first preface, "The object of these sketches is to awaken sympathy and feeling for the African race, as they exist among us; to show their wrongs and sorrows under a system so necessarily cruel and unjust as to defeat and do away with the good effects of all that can be attempted for them, by their best friends, under it."[88] Unlike most authors, Stowe did not limit such direct appeals to her readership to the preface. Instead, throughout the novel she repeatedly disrupted the flow of the narrative with authorial interventions that challenge her readers to put themselves in the shoes of her suffering characters. Describing the scene in which Tom selflessly submits to Mr. Shelby's decision to sell him to Haley rather than see the whole plantation broken up, Stowe explicitly asks her readers to connect it to similar pain that they have suffered: "Sobs, heavy, hoarse and loud, shook the chair, and great tears fell through his fingers on the floor; just such tears, sir, as you dropped into the coffin where lay your first-born son; such tears, woman, as you shed when you heard the cries of your dying babe."[89]

Having lost her son Charley a few years before writing *Uncle Tom's Cabin*, Stowe urges her readers to identify with Tom and his family's plight by drawing on their own emotional reserves. Later, she concludes a passage in which Eliza debates whether she has the strength necessary to run away with Harry from being sold down the river with another direct question to her audience. "If it were *your* Harry, mother, or your Willie, that were going to be torn from you by a brutal trader, tomorrow morning ... how fast could *you* walk?" she asks. "How many miles could

[87] HBS, *Minister's Wooing*, 88; Clark, "Sacred Rights of the Weak," 492; HBS, *Uncle Tom's Cabin*, 220.

[88] HBS, "First Edition Preface," in *Uncle Tom's Cabin* (Boston: Jewett & Co., 1852), http://utc.iath.virginia.edu/uncletom/uteshbsbt.html.

[89] HBS, *Uncle Tom's Cabin*, 90–91.

you make in those few brief hours, with the darling at your bosom, –
the little sleepy head on your shoulder, – the small, soft arms trustingly
holding on to your neck?" Finally, while Stowe wrestles directly with
the question of what individuals can do to solve the problem of slavery
toward the end of the novel, she makes her classic appeal that "there
is one thing that every individual can do, – they can see to it *they feel
right*. An atmosphere of sympathetic influence encircles every human
being; and the man or woman who *feels* strongly, healthily and justly,
on the great interests of humanity, is a constant benefactor to the human
race." Feeling right and identifying with the tragic victims of slavery, she
implies, can help individuals build a culture where the Toms of the world
do not have to die.[90]

At other points, Stowe encourages sympathetic identification
with others with more subtlety. Eva's death, for example, is largely
conveyed through the experiences of her family members and their
bondspeople. While Eva stoically faces her imminent demise, hand-
ing each of the household "servants" a lock of her curls, they burst
out with "groans, sobs, and lamentations." Later, Stowe lingers on the
shared anguish of Augustine St. Clare and Tom as Eva is at death's
door. "O, Tom, my boy, it is killing me!" cries St. Clare as a crying
Tom squeezes "his master's hand between his own." Meanwhile, Eva
smiles brightly, sighing as she passes away, "O! love, – joy, – peace!"
Stowe employs a similar dynamic in Tom's death scene, which is represented first through the eyes of Sambo and Quimbo and later through
those of George Shelby, the son of his former master. Amid savagely
beating Tom, the two drivers are overcome with the wickedness of
their actions. Shortly thereafter, Shelby arrives, hoping to buy Tom
and return him to his old Kentucky home. Stowe affords the reader a
quick glimpse into the heart of Tom, who is at once overjoyed by the
news that he has not been forgotten by the Shelby plantation, while
nonetheless looking forward – even more than Eva – to his imminent
demise. Yet again Stowe is concerned with the emotional impact of his
death on those who surround him, explicating how his death converts

---

[90] HBS, *Uncle Tom's Cabin*, 105, 624; Marianne Noble, "Sentimental Epistemologies
in *Uncle Tom's Cabin* and *The House of the Seven Gables*," in *Separate Spheres No
More: Gender and Convergence in American Literature, 1830–1930*, ed. Monika M.
Elbert (Tuscaloosa: University of Alabama Press, 2000), 268; Laura Hanft Korobkin,
Sentimentality and Nineteenth-Century Legal Stories of Adultery (New York: Columbia
University Press, 1998), 78–80.

Sambo and Quimbo to Christianity while pushing George to swear before God that he "will do *what one man can* to drive out this curse of slavery from my land!"[91]

Viewed through the lens of sentimental identification, then, these death scenes compel Stowe's readers to put themselves not so much in the shoes of her martyrs, but rather those of the mere mortals who surround them. By focusing on the emotional toil of Tom and Eva's deaths on those who witnessed them as well as their impact on friends, family, and others, Stowe offered a primer on the tragedy of the institution of slavery. She did not encourage her audience to strive to live up to Eva and Tom's impossibly high example so much as to understand the acute suffering that it inevitably entailed. This tragic thread extended even to the conversions that resulted from their deaths. On the surface, Eva's death scene seems to be a turning point in the novel, after which those close to her would never be the same. But while Eva helps convert Topsy to Christianity in her final days, she fails utterly to effect larger changes, not least of which is the goal for which she died: the liberation of the St. Clare slaves. Even the promise to free Uncle Tom, which Eva elicits from her father at her deathbed, comes up empty as Augustine is killed in a fight before he can finalize the emancipation.

Tom's martyrdom, too, achieves at best limited practical results regarding slavery. George pledges himself to the antislavery cause and knocks brutal Legree to the ground. Yet when the Legree slaves who bury Tom ask the young master to save them from the "hard times" on the Red River plantation by buying them, he replies, "I can't! – I can't! … it's impossible!" George does play the role of liberator on his own plantation in Kentucky. But here, too, we are left with a sense of ambivalence about what Stowe's sentimental martyr can truly achieve. After being liberated, the Shelby slaves stay on as wage laborers, declaring, "We don't want to be no freer than we are. We's allers had all we wanted. We don't want to leave de ole place, and Mas'r and Missis, and de rest!" Aside from helping Cassy and Emmeline escape, the only concrete blow against slavery that Tom manages to strike leads to the creation of a free labor version of the plantation ideal trumpeted by proslavery apologists like George Fitzhugh. In the end, it is difficult to

---

[91] Glenn Hendler, *Public Sentiments: Structures of Feeling in Nineteenth-Century American Literature* (Chapel Hill: University of North Carolina Press, 2001), 4; HBS, *Uncle Tom's Cabin*, 418, 427–428, 585, 593.

escape the fact that even Christ-like martyrs are no match for the power of institutionalized slavery in *Uncle Tom's Cabin.*[92]

George and Eliza as Resistant Rebels

The tragic role played by Tom in Stowe's sentimental drama raises the question of whether, indeed, she meant him to serve as a heroic model. Garrison, for one, had no doubt that she did. "His character is sketched with great power and rare religious perception," he wrote. "It triumphantly exemplifies the nature, tendency and results of CHRISTIAN NON-RESISTANCE." But on this issue the abolitionist editor also challenged Stowe, wondering whether she believed "in the duty of non-resistance for the white man, under all possible outrage and peril, as well as for the black man." Highlighting the gap between the suffering submission of black Uncle Tom and the heroic journey and fighting spirit of mixed-race George Harris, he asked, "Is there one law of submission and non-resistance for the black man, and another law of rebellion and conflict for the white man?"[93]

Garrison's reading of *Uncle Tom's Cabin* underscores a critical point: Along with Tom the martyr, Stowe proffered an altogether different tale of heroism. The plotline of runaway slave George Harris, who personified the martial valor that so appealed to her fellow New Romantics, further reveals Stowe's ambivalence about the appropriate response to slavery, at least for those with Anglo-Saxon ancestry.

At the outset of the novel George faces the same dilemma as Tom. While the latter is to be sent down the river with a slave trader, the former – a "talented young mulatto man" who had invented a labor-saving machine, not unlike Eli Whitney's cotton gin – has to leave his job in a bagging factory for "a life of toil and drudgery" on his master's farm. An autodidact, George shows a "zeal for self-improvement," which keeps him from being bogged down in bondage's "toil and discouragements." Whereas Tom feels obligated to honor his duty to obey his master, at least to a point, George questions the right of another man to own him: "My master! and who made him my master? ... I'm a man as much as he is." When his wife Eliza reminds him that Christianity teaches obedience to

---

[92] HBS, *Uncle Tom's Cabin* 593, 616; Douglas, *Feminization of American Culture*, 4; Jennifer L. Jenkins, "Failed Mothers and Fallen Heroes: The Uses of Domesticity in *Uncle Tom's Cabin*," *ESQ: A Journal of the American Renaissance* 38 (2nd qt. 1992): 172; McKanan, *Identifying the Image of God*, 162.

[93] *Liberator*, Mar. 26, 1852.

one's master, George replies, "I an't a Christian like you, Eliza; my heart's full of bitterness, I can't trust in God." Determined that he cannot remain a slave, he announces to his wife, "I'll *die* first! I'll be free, or I'll die!"[94] George Harris, then, follows a different moral compass than Tom, one more attuned to worldly conditions than to Christian obedience and self-sacrifice.

Unlike Tom, George does not shrink from violent confrontation with those who would keep him chained. When Mr. Wilson, a white southerner who is sympathetic to his plight, expresses concerns about the repercussions that the young runaway faces if caught, George opens his coat to reveal two pistols and a bowie knife, insisting he is prepared to ensure his success, whatever the cost. Upon hearing Mr. Wilson's appeal to the laws of the land, George replies, "My country again! Mr. Wilson, *you* have a country; but what country have *I*, or any one like me, born of slave mothers? What laws are there for us? We don't make them, – we don't consent to them, – we have nothing to do with them; all they do for us is to crush us, and keep us down." In this passage, Stowe may have consciously been echoing Douglass, who just a few years earlier had declared, "I have no patriotism, I have no country. What country have I?" She later admitted that George was modeled, in part, on the life of her fellow romantic reformer, who so famously expounded upon this theme in his Fifth of July jeremiad.[95]

In a chapter titled "The Freeman's Defence," Stowe pursues the question of martial resistance directly. Befriended by a group of pacifist Quakers, the Harrises are forced to wrestle with the nonresistant beliefs that animate characters like Uncle Tom. Though George says that he is not looking for a fight, preferring to leave the United States peacefully, he refuses to allow either himself or his family to return to bondage. Reflecting on the fact that his sister had been auctioned off in New Orleans, he remarks, "I know what they are sold for; and am I going to stand by and see them take my wife and sell her, when God has given me a pair of strong arms to defend her?" Hearing this, one of his Quaker companions wonders whether this situation is the exception that proves the nonresistant rule. "If man should *ever* resist evil," he states, "then

[94] HBS, *Uncle Tom's Cabin*, 54, 57, 604, 60, 62, 64.

[95] HBS, *Uncle Tom's Cabin*, 185; FD, "The Right to Criticize American Institutions, speech before the American Anti-Slavery Society, May 11, 1847, in *LWFD*, 1: 236; William B. Allen, *Rethinking Uncle Tom: The Political Philosophy of Harriet Beecher Stowe* (Lanham, MD: Lexington Books, 2009), 105n9; HBS, *Key to Uncle Tom's Cabin*, 16–17.

George should feel free to do it now: but the leaders of our people taught a more excellent way; for the wrath of man worketh not the righteousness of God; but it goes sorely against the corrupt will of man, and none can receive it save they to whom it is given. Let us pray to the Lord that we be not tempted."[96]

Not long after, when slave catchers chase down the Harrises and their Quaker companions, George takes his stand, issuing what Stowe calls "his declaration of independence." "I am George Harris," he announces. "A Mr. Harris, of Kentucky, did call me his property. But now I'm a free man, standing of God's free soil; and my wife and my child I claim as mine.... You can come up, if you like; but the first one of you that comes within the range of our bullets is a dead man, and the next, and the next; and so on till the last." After one of the slave catchers replies, "We've got the law on our side, and the power, and so forth," George, having already thrown off the shackles of slavery, rejects the laws and the country that helped put him in bondage in the first place. "We don't own your laws; we don't own your country," he says. "We stand here as free, under God's sky, as you are; and, by the great God that made us, we'll fight for our liberty till we die." [97] In classic New Romantic fashion, George strikes his martial pose on higher law grounds. Shortly thereafter, he proves true to his word, shooting a burly slave catcher with his pistol.

Although George's dramatic escape takes a secondary role in the novel to Tom's tragic tale, Stowe leaves little doubt about her admiration for the former's escapades. In the months before she began to write *Uncle Tom's Cabin*, Stowe had begun revisiting the historical romances of her youth. "The children study English history in school," she wrote her sister-in-law Sarah Buckingham in late 1850, "and I am reading Scott's historical novels in their order." Having just finished *The Talisman*, *The Abbot*, and *Ivanhoe*, Stowe must have had medieval knights on the brain. Little wonder, then, that she counterbalanced Tom's martyrdom with George's tale of martial heroism. In a passage in which her own voice and George's combine into a single chorus, Stowe depicts her resistant rebel as no different from a host of European and American freedom fighters. If he had been "a Hungarian youth," escaping Austria into America, declares George, his militant stand would have been interpreted as "sublime heroism." Yet Americans tended to portray runaway slaves as dangerous

---

[96] HBS, *Uncle Tom's Cabin*, 288.
[97] HBS, *Uncle Tom's Cabin*, 298.

lawbreakers. Since he "was a youth of African descent, defending the retreat of fugitives through America into Canada, of course we are too well instructed and patriotic to see any heroism in it; and if any of our readers do, they must do it on their own personal responsibility." Later in the novel, Stowe again highlights the heroic nature of resistance to bondage. When runaways brave torture and death by escaping and, in some cases, returning to "that dark land" to save their wives, sisters, and mothers, she insists, they are performing "deeds of heroism," not acting like criminals.[98]

Unsurprisingly, Stowe viewed martial heroism through the prism of nineteenth-century gender mores. Runaway husbands and fathers return to save their wives and daughters, not the other way around. Even so, Stowe broke new ground by creating female characters with complex motives. Combining the sort of rebellious heroines one could find in the pulp novels of the period – fallen women, adventure feminists, seductresses – with traditional exemplars of morality and chastity that populated most sentimental novels, she offered what David Reynolds calls "multilayered heroines."[99] George's wife Eliza is, at once, a loving, devoted mother and a brave heroine, who manages to single-handedly free her child and herself. And, importantly, Eliza is the protagonist in the book's most spectacular – if not melodramatic – scene.

On the run from slave trader Haley and his henchmen, Eliza is forced to flee across the icy Ohio River, "stumbling – leaping – slipping – springing upwards again" from one ice fragment to the next, ever clutching young Harry. Stowe's gendered conception of heroism prevented her from overtly characterizing this escape as heroic; instead, she called it "a desperate leap" that was produced by "madness" and "despair." Nevertheless, Eliza's successful jump highlights the degree to which Stowe was of two minds about the appropriate response to slavery for men and women alike. While Tom's pacifist persuasion leaves him at the mercy of Legree's brutal hand, Stowe's runaways (George, Eliza, Henry, Cassy, and Emmeline) are the characters who emerge not only free and unscathed but reunited with their loved ones. When we examine George's fate – a safe and happy family, Christian conversion, university study in

---

[98] HBS to Sarah Buckingham, Dec. 17, [1850], in Jeanne Boydston, Mary Kelley, and Anne Margolis, *The Limits of Sisterhood: The Beecher Sisters on Women's Rights and Woman's Sphere* (Chapel Hill: University of North Carolina Press, 1988), 79; Kelley, *Learning to Stand and Speak*, 249; HBS, *Uncle Tom's Cabin*, 299, 606.

[99] Reynolds, *Mightier than the Sword*, 47.

France – next to Tom's tragic demise, it is difficult to conclude that non-resistant moral suasion was her preferred antislavery mode.[100]

The central question that remains is whether Stowe meant to delimit martial heroism to white and mixed-race individuals alone. After all, she goes to great lengths to associate Harris's resistance with his white blood. Born of a white father and slave mother, Harris, writes Stowe, "inherited a set of fine European features, and a high, indomitable spirit" from his father, while "receiv[ing] only a slight mulatto tinge, amply compensated by its accompanying rich, dark eye," from his mother.[101] In her *A Key to Uncle Tom's Cabin*, Stowe further linked George's enterprising nature, intelligence, and militancy to his white ancestry. Responding directly to the critique that "the character of George has been represented as overdrawn," she insisted: "In regard to person, it must be remembered that the half-breeds often inherit, to a great degree, the traits of their white ancestors." George's seemingly remarkable characteristics, Stowe reminded her readers, can reasonably be attributed to his father's white blood. Moreover, as George Fredrickson has pointed out, the only other characters who actively seek to free themselves in *Uncle Tom's Cabin* – Eliza, Cassy, and Emmeline – are of mixed race. It seems only fair to conclude that Stowe had doubts about the capacity of her full-blooded black characters to overcome what she thought was an inherent passivity.[102]

At the same time, Stowe, like the rest of the New Romantics, did not think that racial difference was entirely fixed. Despite frequently discussing the "natural" or "innate" characteristics of different races, she provided conceptual room for environmental factors. When comparing Eva and Topsy in *Uncle Tom's Cabin*, for example, she noted that "the Saxon" was "born of ages of cultivation, command, education, physical and moral eminence," while "the Afric" was "born of ages of oppression, submission, ignorance, toil and vice!" The yawning gap between Eva and Topsy, implied Stowe, was to a certain extent the result of historical circumstances. She also joined Parker and Douglass in rejecting pseudo-scientific theories that traced racial difference to separate origins or bloodlines.[103]

---

[100] HBS, *Uncle Tom's Cabin*, 118, 117, 561; Hedrick, *Harriet Beecher Stowe*, 213; McPherson, "Tom on the Cross," 28; Reynolds, *Mightier than the Sword*, 47–48.

[101] HBS, *Uncle Tom's Cabin*, 182.

[102] HBS, *Key to Uncle Tom's Cabin*, 13; Fredrickson, *Black Image in the White Mind*, 117.

[103] HBS, *Uncle Tom's Cabin*, 361–362, 268.

What is more, by the mid-1850s Stowe seemed to have changed her mind about the potential of African American men to display the aggressive qualities that racialists usually ascribed only to whites. In her introduction to William Cooper Nell's *The Colored Patriots of the American Revolution*, Stowe wrote of the bravery of black soldiers during the American battle for independence. "This little collection of interesting incidents," she insisted, "made by a colored man, will redeem the character of the race from this misconception, and show how much injustice there may often be in a generally admitted idea." Stowe hoped the book would help to convince white Americans – whether friend or foe of African Americans – that their black counterparts had demonstrated patriotism and bravery and deserved equal rights and opportunities. She also thought that it could serve as a model for black Americans: "Let them emulate the noble deeds and sentiments of their ancestors, and feel that the dark skin can never be a badge of disgrace, while it has been ennobled by such examples."[104]

The protagonist in Stowe's second antislavery novel further illustrates her doubts about inherent black passivity. Written just as sectional tensions boiled over into armed conflict on the plains of Kansas and in the halls of Washington, *Dred: A Tale of the Great Dismal Swamp* evokes the rising tide of violence in the mid-1850s. The first half of Stowe's novel is the sentimental story of Nina Gordon, a southern mistress who entertains a variety of suitors on her plantation. The second half, which unfolds amid the backdrop of proslavery lynch mobs and the caning of Charles Sumner, follows the exploits of its titular protagonist, an escaped slave whom Stowe calls "the hero of the book."[105] In some ways, Dred closely resembles Uncle Tom. "A tall black man, of magnificent stature and proportions," he, too, is devoutly religious. Yet Dred displays other characteristics that align him more closely with such slave rebels as Madison Washington, George Harris, or Martin Delany's Henry Blake, whom we will consider later, than Stowe's sentimental martyr.

The son of would-be insurrectionist Denmark Vesey, Dred has "the muscles of a gladiator" and a burning intensity to make him seem like "one of the wild old warrior prophets of the heroic age." In a sharply drawn contrast to Tom's New Testament pacifism, Dred embraces his

---

[104] HBS, introduction to William Cooper Nell, *The Colored Patriots of the American Revolution* (Boston: Robert F. Wallcut, 1855), 5–6.
[105] HBS, *Dred: A Tale of the Great Dismal Swamp* (1856; repr., Edinburgh: Edinburgh University Press, 1999), 613; HBS and Calvin Stowe to Mr. Phillips, June 11, 1856, BPL.

father's Old Testament militancy, carrying a bowie knife, a hatchet, and a rifle. Retreating to the Great Dismal Swamp after killing an overseer bent on subduing him, Dred's "solitary companion" is his father's Bible, a spiritual guide that to him is "not the messenger of peace and good-will, but the herald of woe and wrath!"[106] Dred, who organizes fellow runaways into a revolutionary maroon community in the swamp, is killed before he is able to initiate the slave rebellion he prophesized. Nevertheless, he represents a prepotent refutation of the assumption that people of African descent were meek and subservient by nature.

What stands out most to the modern reader about Stowe's portrait of Dred are the ways in which she employed elements we associate with popular romanticism to craft her rebuttal to this key pillar of nineteenth-century racial theory. Like a classic Byronic hero, Dred is a tortured outcast who finds solace not among the rest of humanity but rather in the wilds of the powerful and untamed natural world. In a vague but telling passage, she writes, "As the mind, looking on the great volume of nature, sees there is a reflection of its own internal passions, and seizes on that in it which sympathizes with itself, – as the fierce and savage soul delights in the roar of torrents, the thunder of avalanches, and the whirl of ocean storms, – so is it in the great answering volume of revelation." Wandering through the swamp for weeks on end in trance-like states, Dred lives in complete "sympathy and communion with nature." "His life passed in a kind of dream," explains Stowe.[107]

Such passages have led some scholars to insist that the novelist was incapable of portraying black militancy as anything other than a "species of insanity," but this reading misses the positive elements in Stowe's depiction of Dred's mental state.[108] The slave rebel, she maintains, occupies the "twilight-ground between the boundaries of the sane and insane, which the old Greeks and Romans regarded with a peculiar veneration." She contrasts "the hot and positive light of our modern materialism, ... which searches out and dries every rivulet of romance," with Dred's "state of exaltation and trace, which yet appeared not at all to impede the exercise of his outward and physical faculties." Hardships that would be unbearable to the average person, Stowe continued, are for him "an ordinary condition." Indeed, she writes that "the African race are said

[106] HBS, *Dred*, 261, 274, 276.
[107] HBS, *Dred*, 276, 354; 276; Crozier, "Harriet Beecher Stowe and Byron," 197; Fredrickson, *Black Image in the White Mind*, 112–113; Hedrick, *Harriet Beecher Stowe*, 258.
[108] Sundquist, *To Wake the Nations*, 79; Fredrickson, *Black Image in the White Mind*, 112–113.

by mesmerists to possess in the fullest degree, that peculiar temperament which fits them for evolution of mesmeric phenomena."[109] Thus, insofar as Dred casts doubt on some romantic racialist conclusions, he also bespeaks Stowe's belief in the unique religious gifts of African people. Stowe's classic portrait of black militancy, in sum, was as much the product of her romantic frame of mind as was Uncle Tom.

Ambivalence, in the end, was Harriet Beecher Stowe's defining trait. Like all of her siblings, she worked hard to live up to her father's expectations. At the same time, Stowe modified – if not rejected outright – many of the messages he sought so strenuously to impart. By the 1850s, she had become an immediate abolitionist, who publicly advocated a Christocentric theology that was closer to her father's liberal Boston adversaries than his modified Calvinism. Nonetheless, Stowe remained nominally committed to her father's modified version of Calvinism throughout his life.

In a similar fashion, Stowe stretched the boundaries of the nineteenth-century gender roles to which she had long subscribed. She agreed with her sister Catharine that the most important role a woman could play was to be a mother and caregiver in the home. When *Uncle Tom's Cabin* became a blockbuster, however, Stowe was transformed into a public figure, assuming a position of international prominence that implicitly challenged separate spheres ideology. Soon, Stowe assumed an active, though calibrated, role in the political realm. In response to Stephen Douglas's Kansas-Nebraska bill, she insisted that it was the "duty" of American women to use their "social influence" in the burgeoning sectional crisis. Stowe then did her best to live up to this admonition, helping to distribute two anti-Nebraska Act petitions – one to men, the other to women – that spring. For the rest of the decade she would keep one foot well placed in the political struggle against slavery.[110]

Stowe's characteristic ambiguity was on full display in *Uncle Tom's Cabin*. In contrast to the invective that poured forth each week from the pages of Garrison's *Liberator*, Stowe balanced her trenchant critique of southern slavery with a sensitive portrayal of the burdens faced by slaveholders. She embraced – and through sheer popularity, her novel did much to reinforce – troubling stereotypes about, and caricatures of, African

---

[109] HBS, *Dred*, 353–354; Meer, *Uncle Tom Mania*, 227–228.
[110] HBS, "An Appeal to Women of the Free States of America, on the Present Crisis in Our Country," in *OSR*, 455–456; Reynolds, *Mightier than the Sword*, 161–165; Hedrick, *Harriet Beecher Stowe*, 255–256; Stoneham, *In the Shadow of John Brown*, 153.

Americans. But the broader message of *Uncle Tom's Cabin* worked to undermine racial barriers by convincing her readers that all people, even the enslaved, shared a common humanity. Unwilling to follow her fellow New Romantics completely down the perfectionist rabbit hole, she nonetheless created fictional characters that appeared more than human. Tom and Eva's tragic deaths and the Harrises' successful quest for freedom, in turn, underline the novelist's mixed feelings about the most effective means to combat slavery, at least for those with African ancestry. She held in mind two models of romantic heroism: sentimental martyrs, with whom her audience could emotionally identify, and resistant rebels, a more conventionally romantic archetype to which she had been attracted since childhood. Stowe's abolitionist masterpiece, in the end, betrayed a divided heart when it came to solving the problem of slavery.

To its many readers, however, *Uncle Tom's Cabin* was nothing if not clear-cut. Martin Robison Delany, for instance, was convinced that the novel was a colonizationist manifesto, which was rooted in the white author's inability to imagine a future for African Americans in the United States. Yet, in a telling twist, this New Romantic had his own doubts about blacks' place in the nation. Indeed, as we shall see in the next chapter, Delany spent the better part of the 1850s and early 1860s formulating and promoting a plan to build a black enclave abroad.

4

African Dreams, American Realities: Martin Robison Delany and the Emigration Question

In the fall of 1850, as thousands of African Americans were streaming north to Canada for fear that a slave catcher might turn up at their door, Martin Robison Delany went to Harvard.[1] A black abolitionist from Pittsburgh, Delany had been studying and practicing medicine on and off for nearly two decades. No longer burdened by his duties as co-editor of the *North Star*, Delany hoped to follow in the footsteps of James McCune Smith to earn a formal medical degree. Smith had sailed to Glasgow to study medicine; Delany charted a shorter, though far choppier, course. He became one of the first African Americans to attend medical school in the United States.

Harvard was not Delany's first option. By the time he arrived in Boston, he had already been denied admission to medical schools in Pennsylvania and New York. Even nearby Berkshire Medical College – which had recently enrolled several students of color who planned to practice medicine in Liberia – said no. The Massachusetts school refused to educate blacks who intended to stay in the United States and Delany had no plans to move abroad. The dean at Berkshire advised Delany to apply in person to his counterpart at Harvard Medical College, and so, the following day, the black reformer walked into the office of Oliver Wendell Holmes Sr., armed with seventeen letters of recommendation. An imposing figure with ties to half a dozen established New England

[1] Henry Bibb to William Lloyd Garrison, Nov. 20, 1850, in the *Liberator*, Dec. 13, 1850; Hiram Wilson to Garrison, December 4, 1850, in the *Liberator*, Dec. 13, 1850; Fred Landon, "The Negro Migration to Canada after the Passing of the Fugitive Slave Act," *Journal of Negro History* 5 (Jan. 1920): 22 and Robin W. Winks, *The Blacks in Canada: A History, 2nd Edition* (Montreal: McGill-Queen's University Press, 1997), 233–240.

families, Holmes was as comfortable writing poetry as he was dissecting a cadaver. He was, in short, the textbook definition of a Boston Brahmin; he even coined the phrase.[2]

The stocky, jet-black man who sat across from Holmes had a reputation of his own. In the past decade, Delany had edited two newspapers and lectured across the North on the antislavery circuit. The recommendations he brought with him testified both to his medical talents and to his character. One letter from a Pennsylvania doctor with whom Delany had studied implored, "You will subserve the cause of science, justice and humanity if you will accord him the full benefits of Your Institution."[3] Dean Holmes, it seems, agreed, as the thirty-eight-year-old abolitionist soon joined Harvard Medical College's course of lectures, which were already under way.[4]

Just days after Delany was admitted, a Kentucky classmate started making "a fuss."[5] Delany was not the only black face in the lecture hall that winter, to be sure. Isaac H. Snowden and Daniel Laing Jr., African American students who were sponsored by the American Colonization Society (ACS) and planned to emigrate to Liberia once they finished their two terms of study, had attended classes for several weeks without eliciting any formal protests. But Delany's decision to join them appears to have been too much to handle for the Kentuckian and a number of

[2] Holmes's 1861 novel *Elise Venner* tells the story of a former medical student from the "Brahmin caste of New England." Oliver Wendell Holmes, *Elsie Venner: A Romance of Destiny*, in *The Works of Oliver Wendell Holmes* (Boston: Houghton, Mifflin, 1892), 5: 4; Menand, *Metaphysical Club*, 6.

[3] William Lloyd Garrison to Helen E. Garrison, Aug. 16, 1847, in *WGL*, 3: 510–511; Frank [Frances] A. Rollin, *Life and Public Services of Martin R. Delany, Sub-Assistant Commissioner Bureau Relief of Refugees, Freedmen, and of Abandoned Lands, and Late Major 104th U. S. Colored Troops* (1868; repr., New York: Arno Press, 1969), 22; Francis J. LeMoyne, quoted in Ullman, *Martin R. Delany*, 114.

[4] Edwin P. Hoyt, *The Improper Bostonian: Dr. Oliver Wendell Holmes* (New York: William Morrow and Co., 1979), 143–146; *Chronotype*, Dec. 7, 1850, reprinted in *Liberator*, Dec. 27, 1850. My account of Delany's experience at Harvard draws on Nora N. Nercessian, *Against All Odds: The Legacy of Students of African Descent at Harvard Medical School before Affirmative Action, 1850–1968* (Hollis, NH: Harvard Medical School and Puritan Press, 2004), 7–23; Doris Y. Wilkinson, "The 1850s Harvard Medical Dispute and the Admission of African American Students," *Harvard Library Bulletin*, New Series, 3 (Fall 1992), 13–27; Philip Cash, "Pride, Prejudice, and Politics," in *Blacks at Harvard: A Documentary History of African-American Experience at Harvard and Radcliffe*, ed. Werner Sollors, Caldwell Titcomb, and Thomas A. Underwood (New York: New York University Press, 1993), 22–31, Ullman, *Martin R. Delany*, 113–121; and Sterling, *Making of an Afro-American*, 122–135.

[5] Joseph Tracey to William McClain, Dec. 25, 1850, quoted in Ullman, *Martin R. Delany*, 117.

his colleagues. After several hastily organized meetings, about a third of the class signed a resolution that deemed "the admission of blacks to the medical Lectures highly detrimental to the interests, and welfare, of the Institution of which we are members." They worried that the black students would tarnish Harvard's reputation and complained about being forced to attend class alongside people with whom they would not even dine. Although a larger contingent of students dissented from this petition, the faculty agreed to consider the matter.[6]

The faculty initially refused to buckle, but after a few weeks they forged a hollow compromise. Delany, Laing, and Snowden were permitted to complete the winter term, although they would not be allowed to enroll for the required second term. "The presence of colored persons at the Medical Lectures had proved a source of irritation and distraction during the present session more general and serious than might have been apprehended," explained the faculty. A letter sent by fifteen students who threatened to leave Harvard "in the event of negroes being allowed again to become members of the school" surely played a role in this decision.[7]

Despite Boston's reputation as the epicenter of American reform, this expulsion went largely unchallenged, at least in public. Local abolitionists circulated a petition that protested Harvard's unwillingness to "open the classes of the Undergraduates and those of the Schools of Theology, Law, Medicine and Science, to all persons, without distinction of color." Yet this petition – which did not mention Delany, Laing, or Snowden by name – went nowhere. It took nearly two decades for black students to be admitted again into Harvard Medical School.[8]

As far as we know, Delany never wrote about his Boston winter of discontent.[9] Doubtless it reinforced his growing alienation from the United

[6] *Chronotype*, Dec. 7, 1850, reprinted in the *Liberator*, Dec. 27, 1850; "Second Series of Resolutions," [Dec. 10, 1850], reprinted in Wilkinson, "1850s Harvard Medical Dispute," 21; *Boston Daily Journal*, Dec. 19, 1850. The news that the faculty admitted the medical college's first female student also played a role in the protests. *Boston Medical and Surgical Journal* 43 (Dec. 18, 1850): 406.

[7] *Boston Daily Journal*, Dec. 17, 1850; Harvard Medical School faculty to the American Colonization Society, [December 1850], reprinted in Wilkinson, "1850s Harvard Medical Dispute," 24; Letter to the Medical Faculty of Harvard University, n.d., quoted in Wilkinson, "1850s Harvard Medical Dispute," 26.

[8] *Liberator*, Mar. 7, 1851; Wilkinson, "1850s Harvard Medical Dispute," 27.

[9] Our understanding of Delany's Harvard career, like many episodes in his life and career, suffers from the paucity of extant manuscripts and correspondence written by Delany. According to early biographer Frances Rollin, many of the black reformer's private papers were destroyed in a mid-1860s fire at Wilberforce University. Rollin, *Life and Public Services*, 309.

States. After all, Harvard's decision to bow to the pressure of a disgruntled southerner and his classmates came on the heels of Congress's decision to bow to the pressure of disgruntled southern slaveholders with the passage of the new fugitive slave law. Delany thought that this odious part of the Compromise of 1850 put all African Americans in chains. "Under the operations of this bill ... no colored person can be safe," he argued at a rally in Allegheny City, Pennsylvania, just two short weeks after the fugitive slave bill became law. "*Who is to judge whether he is free or a bondsman?*" Four years later, Delany insisted that the North was so beholden to the goal of sectional harmony that a federal law legalizing slavery across the country was not far off. In a passage that could easily have been applied to his Harvard expulsion, he lamented, "Let the South but *demand* it, and the North will comply as a *duty* of compromise."[10]

As was the case with many abolitionists, the Fugitive Slave Law of 1850 elicited a bellicose outburst from Delany. In his Allegheny City address, Delany announced that he was willing to resist its enforcement, whatever the consequences. The Revolutionary generation, he told a crowd that included the town's mayor and two members of Congress, offered a lesson for those who inherited their mantle a century later: "A man has a right to defend his castle with his life, even unto the taking of life."[11] Unlike his fellow New Romantics, however, Delany quickly lost hope that runaway slaves and their allies could successfully defend their castles, even if they took up arms. Ultimately, the twin compromises of 1850 – one forged in Boston, the other in Washington – made one thing clear to the Pittsburgh abolitionist: Black Americans had no secure future in the United States, north or south. Soon Delany started calling for black emigration abroad.

Many of Delany's allies viewed this new position as a betrayal. Frederick Douglass believed that any program that sought to remove African Americans from the United States was premised on the racist notion that the country was an Anglo-Saxon nation. Hence, the Rochester abolitionist was shocked when his former partner appeared to align himself with the white-led ACS. And, truth be told, black emigration was a significant departure for Delany. Since the 1830s, he had championed

---

[10] MRD, quoted in *WPA History of the Negro in Pittsburgh*, ed. Laurence A. Glasco (Pittsburgh: University of Pittsburgh Press, 2004), 166; Richard J. M. Blackett, "' ... Freedom, or the Martyr's Grave': Black Pittsburgh's Aid to the Fugitive Slave," *Western Pennsylvania Historical Magazine* 61 (Apr. 1978): 127–128; MRD, "Political Destiny of the Colored Race on the American Continent," in Rollin, *Life and Public Services*, 360.

[11] MRD, quoted in Rollin, *Life and Public Services*, 76; Ullman, *Martin R. Delany*, 112.

black elevation within the United States as loudly as any antebellum perfectionist. Although Delany had long supported the creation of black institutions and organizations in northern communities, never did he seriously entertain the idea of leaving what he called just a few years earlier his "own native land."[12]

Delany, however, was far from a Benedict Arnold when it came to what mattered most to him. On the contrary, his belief in perfectionist self-help persisted throughout the 1850s. What changed for Delany was his optimism that the United States could prove a suitable climate for black uplift. Dismayed by personal and political disappointments of the late 1840s and early 1850s, Delany started exploring locations for a colony where African Americans could thrive. First he looked to Canada and Latin America, before settling on the Niger Valley in western Africa. By freeing blacks from the barriers that the Slave Power was so hastily erecting, Delany believed that emigration would enable African Americans to improve, if not perfect, themselves. Like Parker's flirtation with antislavery violence and Douglass's reassessment of the Constitution, black emigration was, on one level, simply a tactical shift for Delany.

Yet, as was the case with these reformers, Delany's new solution to the problems of black America bespoke new romantic points of emphasis as well. He had always felt a special tie to Africa and, like so many racial theorists of the day, Delany thought that people of African descent were a distinct people whose particular characteristics set them apart from all other races. Once prospects for black Americans grew dim in the 1850s, emigration to Africa only seemed natural to Delany.

Perhaps, he began to reason, black people simply belonged on the continent from which their non-white ancestors came. Perhaps emigration to Africa was God's plan for black Americans. Delany, in short, created a black program of Manifest Destiny, appropriating – and refashioning – the expansionist ideology made famous by groups such as the Young Americans and the southern filibusterers. In addition, like this latter group of expansionist dreamers – who tried to conquer parts of Latin America in the 1850s – Delany conjured up emigration schemes that combined elitist assumptions about native peoples with fantastical visions about what they might find, and hope to accomplish, in foreign lands. The critical difference, of course, was that unlike most filibusterers, who hoped to ensure slavery's survival by spreading it southward, Delany promised to strike a fatal blow to the institution.

[12] MRD to FD, Feb. 24, 1849, in the *North Star*, Mar. 9, 1849, reprinted in *MDR*, 134.

Notwithstanding his quixotic goals, Delany tempered his emigration plans – and his reform philosophy, more generally – with a healthy dose of realism. His promotion of black self-help, for one, reflected not only a perfectionist faith in self-improvement but also a sense of its concrete benefits. He coupled soaring appeals to human potential with sober encouragement of middle-class work ethic and behavior. In similar fashion, Delany pitched African emigration with a curious admixture of romantic symbolism and staid analysis. For these reasons, students of Delany have had trouble reaching a consensus on what he really believed or hoped to accomplish. While some scholars see the black reformer as "the founding father of black nationalism in America," others view him as a bourgeois apologist for Anglo-American values. In fact, Delany could be both – sometimes at the very same time.[13]

Delany, in other words, can appear maddeningly inconsistent to modern interpreters. Oscillating among different ideals, modes of analysis, and solutions to the problems of slavery and antebellum race relations, he followed a path that was neither straightforward nor free from internal contradiction. To some extent, this trajectory reflected the black reformer's internal tensions. Few figures better epitomized Walt Whitman's paean to the capacious self – "Do I contradict myself?/Very well then ... . I contradict myself;/I am large ... . I contain multitudes." Of course, as we have seen, intellectual inconsistency and tactical ambivalence were nothing new for a New Romantic.[14]

---

[13] Theodore Draper, *The Rediscovery of Black Nationalism* (New York: Viking Press, 1969), 40. For Delany as an early progenitor of black nationalism, see Cyril E. Griffith, *The African Dream: Martin R. Delany and the Emergence of Pan-African Thought* (University Park: Pennsylvania State University Press, 1975); Ullman, *Martin R. Delany*; Sterling, *Making of an Afro-American*; Sterling Stuckey, *The Ideological Origins of Black Nationalism* (Boston: Beacon Press, 1972); and Floyd J. Miller, *The Search for a Black Nationality: Black Emigration and Colonization, 1787–1863* (Urbana: University of Illinois Press, 1975). On Delany as an elitist or politically conservative figure, see Nell Irvin Painter, "Martin Delany, A Black Nationalist in Two Kinds of Time," *New England Journal of Black Studies* 8 (Nov. 1989): 37–47; Painter, "Martin R. Delany: Elitism and Black Nationalism," in *Black Leaders of the Nineteenth Century*, ed. Leon Litwack and August Meier (Urbana: University of Illinois Press, 1988), 149–171; Wilson Jeremiah Moses, *The Golden Age of Black Nationalism, 1850–1925* (New York: Oxford University Press, 1978); Dean E. Robinson, *Black Nationalism in American Politics and Thought* (New York: Cambridge University Press, 2011); and Tunde Adeleke, *Without Regard to Race: The Other Martin Robison Delany* (Jackson: University of Mississippi Press, 2003).
[14] Levine, Introduction to *MDR*, 6–7; Walt Whitman, *Walt Whitman's Leaves of Grass* (1855; rpt., New York; Oxford University Press, 2005), 43. For scholars who read Delany as inconsistent or ideologically malleable, see Levine, *Martin Delany, Frederick Douglass*;

What was new – at least among this group of antebellum reformers – was the idea that American prejudice was so deeply engrained in the 1850s that the only future for blacks was to leave the country. Delany, then, seemed to be moving in exactly the opposite direction of Douglass, Parker, Higginson and Stowe, in the decade leading up to the Civil War. While they mounted barricades within the United States, Delany took the antislavery fight abroad. Nevertheless, the black emigrationist worked from much the same intellectual toolbox as these allies. Despite the misgivings of his former co-editor, Delany's black colony was every bit the product of a romantic imagination as the Boston Vigilance Committee, the *North Star*, or *Uncle Tom's Cabin*.

By Any Effective Means

The youngest of five children, Martin Robison Delany was born on May 6, 1812 in Charles Town, a hamlet in northwestern Virginia. His father, Samuel Delany, was an enslaved carpenter who from an early age provided Martin with an intimate glimpse of the inhumanity of slavery. According to the laws of Virginia, however, Delany's status followed that of his free black mother, Pati Peace. Thus, from birth the black abolitionist occupied the shaky middle ground between the two conditions – slavery and freedom – that defined life in the American South.[15]

Although a tiny minority in Virginia in the early 1800s, free African Americans provoked almost as much fear in the state's white population as its large number of enslaved residents. In the wake of slave rebel Gabriel's failed 1800 uprising in Richmond, the state legislature passed harsh measures that limited gun ownership, mobility, and educational opportunities among free black residents. Collectively, these laws sent a clear message to free black Virginians: You may not be slaves, but you are far from free.[16]

Paul Gilroy, *The Black Atlantic: Modernity and Double Consciousness* (Cambridge, MA: Harvard University Press, 1993), 20; and Adeleke, *Without Regard to Race*, esp. 19–39.
[15] Ullman, *Martin R. Delany*, 1–3.
[16] Ira Berlin, *Generations of Captivity: A History of African-American Slaves* (Cambridge, MA: Belknap Press of Harvard University Press, 2003), Table 2, n.p.; Eva Sheppard Wolf, *Race and Liberty in the New Nation: Emancipation in Virginia from the Revolution to Nat Turner's Rebellion* (Baton Rouge: Louisiana State University Press, 2006), 118–127; Sylvia R. Frey, *Water from the Rock: Black Resistance in a Revolutionary Age* (Princeton, NJ: Princeton University Press, 1992), 235; Douglas R. Egerton, *Death or Liberty: African Americans and Revolutionary America* (New York: Oxford University Press, 2009), 247.

Delany's mother Pati, who had an "uppity" reputation around Charles Town according to one biographer, flouted the new restrictions. After purchasing a copy of the *New York Primer and Spelling Book* from a northern peddler, for instance, she taught her children to read and write in violation of Virginia law. Eventually, the Delany children turned their private lessons into a public game, playing school in their mother's garden for all of the white neighbors to see. Rumor of the Delany school spread swiftly through town and soon Pati was summoned to appear in the circuit court. Instead, she packed up her children and fled north, to nearby Chambersburg, Pennsylvania.[17]

Pati's refusal to delimit her children's education may have had something to do with Delany family history, for she and her husband averred royal African ancestry. Samuel's paternal grandfather claimed to have been a Golah chieftain who was captured in a raid, sold to slavers, and transported to America. Pati, too, believed she came from noble African stock. Her father insisted that he was a Mandigo prince named Shango, who hailed from the western part of the continent. Like Delany's paternal grandfather, Shango was said to have been captured, enslaved, and sent in chains to the New World. Yet, according to family lore, Shango was freed and returned to Africa once his lineage was established. Pati's mother, Graci, was also emancipated, but she chose to stay in the United States with her daughter. Several of these claims, to be fair, are far-fetched, and we have no way of knowing for certain whether they are accurate. Nonetheless, one fact is beyond dispute: Delany's perceived ties to African nobility nurtured an early attachment to the continent – an attachment that likely reinforced his determination to build a colony in the Niger Valley in the 1850s.[18]

---

[17] Sterling, *Making of an Afro-American*, 11–23 (quotation 21); Ullman, *Martin R. Delany*, 3–7; Rollin, *Life and Public Services*, 30–37.

[18] Rollin, *Life and Public Services*, 1–22; Sterling, *Making of an Afro-American*, 4–5; Ullman, *Martin R. Delany*, 4–5. Although Delany's first biographer, Frances Rollin, casts some doubt on the veracity of his royal African lineage, she concludes that the New Romantic "fully authenticated" his heritage when he visited west Africa in the late 1850s. In light of *Life and Public Services of Martin R. Delany*'s hagiographic tone and the fact that Delany helped to finance the project and provided the bulk of the biographical information that Rollin used, however, this claim – like much of her biography – should be approached with caution. Still, Rollin's biography is indispensable because of the dearth of Delany letters and manuscripts. Rollin, *Life and Public Services*, 17; William L. Andrews, introduction to *Two Biographies by African-American Women* (New York: Oxford University Press, 1991), xxxiii–xxxiv.

Pati and her children arrived in Chambersburg when Delany was ten years old. By the following year, 1823, Samuel Delany had purchased his freedom and followed his family there. Although far from the promised land, Pennsylvania afforded the newcomers opportunities they were denied in Virginia. Most importantly, now the Delany children could attend school legally. Thriving in the classroom, Martin Delany spent the next four years studying spelling, grammar, American history, and public speaking. He read Aesop's fables, Shakespeare, and Thomas Jefferson. By the end of the decade, Delany had exhausted his educational opportunities in Chambersburg. He spent the next few working his way through a number of odd jobs in central Pennsylvania before heading west to Pittsburgh (Figure 4.1).[19]

Not yet twenty, Delany quickly found a place in the city's black reform circles. He joined the African Education Society, the Moral Reform Society, and the Pittsburgh Anti-Slavery Society. Delany took particular pride in his work with the Philanthropic Society, a vigilance society that assisted poor blacks who lived in Pittsburgh as well as runaway slaves who made their way to western Pennsylvania. The newcomer also cofounded Pittsburgh organizations dedicated to African American education and uplift. The Theban Literary Society, named for the ancient Egyptian city, reflected his immersion in classical Greek and Roman philosophy as well as his lifelong desire to demonstrate the African roots of Western civilization. In 1837, Delany and fifteen others transformed the Theban Literary Society into the Young Men's Literary and Moral Reform Society, which sought to promote "the literary, moral and intellectual improvement of the young and rising generation, the establishment of a library, the promotion of education and morality and instruction in the mechanical arts."[20] Like many romantic reformers, black as well as white, Delany put the perfectionist ideal of self-culture at the center of his social activism.

Delany's first teacher in Pittsburgh, Reverend Lewis Woodson, likely played a role in this emphasis on self-improvement. A leading player in most of the city's black reform organizations, Woodson urged African Americans to improve themselves morally, intellectually, and economically, insisting that "CONDITION and not *color*, is the chief cause of the prejudice, under which we suffer." He placed special emphasis on

[19] Sterling, *Making of an Afro-American*, 24–34; Ullman, *Martin R. Delany*, 5–8.
[20] Ullman, *Martin R. Delany*, 20–31; Sterling, *Making of an Afro-American*, 35–47; Rollin, *Life and Public Services*, 39; Levine, *Martin Delany, Frederick Douglass*, 25; *Colored American*, Sept. 2, 1837.

MAJOR MARTIN R. DELANEY, U. S. A.

FIGURE 4.1. Major Martin Robison Delany, ca. 1865.
Source: Unknown. Courtesy of the Photography Collection, Miriam and Ira D.
Wallach Division of Art, Prints, and Photographs, The New York Public Library,
Astor, Lenox, and Tilden Foundations.

the virtues of hard work, sobriety, and refinement for young African
Americans who sought to improve their lot in life.[21]

Woodson's young protégée echoed these ideas as he became a more
active reformer in the 1830s and 1840s. Delany agreed that racial

---

[21] *Colored American*, Feb. 16, 1839; Miller, *Search for a Black Nationality*, 94–98; Adeleke,
Without Regard to Race, 48.

injustice was not rooted in "the ridiculousness and absurdity of prejudice against color" but rather "prejudice against condition." He also shared his mentor's concern for maintaining Victorian standards of etiquette, decorum, even hygiene. "Of all things in the world, for heaven's sake, give me cleanliness," Delany later wrote. "I see no good reason why people may not be cleanly about their houses and with their persons."[22]

The weight that Delany attached to bourgeois matters like manners and hygiene can make him appear "prissy" to modern scholars.[23] Yet the black reformer leavened such Booker-T.-Washingtonian tributes to cleanliness with Emersonian paeans to the human potential for greatness. Like Douglass, Delany developed a philosophy of black self-help that dovetailed with the romantic theories emanating from Boston and Concord. Delany worried, for instance, that African Americans, inspired by religious lessons of patience and forbearance, succumbed too easily to passive frames of mind. "Brethren," Delany urged black readers of the *North Star* in 1849, "our object is to set you to thinking – thinking *for* yourselves." Earlier that decade, Emerson had a similar point in his seminal essay "Self-Reliance." "To believe your own thought," he wrote, "to believe that what is true for you in your private heart is true for all men, – that is genius."[24]

If Delany echoed Emerson's essay "Self-Reliance," then he anticipated one of the most popular tracts published by the Transcendentalist's Harvard teacher, William Ellery Channing. Based on an 1838 lecture honoring Benjamin Franklin, Channing's "Self-Culture" – as we saw in Chapter 2 – framed individual improvement as a gradual, organic process. Addressed to those "who are occupied by manual labor," the tract also emphasized the democratic implications of self-culture. Channing believed that the United States provided its citizens unsurpassed opportunities for personal elevation, concluding that "in this country the mass

---

[22] MRD to FD, Mar. 22, 1848, in the *North Star*, Apr. 7, 1848; MRD to FD, June 18, 1848, in the *North Star*, July 7, 1848.

[23] Levine, *Martin Delany, Frederick Douglass*, 36.

[24] MRD, "Domestic Economy," [Part I], *North Star*, Mar. 23, 1849, in *MDR*, 151; MRD, "Domestic Economy," [Part II], *North Star*, Apr. 13, 1849, in *MDR*, 153; Ralph Waldo Emerson, "Self-Reliance," in *Emerson's Complete Writings* (New York: H. Wise and Co., 1923), 1: 48. For a perceptive re-interpretation of Booker T. Washington's emphasis on cleanliness and personal hygiene, see Peter A. Coclanis, "What Made Booker Wash(ington)? The Wizard of Tuskegee in Economic Context," in *Booker T. Washington and Black Progress: Up From Slavery 100 Years Later*, ed. W. Fitzhugh Brundage (Gainesville: University Press of Florida, 2003), 81–106.

of the people are distinguished by possessing means of improvement, of self-culture, nowhere else."²⁵

Almost a decade earlier, Delany and his colleagues in Pittsburgh's African Education Society had crafted a constitution that applied democratic self-culture to all Americans, regardless of color. In 1831, they insisted that "the intellectual capacity of the black man is equal to that of the white … he is equally susceptible of improvement."²⁶ Delany and company, in other words, not only shared the perfectionist sensibility – which was popular from Boston to the burned-over district of western New York – they took it a step further. By suggesting that people of every hue possessed the capacity for moral, spiritual, and physical growth, they challenged racial mores of the day, making clear the radical social implications of perfectionism.

Delany did not believe that perfectionist self-help alone would solve the problems of black Americans, however. So, the Pittsburgh abolitionist became involved in political agitation at an early age – far earlier, in fact, than his fellow New Romantics. While first-generation romantic reformers like Garrison were arguing that active participation in the political system amounted to an endorsement of state violence, Delany insisted that the right of suffrage was sacrosanct. In 1841, he organized a statewide black convention to protest Pennsylvania's recent decision to restrict the vote – a privilege that some black male citizens had enjoyed in the state for decades – to white men alone. Defending suffrage on moral and practical grounds, the convention framed the vote as simultaneously a political tool and a measure of a citizen's worth to society. Delany also campaigned actively for the Liberty Party in the 1840s, despite its moderate platform, which called for emancipation in the District of Columbia, the abolition of the interstate slave trade, and an end to the admission of slave states, but little else.²⁷

²⁵ Channing, *Self-Culture*, 3, 6; Howe, *Making the American Self*, 132–133; Rael, *Black Identity and Black Protest*, 131; Adeleke, *Without Regard to Race*, 42–46.

²⁶ African Education Society Constitution, quoted in Sterling, *Making of an Afro-American*, 41–42.

²⁷ Proceedings of the State Convention of the Colored Freemen of Pennsylvania, Held in Pittsburgh, on the 23rd, 24th, and 25th of August, 1841, for the Purpose of Considering Their Condition, and the Means of Its Improvement," in *Proceedings of the Black State Conventions, 1840–1865, Vol. 1: New York, Pennsylvania, Indiana, Michigan, Ohio,* ed. Philip S. Foner and George E. Walker (Philadelphia: Temple University Press, 1979), 106–109; Levine, *Martin Delany, Frederick Douglass*, 25–26; Leon F. Litwack, *North of Slavery: The Negro in the Free States, 1790–1860* (Chicago: University of Chicago Press, 1961), 84–87; Sterling, *Making of an Afro-American*, 75–76; Ullman, *Martin R. Delany,* 40; Johnson, *Liberty Party,* 153–154, 247, 250; Stewart, *Holy Warriors,* 97–104; Howe,

In the same period, Delany sought to expand his reform efforts beyond Pittsburgh by founding two antislavery weeklies: the *Mystery* and later, with Frederick Douglass, the *North Star*. Delany continued to work as a cupper, leecher, and bleeder for Pittsburgh's black community, but he spent the bulk of his time on these ambitious journalistic endeavors. The *Mystery* devoted itself to destroying slavery while also working for "the Moral Elevation of the Africo-American and African race, civilly, politically and religiously." Reflecting its editor's desire to promote the African roots of Western intellectual and cultural traditions, the four-page paper's initial motto was: "AND MOSES WAS LEARNED IN ALL THE WISDOM OF THE EGPYPTIANS."[28]

The *North Star* enabled him to work for black emancipation and elevation on a larger stage. As such, it was an early step toward assuming the national leadership role to which he aspired – a goal that became increasingly important to the reformer over the next decade. Although nominally a co-editor of the new paper, Delany's duties were closer to those of correspondent and subscription agent. He spent most of his year-and-a-half tenure spreading abolitionist gospel, hawking *North Star* subscriptions, and surveying social conditions in states such as Ohio, Pennsylvania, and Michigan. Delany, in other words, served the *North Star* in much the same fashion as Douglass had served the *Liberator* just a few years earlier. But if the *North Star* was really Douglass's paper, Delany still carved an important space in the new journal by writing a series of lengthy letters as he traveled from town to town. These dispatches from his "Western tour," which he sent back to the *North Star* for publication every few weeks, kept Douglass – and, more importantly, the readers of the *North Star* – abreast of his efforts and observations. Moreover, as Robert Levine has convincingly argued, they functioned as a travel narrative, a genre for which nineteenth-century romantics demonstrated a particular affinity.[29]

What Hath God Wrought, 651–653. On black disenfranchisement in Pennsylvania, see Eric Ledell Smith, "The End of Black Voting Rights in Pennsylvania: African Americans and the Pennsylvania Constitutional Convention of 1837–1838," *Pennsylvania History* 65 (Summer 1997): 279–299; and Nicholas Wood, "'A Sacrifice on the Altar of Slavery': Doughface Politics and Black Disenfranchisement in Pennsylvania, 1837–1838," *Journal of the Early Republic* 31 (Spring 2011): 75–106.

[28] MRD, "Prospectus of the *Mystery*," *Mystery*, Dec. 16, 1846, in *MDR*, 30; quoted in Ullman, *Martin R. Delany*, 60.

[29] *North Star*, Jan. 21, 1848; Ullman, *Martin R. Delany*, 81; Levine, *Martin Delany, Frederick Douglass*, 32–33. This section is indebted to Levine's thoughtful reading of Delany's western dispatches. Levine, *Martin Delany, Frederick Douglass*, 32–48.

A popular literary form since the eighteenth century, travel writing was ideally suited to romantic minds. Years before he wrote his masterpiece *Moby-Dick*, Herman Melville penned captivating stories about adventures at sea. Margaret Fuller sought inspiration by traveling through the American West, a journey she recounted in *Summer on the Lakes*. Meanwhile, Fuller's Transcendentalist peer Henry David Thoreau wrote a handful of books – including *Walden* and *Cape Cod* – centered around one sort of romantic excursion or another. Whether real or imagined, focused primarily on internal exploration or losing oneself on the high seas, romantic travel narratives abounded in antebellum America.[30]

Delany's dispatches from the West, to be fair, devoted far less time to spiritual introspection than those written by Melville, Fuller, or Thoreau. One exception is Delany's final letter. Upon returning home to Pittsburgh in early 1849 after touring the Ohio and Pennsylvania countryside for the better part of a year, the *North Star* agent wrote a lengthy account of his experiences crossing the Allegheny Mountains. "These mountains," he noted at the start of his letter, "though common to every traveller from eastern to western Pennsylvania … are so novel and romantic in their appearance and arrangement, and withal so tedious to travel, that a cursory description of them may not be amiss." After carefully describing the Alleghenies, Delany lingered on the spiritual benefits that might accrue from a journey through the range:

It is worth the trip to those who have the means to travel, as the tediousness is lost in contemplation of the scenery around. The soul may here expand in the magnitude of its nature, and soar to the extent of human susceptibility. Indeed, it is only in the mountains that I can fully appreciate my existence as a man in America, my own native land. It is then and there my soul is lifted up, my bosom caused to swell with emotion, and I am lost in wonder at the dignity of my own nature. I see in the works of nature around me, the wisdom and goodness of God. I contemplate them, and conscious that he has endowed me with faculties to comprehend them, I perceive the likeness I bear to him. What a being is man! – of how much importance! – created in the impress image of his Maker.

This remarkable passage, which is so unlike anything else in his western letters, captures Delany in his most romantic vein. According to literary critic George Parks, nothing in the natural world inspired as much

---

[30] Buell, *Literary Transcendentalism*, 188–207; Charles Capper, *Margaret Fuller: An American Romantic Life, Volume II: The Public Years* (New York: Oxford University Press, 2007), 123–156.

outpouring of romantic travel writing as mountain scenery. This is certainly true for Delany, who viewed the Alleghenies, if not mountains in general, as the key to unlocking the perfectionist potential that lay dormant in the human heart. Delany's dispatch piles one evocative image on top of another – his soul expands and soars, his bosom swells with emotion, he begins to appreciate his place in his native land – before culminating with a crescendo that intertwines the individual, the natural world, and the divine. The majesty of both the Allegheny Mountains and God's infinite wisdom and grace seem to empower Delany; in their shadow, he does not feel insignificant but rather formidable. Like Parker, Douglass, and even Stowe on occasion, Delany found celestial potential in his human heart.[31]

Such moments of romantic introspection were few and far between for the *North Star* correspondent, however. More often, Delany's "Western tour" letters were detailed accounts of the challenging social, economic, and political conditions faced by black communities from Wilmington, Delaware, to Detroit, Michigan. Although he noted that some of these communities appeared to be thriving against all odds, his tour as a whole undermined his faith in the reform solutions – self-help, moral suasion, political agitation – Delany had promoted since the 1830s. Increasingly, a more militant response to slavery and racial prejudice seemed warranted.[32]

This new position put Delany at odds with the *North Star*'s pacifist principles. Unlike Douglass, Delany had never pledged himself to nonviolence. Three years before they started working together, in fact, Delany had changed the *Mystery*'s motto to "HEREDITARY BONDSMEN! KNOW YE NOT WHO WOULD BE FREE, THEMSELVES MUST STRIKE THE BLOW." Trading in his appeal to Africa's rich cultural heritage for Byron's militant call to arms, Delany anticipated a move that his New Romantic peers would make in the decade that followed.[33]

---

[31] MRD to FD, Feb. 24, 1849, in the *North Star*, Mar. 9, 1849, reprinted in *MDR*, 133, 134; Levine, *Martin Delany, Frederick Douglass*, 47–48; George B. Parks, "The Turn to the Romantic in the Travel Literature of the Eighteenth Century," *Modern Language Quarterly* 25 (Mar. 1964): 27.

[32] MRD to FD, June 18, 1848, in the *North Star*, July 7, 1848, reprinted in *MDR*, 100; MD to FD, Nov. 18, 1848, in the *North Star*, Dec. 1, 1848, reprinted in *MDR*, 124; MRD to FD, May 7, 1848, in the *North Star*, May 26, 1848, reprinted in *MDR*, 93; MRD to FD, July 14, 1848, in the *North Star*, July 28, 1848, reprinted in *MDR*, 109–115.

[33] Quoted in Ullman, *Martin R. Delany*, 61; Levine, *Martin Delany, Frederick Douglass*, 27.

Delany grew even more militant during his "Western tour." In early 1848, he pushed Douglass to admit that moral suasion was impotent in the face of a slaveholder bent on violating his family members, while pledging, for his part, to use "any effective means" to stop such advances. Later that year, after escaping a white mob in Marseilles, Ohio, he proposed a resolution at a black convention that advised free blacks to study "military tactics ... so as to enable them to measure arms with assailants *without* and invaders within."[34] Then, the following spring, he urged American slaves to join "the oppressed of every nation" in a global war for freedom. "Let him be taught that he dare strike for liberty," advised Delany, "let him know this, and he at once rises up disenthralled – a captive redeemed from the portals of infamy to the true dignity of his nature – an elevated freeman." Although this final line evokes Douglass's famous fight with Covey, Delany knew that his Rochester counterpart would not endorse his militant sentiments. So, he quickly added that this endorsement of slave rebellion was his alone.[35]

Just two months later, Douglass made it clear that such qualifiers were no longer necessary. In the June 29 issue of the *North Star*, he announced that "after the present number, by a mutual understanding with our esteemed friend and coadjutor, M. R. DELANY, the whole responsibility of editing and publishing the NORTH STAR, will devolve upon myself." It is not entirely clear why Delany brought his brief tenure at the *North Star* to a close. Perhaps it was a financial decision. Just the year before Douglass had blamed the paper's mounting debt on Delany's shortcomings as a subscription agent. The departure may also have reflected an emerging rivalry between Douglass and Delany over who was going to be the leading voice in black America. Whatever the case, Delany no longer had to strike a balance between burgeoning militancy, on the one hand, and the ideological commitments of his partners at the *North Star*, on the other. At the dawn of the 1850s, he was free to go wherever his conscience took him.[36]

---

[34] MRD to FD, Feb. 6, 1848, in the *North Star*, Feb. 18, 1848, reprinted in *MDR*, 81; *North Star*, Sept. 29, 1848; Sterling, *Making of an Afro-American*, 111–112. On Delany's experience in Marseilles, see MRD to FD, July 1, 1848, in the *North Star*, July 14, 1848, reprinted in *MDR*, 106–107.

[35] MRD, "Annexation of Cuba," *North Star*, Apr. 27, 1849, reprinted in *MDR*, 165; FD, *Narrative*, 54.

[36] *North Star*, June 29, 1849; Frederick Douglass to Julia Griffiths, Apr. 28, 1848, in *FDPC*, 1: 302–303; Levine, *Martin Delany, Frederick Douglass*, 48–57.

Colonization Fever

Delany welcomed the new decade with raised fists. When the new fugitive slave bill became the law of the land in September, his posture only became more aggressive. Delany said that he would defy the measure at all costs. At a large rally just outside of Pittsburgh, he justified resistance based on the nation's revolutionary tradition. "Honorable mayor," began Delany in an address that anticipated the outsider posture stance that Douglass employed so effectively two years later in his Fifth of July address, "whatever ideas of liberty I may have, have been received from reading the lives of your revolutionary fathers." Delany then explained that he would follow the martial example of the founding generation, regardless of who tried to enforce the law.

If any man approaches [my] house, whether constable or sheriff, magistrate or even judge of the Supreme Court ..., – if he crosses the threshold of my door, and I do not lay him a lifeless corpse at my feet, I hope the grave may refuse my body a resting-place, and righteous Heaven my spirit a home. O, no! he cannot enter [my] house and we both live.[37]

Neither political office, nor force of law, in his mind, legitimated the Fugitive Slave Law of 1850. Few abolitionists took so strident a public stance against the new measure.

In the coming years, Delany proved that he was willing to do more than just talk the talk when it came to resisting slave catchers. In June 1853, he partnered with six others to form an impromptu vigilance committee that helped rescue a fourteen-year-old Jamaican boy who had been lured to the United States by stories of American opportunity. Tennessean Thomas J. Adams had hoped to kidnap the black teenager and sell him into slavery, but the vigilance committee intercepted the boy at the Pittsburgh train depot and helped local officials arrest the would-be kidnapper. Although Adams escaped before he could be put on trial, Delany and three others wrote a letter to the editor of the *Kingston Morning Journal*, warning its readers of this new practice of luring black Jamaican youths to America under false pretenses. By extending masters' hands into the North, they warned, the fugitive slave law made the entire United States slave country: "No colored person in the United States is really free; all are virtually and legally, if not abjectly, slaves. Bury your bones

---

[37] MRD, quoted in Rollin, *Life and Public Services*, 76.

in the sunny clime of your own beautiful isles, rather than come to this *slaveholding, oppressing* country."[38]

Truth be told, Delany had recently started thinking about burying his own bones in the sunny clime of those beautiful isles. The events of the early 1850s only magnified the frustration he had felt a few years earlier while traveling across Pennsylvania, Ohio, and Michigan. First came the new fugitive slave law. Then came Delany's disappointing term at the Harvard Medical School in Boston, where the prejudices of classmates torpedoed his plan to earn a medical degree just as the prejudices of the nation as a whole jeopardized the liberty of black citizens more generally. Adding insult to these injuries, in late 1851, a "distinguished patent attorney" induced Delany to abandon his pursuit of a patent for a device he had invented to move locomotives up steep hills. The attorney told the New Romantic that black Americans, lacking citizenship rights, could not be granted patents in the United States.[39] Increasingly feeling like an outsider wherever he went and whatever he did, Delany began to entertain the idea of emigrating abroad. This was no small thing.

Proposals to solve America's racial problems by removing its African American residents had long been a bugbear of the nation's black community. Colonization's most vigorous proponent in the antebellum period was the ACS, which hoped to remove blacks to Africa. Founded in 1816, the ACS functioned as a big tent when it came to the vexing issue of slavery. Some members hoped African colonization would help destroy slavery in the young republic, while others believed it would shore up the institution by removing troublesome free blacks. The ACS eventually drew the imprimatur of leading clergymen and politicians (including Lyman Beecher, Daniel Webster, and Henry Clay), attracted private and public funding, and established the African colony of Liberia. Under its auspices, approximately six thousand black Americans were emancipated and sent to Liberia between 1820 and 1860.[40]

The ACS and similar colonization efforts proved unpopular with most free blacks from the start. Just months after the organization was founded, African Americans gathered in the District of Columbia, Richmond, and Philadelphia to voice their opposition. Colonization to them was little

---

[38] MRD, et al., to Editor, *Kingston Morning Journal*, May 31, 1853, in *Saturday Visitor*, June 4, 1863, reprinted in *BAP*, 4: 160. Delany later helped to lead one of Canada's most active vigilance groups, the Chatham Vigilance Committee. *BAP*, 2: 29.

[39] Rollin, *Life and Public Services*, 77–78.

[40] Burin, *Slavery and the Peculiar Solution*, x, 1–2, 7, 14; Davis, *Inhuman Bondage*, 256–258.

more than a proslavery attempt to protect the institution's future by eliminating the most vocal opponents of slavery: free blacks. Denouncing the racial assumptions upon which the ACS was constructed, they swore never to separate themselves from their enslaved brethren.[41]

Delany, too, was a strong critic of the ACS. He believed that the organization sought "the exile and expatriation of the entire free colored population and the decrepit helpless slaves." The New Romantic hoped the forces of cosmic justice would wreak havoc on the ACS. Evoking the harrowing imagery of the Middle Passage to undermine the proposed "return" to Africa, Delany declared:

Let the angry storms and beating winds refuse the unjust and cruel transportation; let the dark and crowning clouds of Heaven threaten the scheme with annihilation; let the thundering howls and terrific motion of this raging hurricane reject the wanton traffic, and the repulsive waves of the uncontrollable ocean dash back the putrid carcasses of their deluded victims to the American coast, to bleach and decay upon the soil, enriched by their sweat and blood![42]

Despite this deep antipathy for colonization, Delany occasionally praised ACS initiatives, especially when they provided black leadership roles. In 1846, he wrote positively about a shipping company founded by members of the Maryland State Colonization Society, which aimed to become black owned and operated. Two years later, he celebrated Liberia's declaration of independence, telling Douglass that the republic "is determined to exist without a *master* and *overseer* ... and for this, she is lauded to the skies as an evidence of the capacity of the colored man for self-government." Nevertheless, Delany remained an inveterate opponent of the ACS into the 1850s, when he characterized colonization as a "hydra-headed monster," which "originated in the South, by slaveholders ... and still continues to be carried on under the garb of philanthropy and Christianity, through the medium of the basest deception and hypocrisy."[43]

[41] Miller, *Search for a Black Nationality*, 48–49; Newman, *Freedom's Prophet*, 204; Horton and Horton, *In Hope of Liberty*, 187–190; Davis, *Inhuman Bondage*, 258.

[42] MRD, quoted in Sterling, *Making of an Afro-American*, 89.

[43] Miller, *Search for a Black Nationality*, 119–120; Tomek, *Colonization and Its Discontents*, 202–203; MRD to FD, Jan. 21, 1848, in the *North Star*, Feb. 4, 1848, reprinted in *MDR*, 77; and MRD, "Liberia," *North Star*, Mar. 2, 1849, reprinted in *MDR*, 147; MRD, *The Condition, Elevation, Emigration, and Destiny of the Colored People of the United States* (1852; repr., New York: Arno Press, 1968), 35; MRD, Introduction to William Nesbitt, *Four Months in Liberia* (1855; repr., New York: Arno Press, 1969), 81.

The compromises of 1850, however, got the Pittsburgh activist wondering whether he had too quickly dismissed the idea of leaving the United States. In 1851, he attended the North American Convention of Emigrationists, which promoted "the emigration of free people from the United States, for the settlement of Canada land." Although the convention was careful to distinguish between colonization to Africa, which it deemed "prejudicial against color and pro-slavery," and black-initiated emigration, Delany joined a group of dissenters who argued that emigration was "impolitic."[44]

Despite these protestations, suspicions of Delany's emigration drift were in the air. In January 1852, the Brooklyn correspondent for *Frederick Douglass' Paper* provocatively questioned whether the Pittsburgh reformer has "got the Colonization fever." Reporting on a recent meeting, the correspondent wrote, Delany's "symptoms were strange, and curious inferences have been drawn, who will answer?" Three months later, Delany pleaded a clean bill of health, so to speak, when he volunteered to chair an anti-colonization committee that dismissed "mischievous schemes" to remove blacks from the country. After pledging allegiance to their "native land ... the land of our birth," the group advised their "brethren to stand firm, and contend for 'Life, Liberty and Happiness' in the United States."[45]

But the matter was not settled. Indeed, that very month – April 1852 – Delany published *The Condition, Elevation, Emigration, and Destiny of the Colored People of the United States Politically Considered*, which proposed that black Americans pursue their inalienable rights abroad. Hastily penned in New York City, this powerful appeal for black migration outlined the obstacles African Americans faced, their achievements despite limited opportunities, and, finally, a plan of emigration to Latin America.[46]

In some sections of the book, the New Romantic seemed to single African Americans out as the root of the nation's racial problems. Too often, he argued, blacks let their religious nature get the best of them: "They usually stand still – hope in God, and really expect Him to do that for them, which it is necessary they should do themselves." Over the course of the book as a whole, however, Delany placed blame on

[44] *Voice of the Fugitive*, Aug. 27, 1851; *Voice of the Fugitive*, Sept. 24, 1851.
[45] *Frederick Douglass' Paper*, Jan. 8, 1852; *Frederick Douglass' Paper*, Apr. 29, 1852.
[46] Levine, *Martin Delany, Frederick Douglass*, 61; MRD, *Condition, Elevation, Emigration, and Destiny*, 7.

a hypocritical white nation rather than its black victims. "The United States, untrue to her trust and unfaithful to her professed principles of republican equality, has also pursued a policy of political degradation to a large portion of her native born countrymen, and that class is the Colored People," he wrote. "Denied an equality not only of political, but of natural rights, in common with the rest of our fellow citizens, there is no species of degradation to which we are not subject."[47]

The Fugitive Slave Law of 1850, Delany held, was the culmination of this discriminatory pattern. He reproduced the new law in full and then offered his most detailed explication of the challenges it posed to black freedom. "The most prominent provisions of the Constitution," argued Delany, are those that guarantee its citizenry's person and property. Yet the fugitive slave law violated the Constitution's egalitarian foundations, transforming the black community – north and south, enslaved and free – into a politically impotent "nation within a nation." Thus, he concluded, "We are slaves in the midst of freedom, waiting patiently, and unconcernedly – indifferently, and stupidly, for masters to come and lay claim to us, trusting to their generosity, whether or not they will own us and carry us into endless bondage."

Delany foresaw only three possible responses to this state of affairs: submission, flight, or resistance. "Ponder well and reflect," he advised his readers. Since the late 1840s, Delany had gravitated toward the third option. Just as many of his fellow New Romantics likewise turned to forceful resistance, however, Delany settled on a different solution to the problem of slavery. Drawing on historical precedent – from the "Exodus of the Jews ... from Judea" to the Puritan migration to New England – he determined that the time had come for African Americans to make a new start in a new country.[48]

But where to go? Delany quickly dismissed emigration to the former ACS colony of Liberia. The black republic existed in an unhealthy environment, had proslavery origins, and had failed to establish true independence. Liberia, he concluded, "*is not* an independent nation at all; but a poor *miserable mockery* – a *burlesque* on a government – a pitiful dependency on the American Colonizationists." Still beholden to southern slaveholders, it is "unworthy of any respectful consideration from

[47] MRD, *Condition, Elevation, Emigration, and Destiny*, 37–38, 14, 12.
[48] MRD, *Condition, Elevation, Emigration, and Destiny*, 155–156, 159.

us." As such, Delany concluded that "we must not leave this continent; America is our destination and our home."[49]

Emigration to Canada also had its drawbacks. Although a significant black community already existed in Canada West, he thought the United States was determined to annex Canada, which would result in "disfranchisement, degradation, and a delivery up to slave catchers and kidnappers" for its black residents.[50] Thus, Delany concluded that Central America, South America, or the West Indies were the best spots for the nation's black population. These regions had significant agricultural resources, large black populations, and far less racial prejudice than the United States. Go south, he advised African Americans.[51]

The Work of Our Own Hands

At first blush, Delany's emigration manifesto appears an outright rejection of the reform program that he had endorsed for decades. Since the 1830s, he had argued that African Americans – free and enslaved alike – should work for improvement within the United States. Now Delany was calling for black emigration abroad. Unsurprisingly, a number of his abolitionist allies did not take kindly to *Condition, Elevation, Emigration, and Destiny.*

The *Pennsylvania Freeman* wrote that the book was "bunglingly and egotistically presented," concluding that for Delany's "own credit, and that of the colored people," the paper wished "it had never been published."[52] The *Liberator*'s review was not quite so negative. *Condition, Elevation, Emigration, and Destiny* "contains so many valuable facts and cogent appeals that its dissemination cannot fail to remove many groundless prejudices, and enlighten many a benighted mind," wrote Garrison. Yet the editor took issue with its central thesis. Comparing its emigration program to colonization, Garrison maintained that Delany's "arguments for a removal have long since been anticipated by the Colonization Society." "We are desirous of seeing neither white nor black republics," he concluded, "and we maintain that all who love mankind impartially should aim to break down every

---

[49] MRD, *Condition, Elevation, Emigration, and Destiny*, 169, 34–35, 170.
[50] MRD, *Condition, Elevation, Emigration, and Destiny*, 174–175. Canada West later became the province of Ontario, Canada.
[51] MRD, *Condition, Elevation, Emigration, and Destiny*, 179–181.
[52] *Pennsylvania Freeman*, Apr. 29, 1852.

unnatural barrier, and bear their testimony against whatever is clannish or exclusive in spirit."[53]

While the *Pennsylvania Freeman* and the *Liberator* published critical reviews of Delany's new book, *Frederick Douglass's Paper* did not even acknowledge its publication. Delany sent Douglass a copy of *Condition, Elevation, Emigration, and Destiny* not long after it was published, but, much to Delany's disappointment, his old partner made no mention of the book in his paper. Up until this point, noted Delany in a letter to Douglass, his paper had always given some notice of the books it received, regardless of whether it agreed with them or not. "But you heaped ... a cold and deathly silence" upon my study, he complained. Was Delany being treated differently, he wondered, because he was black?[54]

Delany may have had Stowe in mind when he raised this slight, for just a few months earlier *Frederick Douglass's Paper* had heaped not cold silence but warm praise upon *Uncle Tom's Cabin*. "The friends of freedom owe the Authoress a large debt of gratitude for this essential service rendered by her to the cause they love," announced the paper in its "Literary Notices" section. Stowe "has evinced great keenness of insight into the workings of slavery and a depth of knowledge of all its various parts, such as few writers have equaled, and none, we are sure, have exceeded." Delany, whose book was published just one month after Stowe's novel, could not help but feel snubbed by his old partner.[55]

This disparate treatment helps explain Delany's decision to send a series of letters criticizing Stowe and her novel to Douglass the following year. As we saw in Chapter 3, Delany believed that white reformers like Stowe could not fully understand the plight of African Americans and, as such, they had no business taking the lead in efforts to uplift the black race. Why, he asked, do African Americans ignore "the *intelligent* and *experienced* among *ourselves*" and instead look for solutions from white reformers? Delany also questioned Stowe's celebration of a Christlike Tom figure and her seeming endorsement of colonization by sending George Harris and his family to Africa at the end of the novel. "Is not Mrs. Stowe a *Colonizationist*? having so avowed, or at least subscribed

[53] *Liberator*, May 7, 1852.

[54] MRD to FD, July 10, 1852, in *Frederick Douglass' Paper*, July 23, 1852, reprinted in *MDR*, 222.

[55] *Frederick Douglass' Paper*, Apr. 8, 1852; Levine, *Martin Delany, Frederick Douglass*, 70–74.

to, and recommended their principles in her great work of Uncle Tom," asked the newly minted emigrationist.[56]

Douglass printed these letters, and then issued two sharp responses. Delany's dismissal of Stowe because she was white, insisted the Rochester editor, was as misguided as the argument that she was a colonizationist at heart. Minimizing the significance of the Harrises' emigration to Africa late in the novel, Douglass wrote, "We shall not ... allow the sentiments put in the brief letter of GEORGE HARRIS, at the close of Uncle Tom's Cabin, to vitiate forever Mrs. Stowe's power to do us good."[57]

Douglass's responses also acknowledged *Condition, Elevation, Emigration, and Destiny* for the first time. Although "in many respects, an excellent" book, conceded Douglass, it "leaves us just where it finds us, without chart or compass, and in more doubt and perplexity than before we read it." He accused his former partner of the very crime for which he had indicted Stowe. "A little while ago, brother Delany was a colonizationist," wrote Douglass. "Yet, we never suspect his friendliness to the colored people; nor should we feel called upon to oppose any plan he might submit, for the benefit of the colored people." Then Douglass took the gloves off:

We don't object to colonizationists because they express a lively interest in the civilization and Christianization of Africa; nor because they desire the prosperity of Liberia; but it is because, like brother Delany, they have not sufficient faith in the people of the United States to believe that the black man can ever get justice at their hands on American soil.[58]

Both Delany and the ACS, from Douglass's vantage point, lacked faith in the potential for black uplift in America.

This accusation must have stung Delany, who for decades had argued exactly the opposite. Still, Douglass had a point. Once optimistic about the future of black Americans in the United States, Delany, by the early 1850s, had grown as pessimistic about a biracial America as any colonizationist. Although he rejected the ACS's premise that the United States had been founded as a white republic, Delany similarly forecasted a monochromatic future for the nation.

---

[56] MRD to FD, Mar. 20, 1853, in *Frederick Douglass' Paper*, Apr. 1, 1853, reprinted in *MDR*, 224; MRD to FD, Apr. 15, 1853, in *Frederick Douglass' Paper*, Apr. 29, 1853, reprinted in *MDR*, 230–231; MRD to FD, Apr. 18, 1853, in *Frederick Douglass' Paper*, May 6, 1853, reprinted in *MDR*, 232.

[57] *Frederick Douglass' Paper*, May 6, 1853.

[58] *Frederick Douglass' Paper*, Apr. 1, 1853; *Frederick Douglass' Paper*, May 6, 1853.

If, however, Delany had given up his faith in the American public to treat its black citizenry justly, he had not lost hope in perfectionist self-help. As Delany made clear two years later, he still thought that every individual had "infinite" capacity for self-improvement if only given the opportunity.[59] Put simply, emigration, to him, was a way for African Americans to wrest control of their lives from both those who held them down and those who sought to lend them a hand. Like the *Mystery* and the *North Star*, it would be a black-led endeavor. "Our elevation must be the result of *self-efforts*, and work of our *own hands*," he wrote. Colonizationists wanted to rid themselves of African Americans to create an all-white nation; his primary goal, in contrast, was to foster black uplift, wherever it was possible. "Go with the fixed intention – as Europeans came to the United States – of cultivating the soil, entering into the mechanical operations, keeping of shops, carrying on merchandise, trading on land and water, improving property," he urged, "in a word, to become the producers of the country, instead of the consumers."[60]

In typical fashion, Delany balanced such level-headed counsel with high-flying visions of the individual and social transformations that would be wrought by emigration. Black migrants were not abandoning the millions of African Americans who still toiled on the plantations of the South, he claimed. "We believe it to be the duty of the Free, to elevate themselves in the most speedy and effective manner possible; as the redemption of the bondman depends entirely upon the elevation of the freeman," wrote Delany. "Therefore, to elevate the free colored people of America, anywhere upon this continent; forebodes the speedy redemption of the slaves." Delany, however, said next to nothing about how black progress abroad would emancipate the enslaved back home in *Condition, Elevation, Emigration, and Destiny*, concluding simply, "Let us apply, first, the lever to ourselves; and the force that elevates us to the position of manhood's considerations and honors, will cleft the manacle of every slave in the land."[61] Delany's faith in perfectionist self-help, in sum, remained as strong – if also as naïve – as ever.

Two years later, he further developed his emigration rationale at a black convention in Cleveland. In late August 1854, more than 100 African American men and women gathered in the Ohio city "to consider

[59] MRD, "Political Destiny," 338.
[60] MRD, *Condition, Elevation, Emigration, and Destiny*, 45, 187; Tomek, *Colonization and its Discontents*, 187–218.
[61] MRD, *Condition, Elevation, Emigration, and Destiny*, 205–206.

the expediency, and devise of a practical plan of emigration to Central or
South America."[62] Delany was the convention's president *pro tem*, chairman of the business committee, and the meeting's keynote speaker. It was
to be, according to one biographer, "Delany's show from beginning to
end."[63]

On the second day of the National Emigration Convention, Delany
delivered his keynote address, the "Political Destiny of the Colored Race
on the American Continent." Revisiting key points he had made two years
earlier, Delany traced the social and political marginalization of black
Americans in the United States. "A people, to be free, must necessarily be
their own rulers," he argued in Byronic fashion, "that is, *each individual*
must, in himself, embody the *essential ingredient* – so to speak – of the
sovereign principle which composes the *true basis* of his liberty." The
"diseased" American body politic, infected with racial prejudice, needed
the "healing balm" of emigration, which the black physician concluded
was the "remedy" for "this disease." He thought Canada could provide
short-term relief but, over the long haul, he held that "attention must be
turned in a direction towards those places where the black and colored
man comprise, by population, ... the *ruling element* of the body politic." Once again, Delany endorsed emigration to Central America, South
America, and the West Indies, which remained, to him, the areas most
conducive to moral, mental, and physical development as well as the free
"enjoyment of civil and religious liberty."[64]

Following his own prescription, Delany left Pittsburgh for Chatham,
Canada West, a few years later. Since more than a third of Chatham's
four thousand residents were free blacks and runaway slaves, Delany
knew he would find a community that was sympathetic to his reform
agenda as well as in need of his medical skills. The Canadian town also
promised better educational opportunities than Pittsburgh's segregated
schools for Delany's growing family. Finally, Canada's "proximity" made
it a convenient place to test out black emigration. Nevertheless, as Delany
suggested in "Political Destiny," in his mind Canada was a temporary
solution. Soon he would outline a grander expedition, although not to
Latin America, but rather to the Niger Valley in western Africa.[65]

---

[62] *National Era*, Oct.12, 1854.
[63] Levine, *Martin Delany, Frederick Douglass*, 93–94; Sterling, *Making of an Afro-
American*, 154.
[64] MRD, "Political Destiny," 329–333, 352.
[65] Ullman, *Martin R. Delany*, 183; Sterling, *Making of an Afro-American*, 159–161; S.
Cameron and L. A. Falk, "Some Black Medical History: Dr. Martin R. Delany's Canadian

My Duty and Destiny Are in Africa

A couple of weeks after the *Liberator* reviewed *Condition, Elevation, Emigration, and Destiny*, Delany wrote a public letter to the paper, clarifying his positions. Although he appreciated the "very favorable and generous notice," Delany took issue with the suggestion that he thought blacks and whites were incompatible. "I am not in favor of caste, nor a separation of the brotherhood of mankind, and would as willingly live among white men as black, if I had an *equal possession and enjoyment* of privileges," the New Romantic told Garrison and his readers. But Delany added that he would "never be reconciled to live among them, subservient to their will – existing by mere *sufferance*, as we, the colored people, do in this country."[66]

Delany had no fundamental desire to live apart from American's white citizens; he simply wanted to locate a place where black self-help was truly viable. Viewed this way, his decision to build a black colony abroad was motivated by – in the terms used by migration scholars – the *push* of racial prejudice. Yet there were other factors – some age-old, others newly emergent – that *pulled* Delany toward emigration, especially to Africa, which he embraced as a destination in the late 1850s. Weaving together his romantic attachment to African history and culture and heroic black leadership, on the one hand, with burgeoning theories of racial difference and the tropes of Manifest Destiny, on the other, Delany formulated a black emigration program that was not just an accommodation to reality but also a desirable goal in and of itself.

Desperate times produce unlikely bedfellows. Take the surprising similarity between Delany's black emigration scheme and Manifest Destiny, the era's most influential doctrine of white imperial expansion. Many antebellum Americans – but especially Jacksonian Democrats and the artists and intellectuals associated with the Young American Movement – believed that God had foreordained the Anglo-Saxon people and their liberal institutions and values to move westward across the continent. In July 1845, John L. O'Sullivan's *United States Magazine and Democratic Review* captured this expansionist vision in a catchy two-word phrase, when it suggested that the recent annexation of Texas was "the fulfilment [*sic*] of our *manifest destiny* to overspread the continent

Years as Medical Practitioner and Abolitionist (1856–1864)," unpublished manuscript, Dorothy Sterling Papers, Amistad Research Center (ARC), Tulane University, New Orleans, LA; *Provincial Freeman*, Feb. 23, 1856; *Provincial Freeman*, Oct. 13, 1855.
[66] MRD to Garrison, May 14, 1852, in the *Liberator*, May 21, 1852.

allotted by Providence for the free development of our yearly multiplying millions."[67]

There was, of course, a rich irony to the American expansionists' liberal professions. Despite promising the expansion of freedom and democracy, they ignored Native American and Mexican populations in the West, imagining the American continent as an empty space waiting to be filled by "multiplying millions" of Anglo-Saxons. Moreover, as many abolitionists pointed out, Manifest Destiny provided cover for not just the appropriation of non-white land but also the westward expansion of slavery.[68]

Notwithstanding such regressive features, a number of antebellum reformers echoed ideas we associate with Manifest Destiny. As we have seen, Theodore Parker equated Anglo-Saxon culture with the march of liberty. So, too, did Frederick Douglass, who believed that Anglo-Saxon people had a special gift for democracy that set countries like the United States apart from nations established by "Latin races," which lacked "the full comprehension of the principles of republicanism." Although these New Romantics had serious concerns about Anglo-Saxon aggression and "love of power," they agreed that these racial characteristics made white domination of the American continent all but inevitable.[69]

Even abolitionists who did not see Anglo-Saxon expansion as foreordained were drawn to the rhetoric of Manifest Destiny. In 1848, black clergyman Henry Highland Garnet insisted the impending U.S. victory in the war with Mexico represented not the triumph of the white race but rather the end to the purity and domineering ways of the Anglo-Saxon race. Garnet predicted that "the dark-browed and liberty-loving" Mexican people would add more color to the already mixed-race United States and, in the process, inaugurate a more peaceful and democratic culture. "This republic, and this continent, are to be the theatre in which the grand drama of our triumphant Destiny is to be enacted," concluded Garnet. A decade and a half later, black emigrationist Richard Harvey Cain adopted the expansionist slogan wholesale in a lecture titled,

---

[67] "Annexation," *United States Magazine and Democratic Review* 17 (July 1845): 5. Emphasis mine. Although this article has long been attributed to O'Sullivan, there is some evidence that political journalist Jane Storm wrote it. Howe, *What Hath God Wrought*, 703.

[68] Howe, *What Hath God Wrought*, 704–705; Horsman, *Race and Manifest Destiny*, 219.

[69] FD, "Our Southern Sister Republic," in *LWFD*, 4: 259; FD, "In Law Free, In Fact, A Slave: An Address Delivered in Washington, D.C., on 16 April 1888," in *FDP*, 5: 360; Martin, *Mind of Frederick Douglass*, 198–199; Bay, *White Image in the Black Mind*, 66–71; Dain, *Hideous Monster of the Mind*, 249–256.

"Manifest Destiny of the African Race." Cain saw the creation of a black colony in Africa as the fulfillment of God's plan for his race.[70]

Delany, too, outfitted black emigration in Manifest Destiny garb. In the early 1850s, he imagined the New World as the place where non-whites were destined by God to predominate. "The continent of America," Delany admitted in *Condition, Elevation, Emigration, and Destiny*, "seems to have been designed by Providence as an asylum for all the various nations of the earth." But Delany thought that Africans had a special claim to the region, highlighting the fact that they were "among the earliest and most numerous class who found their way to the New World." He also pointed to the African appearance of some pre-Columbian Americans, a factor that he thought meant Native Americans had African origins and thus the black race had "greater claims to this continent" than did Anglo-Saxons. "We are not inclined to be superstitious," concluded Delany, "but say, that we can see the 'finger of God' in all this." While Jacksonian Democrats viewed the U.S.'s burgeoning white populace as evidence of Anglo-Saxon dominance, Delany saw something similar in "the vast colored population" to the south. You have more than 21 million colored "brethren" in Central and South America, he told his fellow black Americans: "They are precisely the same people as ourselves and share the same fate with us."[71]

Toward the end of the 1850s, Delany began proposing emigration not to Central America, South America, or the West Indies but rather to Africa. Despite this change of destination, Delany continued to use the language of Manifest Destiny to describe his emigration impulse. "My duty and destiny are in Africa," he explained to a fellow black emigrationist, "the great and glorious (even with its defects) land of your and my ancestry."[72]

Delany never explained what triggered his decision to trade emigration to the south for emigration across the Atlantic, although it likely had

[70] Henry Highland Garnet, quoted in Robert S. Levine, *Dislocating Race & Nation: Episodes in Nineteenth-Century American Literary Nationalism* (Chapel Hill: University of North Carolina Press, 2008), 127; Bernard E. Powers Jr., "'I Go to Set the Captives Free'": The Activism of Richard Harvey Cain, Nationalist Churchman and Reconstruction-Era Leader," in *The Southern Elite and Social Change: Essays in Honor of Willard B. Gatewood Jr.*, ed. Randy Finley and Thomas A DeBlack (Fayetteville: University of Arkansas Press, 2002), 37.

[71] Levine, *Martin Delany, Frederick Douglass*, 66–67; MRD, *Condition, Elevation, Emigration, and Destiny*, 171–173, 181.

[72] MRD to James T. Holley, Jan. 15, 1861, in *Chatham Tri-Weekly Planet*, Jan. 21, 1861, reprinted in *MDR*, 365.

something to do with the infamous 1857 *Dred Scott* ruling, which gave discrimination against African Americans the Supreme Court's stamp of approval. In his novel *Blake; or, the Huts of America*, which appeared serially between 1859 and 1862, Delany suggested that *Dred Scott* reinforced the fugitive slave law, rendering "every free black in the country, North and South ... slaves-at-large, whom any white person may claim at discretion."[73] Whatever the proximate reason, colonization to Africa was a natural fit, for it enabled Delany to combine his sense that black emigration was predestined by God with his abiding interest in African history and culture.

Delany had long evinced pride in his family's royal African roots – however real, in fact, they were. He had fantasized about "going to Africa, the land of [his] ancestry" as early as the 1830s, when the black reformer made a pact with a friend to visit the continent.[74] In the years that followed, Delany chose names for his seven children – Toussaint L'Ouverture, Charles Lenox Remond, Alexander Dumas, Saint Cyprian, Faustin Soulouque, Ramses Placido, Ethiopia Halle Amelia – that either evoked Africa or paid homage to famous individuals of African descent.[75]

Since his first days in Pittsburgh, Delany had also displayed signs of what Ali A. Mazuri calls the "*romantic gloriana*" strain of black nationalism. In contrast to twentieth-century black nationalists – who often touted the "the simplicity of rural African village life" – nineteenth-century black nationalists celebrated the monumental achievements of ancient Egyptian and Ethiopian societies. Certainly Delany fits this portrait. In the 1830s and 1840s, he founded organizations, such as the Theban Literary Society, and produced publications, like the *Mystery*, that emphasized the African roots of Judeo-Christian values and Western civilization and culture. As a founding member of Pittsburgh's chapter of the black Freemasons, Delany delivered a lengthy lecture in 1853, which suggested that the secretive fraternal organization was "first established" by priests from the early "Egyptian and Ethiopian dynasties." Later, he called the "African library" of ancient Alexandria "the depository of the

[73] MRD, *Blake; or, The Huts of America* (Boston: Beacon Press, 1970), 61.

[74] MRD, *Official Report of the Niger Valley Exploring Party*, in *Search for a Place: Black Separatism and Africa, 1860*, ed. Howard H. Bell (Ann Arbor: University of Michigan Press, 1969), 32.

[75] Rollin, *Life and Public Services*, 15–18, 29.

earliest gems of social, civil, political, and national progress, the concentrated wisdom of ages."[76]

Even as Delany disavowed any intention to leave the Americas in the early 1850s, he provided hints that his heart lay on the other side of the Atlantic. To take one example, Delany concluded *Condition, Elevation, Emigration, and Destiny*, which formally supported Latin American emigration, with an appendix outlining a project to explore the eastern coast of Africa. "In Eastern Africa must rise up a nation, to whom all the world must pay commercial tribute," he wrote.[77] A couple of years later, to take another, Delany seems to have been involved in "Secret Sessions" at the Cleveland emigration convention, which quietly agreed that Africa was their ultimate destination. Although the ACS had tainted Africa as a destination in the minds of many black emigrationists, Delany later explained that the leaders of the convention were strong proponents of "the regeneration of Africa." As such, while "the first shell thrown" by their "great gun" was aimed "at the American Continent," they held Africa "*in reserve, until by the help of an All-wise Providence*" a black colony might be established there.[78]

In seeking to establish a "colored" nation – whether in Latin America or Africa – Delany displayed a fondness not just for Manifest Destiny rhetoric but also for the romantic racial nationalism on which the expansionist ideology rested. This is not to say that Delany rejected the color-blind claims of years past. In the *Condition, Elevation, Emigration, and Destiny*, for instance, he wrote, "We believe in the universal equality of man, and believe in that declaration of God's word, in which it is there

---

[76] Ali A. Mazrui, "Islam and Afrocentricity: The Triple Heritage School," in *Africanity Redefined: Collected Essays of Ali A. Mazrui*, ed. Ricardo Rene Laremont and Tracia Leacock Seghatolislami (Trenton, NJ: Africa World Press, 2002), 1: 110–111; Teshale Tibebu, *Edward Wilmot Blyden and the Racial Nationalist Imagination* (Rochester, NY: University of Rochester Press, 2012), 9; Gilroy, *Black Atlantic*, 26; MRD, "The Origin and Objects of Ancient Freemasonry: Its Introduction into the United States, and Legitimacy among Colored Men. A Treatise Delivered Before St. Cyprian Lodge, No. 13, June 24th A.D. 1853 – A.L. 5853," in *MDR*, 53; Stephen Kantrowitz, "'Intended for the Better Government of Man': The Political History of African American Freemasonry in the Era of Emancipation," *Journal of American History* 96 (Mar. 2010): 1006–1007; MRD, "The International Policy of the World towards the African Race," in Rollin, *Life and Public Services*, 325.

[77] MRD, *Condition, Elevation, Emigration, and Destiny*, 11–12, 209–214 (quotation 214).

[78] MRD, *Official Report*, 32–33; *MDR*, 315–317; Miller, *Search for a Black Nationality*, 172.

positively said, that 'God had made of one blood all the nations that dwell on the face of the earth.'"[79]

Still, in the 1850s Delany often coupled such affirmations of Enlightenment universalism with assertions of fundamental racial difference. Just one page after stating that God had created all men equal, he echoed one of the era's most pervasive romantic racialist claims. "The colored races are highly susceptible of religion," Delany insisted, "it is a constituent principle of their nature, and an excellent trait in their character."[80] Two years later, in his address to the Cleveland emigration convention, he went further than this, outlining a clear statement of fundamental racial difference. "The truth is," Delany told the black delegates, "we are not identical with the Anglo-Saxon, or any other race of the Caucasian or pure white type of the human family, and the sooner we know and acknowledge this truth the better for ourselves and posterity." He opined that all races and ethnicities "have their native or inherent peculiarities" and each race should "cultivate" its unique gifts, "develop them in their purity, to make them desirable and emulated by the rest of the world." White people may excel at mathematics, sculpture, architecture, and commerce, but "the black race will yet instruct the world" in languages, oratory, poetry, metaphysics, theology, and legal jurisprudence."[81]

Like the rest of the New Romantics, Delany was not your run-of-the-mill nineteenth-century racialist. While Romantic ethnographers and theorists, including Herder, Schleiermacher, and Joseph Arthur de Gobineau, viewed racial difference as fundamental and fixed, Delany, in the antebellum period, preferred environmental explanations – particularly the disparate effects of climate, culture, and experience – for the peculiar gifts displaced by different nations or races. Moreover, he rejected a number of the stereotypes associated with romantic racialism. Unlike Parker, who called Africans "a feeble tribe of men," the black emigrationist believed that people of the African diaspora have "proven themselves ... superior physically to any living race of men – enduring fatigue, hunger, and thirst – enduring change of climate, habits, manners and customs, with infinitely far less injury to their physical and mental system, than any other people on the face of God's earth." Indeed, Delany concluded that Africans "are a *superior race*," whose unique physical gifts give them the

---

[79] MRD, *Condition, Elevation, Emigration, and Destiny*, 36.
[80] MRD, *Condition, Elevation, Emigration, and Destiny*, 37–38.
[81] MRD, "Political Destiny," 334–335.

"right and duty" to live wherever they so choose.[82] Our fathers' generation, he told black reformers in 1854, "admitted themselves to be inferi-
ors" to the Anglo-Saxon. "They felt themselves happy to be permitted to
beg for rights." But that was the past. "We demand [rights] as an innate
inheritance" and "we barely acknowledge the whites as equals, perhaps
not in every particular," he bragged. This "pride of race," in turn, led
Delany on occasion to suggest that "pure" black reformers like him were
better suited to lead the antislavery fight than mixed-blood counterparts
like Frederick Douglass.[83]

Such statements opened up Delany to a torrent of criticism, much of
it from fellow black reformers. His friend Daniel Alexander Payne concluded that the New Romantic might have been as influential as Douglass
"had his love for humanity been as great as his love for his race." And
Douglass, perhaps smarting over Delany's comments about mixed-race
leadership, wrote in 1862 that his one-time partner "has gone about the
same length in favor of black, as the whites have in favor of the doctrine of
white superiority." Black novelist William Wells Brown went so far as to
suggest that Delany was the nation's most influential black chauvinist.[84]

Although not entirely unfounded, these critiques overlook the strategic
motivations for Delany's cultural chauvinism. The black emigrationist
was careful to note the implications of ignoring the era's prevailing racial
sentiments. "Our friends in this and other countries, anxious for our elevation, have for years been erroneously urging us to lose our identity as
a distinct race, declaring that we were the same as other people," Delany
reminded his black audience in 1854, "while at the very same time their
own representative was traversing the world, and propagating the doctrine in favor of a *universal Anglo-Saxon predominance*." Reformers
who preached racial equality, in other words, inadvertently aided and
abetted "Anglo-Saxon rule" by losing sight of the question upon which
antebellum racial politics turned. "Endeavor to shun it as we may," he
declared two years later, "we cannot ignore the fact, that the world is at
present more or less, enquiring into the condition of the colored races,

[82] TP, "Nebraska Question," 338; MRD, *Condition, Elevation, Emigration, and Destiny*,
55–56, 202.
[83] MRD, "Political Destiny," 351; Rollin, *Life and Public Services*, 19, 22; Fredrickson,
Black Image in the White Mind, 120–121; Bay, *White Image in the Black Mind*, 65;
Levine, *Martin Delany, Frederick Douglass*, 55–56, 230.
[84] Daniel Alexander Payne, *Recollections of Seventy Years* (1888; repr., New York: Arno
Press, 1968), 160; *Douglass's Monthly*, Aug. 1862, p. 695; William Wells Brown, "The
Colored People of Canada," in *BAP*, 2: 472; Levine, introduction to *MDR*, 3.

as a distinct people from the white races." To some extent, Delany's emphasis on racial difference was a calculated response to the claims of white supremacy rather than "an expression of cultural nationalism that would be familiar to late-twentieth-century audiences."[85]

Yet Delany did not simply argue for racial equality. Instead, he and a handful of like-minded black reformers reversed antebellum America's racial polarity. Positing the African race as the highest rung on the ladder of civilization, they concluded that Anglo-Saxons were violent, predatory, and reprobate, while Africans were moral, upright, and destined to redeem the world. As was the case with O'Sullivan, the Young Americans, and so many supporters of Manifest Destiny, then, Delany's emigration plan was rooted in the idea that *his* race was not just different from, but also superior to, its counterparts. Even more, like the most controversial expansionists of the era, the southern filibusters, Delany outlined a program that was as grandiose as it was elitist.[86]

In the 1850s, men such as Narciso López, John Quitman, Pierre Soulé, and William Walker dreamed up wild plans to lead revolutions in Cuba, Sonora, and Nicaragua. Intoxicated by visions of Anglo-Saxon superiority, divine will, and heroic adventure in exotic lands, these "self-appointed agents of Manifest Destiny" cast themselves as latter-day knights who would sail south to subdue inferior peoples. "Regarding the magnificent country of tropical America, which lies in the path of our destiny on this continent, we may see an empire as powerful and gorgeous as ever was pictured in our dreams of history," wrote filibuster promoter Edward Pollard. "It is an empire founded on military ideas; representing the noble peculiarities of Southern civilization."[87]

Delany's emigration schemes betrayed a similar propensity for fantastical flights of fancy coupled with a cool indifference to the desires of local populations. Like the southern filibusters, he pitched African

---

[85] MRD, "Political Destiny," 334; *Provincial Freeman*, May 31, 1856; Rael, *Black Identity and Black Protest*, 51.

[86] Frederickson, *Black Image in the White Mind*, 71–82; Dain, *Hideous Monster of the Mind*, 197–226; Bay, *White Image in the Black Mind*, 42–44, 64–66, 71–74, 220–226.

[87] Charles H. Brown, *Agents of Manifest Destiny: The Lives and Times of the Filibusters* (Chapel Hill: University of North Carolina Press, 1980), 18; Robert E. May, *Manifest Destiny's Underworld: Filibustering in Antebellum America* (Chapel Hill: University of North Carolina Press, 2002); William W. Freehling, *The Road to Disunion, Volume 2: Secessionist Triumphant, 1854–1861* (New York: Oxford University Press, 2007), 145–167; John Hope Franklin, *The Militant South, 1800–1861* (Boston: Beacon Press, 1964), 98–99; Osterweis, *Romanticism in the Old South*, 172–185; Edward Pollard, quoted in Walter Johnson, *River of Dark Dreams: Slavery and Empire in the Cotton Kingdom* (Cambridge, MA: Belknap Press of Harvard University Press, 2013), 310.

exploration as a "great adventure" in a foreign locale. Although his official emigration proposals lacked the martial spirit and knightly aura that animated filibusterer propaganda, Delany nonetheless advertised colonization as something to satisfy African Americans' deepest yearnings, insisting that "every people should be the originators of their own designs, the projector of their own schemes, and creators of the events that lead to their destiny – the consummation of their desires."[88]

Even when unconsummated, Delany's desires could be wild. While writing *Condition, Elevation, Emigration, and Destiny* in New York City, for instance, the black reformer learned that he had been elected mayor of the Nicaraguan port city of Greytown as well as "civil governor of the Mosquito reservation, and commander-in-chief of the military forces of the province!" Or, at least that is what Delany told his biographer Frances Rollin a decade later. According to her account, the Nicaraguan convention that elected the New Romantic also instructed him to "bring with him his own *council of state* as the native material" was not up to the task. Delany, it seems, was so taken with this idea that he spent the next eight months traveling across the United States searching in vain for African Americans who would accompany him to Greytown and help him rule. Although no evidence exists that such an election took place, the fact that Delany believed that he had been selected for high political offices by residents of a place that he had never visited speaks to his imagination, if not also his credulity.[89]

It also speaks to his long-standing desire to play the role of black redeemer. Since his days writing for the *North Star*, Delany had maintained that intelligent black male leaders were essential to any successful program of African American emancipation and uplift. At times, he pointed to a small cadre of reformers, including Henry Highland Garnet, Charles L. Remond, and Douglass, who would take the lead in these efforts. In other moments – especially those in which Delany emphasized his own "pure" blackness – the New Romantic implied that he alone was capable of saving the black race. This romantic self-conception emerges most fully in his 1859–1862 novel, *Blake*, which chronicles the exploits of Henry Blake, a Cuban-born free black who – after being kidnapped and sold into slavery in Mississippi – travels across the American South and the West Indies plotting a clandestine slave revolt. A resistant rebel

---

[88] MRD, *Condition, Elevation, Emigration, and Destiny*, 209; MRD, *Official Report*, 45.
[89] Rollin, *Life and Public Services*, 80–82 (quotations 80); Levine, *Martin Delany, Frederick Douglass*, 62–63; Minardi, *Making Slavery History*, 153.

in the mold of Douglass's Madison Washington and Stowe's Dred, Blake can also be read as a fictional proxy for Delany himself. He is a bold, dark-skinned, intelligent leader who, in contrast to most of the novel's enslaved characters, neither speaks in dialect, nor embraces the spiritual beliefs and practices that Delany thought held most slaves down. Although Blake hopes to foster slave insurrection in the Deep South and the West Indies, he remains aloof from the slave plantations and maroon communities he visits. Delany's hero enlists a few lieutenants in his plot, but makes it clear that he has the unique capacity "to redeem" his people. "I come to bring deliverance to the captive and freedom to the bond," Blake says at the end of the novel. "Your destiny is my destiny."[90]

Delany approached his emigration project in a similar spirit. Like the filibusterers, he paid little mind to the desires of the natives among whom he hoped to settle. The colonizing perspective that allowed him to believe that the Nicaraguan people had chosen a foreign leader whom they had never met emerged again in Delany's plans for African emigration. In his 1852 outline to explore the eastern coast of the continent, for instance, he wrote that the venture should be organized by a "Confidential Council" made up of "a limited number of known, worthy gentlemen" who had "the right to project any scheme they may think proper for the general good of the whole people – provided that the project is laid before them after its maturity." This council would be empowered to appoint a Board of Commissioners of "decided qualifications" – physicians, botanists, chemists, geologists, geographers, and surveyors – to lead the African expedition. Although led by educated free blacks like him, Delany's emigration plan left room for input to the African American population as a whole. The same cannot be said for the African people among whom his "enlightened freemen" would settle, however. Delany, in fact, did not mention native-born Africans in his plan at all. Instead, he framed eastern Africa as a "long neglected" and "little known" wonderland of abundant natural resources, not unlike the western frontier and Central and South

---

[90] Levine, introduction to *MDR*, 17; Tomek, *Colonization and its Discontents*, 207; Carla L. Peterson, *Doers of the World: African-American Women Speakers and Writers in the North (1830–1880)* (New York: Oxford University Press, 1995), 169–170; Kameelah L. Martin, "Hoodoo Ladies and High Conjurers: New Directions for an Old Archetype," in *Literary Expressions of African Spirituality*, ed. Carol P. Marsh-Lockett and Elizabeth J. West (Lanham, MD: Lexington Books, 2013), 120–121; Levine, *Martin Delany, Frederick Douglass*, 191–200; MRD, *Blake*, 9 15–17, 102, 114–115, 136–139, 251, 290 (quotations 251, 290).

America in the minds of American expansionists. The black reformer concluded his outline of the expedition by arguing that the black race's unique characteristics gave them a special claim to set out and make themselves into the "*lords*" of whatever "terrestrial creation" they chose. "The land is ours – there it lies with inexhaustible resources," he insists, "let us go and possess it." It seems unlikely that he gave even a second thought to those who counted eastern Africa as theirs already.[91]

Delany displayed a similar indifference to the interests and input of west Africans as he raised money for – and then led – an expedition to their region in the late 1850s. Influenced by several recent African travel accounts, including Thomas J. Bowen's *Central Africa: Adventures and Missionary Labors in Several Countries in the Interior of Africa, 1849–1856*, he started planning his exploratory mission to the western part of the continent in 1858.[92]

Initially, Delany hoped that the Niger Valley Exploring Party, like the colony it established, would be the product of black hands, minds, and wallets.[93] His inability to secure funding from black sources, however, led Delany to cast his net wider. In June, he reached out to Stowe's brother Henry, who had connections to the white evangelical American Missionary Association (AMA). "Our determination is, to build up an Enlightened and Christian Nationality in the minds of these tractable and docile people, which shall not cease till its influence shall have reached the remotest parts of that extensive and interesting county," he wrote Beecher.[94] Like countless colonizers and missionaries, Delany imagined native Africans as submissive primitives who needed molding by their more civilized brethren.

This attitude persisted when Delany finally visited Africa the following year. The AMA had turned him down – most likely because it had doubts about the Christian bona fides of a man who readily admitted that he was not a "religious howler" – and so Delany turned to an even more unlikely

---

[91] MRD, *Condition, Elevation, Emigration, and Destiny*, 210–212, 214; Levine, *Martin Delany, Frederick Douglass*, 62–63, 185–186.

[92] R. J. M. Blackett, *Building an Antislavery Wall: Black Americans and the Atlantic Abolitionist Movement, 1830–1860* (Baton Rouge; Louisiana State University Press, 1983), 175.

[93] Dr. Joseph Hobbins to the Royal Geographic Society, June 7, 1858, with letter by MRD, May 31, 1858, Royal Geographical Society Papers, London, UK.

[94] MRD to Henry Ward Beecher, June 17, 1858, American Missionary Association Archives (AMAA), ARC.

source: the ACS. With the help of his partner Robert Campbell, Delany acquired support from this long-time nemesis.[95]

The New Romantic set sail for Africa in the summer of 1859, aboard the Liberian-owned ship, the *Mendi*. Delany spent the next nine months touring Liberia and Yoruba (what is today southwest Nigeria), meeting up with Campbell in the Yoruban city of Abeokuta. There, the two reformers negotiated a treaty with the *alake* (king) and his chiefs that empowered their black emigrants to settle among the Egba people who lived in the region. The ambiguously worded document they produced seemed to give the Niger Valley Exploring Party both legal title to Egba land and full legal autonomy on that land. In exchange for these concessions, the settlers promised to "bring with them ... Intelligence, Education, a Knowledge of the Arts and Sciences, Agriculture, and other Mechanical and Industrial Occupations, which they shall put into immediate operation, by improving the lands, and in other useful vocations."[96]

It is as if Delany and Campbell were operating straight out of the European colonizer's handbook. Their treaty, for one, ignored Egba tradition, which held that property was owned by kinship groups and their descendants and thus could not be transferred to another individual or group, even by a chief or king. Secondly, the emigrationists gave up on the idea of fostering black migration to Africa en masse, promising instead just to bring but a chosen few, who would take the lead in transforming the backwards region and its people. As Delany later explained, the document was signed "with the express understanding that no heterogeneous nor promiscuous 'masses' or companies, but select and intelligent people of high moral as well as religious character were to be induced" to move to Africa. Like Delany's letter to Beecher, the treaty posited the Egba people as an inferior people in need of civilization – science, technology, Christianity – that only elite free emigrants could provide.[97] In 1854, Delany had declared his intention to move to a place where black men could be "the *ruling element* of the body politic." Now he made it clear who, in the end, would do the ruling. "Our policy must be ... *Africa for the African race, and black men to rule them*," he wrote in the official report on his African venture, adding, "by black men I mean,

---

[95] MRD to George Whipple, July 1858, AMAA, ARC; Levine, *Martin Delany, Frederick Douglass*, 183–184.

[96] Miller, *Search for a Black Nationality* 182; MRD, 316–317, 332; Richard J. M. Blackett, "Martin R. Delany and Robert Campbell: Black Americans in Search of an African Colony," *Journal of Negro History* 62 (Jan. 1977): 1–25; MRD, *Official Report*, 77–78.

[97] MRD, *Official Report*, 77; Miller, *Search for a Black Nationality*, 213–214.

men of African descent who claim an identity with the race." What he really meant, of course, was elite black men like him. As Nell Painter has written, Delany's emigration plan "was a paternalistic, not a democratic, scheme."[98]

It was not, however, identical to the expeditions proposed by southern filibusters – expeditions that Delany himself had long denounced. Since he started talking about moving to Latin America, he had been an outspoken critic of filibusterism in the region. He protested Narciso López's attempt to seize power in Cuba in 1851 and, a few years later, William Walker's invasion of Lower California and Nicaragua. "The marauding crusade in Cuba" failed because the Spanish government wisely employed "colored soldiery," cheered Delany in 1855. He also wrote positively of the local population's successful resistance of "the despicable puerile attempt by the buccaneer Walker, to overthrow the governments of Lower California and Nicaragua."[99]

This line of critique, in turn, underscores a critical difference between what Robert Levine calls Delany's "black filibusterism" and its southern white counterpart. Insofar as Delany framed black emigration as an antislavery measure, white filibusters viewed their efforts as essential to the future of the peculiar institution across the Americas. Not every southern filibuster was focused squarely on extending slavery – some framed their missions as about expanding American markets, while others viewed them as ridding the Western Hemisphere of the despotic and illiberal influence of the Spanish crown. Yet, as historian John Ashworth reminds us, "the interests of slavery were never far from the surface" of the filibuster campaigns of the 1850s.[100]

Delany, in contrast, consistently argued that his black nation – whether located in Latin America or Africa – would aid not only blacks who left America but also those who remained behind. In *Condition, Elevation, Emigration, and Destiny*, he wrote that black emigration to a country like Nicaragua or New Grenada would be a first step toward breaking

[98] MRD, "Political Destiny," 333; MRD, *Official Report*, 121; Levine, *Martin Delany, Frederick Douglass*, 183–187; Painter, "Martin R. Delany," 160. Just months before he signed his treaty with the Egba *alake*, Delany had presented African emigration as a mass movement by which "six hundred thousand free colored men of the North" would move to Africa. Yet after the treaty, Delany repeatedly reaffirmed his commitment only to bring elite blacks. *Weekly Anglo-African*, Oct. 1, 1859; *Chatham Tri-Weekly Planet*, Jan. 21, 1861; MRD to James Theodore Holley, Jan. 15, 1861, in *BAP*, 2: 439.

[99] MRD, "Political Aspect of the Colored People of the United States," in *MDR*, 287.

[100] Levine, *Martin Delany, Frederick Douglass*, 203; Johnson, *River of Dark Dreams*, 366–394; Ashworth, *Slavery, Capitalism, and Politics*, Vol. 2, 394.

"the manacle of every slave in the land." A decade later, he called African emigration "a powerful handmaid" to those who were "contending for our rights in America."[101] Early on, Delany did not elaborate much on how black emigration would help slaves within the United States, but he became more explicit as he set his sights on western Africa in the late 1850s. The black abolitionist believed that the region's fertile soil, warm climate, and industrious people made it an ideal place to grow cotton, while the settlers he would bring there would provide the commercial, agricultural, and scientific expertise to build a thriving cotton economy. By offering an alternative, free-labor source of cotton, his African colony would function as part of the Free Produce movement, which called for the boycott of all products made by slave labor. Emigration, in short, would enable black Americans and their African counterparts to beat King Cotton at its own game, destroying American slavery in the process.

Delany developed this antislavery vision for black emigration most fully on tour in Great Britain, which he visited after leaving Africa in the spring of 1860. The New Romantic tailored his arguments to England's cotton manufacturers and abolitionists, both of whom were worried about their nation's dependence on a slave-grown product. "If John Brown had been successful and the influence had been spread ... through the whole coast of America," he told the English lords of the loom, "the mills of Manchester, Leeds, and Glasgow, must have stopped, for the next year at least, for want of cotton." Why not support cotton grown by free laborers in Africa? Meanwhile, Delany advised British opponents of slavery that his colony would cripple both the international slave trade and slavery within the United States. "His scheme would not only put down the foreign slave trade, but would have a reflex influence on the domestic slave trade in America, because the raising of cotton in Africa would certainly supersede the raising of cotton," in the United States, reported the *Glasgow Herald*. And if Americans "could not raise cotton they would have very little use for their slaves," he ventured, "for sugar would not keep many of them in labour."[102] In the end, we should not lose sight of the fact that Delany's emigration program – albeit as elitist

[101] MRD, *Condition, Elevation, Emigration, and Destiny*, 206; MRD, *Official Report*, 116.
[102] Blackett, *Building an Antislavery Wall*, 176–186; Miller, *Search for a Black Nationality*, 226–227; *Glasgow Examiner*, Oct. 27, 1860; *Glasgow Daily Herald*, Oct. 9, 1860.

and grandiose as any filibusterer venture – aimed not to save but rather to destroy slavery.

Founding a Corps D'Afrique

After leaving Africa in early 1860, Delany spent the next few years spreading the gospel of black emigration in towns across Great Britain, Canada, and the United States.[103] By March 1863, it was Chicago's turn. The New Romantic offered his regular course of lectures on western Africa in the midwestern city, outlining the region's social and cultural practices as well as its economic prospects. Delany was keen to correct the "erroneous notions" about Africa and its people that could be found in "American school-books," reported the *Chicago Tribune*. The newspaper's account of his first lecture placed particular emphasis on Delany's distinctive attire and avowed racial pride. "The dress which the Doctor wore on the platform was a long, dark-colored robe with curious scrolls upon the neck as a collar," wrote the *Tribune*. Delany explained that it was "the wedding dress of a Chief," which had embroidery that "had a specific meaning well understood in high African circles." The black emigrationist, for his part, judged the dashiki "becoming" and "fitting" for "the occasion." Delany's sartorial pride befitted the broader message he hoped to impart about African society and culture. "He was not ashamed, he said, to be called a negro," reported the *Tribune*. "If curly hair and a black face helped to make a negro, then he was a negro, and a full-blooded one at that."[104]

Two years into the American Civil War, then, Delany appeared bound and determined to move to Africa. As white America suffered through the nightmares of Shiloh, Antietam, and Fredericksburg, he was dreaming of building a black nation abroad. Espousing the virtues of Africa, while wearing an elaborately embroidered dashiki, Delany embodied the romance of black emigration to his audiences. No wonder scholars in the 1960s and 1970s – in search of the early progenitors of Pan-Africanism and Black Power – styled him "the father of black nationalism and the epitome of proud blackness."[105]

---

[103] *Glasgow Examiner*, Oct. 27, 1860; *Glasgow Daily Herald*, Oct. 9, 1860; *Chatham Tri-Weekly Planet*, Mar. 29, 1861; *Pine and Palm*, Apr. 3, 1862; *Douglass's Monthly*, Aug. 1862, p. 695.

[104] *Chicago Tribune*, Mar.19, 20, 21, 1863 (quotations Mar. 20); *Christian Recorder*, May 9, 1863; Miller, *Search for a Black Nationality*, 261–263.

[105] Painter, "Martin R. Delany," 149.

But Delany never left for Africa. Instead, he firmly planted his stake in United States soil. Just weeks after touting the African continent in Chicago, in fact, Delany started recruiting black soldiers for the U.S. Army. "The Governor of Massachusetts, embracing the earliest instant in which the patriotic blacks of our country can be enrolled among the defenders of endangered liberty, is receiving all able-bodied black men," reported the *Chicago Tribune* on April 15, 1863. Interested parties were directed to seek out Delany or one of his colleagues.[106] Like Douglass and a number of other prominent black reformers, the New Romantic had signed on as an agent for one of the first northern black regiments – the Fifty-fourth Massachusetts – thereby demonstrating a newfound commitment to finding a place for African Americans within the United States. The following year Delany permanently relocated back to the United States, buying a home in Wilberforce, Ohio.[107]

Delany's abrupt abandonment of black emigration – a goal he had been working toward for the better part of a decade – is striking. In light of the larger trajectory of his reform career, however, it is not surprising. As we have seen, throughout the 1830s and 1840s Delany had been committed to the idea that perfectionist self-help was possible within the United States. He lost faith in the early 1850s, but the black reformer's optimism swiftly returned in 1863.

How do we explain this change of heart? Delany's new thinking seems a direct response to the changes inaugurated by Lincoln's final Emancipation Proclamation. On January 1, 1863, the president had, for the first time, publicly committed himself – and the nation – to immediate emancipation. Although his proclamation applied only to slaves in rebel territories, it sent a sure signal that the War Department intended not simply to preserve the Union but also to bring slavery to a close. What is more, the Emancipation Proclamation called for the recruitment and arming of black men.

Lincoln's proclamation gave new life to Delany's faith that armed struggle could be a vehicle for black empowerment – a theme he explored most fully in his novel, *Blake*. This serialized story imagined a hemispheric-wide slave revolt led by Henry Blake, the titular hero who so resembled its author's self-perception. After escaping from his Mississippi plantation, Blake travels across the Deep South, "sowing the seeds of future devastation and ruin to the master and redemption to the slave."

---

[106] *Chicago Tribune*, Apr. 15, 1863.
[107] Ullman, *Martin R. Delany*, 291.

Like Stowe's Dred, Blake convenes in the Dismal Swamp with runaways –
men who held "black rebels" like Nat Turner, Denmark Vesey, and slave
rebel Gabriel in "sacred reverence." "I am not fit, brother, for a spiritual
leader," he tells one recruit, "my warfare is not Heavenly, but earthly."
Eventually, Blake returns to Cuba, where he gathers a large group of followers who declare him "General-in-Chief of the army of emancipation
of the oppressed men and women of Cuba!" The novel ends with Blake's
slave rebellion looming, yet unfulfilled, although not before its martial
hero lays bare his plan to lead a "war upon whites."[108]

At the Civil War's outset, Delany hoped that he might play the role of
Blake and build an army of emancipation. While on the lecture circuit in
the fall of 1861, he visited white abolitionist Asa Mahan, whom he hoped
to convert to his latest antislavery plan: to create a black Union division inspired by a famous North African fighting force. Delany's "corps
d'Afrique" was modeled on the Zouaves, an elite French unit renowned
for its valor, martial prowess, and distinctive uniforms (they wore fezzes,
baggy red trousers, and loose jackets). In the mid-1800s, the Zouaves,
which originally consisted largely of North African Zouaoua tribesmen,
had gained an international reputation for their daring exploits in French
campaigns in Italy and Crimea. As a *rage militaire* swept the Union
and the Confederacy in the first months of the war, the swashbuckling
Zouaves proved irresistible to Americans of all stripes. Indeed, by the
end of the war, some fifty American Zouave regiments – white and black,
Union and Confederate – had followed in the exotic footsteps of the
French North African unit.[109]

If Delany had had his way, one of the first Zouave outfits would have
been a black one that he commanded. In his conversation with Mahan,
Delany stressed the African origins of Zouaves, insisting that their unique
fighting style had become a staple not only of the French military but
also those who fought for the black nation of Haiti. The Haitian army,
he explained, employed "peculiar tactics," which involved loading and
firing their weapons while throwing themselves on the ground. "This

[108] MRD, *Blake*, 83, 112–113, 103, 241, 290; Levine, *Martin Delany, Frederick Douglass*,
191–197, 210–211; Tomek, *Colonization and its Discontents*, 207.
[109] Rollin, *Life and Public Services*, 141–142; James M. McPherson, *For Cause and
Comrades: Why Men Fought in the Civil War* (New York: Oxford University Press,
1997), 16; Wayne Wei-siang Hsieh, *West Pointers and the Civil War: The Old Army
in War and Peace* (Chapel Hill: University of North Carolina Press, 2009), 121; Adam
Goodheart, *1861: The Civil War Awakening* (New York: Knopf, 2011), 193; Robin
Smith, *American Civil War Zouaves* (Oxford: Osprey, 1996), 2–3.

was, doubtless, nothing but the original Zouave tactics introduced long years ago by native Africans among these people," Delany concluded. According to Rollin, Mahan was so fond of Delany's corps d'Afrique that he said he would take the idea to President Lincoln and, if approved, help the black reformer recruit and lead the unit.[110]

As with other bold visions put forth by Delany, this plan never came to fruition. But the meeting with Mahan demonstrates that, in the very first months of the Civil War, the black reformer was thinking about how to turn the conflict into a vehicle of emancipation in which black men played a big part. At an 1862 meeting in New York Shiloh Church, to take another example, he told a black audience that "if Great Britain or any other power undertook to raise the blockade to assist the South, at the expense of liberty of the blacks, then let our war cry be 'insurrection' and let the government not interfere."[111]

Delany, to be sure, did not give up on black emigration at the start of the conflict. In a September 1861 letter published in the *Weekly Anglo-African*, he wrote, "my destiny is fixed in Africa, where my family and myself, by God's providence, will soon be happily situated." The following January, he reaffirmed that since "duty and obligations call me to Africa, I cannot hope to be long on this continent." Yet, however much he still viewed African emigration through the lens of Manifest Destiny, Delany was not one to let other options pass by. Indeed, as he told Douglass when he visited the editor at his Rochester home in the early years of the war, Delany believed "a signal providence directed" Lincoln's course as well.[112]

The final Emancipation Proclamation brought the president's providential course together with Delany's own. By turning the Civil War into a fight against slavery in which black men could play a prominent part, Lincoln opened the door for the man Douglass once called "the intensest embodiment of black Nationality" to take up the Union cause.[113] A recruitment poster that Delany produced as a Union recruiter highlights what had changed for him by this point – and what remained the same.

[110] Rollin, *Life and Public Services*, 142–143 (quotations 143); Matthew J. Clavin, *Toussaint Louverture and the American Civil War: The Promise and Peril of a Second Haitian Revolution* (Philadelphia: University of Pennsylvania Press, 2010), 131.

[111] Rollin, *Life and Public Services*, 134; *Weekly Anglo-African*, Jan. 25, 1862.

[112] MRD to Robert Hamilton, Sept. 28, 1861, in the *Weekly Anglo-African*, Oct. 5, 1861, reprinted in *MDR*, 369; MRD to James McCune Smith, Jan. 11, 1862, reprinted in *MDR*, 371; *Rollin, Life and Public Services*, 139.

[113] *Douglass's Monthly*, Aug. 1862, p. 695.

The year 1863 was, in many ways, a brand new day for black Americans. "The hour you have so long waited for has struck," maintained Delany. "Your country calls you. Instead of repelling, as hitherto, your patriotic offers, she now invites your services." Having been made to feel unwelcome in the nation's cities, towns, and universities for decades, the black reformer noted this new departure with appropriate enthusiasm.

Nonetheless, age-old challenges remain. "Your enemies" have maligned your martial spirit, he told potential recruits, saying, "oh, the negro won't fight; he's a coward naturally." Although the "valor" of black soldiers on "a dozen bloody fields" has proven such accusations false, much more work remains to be done, insisted Delany. Volunteer for the state of Rhode Island, he urged black men, and you will have the opportunity not only to follow in the heroic footsteps of the Massachusetts Fifty-fourth but also to come to the aid of your downtrodden brothers and sisters in chains. "The millions of your brethren still in bondage implore you to strike for their freedom," declared Delany. "Will you heed their cry?"[114]

Many did. Over the next few years, Delany became one of the most successful black Union recruiters, joining a distinguished group that included Douglass, William Wells Brown, John Mercer Langston, Henry Highland Garnet, and Mary Ann Shadd Cary. In October 1863, the *Chicago Tribune* praised "the earnest and energetic efforts being put forth by Mr. Delaney [sic] ... towards the enlistment of volunteers for the Artillery Brigade, to be composed entirely of colored men." Delany, who was the first African American to earn a state recruitment contract, eventually helped fill regiments not only from Rhode Island but also from Ohio, Massachusetts, and Connecticut. This record of success inspired the New Romantic to seek to expand his recruitment efforts into parts of the Confederacy. That December, he wrote Secretary of War Edwin M. Stanton with a proposal to head south "to recruit Colored Troops in any of the Southern or seceded states."[115]

Delany did not receive an official response from the War Department. A little over a year later, however, he made a similar proposal to Stanton's boss. According to Rollin's account, Delany visited the White House in February 1865 to pitch Lincoln on a plan to form a new black army, which would be "commanded entirely by black officers, except such

---

[114] MRD, recruitment poster, reprinted in Sterling, *Making of an Afro-American*, 234–235.

[115] *Chicago Tribune*, Oct. 2, 1863; MRD to Edwin M. Stanton, Dec. 16, 1863, in *BAP*, 5: 261.

whites as may volunteer to serve." He predicted that this black army could "penetrate through the heart of the South, and make conquests, with the banner of Emancipation unfurled, proclaiming freedom as they go, sustaining and protecting it by arming the emancipated, taking them as fresh troops, and leaving a few veterans among the new freedmen, when occasion requires." At last, the Union would benefit from the full weight of the millions of slaves who still lived behind Confederate lines. Lincoln responded enthusiastically to this proposal, saying this "is the very thing that I have been looking and hoping for; but nobody offered it." Turning toward Delany, he then asked, "Will you take command?" The New Romantic replied humbly, "If there be none better qualified than I am, sir, by that time I will."[116]

Like so much of Rollin's biography, which, of course, was written under her subject's watchful eye, it is difficult to take this story at face value. After all, it depicts Delany – a long-time aspirant to the role of romantic black redeemer – being asked to play this very role, and by the president no less. Whether this story unfolded as the biography suggests, however, one thing is certain: Not long after his meeting with Lincoln, Delany was appointed as the Union Army's first black major. Four years after proposing his corps d'Afrique to Asa Mahan, then, the black reformer was on the verge of personally seeing this vision through.[117]

Before he headed off to the front, Major Delany paid a visit to his new home in Ohio, where he gave a speech "in full uniform." A white reporter described the remarkable scene: "Major Delany ... is black – black as the blackest – large, heavy set, vigorous, with a bald, sleek head, which shines like a newly polished boot. And he wears brass buttons and shoulder straps! and is an officer in the army of the Union! These sentences record the history of the progress of the country during the war!" African Americans elsewhere got their own glimpse of this striking encapsulation of the changes wrought by the Civil War that spring. To honor Delany's recent commission, the *Weekly Anglo-African* advertised a twenty-five cent postcard portrait of Delany in uniform.[118]

[116] Rollin, *Life and Public Services*, 168–170.
[117] Levine, *Martin Delany, Frederick Douglass*, 222–223.
[118] Rollin, *Life and Public Services*, 173–174; Ullman, *Martin R. Delany*, 300; "The Colored Citizens of Xenia Their Prowess and Their Patriotism Major Delany – A Negro 'in Full Uniform' His Speech," in *MDR*, 388–389; Maurice O. Wallace, *Constructing the Black Masculine: Identity and Ideality in African American Men's Literature and Culture, 1775–1995* (Durham, NC: Duke University Press, 2002), 72–74.

Just two years removed from touring the North in support of emigration to the Niger Valley, the newly minted U.S. Army major left for the warfront, where he would try to put the United States back together. In trading his African dashiki for Union blue, Delany turned his back on his scheme to build a black colony – and with it, the romantic dreams that pulled him toward the African continent and its people and culture. But this did not mean that Delany gave up romantic reform. He was still committed to perfectionist self-help, to the virtues of martial heroism, and to the immediate destruction of the institution of slavery. By heading off to war, he hoped to bring these ideals together, leading a black mission that would simultaneously improve the lives of its participants and, once and for all, crush slavery.

Martin Robison Delany never got his chance to march a black army deep into the heart of the Confederacy, however. Just months after he arrived in South Carolina, the war came to a close, and so the black reformer spent most of his tour of duty helping former slaves adjust to their new lives as a Freedmen's Bureau agent. Despite his preoccupation with playing the role of black emancipator, Delany perhaps found some small measure of solace in the fact that another New Romantic had already tried much the same thing in much the same place. Two years earlier, U.S. Colonel Thomas Wentworth Higginson had led the nation's original black regiment, which was stationed in the South Carolina Sea Islands, on a series of raids into rebel-controlled portions of the southeast.

5

Thomas Wentworth Higginson's War on Slavery

Preston Brooks marched into the Senate chamber in Congress with a score to settle. Smoke from the day's session still hung in the air as the representative from South Carolina made his way to the desk of Charles Sumner. Two days earlier, on May 20, 1856, the Massachusetts senator had concluded a fiery jeremiad about the sins of southern slaveholders. Adding insult to injury, the senator had singled out Brooks's cousin, Senator Andrew P. Butler, who at the time was at home recovering from a stroke. The elderly, infirm South Carolinian went to bed with "the harlot slavery," declared Sumner. This brazen reference to the lurid underbelly of slavery was too much for Butler's kin. So, Brooks set out to teach the Yankee scoundrel – and his fellow southerners – a lesson. As the chamber emptied, Sumner sat at his desk poring over paperwork. Brooks approached the senator with a sturdy cane and proceeded to hit him with all of his might. Stunned, Sumner struggled to free himself from beneath his desk, which was bolted to the floor. His assailant, in the meantime, unleashed a flurry of blows that did not stop until after his cane had shattered into pieces. The brutal assault left Sumner bloody and senseless.[1]

The South cheered the attack. At last, southern honor had been vindicated. Had he been a worthy adversary, Brooks might have challenged the Massachusetts senator to a duel. In white Southern eyes, however, Sumner was no better than a slave or a dog. A caning fit the bill nicely.

---

[1] Donald, *Charles Sumer and the Coming of the Civil War*, 293–311, Williamjames Hull Hoffer, *The Caning of Charleston Sumner: Honor, Idealism, and the Origins of the Civil War* (Baltimore: Johns Hopkins University Press, 2010), 7–35; Potter, *Impending Crisis*, 209–211, 220–221.

The *Richmond Enquirer* called "the act good in conception, better in execution, and best of all in consequence."[2]

Northern reformers, unsurprisingly, were of a different mind. Brooks's assault – and his region's response to it – underscored the illiberal nature and inherent brutality of southern culture to them. "Freedom of speech is beat down in the Senate," decried Douglass. Stowe was struck by the way the South, and South Carolina in particular, rushed to embrace Preston Brooks. "When *Uncle Tom* was published, sentimental humanity was shocked that its author could represent a Legree beating defenceless Uncle Tom on the head with a cow-hide," she wrote. But after Brooks's attack, "the chivalry of South Carolina presented the ruffian with a cane, bearing the inscription, 'Hit him again.'" Parker expressed greater concern about the impact such incidents had on the North. Since the caning of Sumner, he noted in 1858, only one antislavery voice had dared to speak in Congress. "The slave power," bellowed Parker, "dealt the blows upon one Northern man, and nearly silenced all the rest!"[3]

Parker's protégé, Thomas Wentworth Higginson, had been making similar complaints for years. The antislavery movement, he had declared in 1854, has suffered one humiliating defeat after the next: Texas annexation, the Mexican War, the Fugitive Slave Law of 1850, and the rendition of fugitive slaves across the North. In each case, abolitionists' "utter indignation" proved ineffectual. "Each time men have eaten the bravest words they ever spoke, with the same quiet resignation," he lamented. The problem, Higginson believed, was not merely antislavery silence, but rather the reliance on words alone. When he visited a recovering Sumner several months later, Higginson was struck by the contrast between the "heroic tones" of the senator's "unchanged voice" and the "wreck of what was once CHARLES SUMNER ... even after months of convalescence, so weak and tottering." Northern words, however eloquent, were no match for southern sticks.[4]

Yet Higginson also thought the caning was a blessing in disguise. For "the assault on Mr. Sumner," though tragic, "has done more than all the

---

[2] *Richmond Enquirer*, June 9, 1856, quoted in McPherson, *Battle Cry of Freedom*, 151.

[3] FD, "Is the Plan of the American Union Under the Constitution, Anti-slavery or Not? A Debate Between Frederick Douglass and Charles Lenox Remond in New York, New York, on 20, 21 May 1857," in *FDP*, 3: 169; HBS, introduction to *Dred; A Tale of the Great Dismal Swamp in Two Volumes* (London: Sampson Low, Son & Co., 1856), 1: iv; TP, "Aspect of Slavery in America," 291.

[4] *Liberator*, Feb. 2, 1854; TWH, in *Proceedings of the State Disunion Convention, Held at Worcester, Massachusetts, January 15, 1857* (Boston: Massachusetts State Disunion Committee, 1857), 26.

outrages of the Slave Power put together to divide this Union." As he reasoned not long after the brutal attack, "men will bear an injury to their
principles or their interests more easily than a wrong done their pride."[5]
Finally, he hoped, antislavery forces would adopt a forceful response to
slavery. Finally, they would hit back.

Over the course of the 1850s, Higginson had been doing just that.
A Harvard-educated minister, he had gained a national reputation as a
militant abolitionist rather than as a theologian or scholar. Higginson
ran for Congress as a Free Soil candidate in 1850 and, as a leader of the
Boston Vigilance Committee (BVC), worked to assist fugitive slaves in
several high-profile cases. The tall, handsome abolitionist carried a life-
long scar on his face after an ill-fated attempt to free Anthony Burns in
1854. Two years later, Higginson traveled to "Bleeding Kansas" to aid
free-state settlers in their war against Border Ruffians. Later in the decade, he helped plan and finance John Brown's raid at Harpers Ferry. By
late 1862, he was headed to the South Carolina Sea Islands to assume
command of the nation's first regiment of former slaves, the First South
Carolina Volunteers. "This undertaking will be more easy to me than
to almost any one," wrote the newly appointed colonel in his journal,
"because it falls so remarkably into the line of all my previous preparations" (Figure 5.1).[6]

The path Higginson traveled in the 1850s and early 1860s – from
Transcendentalist minister committed to pursuits of the mind to army officer embracing those of the body – resembled that tread by many romantic reformers in the run-up to the Civil War. As the political victories
of the Slave Power accumulated, frustrations with traditional solutions
mounted. Nonetheless, most abolitionists – including all of Higginson's
fellow New Romantics with the exception of Delany – were reluctant
to translate their growing militancy, however impassioned, into concrete
action. Higginson had no such reservations.

He also formulated a more systematic rationale for antislavery violence
than did any of his colleagues. Like them, Higginson believed that higher
law doctrine opened the door to extralegal acts in cases in which the
government aligned against God's law. And he, too, found inspiration in
nature, self-culture, and the virtues of martial valor. What set Higginson
apart, beyond his willingness to take up the sword himself, was the way
he turned these romantic notions into an explicit justification for going to

5 *Liberator*, Aug. 8, 1856.
6 TWH, Journal, Nov. 23, 1862, in *CWJ*, 42.

FIGURE 5.1. Colonel Thomas Wentworth Higginson, ca. 1862–1864.
Source: Photomechanical by unknown photographer, n.d. Courtesy of the Massachusetts Historical Society, Portraits of American Abolitionists, photograph number 81.323.

war against slavery. Like many romantics, Higginson thought that there was an organic connection between the material and spiritual realms. But he placed greater emphasis on body culture – a rigorous program of physical exercise – than immersion in the natural world. As such, Higginson came to conclude that by actively, even violently, resisting the forces of slavery, reformers could avoid the artificial separation of mind and body.

Higginson's concern for the way that resistant abolitionism aided reformers' personal development, in turn, reflected the primacy he gave to the romantic ideal of self-culture. In contrast to Transcendentalists like Emerson and Thoreau, Higginson saw no fundamental tension between self-cultivation and social reform. Instead, he framed forceful resistance to slavery as the means by which reformers and slaves alike could work to improve themselves and to perfect their culture. On the one hand, by risking their own lives in the fight to end slavery, abolitionists and rebellious slaves were following a path toward a greater personal development. On the other hand, resistant abolitionism enabled opponents of slavery to turn self-culture into the very means by which to achieve social and political change for others. If antislavery forces – whether enslaved or free – actively resisted slavery, they could not only break all the chains (literal and figurative) that bound them, they could also destroy the barriers that kept America from fulfilling its destiny. Even the body politic, Higginson held, could benefit from a forcible response to slavery, for resistance would root out the corrosive institution while, at the same time, reinvigorate the waning civilization of the North. Higginson thus had high hopes for the Civil War: If waged for the right reasons and in the right way, it could elevate reformers, emancipate slaves, and save the nation.[7]

Standing on the Shoulders of Giants

Thomas Wentworth Higginson was a latecomer to romanticism. Born in 1823 in Cambridge, Massachusetts, into a prominent though no longer wealthy family, he all but grew up on the Harvard College campus, where his father, Stephen Higginson Jr., was steward. Higginson, in other words, came of age amid the confrontation between such Transcendentalists as Emerson, Parker, and Ripley and the conservatives who controlled Harvard.[8]

Higginson passed Harvard College's entrance examinations in August 1837, before he turned fourteen. Not long after, Emerson delivered his infamous "American Scholar" address at the school's annual Phi Beta Kappa meeting. Taking direct aim at a young nation's intellectual culture, which his host had helped to construct, Emerson lamented that American letters were too subservient to the Old World. "Meek young men grow up in libraries, believing it their duty to accept the views, which Cicero, which Locke, which Bacon, have given, forgetful that Cicero, Locke, and

---

[7] By exploring how Higginson applied the romantic ideal of self-culture to the social problem of slavery, this chapter joins recent scholarship that challenges the long-standing assumption that Transcendentalists were divided into two distinct camps: associationists and Emersonian individualists. On this division, see Perry Miller, ed., *The Transcendentalists: An Anthology* (Cambridge, MA: Harvard University Press, 1950), 464 and Gura, *American Transcendentalism*, xiv. For works that complicate this dichotomy, see Richard Francis, *Transcendental Utopias: Individual and Community at Brook Farm, Fruitlands, and Walden* (Ithaca, NY: Cornell University Press, 1997), ix-xi, 42–43; Adam-Max Tuchinsky, "'Her Cause Against Herself': Margaret Fuller, Emersonian Democracy, and the Nineteenth-Century Public Intellectual," *American Nineteenth Century History* 5 (Spring 2004): 66–99; Tuchinsky, *Horace Greeley's New-York Tribune*, 64–72, 257n20; and Albert J. Von Frank, "On Transcendentalism: Its History and Uses," *Modern Intellectual History* 6 (Apr. 2009): 189–205.

[8] Edelstein, *Strange Enthusiasm*, 1–17.

Bacon were only young men in libraries, when they wrote those books," he announced.[9]

Higginson initially paid little mind to this intellectual revolution fomenting around him. Instead, he spent his time mastering Greek, Latin, mathematics, and history. Although the young student supplemented this traditional curriculum with a healthy regime of football and ice hockey, he spent enough time in the library to finish second in his class. Higginson's academic career, in short, exemplified just the sort of regime that so troubled Emerson. Though far from meek, he grew up in the library.[10]

Not long after graduation in 1841, however, Higginson caught the romantic bug. He had been exposed to Byron growing up, and, over the next few years, he ranged widely through the European theologians and poets who were all the rage in Boston's avant-garde circles. While working as a teacher and later studying as a Harvard Divinity School student, Higginson spent his free time with the works of Madame de Staël and Carlyle. He taught himself German in order to read Goethe and Schiller in their native tongue. Inspired by Coleridge and Thomas De Quincey, Higginson experimented with opium. He also engaged romantics closer to home. He became friends with Transcendentalist ministers James Freeman Clarke and William Henry Channing, visited Brook Farm, and began reading the *Dial*, which exposed him to the work of Emerson, Fuller, Ripley, and Parker. Soon Higginson was living on a diet of Transcendentalism. "The usual dose of Emerson & to bed," he noted in his journal in 1842.[11]

The radical ideas and experimental literary forms associated with romanticism were a "revelation" to Higginson. He hoped to follow in the footsteps of Emerson – whose intellectual powers and "moral nature" he found second to none – and pursue a literary career. But Higginson doubted his talent for writing, even more so after Emerson himself declined to publish his verse in the *Dial*.[12]

[9] Ralph Waldo Emerson, "The American Scholar," in *The Collected Works of Ralph Waldo Emerson*, ed. Robert E. Spiller (Cambridge, MA: Belknap Press of Harvard University Press, 1971), 1: 56.

[10] Edelstein, *Strange Enthusiasm*, 18–34.

[11] Edelstein, *Strange Enthusiasm*, 35–45 (quotation 38); Anna Mary Wells, *Dear Preceptor: The Life and Times of Thomas Wentworth Higginson* (Boston: Houghton, Mifflin, 1963), 45; Brenda Wineapple, *White Heat: The Friendship of Emily Dickinson and Thomas Wentworth Higginson* (New York: Knopf, 2008), 23.

[12] TWH, *Contemporaries* (Boston: Houghton, Mifflin, 1899), 10; TWH to Ralph Waldo Emerson, July 6, 1864, Huntington Library (HUNT), San Marino, CA; Mary

Ultimately, Higginson settled on a different vocation. Listening to Sunday sermons by Clarke, and especially Parker, convinced the young romantic that "one might accomplish something and lead a manly life even in the pulpit."[13] So, Higginson enrolled at Harvard Divinity School in 1844. His second stint at Harvard was not quite as smooth as his first, however. Still the heart of mainstream Unitarianism, the Divinity School continued to emphasize supernatural rationalism, an awkward combination of reason and scriptural revelation that made little sense to Higginson. He was becoming an idealist, a firm believer in romantic intuition. "Take away the Bible from the world," Higginson announced in the 1850s, "and you do not take away conscience ... the distinction between right and wrong is a plant of universal growth."[14]

Yet Higginson devoted far less attention to rarefied theological disputes than did his fellow Transcendentalists. His primary concern, instead, was social action. When Higginson graduated as a young man from Harvard Divinity School, for instance, he urged his fellow ministers to spend less time on biblical exegesis and more time serving humanity.[15]

Higginson followed his own advice and paid the price. Chosen to serve as a minister of the First Religious Society of Newburyport, Massachusetts, he opened his church to radical ideas and activists to the consternation of the congregation's conservatives. Having been converted to the antislavery cause by Lydia Maria Child's 1833 book, *An Appeal in Favor of That Class of Americans Called Africans*, the new minister invited Parker, who became a mentor to him, and fugitive slave William Wells Brown to speak from his pulpit.[16]

Higginson regularly addressed controversial topics too. In a Thanksgiving address in 1848, he chastised his largely Whig congregation for backing Mexican War hero Zachary Taylor – "a mere warrior, a mere slaveholder" – in his successful bid for the presidency. He then pledged to follow a new course in his weekly sermons. "I listened this week to Frederick Douglass," Higginson explained. "And as I sat and looked at that extraordinary man, and trembled before the volcanic

Thacher Higginson, *Thomas Wentworth Higginson: The Story of His Life* (Boston: Houghton, Mifflin, 1914), 64–65; TWH, "My Literary Neighbors," *Outlook* 61 (Feb. 4, 1899): 296.

[13] TWH, *Cheerful Yesterdays*, 97.

[14] Edelstein, *Strange Enthusiasm*, 53–67; TWH, "Scripture Idolatry," in *WTH*, 348.

[15] Edelstein, *Strange Enthusiasm*, 56–58, 66–67; TWH, "The Clergy and Reform," in *WTH*, 328.

[16] TWH to Frederic Bancroft, [Nov. 14, 1910], Frederic Bancroft Papers, RBML, CU; Edelstein, *Strange Enthusiasm*, 83–86; Butler, *Critical Americans*, 24.

words in which the accumulated wrongs of an outraged race burst their way through his soul ... I felt ... as if I were a recreant to humanity ... to let one Sunday pass in the professed preaching of Christianity, and leave the name of SLAVERY unmentioned." While abolitionists cheered this sermon, his congregation found it a hard Thanksgiving meal to swallow. Seats in the church began going unfilled and, by the following year, the minister had resigned.[17]

Higginson found a more suitable pulpit in Worcester, Massachusetts, a few years later. Liberal, non-sectarian, and socially engaged, the Free Church was modeled on Parker's Twenty-Eighth Congregational Society.[18] The new minister was a perfect fit. Higginson was becoming involved in a range of social movements, including temperance, peace, adult education, and women's rights. But one purpose stood above all others. "The Anti-Slavery agitation dwarfs every other political question," he claimed in 1853.[19]

Higginson's emerging antislavery sympathies had led him to take an active role in the Free Soil movement in 1848. Two years later, he ran for Congress on the Free Soil ticket. Higginson's campaign was largely symbolic, however, as he put more stock in moral consistency than in winning votes. "We believe the anti-slavery principle to be of more importance than any thing else now at issue before the American people," he announced early in his campaign, "and upon it we are willing to stand, if need be alone." In the end, Higginson did not stand alone – he received 21 percent of the vote – but still finished third in the race for Congress.[20]

As Higginson became more actively involved in the antislavery movement, he broke ranks with many New England romantics. Some had profound doubts about abolitionism. Nathaniel Hawthorne, for instance, maintained that he would never "feel any preeminent ardor" for the antislavery cause.[21] Other romantics worried about the personal impact of taking up the fight against slavery. Emerson found social reform

---

[17] TWH, *Man Shall Not Live By Bread Alone: A Thanksgiving Sermon* (Newburyport, MA: Charles Whipple, 1848), 6, 9; Edelstein, *Strange Enthusiasm*, 90–95.

[18] TWH to TP, June 24, 1852, HUNT; Edelstein, *Strange Enthusiasm*, 129–130.

[19] Edelstein, *Strange Enthusiasm*, 124–125; TWH, *Cheerful Yesterdays*, 120–121; TWH, *The Unitarian Autumnal Convention: A Sermon* (Boston: Benjamin B. Mussey & Co., 1853), 5.

[20] TWH to TP, Sept. 11, 1848, HUNT; *Newburyport Daily Evening Union*, Oct. 8, 1850; Edelstein, *Strange Enthusiasm*, 107.

[21] Nathaniel Hawthorne, quoted in John Stauffer, "Fighting the Devil with His Own Fire," in *Abolitionist Imagination*, 62.

movements like abolitionism futile if undertaken before personal reform, insisting that if individuals did not start by transforming themselves, then they risked being used – even degraded by – reform movements. "Though I sympathize with your sentiment and abhor the crime you assail," Emerson wrote to reformers, "I shall persist in wearing this robe, all loose and unbecoming as it is, of inaction." Even as he became more committed to the antislavery movement in the 1850s, the high priest of self-reliance continued to write privately about the costs of dedicating one's life to social action. Emerson's protégé Thoreau also had an individualistic vision for reform. "Nothing can be affected but by one man," he wrote. "In this matter of reforming the world, we have little faith in corporations."[22]

Though a close colleague of Emerson and Thoreau, Higginson worried that their emphasis on self-culture could lead to self-absorption, even moral bankruptcy. "The effect of Transcendentalism on certain characters, a minority of its adherents, was seemingly disastrous," he confessed later in life. Here, Higginson sounded like Stowe when she contrasted Byron's "high wrought" idealism with Dickens's more grounded and humanistic fiction.[23]

In *Uncle Tom's Cabin*, Stowe sought to fuse these disparate impulses, anchoring the soaring passion of a romantic with the social engagement of a realist. Higginson, for his part, believed that the antislavery movement provided a similar solution to his fellow Transcendentalists. A counterbalance to moral apathy and narcissism, "the perpetual tonic of the anti-slavery movement" forced these artists and intellectuals to reckon with a pressing social question. "At every crisis brought on" by slavery, Higginson maintained, "it turned out that mere moral purpose might impart to these pacific social reformers a placid courage which rose on occasion to daring."[24]

Abolitionism, in short, was Higginson's solution to the impasse that stymied the romantic mind. While Emerson's fears led him to wrap about

---

[22] Ralph Waldo Emerson, "Reforms," in *The Early Lectures of Ralph Waldo Emerson*, ed. Robert E. Spiller, Stephen E. Whicher, and Wallace E. Williams (Cambridge, MA: Harvard University Press, 1972), 3: 266; James H. Read, "The Limits of Self-Reliance: Emerson, Slavery, and Abolition," in *A Political Companion to Ralph Waldo Emerson*, ed. Alan M. Levine and Daniel S. Malachuk (Lexington: University of Kentucky Press, 2011), 152–184; Henry David Thoreau, quoted in Petrulionis, *To Set This World Right*, 25.

[23] TWH, "The Sunny Side of the Transcendental Period," in *WTH*, 572; Caleb Crain, "The Monarch of Dreams," *New Republic*, May 8, 2001, 43–44; *New-York Evangelist*, July 13, 1843.

[24] TWH, "Sunny Side of the Transcendental Period," 571.

himself a robe of inaction, Higginson tailored a different suit from the same thread. "We all need action," maintained the second-generation Transcendentalist in 1849. "This is shown by the way it transforms us."[25] Participation in the antislavery movement, in his eyes, was a path by which reformers could simultaneously perfect themselves and society. Higginson thus turned the Emersonian dilemma on its head, positing social reform as an opportunity for – rather than barrier to – self-culture. "It is worth being a reformer, for the sake of getting the habit of thinking for one's self. One soon learns the inconsistencies of others and is glad to take each one on his best side," he wrote in 1850. Five years later, he maintained that the fight against slavery was the enlightened avenue out of the dusty library that constrained the American mind. "We have something more important to do in this age than be mere scholars," he announced, for "without the antislavery movement, our literary men would have been what the literary men of England in the last century were, a slavish race."[26]

Words Are Nothing

By the early 1850s, Higginson had settled comfortably into a new town, pulpit, and role. With his liberal Worcester congregation behind him, the young minister was free to immerse himself in the antislavery struggle, which became all consuming. The recently passed fugitive slave law, as we have seen, raised the stakes for all of the New Romantics. Like Parker, Higginson joined the BVC after its passage, quickly becoming one of the large committee's most militant voices.

He was often frustrated that the vigilance committee was not, in fact, vigilant enough. After Thomas Sims was arrested in April 1851, he later complained, the BVC failed "to undertake any positive action in the direction of forcible resistance to authorities." Half of the BVC "were non-resistants, as was their great leader, Garrison, who stood composedly by his desk preparing his next week's editorial," placidly looking "beyond the rescue of an individual to the purifying of a nation," explained Higginson. Much of the rest of the group were political abolitionists, who "were extremely anxious not to be placed for one moment outside the pale of good citizenship." With so few members willing to

---

[25] TWH, Journal, May 1849, Thomas Wentworth Higginson Papers (TWHP), HL.
[26] *Newburyport Daily Evening Union*, Dec. 19, 1850; *Liberator*, June 8, 1855.

act decisively, the BVC failed to prevent Sims from being sent back to Georgia.[27]

Three years later, when runaway Anthony Burns was captured in Boston, Higginson was determined not to let the BVC get bogged down again in empty debate. The day Burns was apprehended, Samuel May Jr. summoned Higginson from Worcester. The committee, May explained, had already convened and a mass meeting was in the works for the following night. "Come strong," he recommended.[28] Higginson did his best. First, he spread the word to Worcester supporters, including his congregant Martin Stowell, who had helped to free the fugitive slave Jerry in Syracuse three years earlier. They were to gather as many local men as possible and bring them along to Boston.

The following morning, May 25, 1854, Higginson set out for Boston. There he found the BVC just as paralyzed as it had been three years earlier. "There was not only no plan of action," he later noted, "but no set purpose of united action." At one point, half of the committee left the meeting in order to stare down the slave catchers who were passing nearby, as if "pointing the finger of scorn" might make a difference to men who made their living capturing runaways. Even purged of timid members, the BVC could not reach a consensus on what to do. Some talked about a rescue the following day, but the details were left undecided.[29]

One thing seemed certain to Higginson: If Burns were to be liberated, then Worcester men needed to take the lead. Fortunately, Stowell arrived on the train from Worcester in the early evening with close to fifty antislavery soldiers. After receiving a quick update from Higginson, Stowell formulated a plan to raid the Boston courthouse during the evening's rally at nearby Faneuil Hall. If word of the attack could be spread quickly, then the "whole meeting" might rush "pell-mell to Court Square, ready to fall in behind the leaders and bring out the slave." Convinced that the element of surprise was essential, Higginson consented to the plan and the two abolitionists got to work. He purchased a dozen axes from a local dry-goods store, which would be stashed near the courthouse door, and headed to Faneuil Hall to apprise other BVC members of their impromptu plan. Stowell went to find more men.

The crowd of five thousand that had squeezed into Faneuil Hall precluded any attempt to meet collectively with the other BVC leaders, but

[27] TWH, *Cheerful Yesterdays*, 139–145 (quotations 139, 140).
[28] Samuel May Jr. to TWH, May 25, 1854, BPL.
[29] TWH, *Cheerful Yesterdays*, 147–149 (quotations 148).

Higginson managed to alert Parker and Samuel Gridley Howe, both of whom he said "gave a hasty approval" to the plot. The Worcester minister then left Faneuil Hall, making his way to Court Square, where some twenty-five abolitionists, black and white, waited. Back at Faneuil Hall, Wendell Phillips and Parker worked the large crowd into a lather. When John Swift, whom Higginson had chosen to give the signal, shouted that a rescue attempt was under way, much of the audience stormed out of Faneuil Hall's lone exit. The plan was in motion.[30]

Not long after, Higginson and his allies heard the crowd rush toward them. The axes the minister had purchased were swiftly distributed, while Stowell and black abolitionist Lewis Hayden drew pistols. In the meantime, Higginson and ten others picked up a large wooden beam, a battering ram they would use to break open the courthouse door. It worked. After forcing open a narrow space through which just one man could enter, Higginson looked at Hayden, who stood next to him. A runaway from Kentucky and BVC agent, Hayden exemplified black militancy in the 1850s. "He did not even look at me," Higginson later remembered, "but sprang in first, I following." Inside, the two would-be rescuers stood face to face with a half-dozen policemen, who immediately attacked them with billy clubs and, perhaps, swords.

No one else managed to make it through the small hole in the door. As shots from Stowell and Hayden rang out, the two abolitionists were forced back out of the courthouse. Blood dripped from a deep cut on Higginson's chin as he emerged, a life-long reminder of the battle on the streets of Boston. The minister fared better than James Batchelder, a courthouse guard who was killed by either a sword or a bullet wound.[31]

One short week after this brazen attempt to free Burns, the runaway was marched in chains through the streets of Boston to be put aboard a ship bound for Virginia. Accompanying the prisoner was a military and police force, the sheer size of which betrayed an ample supply of caution, if not fear. Huge crowds lined the streets and heard drunken renditions of the minstrel song "Carry Me Back to Old Virginny" and shouts of "Shame! Shame! Kidnappers! Kidnappers!"[32]

[30] TWH, *Cheerful Yesterdays*, 149–151 (quotations 150); Von Frank, *Trials of Anthony Burns*, 52–61.

[31] TWH, *Cheerful Yesterdays*, 152–158 (quotation 153–154); Von Frank, *Trials of Anthony Burns*, 62–71; Edelstein, *Strange Enthusiasm*, 154–160. On Hayden, see Kantrowitz, *More Than Freedom*.

[32] Von Frank, *Trials of Anthony Burns*, 212–218; quoted in Steven Lubet, *Fugitive Justice: Runaways, Rescuers, and Slavery on Trial* (Cambridge, MA: Belknap Press of Harvard University Press, 2010), 215.

Just two days later, on Sunday, June 4, Parker addressed the rendition of Anthony Burns in a sermon at Boston Music Hall. Placing blame at the complacent feet of the city's political and economic elite, he was particularly angry with Massachusetts judge Edward Greely Loring, whom Parker called the "prime mover" in "this mock trial." Even Parker's old whipping boy, Daniel Webster, though dead nearly two years, could not escape his opprobrium. "Daniel Webster lies buried at Marshfield; but his dead hand put the chain on Anthony Burns," the minister insisted. "Last winter it was proposed to build him a monument. He needs it not ... Daniel Webster ... had his monument last Friday." The path Burns had taken through the streets of Boston out into the sea would stand as a fitting testament to Webster's tainted legacy.[33]

While Parker highlighted the tragedy of Burns's rendition, Higginson had a more positive take. Although disappointed by the failure to free Burns, he stressed that their well-conceived plan had come "within an inch of success." "If no attempt had been made," Higginson concluded the following summer, "we should have had the ineffable disgrace of seeing Burns marched down State street under a corporal's guard only, amidst a crowd of irresolute semi-abolitionists, hooting, groaning, and never striking a blow."[34]

What is more, Higginson relished the event's symbolic power. "The strokes on the door of the Court House that night," he preached from his Worcester pulpit, "went echoing from town to town, from Boston to far New Orleans, like the first drum beat of the Revolution – and each reverberation throb was a blow upon the door of every Slave-prison of this guilty Republic." Years later, he would remember this event as a sort of Fort Sumter before Fort Sumter: "In all the long procession of events which led the nation through the Kansas struggle, past the John Brown foray, and up to the Emancipation Proclamation, the killing of Batchelder was the first act of violence."[35]

Higginson did not embrace bloodshed unequivocally. "I do not like even to think of taking life," he admitted, "only of giving it." At the same time, he celebrated the physical, active nature of the attempt to

[33] TP, *The New Crime Against Humanity: A Sermon, Preached at the Music Hall, in Boston, on Sunday, June 4, 1854* (Boston: Prentiss and Sawyer, 1854), 44, 53, 60–61; Von Frank, *Trials of Anthony Burns*, 261–262.

[34] TWH to Garrison, Aug. 19, 1855, in the *Liberator*, Aug. 24, 1855.

[35] TWH, *Massachusetts in Mourning: A Sermon, Preached in Worcester, on Sunday, June 4, 1854* (Boston: Prentiss and Sawyer 1854), 4–5; TWH, *Cheerful Yesterdays*, 155.

free Burns. "Words are nothing – we have been surfeited with words for twenty years," he insisted. "I am thankful that this time there was action also ready for Freedom. God gave men bodies, to live and work in.... He gave us higher powers, also, for weapons, but, in using those, we must not forget to hold the lower ones also ready."[36]

This call to action was not a new theme. A half-decade earlier, Delany had written much the same thing in the pages of the *North Star*. Frustrated with African Americans who believed that "prayers and supplications" were the solution to their problems, the black abolitionist argued that since slavery was "a temporal and physical act" it "required temporal and physical means."[37] The rendition of Anthony Burns led his fellow New Romantic to the same conclusion: The solution to the problem of slavery demanded not just the methods of the mind but also those of the body. Put another way, measures such as the Fugitive Slave Law of 1850 would never be defeated by legislative means; they "can only be repealed by ourselves, upon the soil of Massachusetts."[38]

Two years later, Higginson demonstrated his newfound commitment to violent confrontation with proslavery forces, though this time on different soil. As secretary of the Worcester County Kansas Committee and New England agent for the Massachusetts Kansas Aid Committee, he raised money to outfit free-state emigrants to the Kansas territory. Convinced that Eli Thayer's New England Emigrant Aid Society did not adequately prepare settlers for the armed struggle they faced, Higginson bought dozens of rifles, muskets, revolvers, and knives. He even purchased a cannon for the cause. "I am one of those who believes that the whole question is ultimately to be settled by force, not politics," he wrote shortly before heading out to "Bleeding Kansas" in the fall of 1856.[39]

There he found a territory plagued by "perpetual guerilla warfare" between free-state emigrants, like John Brown, and proslavery Border Ruffians. In dispatches Higginson wrote for the *New-York Tribune*, he maintained that the former held the moral high ground in Kansas, fighting a largely defensive war. But if the antislavery man was a dove, the Transcendentalist reminded his readers, he nonetheless "carried a Sharp's

---

36 TWH, *Massachusetts in Mourning*, 4.
37 MRD, "Domestic Economy, [Part II], *North Star*, Apr. 13, 1849, reprinted in *MDR*, 152–153.
38 TWH, *Massachusetts in Mourning*, 11–12.
39 TWH, *Cheerful Yesterdays*, 196–204; Edelstein, *Strange Enthusiasm*, 186–193; Wells, *Dear Preceptor*, 100–101; TWH to William Penn Clarke, Aug. 1856, JBM, RBML, CU.

rifle under his wing."⁴⁰ Higginson, for his part, fired his gun once in
Kansas – and at a hawk not at a Border Ruffian. Nevertheless, he savored
the fantasy of fighting proslavery forces on the frontier. "Imagine me also
patrolling as one of the guard for an hour every night, in high boots amid
the dewy grass, rifle in hand & revolver in belt," he wrote his mother.
Many of his friends and colleagues conjured up similar visions of martial
heroism when they thought of Higginson in Kansas, regularly referring to
him as "general" after he returned from the territory.⁴¹

"Bleeding Kansas" convinced Higginson that war on slavery was imminent, a position that left him at odds with not only moderate opponents
of slavery but also his Garrisonian allies in Boston. Indeed, the Worcester
minister began publicly questioning the viability of moral suasion among
his nonresistant brethren. Abolitionists have been struggling for two
decades against slavery to little avail, he complained at a gathering in
Boston. Though he valued moral suasionists' work, as the 1850s wore
on, they appeared anachronistic to Higginson.⁴² Having once endorsed a
two-pronged antislavery approach comprising both political and moral
agitation, Higginson found the use of such "higher powers" equally
wanting by the late 1850s. Opponents of slavery, he lamented, spent too
much time debating issues such as whether or not the Constitution was a
proslavery document. "All the intellect, all the genius, all the learning ever
expended upon the point of Constitutional interpretation, are not worth,
in the practical solution of the slavery question, a millionth part so much
as the poorest shot that ever a fugitive slave fired at his master," he concluded. Committed to the higher law like his fellow New Romantics,
Higginson eventually settled on what he termed "lower" powers.⁴³

The Sensation of Being Free Men

Most of the reformers explored in this book had trouble endorsing
antislavery violence without reservation. In contrast, by the late 1850s,
Higginson was not only calling for armed resistance but also providing

---

⁴⁰ TWH, *Cheerful Yesterdays*, 209; *New-York Tribune*, Oct. 10, 1856. Higginson's dispatches from Kansas are reproduced as "A Ride Through Kanzas," in *WTH*, 74–100.
⁴¹ TWH to Louisa Higginson, Sept. 24, 1856, TWHP, HL; TWH, note, on a letter from James
   Russell Lowell to TWH, Dec. 25, [1859?], HUNT; TP to TWH, Apr. 7, 1858, HUNT.
⁴² *Liberator*, May 9, 1856; *Liberator*, Aug. 8, 1856; *Liberator*, Feb. 5, 1858.
⁴³ TWH, *Address to the Voters of the Third Congressional District*, 3; TWH, *New
   Revolution*, 8; TWH, *Massachusetts in Mourning*, 4.

an explicit justification for this position. Grounded in higher law doctrine, his burgeoning militancy drew on – and imaginatively combined – three other romantic points of emphasis: organicism, self-culture, and martial heroism.

Like many romantics in the United States and Europe, Higginson believed that the world is not neatly divided into material and moral realms but rather united in a single, organic whole. Following in the footsteps of Emerson, he found powerful confirmation of this idea in Emmanuel Swedenborg's "doctrine of correspondence." We have already seen how the Swedish visionary's racial theories, via Alexander Kinmont, likely influenced Stowe. Swedenborg had a clearer impact on the New England Transcendentalists. Emerson echoed the Swede in concluding that "every natural fact is a symbol of some spiritual fact," while Higginson called the doctrine of correspondence "as old and familiar as the senses of mankind." To Higginson, the natural world was an "inexpressible wonder & delight," with "boundless stores of thought," overshadowing everything else. "Were it possible to eliminate from my writings – such as they are – the element contributed by woods, the boat & the gymnasium – there would not be much left," he held in 1860.[44]

Toward the end of the 1850s, Higginson turned this impulse to commune with nature in on itself, publishing a number of essays in the *Atlantic Monthly* that devoted more attention to the physical body than the external world that surrounded it. He found the same sort of inspiration in the human form that other romantics looked for in nature. Watching water rush by in Brattleboro, Vermont, Higginson mused, "Man's body ... is like a waterfall – a constant stream of fresh particles gliding through – & yet the same form always."[45]

This focus on the human body reflected Higginson's abiding concern for the romantic project of self-culture as well. Higginson believed that self-culture meant more than just mental or moral improvement – the body, too, had to be developed. As manual labor on the small farm gave way to white-collar work in the city, minds became better honed, but hands and bodies softened. Thus, Higginson insisted that his fellow citizens needed to find "some other form of physical activity to restore the

---

[44] Packer, *The Transcendentalists*, 48; Gura, *American Transcendentalism*, 59–64; Chadwick, *Theodore Parker*, 300–301; Emerson, *Nature*, 26; TWH, "Man and Nature," *Christian Examiner* 53 (July 1852): 123; Higginson, Field Book, July 23, 1861, May 20, 1860, and Sept. 18, 1860, TWHP, HL.

[45] Higginson, Field Book, Oct. 26, 1860, TWHP, HL.

equilibrium."[46] The minister, in fact, became something of a body culture prophet, gaining a cohort of converts in his hometown according to one account. After spending a month with friends in Worcester in early 1859, abolitionist Sallie Holley regaled a friend with stories about Higginson's new success. Much of the town in the winter now headed out to the local pond to ice skate. Some called it "Higginson's Revival."[47]

Eventually, the Transcendentalist minister applied these ideas to the fight against slavery. Physical resistance, he came to believe, was not just a practical response to the challenge posed by those who defended slavery; it promised personal benefits as well. In an 1859 *Atlantic Monthly* essay, Higginson urged sickly office workers to follow in Free Soilers' footsteps and go west. Take just a horse and a revolver, he urged readers, and follow "distinct instructions to treat any man as a Border Ruffian who should venture to allude to the subject of disease in your presence." The free-state battle in Kansas, in other words, promised personal as well as social transformation. By traveling west to fight Border Ruffians, abolitionists could improve themselves while they worked to free bondsmen.[48]

Higginson claimed to have witnessed just this sort of personal windfall among the emigrants he found in Kansas when he visited in 1856. "What is most striking," he insisted, is the fact that "the same persons whom you saw a year ago in Boston, indolent and timid, are here transformed to heroes." The frontier fight, in short, was an opportunity to display – and enjoy the attendant personal benefits of – martial valor. "In Kansas, nobody talks of courage, for everyone is expected to exhibit it."[49]

Like the rest of the New Romantics, Higginson regularly appealed to antislavery heroism. But whereas Douglass, Stowe, and Delany constructed fictional or semi-fictional antislavery rebels, Higginson confined himself to the historic record. He characterized Wendell Phillips and John Brown as "the heroic type" and "one of the age's prime heroes," respectively, and he insisted that the dangerous mobs that pioneering abolitionists such as

---

[46] TWH, *Massachusetts in Mourning*, 14–15; TWH, "Gymnastics," *Atlantic Monthly* 7 (Mar. 1861): 285.

[47] Sallie Holley to Mrs. Samuel Porter, Feb. 28, 1859, *A Life for Liberty: Anti-Slavery and Other Letters*, ed. John White Chadwick (New York: Putnam's, 1899), 166–167 (quotation 167); *New York Times*, Jan. 13, 1893. Parker and Stowe likewise emphasized both physical and moral cultivation. See TP, "Chief Sins of the People," 314 and HBS, "Bodily Religion: A Sermon on Good Health," *Atlantic Monthly* 18 (July 1866): 92.

[48] TWH, "A Letter to a Dyspeptic," *Atlantic Monthly* 3 (Apr. 1859): 469. See also TWH, "Theodore Parker," *Atlantic Monthly* 6 (Oct. 1860): 450–451 and TWH, "Saints and their Bodies," 585.

[49] TWH to Dabney family, Oct. 9, 1856, in *LTH*, 142; *New-York Tribune*, Oct. 17, 1856.

Garrison braved gave "the early anti-slavery period ... something of the heroic quality."[50] Yet true heroism, for Higginson, involved more than just the moral courage to stand up for what is right. He also stressed physical courage – the bravery that emerges in the face of mortal danger – which, in times of crisis, kept chaos at bay.[51]

As was the case with Stowe, this emphasis on martial heroism drew on Higginson's life-long love for Walter Scott's historical romances. As a young boy, he had listened to his mother read Scott's tales of the chivalric knights heading off to battle. Later, while serving as a colonel in the Civil War, he compared a raid on a "rebel camp" to the daring exploits chronicled in the Romantic's novels about warfare on the Scottish border. As late as 1903, Higginson lauded "Scott's novels" and "Border ballads" as an important source of inspiration for young American boys. In this way, the Transcendentalist found an unlikely bedfellow in southern planters, whose emphasis on honor and martial virtues was also reinforced by their enthusiasm for Scott.[52]

Higginson and his Confederate counterparts did not see eye to eye on who might benefit from martial valor, however. For the latter, only white southern men had the makings of a cavalier. The New Romantic, in contrast, insisted that the benefits of physical vigor and martial valor were open to all. As much as he believed that resistant antislavery would revitalize a minister or reformer, he thought that resistance was doubly important to the enslaved. Indeed, he argued that if slavery was to be toppled, then black rebellion had to be the engine. "Never in history was there an oppressed people who were set free by others, and it will not begin here and now," he told the New York Anti-Slavery Society in 1858. Too often, the minister implored fellow white abolitionists, the courage of runaway slaves and "the heroes of St. Domingo" are forgotten. "I declare it, as my solemn conviction, from years of acquaintance with that underground railroad, years of intercourse with fugitive slaves, that if the truth could be fairly told to-day, we white Anglo-Saxons on this continent must yield the palm of native heroism to the negro," announced Higginson to cheers from the gallery.[53]

[50] TWH, *Contemporaries*, 278, 238, 245.
[51] TWH, "Physical Courage," *Atlantic Monthly* 2 (Nov. 1858): 730.
[52] Edelstein, *Strange Enthusiasm*, 11; TWH, Journal, Mar. 28, 1863, in *CWJ*, 118; Looby, introduction to *CWJ*, 8; TWH and Henry Walcott Boynton, *A Reader's History of American Literature* (Boston: Houghton, Mifflin, 1903), 269; Franklin, *Militant South*, 194; Osterweis, *Romanticism and Nationalism in the Old South*, 82–102.
[53] *Liberator*, May 28, 1858.

To advance this cause, he published a series of slave rebellion narratives in the *Atlantic Monthly*. These essays underscored the bravery and fighting prowess of the maroon communities of Jamaica and Surinam as well as the examples of Nat Turner, Denmark Vesey, and the slave rebel Gabriel. Walking a narrow tightrope, Higginson sought to undermine romantic racialist notions of black docility, while not depicting rebellious slaves as irrational, bloodthirsty savages. Viewed as a whole, moreover, his slave rebellion narratives underscored one theme: By striking for their own freedom, slaves dropped the baggage that went hand in hand with bondage.[54] Slavery, to Higginson's mind, emasculated the enslaved to a far greater extent than civilization did the northern intellectual or businessman. Yet he did not think such evidence corroborated negative racial stereotypes of the day; rather, he insisted that slaves tended to overcome the deleterious effects of bondage. "Desperate emergencies," wrote Higginson, often spurred a remarkable transformation in slaves: "The black man seems to pass at one bound ... from cowering pusillanimity to the topmost height of daring. The giddy laugh vanishes, the idle chatter is hushed, and the buffoon becomes a hero."[55] What some took to be an inescapable fact – slave docility – could be thrown off at a moment's notice. Contesting the period's racial assumptions about African ancestry, Higginson's *Atlantic Monthly* slave narratives amplified the lesson taught by such fictional characters as Madison Washington, George Harris, and Henry Blake: Blacks possessed the heroic capacity to break their chains, rebel, and thereby transform themselves and the world around them.

Higginson's ideas about body culture and heroic self-transformation also challenged prevailing gender norms, at least in theory. Although he took men as the subjects of his body culture articles, he insisted that "the same principles apply to women." The minister even wrote a hagiographic article about the heroic military leadership displayed by Anne Marie Louise D'Orléans in seventeenth-century France.[56] Still, we should not overlook the fact that in practice women were all but excluded from the possibilities for self-transformation promised by martial heroism.

---

[54] TWH, "The Maroons of Jamaica," *Atlantic Monthly* 5 (Feb. 1860): 213–222; TWH, "The Maroons of Surinam," *Atlantic Monthly* 5 (May 1860): 549–557; TWH, "Denmark Vesey," *Atlantic Monthly* 8 (June 1861): 728–744; TWH, "Nat Turner's Insurrection," *Atlantic Monthly* 8 (Aug. 1861): 173–187; TWH, "Gabriel's Defeat," *Atlantic Monthly* 10 (Sept. 1862): 728–744.

[55] TWH, "Physical Courage," 732.

[56] TWH, "The Health of Our Girls," *Atlantic Monthly* 9 (June 1862): 731; TWH, *Woman and Her Wishes: An Essay* (New York: Fowler and Wells, 1853), 8; TWH, "Mademoiselle's Campaign," *Atlantic Monthly* 2 (July 1858): 193–207.

This was, after all, a period in which women reformers like Lydia Maria Child and the Grimké sisters faced catcalls from antislavery allies for being so bold as to speak their mind at public rallies. Resistant abolitionism, to be sure, entailed a more direct and thorough assault on the literal and psychological barriers of separate spheres ideology.

So, despite his arguments to the contrary, the personal transformation for which Higginson called was highly gendered. It was the means by which to become not so much a better person as a better man. "Ever since the rendition of Anthony Burns, in Boston," he wrote in 1856, "I have been looking for *men*." A year later, Higginson linked his militant antislavery impulse to manliness in no uncertain terms: "If we have not got the tongue of [abolitionist] Stephen Foster, we must take the next sharpest thing; if we cannot roll out the cannon balls that come, every week, out of *The Liberator*, we must take pistol bullets. Anything, any weapon, so that for one instant in our lives we may know the sensation of being free men!"[57]

Disunion and John Brown's Raid

Higginson's concern with the corruption of the body was not limited to the poor health of northern men. Since the early 1850s, he had repeatedly described the United States as a body stricken with the disease of slavery. Shortly after the passage of the Kansas-Nebraska Act, Higginson advocated a homeopathic remedy. While some reformers put their faith in trying to cure the body politic by "the suppression of agitation in the system," his approach would give "for any symptom the medicine that would produce the symptom," and thereby cure "the disease by helping it to do its work in the shortest possible time." Southern proslavery action, in other words, must be met head on, not suppressed by means of compromise. Martin Delany thought that emigration could be "a healing balm to a sorely diseased body," but Higginson had a more invasive cure

[57] *New-York Tribune*, Oct. 17, 1856; *National Antislavery Standard*, June 20, 1857. Some scholars have argued that rhetoric like this, when coupled with the conflict and violence of the 1850s, suggest a "masculinization" of abolitionism in that decade. See James Oliver Horton and Lois E. Horton, "The Affirmation of Manhood: Black Garrisonians in Antebellum Boston" in *Courage and Conscience: Black And White Abolitionists in Boston*, ed. Donald Jacobs (Bloomington: Indiana University Press, 1993), 128–50 and Chris Dixon, *Perfecting the Family: Antislavery Marriages in Nineteenth-Century America* (Amherst: University of Massachusetts Press, 1997), 157–202.

in mind. He supported disunion, a sort of radical amputation that would provoke war with slaveholders.[58]

In early 1857, Higginson organized a Disunion Convention in Worcester, which he hoped might be a first step toward such a procedure. Called in response to the election of doughface Democrat James Buchanan to the presidency, the convention brought together a range of New England abolitionists who were willing to explore, "the practicability, probability, and expediency, of a Separation between the Free and Slave States." Many of the reformers who assembled in Worcester believed disunion could be achieved peacefully. "The dissolution of the Union will paralyze the power of the master," argued William Lloyd Garrison, "and, therefore, render emancipation certain, by a geographical necessity." Higginson agreed that freedom would triumph in the long term, but he did not glide as quickly over the political chaos and violence that might ensue with disunion as did his pacifist counterpart. Bellicose language suffused his convention address. "You say we are 'weak'.... Give us five years, and let us see," he intoned. "You say, 'Oh, they come together, and try to get up a great flame; but some are old flints, that won't strike fire, and some are young steel, that won't give out sparks'.... [A]ll we ask is, Open the doors of your powder magazine, and let us try!" Using such vivid imagery, Higginson seemed to savor the prospect of a bloody struggle: "The vast antagonistic powers are brought into collision – the earthquake comes – and all we disunionists say is, if it is coming, in God's name, let it come quickly!" With characteristic bravado, he roared to loud applause, "Give me a convention of ten men who have drawn the sword for the right, *and thrown away the scabbard*, and I will revolutionize the world."[59]

Militant posturing was nothing new for the Worcester abolitionist, but Higginson may have had in mind a different revolutionary leader. After all, sitting in the hall that day was John Brown. Earlier that month, the Transcendentalist had compared "Old Captain Brown" to the heroes of the American Revolution, telling a largely pacifistic crowd that Brown "swallows a Missourian whole, and says grace after the meat."[60] One week later, in the days leading up to the Disunion Convention, Higginson met for perhaps the first time the man who had been dining on Border Ruffians.[61]

---

[58] *Liberator*, Feb. 2, 1854; MRD, "Political Destiny," 331–332; *Liberator*, Nov. 2, 1855.
[59] *Proceedings of the State Disunion Convention*, 3, 41, 29, 31, 29.
[60] Edelstein, *Strange Enthusiasm*, 203; *Liberator*, Jan. 16, 1857.
[61] TWH, *Cheerful Yesterdays*, 216–217; Edelstein, *Strange Enthusiasm*, 196.

Higginson was not the only New Romantic who found common cause with Brown in the late 1850s. At Brown's behest, Delany had helped organize a convention to entice volunteers to join the white abolitionist's war against slavery in May 1857. And Douglass had met with Brown on several occasions over the last decade. Brown even invited Douglass to join him on a raid at Harpers Ferry as he made his final preparations in Chambersburg, Pennsylvania, but the black reformer declined, fearing that the grizzled militant was taking his men "into a perfect steel-trap."[62]

Theodore Parker, too, was a close confidant of Brown, joining with Higginson, Franklin Sanborn, Gerrit Smith, George Stearns, and Samuel Gridley Howe, to form the so-called Secret Six. This clandestine committee helped Brown formulate his plan to combat slavery, raising almost $4,000 to outfit his rebellion. Although Brown kept the precise details of the plan vague, he described it as similar to the Underground Railroad "business on a *somewhat extended* scale" in a letter to Higginson. Brown had long hoped to take a couple dozen men into the Appalachian Mountains to establish a base from which he could raid local plantations. Some slaves they liberated would be spirited north, while the rest would supplement the army he was building in the mountains. Having studied the slave insurrections and maroon colonies of the West Indies, Brown was sure that the enslaved must be active participants in their own liberation.[63]

Higginson, of course, concurred. Yet when Brown first approached him for assistance, the minister balked. Reluctant to turn over the $3,000 held by the Worcester County Kansas Committee without hearing the details of Brown's plan, Higginson also had misgivings about his counterpart's poor financial track record. The minister's attention, moreover, was focused squarely on the national disunion convention that he hoped to hold in Cleveland in late 1857. In contrast, Franklin Sanborn, a Transcendentalist schoolmaster from Concord with whom Higginson had worked to assist Kansas settlers, had no doubts about Brown. "I believe

---

[62] Rollin, *Life and Public Services*, 85–90; Reynolds, *John Brown, Abolitionist*, 248–264, 299–300; Blight, *Frederick Douglass' Civil War*, 95–96; FD, *Life and Times*, 389.

[63] Brown to Higginson, Feb. 12, 1858, in *John Brown: The Making of a Revolutionary: The Story of John Brown in His Own Words and in the Words of Those Who Knew Him*, ed. Louis Ruchames (New York, Grosset & Dunlap, 1959), 118–119; TWH, "The Route to North Elba," in Redpath, *Public Life of Capt. John Brown, with an Auto-biography of his Childhood and Youth* (Boston: Thayer and Eldridge, 1860), 62; FD, *Life and Times*, 340–341; TWH, *Cheerful Yesterdays*, 220–221; Rossbach, *Ambivalent Conspirators*, 4.

he is the best Disunion champion you can find," he wrote to Higginson in September. With an army of just 100 men, continued Sanborn, Brown "will do more to split the Union than a list of 5,000 names for your [Disunion] convention – as good as that is."[64]

It did not take much to convince Higginson. He later wrote that Brown and his proposed incursion seemed something out of the Walter Scott tales that he read as a child. But it was not simply the thrill of mountain refuges and guerilla warfare that appealed to the Worcester abolitionist. Brown had intimate knowledge of the Alleghenies from his youth and he showed Higginson "rough charts of some of those localities and plans of connected mountain fortresses which he had devised." The New Romantic judged his initial plan entirely practicable. By early 1858, he had committed himself to Brown's cause, pledging to buy a $100 share in the enterprise.[65]

Falling into old patterns, Higginson swiftly became the most militant voice in Brown's ear. This time he had little patience with Brown's decision to postpone his venture. In the spring of 1858, Brown and his co-conspirators feared that Hugh Forbes, an English soldier of fortune who had helped train Brown's recruits, might compromise the plan to invade Virginia. Believing that he was never adequately compensated, Forbes blanketed the North with letters to reformers and politicians, many of whom knew next to nothing about Brown. Although these pleas did little more than discredit Forbes in the eyes of his skeptical correspondents, most of the Secret Six were alarmed. Parker, Sanborn, and Stearns urged Brown to delay the raid until the following year. Gerrit Smith went further. "I never was convinced of the wisdom of his scheme," he admitted to Sanborn. "But as things now stand, it seems to me it would be madness to attempt to execute it."[66]

Among Brown's backers, only Higginson urged him to stay the course. Forbes "can do as much harm next year as this," he wrote John Brown's son Jason. "*If the thing is postponed, it is postponed forever.*" Higginson, in fact, wished he had the means to advance the venture more quickly. "If

[64] Rossbach, *Ambivalent Conspirators*, 86–87; Franklin Sanborn to TWH, Sept. 28, 1857, quoted in Edelstein, *Strange Enthusiasm*, 207.

[65] TWH, *Cheerful Yesterdays*, 219–221 (quotation 220); Edelstein, *Strange Enthusiasm*, 210.

[66] TWH, memorandum, June 1, 1858, BPL; TWH to [John Brown], Oct. 29, 1858, BPL; Reynolds, *John Brown, Abolitionist*, 247–248; Edelstein, *Strange Enthusiasm*, 210–216; Rossbach, *Ambivalent Conspirators*, 132–133; Gerrit Smith to Franklin Sanborn, May 7, 1858, in *The Life and Letters of John Brown*, ed. Franklin Benjamin Sanborn (Boston: Roberts Brothers, 1891), 458.

I had the wherewithal I would buy out the other stockholders & tell our veteran to go on," he told Parker two weeks later. "As it is, I can only urge it to the extent of my investment."[67]

Higginson's frustrations with his co-conspirators were likely matched by Brown's own frustrations with him, for the New Romantic often answered the abolitionist warrior's requests for aid with apologies – but few funds. Although he could not offer financial assistance, Higginson wrote Brown in May 1859 that he would gladly assist him in person, if not for "other ties." Most likely his wife Mary's poor health was the pre-eminent "tie" that kept him from joining Brown, but he also wondered whether his fellow Secret Six conspirators' reluctance had undermined the prospects of the mission. "I long to see you, with adequate funds in your hands, set free from timid advisers, & able to act in your own way," insisted the minister.[68]

These hopes were soon realized. By the summer of 1859, Brown had recruited more than twenty men, including three of his sons and two former slaves. He had also arranged to purchase and ship some 400 Sharps rifles and revolvers to Chambersburg, a town in southern Pennsylvania, and rented a Maryland farmhouse just five miles from Harpers Ferry, Virginia. It is not clear whether Higginson knew the precise details of Brown's plot to raid the United States arsenal in the small town at the confluence of the Shenandoah and Potomac rivers. The minister, in fact, later disavowed knowledge of the target, writing, "Nobody mentioned Harper's Ferry." Yet he and Sanborn were familiar enough with the specifics of the plan to send Francis Jackson Merriam, a last-minute recruit, to the Maryland farmhouse where Brown was making his final preparations.[69]

Regardless, Higginson was thrilled when he first heard news of the Harpers Ferry raid, calling it "the most formidable slave insurrection that has ever occurred."[70] He hoped that Brown might establish an outpost in the Appalachian Mountains that resembled the maroon colonies in Jamaica and Guiana. Brown and the eighteen colleagues that followed him into Harpers Ferry on the night of October 16, 1859 had managed to secure the town and capture its federal arsenal in short order. But the

[67] TWH to [Jason Brown], May 7, 1858, BPL; TWH to TP, May 18, 1858, BPL.
[68] Edelstein, *Strange Enthusiasm*, 217–218; TWH to [John Brown], May 1, 1859, BPL.
[69] TWH, *Cheerful Yesterdays*, 222–223 (quotation 223); Edelstein, *Strange Enthusiasm*, 217–220; TWH to [John Brown], May 1, 1859, BPL; Reynolds, *John Brown, Abolitionist*, 288–307.
[70] TWH to Louisa Higginson, Oct. 1859, TWHP, HL.

initial success did not last long. Local slaves failed to flock to Brown's side in large numbers and, by the following day, his well-armed band had retreated to an engine room, surrounded by a dozen local rifle companies and nearly 100 marines. When Brown refused to surrender, the marines, under the command of Robert E. Lee, stormed the engine house, subduing Brown and his co-conspirators. Seventeen people, ten of whom were Brown's men, died during the raid.[71]

After the abject failure at Harpers Ferry, many of Brown's supporters sought to distance themselves from the militant abolitionist. Three members of the Secret Six – Sanborn, Howe, and Stearns – fled north to Canada. Douglass, who had been warned that two investigators had been dispatched to Rochester to interrogate him, also escaped to Canada, before sailing for England. Meanwhile, Smith and Howe publicly insisted that they had no knowledge of Brown's plans.[72]

In contrast, Higginson, although potentially indictable for treason, stood his ground. Three decades later Douglass praised the Transcendentalist for his bravery, saying that he was "one of the few staunch friends of the old hero of Ossawatomie." Behind closed doors, Higginson castigated several of his co-conspirators for their unwillingness to admit their support for the raid. In a letter to Howe, he called it "the extreme of baseness in us to *deny* complicity with Capt. Brown's general scheme." And when Sanborn pushed Higginson to hold his tongue in public, he acerbically replied, "Sanborn, is there no such thing as *honor* among confederates?" How, asked the Worcester abolitionist, can we worry about saving ourselves "when the nobler man whom we have provoked on into danger is the scapegoat of that reprobation – & the gallows too?"[73]

Higginson was not entirely selfless. In a callous moment not long after the raid he privately acknowledged, "I don't feel sure that his acquittal or rescue would do half as much good as being executed; so strong is the *personal* sympathy with him." (Brown, for his part, said much the same thing to his brother not long after he was sentenced to hang.)[74] In the months that followed, however, Higginson evinced a compassionate side. He helped to arrange and raise money for Brown's legal counsel and explored a number of different plans to free the abolitionist

[71] McGlone, *John Brown's War Against Slavery*, 1–9.
[72] Reynolds, *John Brown, Abolitionist*, 342–343.
[73] *Boston Daily Globe*, Nov. 4, 1888; TWH to Samuel Gridley Howe, Nov. 15, 1859, BPL; TWH to Franklin Sanborn, Nov. 17, 1859, BPL.
[74] TWH to Louisa Higginson, Oct. 23, 1859, TWHP, HL; John Brown to Jeremiah Brown, Nov. 12, 1859, in Sanborn, *Life and Letters of John Brown*, 588.

and his fellow raiders. Shortly after Brown was condemned to death in Charlestown, Virginia, Higginson traveled to the Brown farm in North Elba, New York, where he enlisted the prisoner's wife Mary in an effort to persuade her husband to go along with an escape plan. But Brown, who had come to believe that his martyrdom would be his most effective blow against slavery, objected to any efforts to break him out of jail and, in the end, no attempts were made. After Brown's execution in early December, Higginson hatched a scheme to liberate the two conspirators who remained in jail. He even traveled under an assumed name to Harrisburg, Pennsylvania, to lay the groundwork for the mission. In the face of a vigilant Virginia countryside and heavy snow, however, this escapade, too, was abandoned.[75]

As Higginson worked covertly to rescue Brown, he launched a public campaign to salvage his reputation. David Reynolds has recently made the case that Thoreau "alone took the risk of publicly defending" Brown in the immediate aftermath of Harpers Ferry, citing the Transcendentalist's impassioned talk, "A Plea for Captain John Brown," which was first delivered in Concord on October 30.[76] But pride of place in offering public support for John Brown really belongs to another Massachusetts romantic. On October 25 – five days before Thoreau put his reputation on the line in Concord – Higginson took the stage at Worcester's Brinley Hall. There, before a packed house, he lauded the Harpers Ferry raid and the brave man who led it. Higginson claimed that "nine out of ten of the republicans at Worcester sympathized with the insurrection," adding that his only regret was that "Captain Brown was not successful" (Figure 5.2).[77]

Higginson beat Thoreau to the punch, but Reynolds's larger point – that the Transcendentalists did much to resurrect Brown's reputation – still holds. In the first few days after the raid, most northerners had scrambled

---

[75] TWH, et al., "Circular Letter," Nov. 2, 1859, BPL; Oswald Garrison Villard to TWH, Dec. 8, 1907 and TWH to Oswald Garrison Villard, Jan. 10, 1908, JBM, RBML, CU; *New-York Tribune*, Nov. 8, 1859; TWH, *Cheerful Yesterdays*, 226–235; Edelstein, *Strange Enthusiasm*, 227–236.

[76] Reynolds, *John Brown, Abolitionist*, 346; David S. Reynolds, "Transcendentalism, Transnationalism, and Antislavery Violence: Concord's Embrace of John Brown," in *Emerson for the Twenty-First Century*, ed. Barry Tharaud (Newark: University of Delaware Press, 2010), 472.

[77] *New York Herald*, Oct. 28, 1859; *Liberator*, Nov. 4, 1859; Rossbach, *Ambivalent Conspirators*, 217. Decades later, Higginson was more critical of Brown's plan. See TWH, *Cheerful Yesterdays*, 223 and TWH, "John Brown at Ossawatomie," *Alexander's Magazine* 2 (Aug. 1906): 25.

FIGURE 5.2.   John Brown portrayed on the front cover of *Frank Leslie's Illustrated Newspaper* shortly after being sentenced to death for his actions at Harpers Ferry. While many northerners denounced Brown, Higginson was among the first to defend the militant abolitionist in public.

Source: *Frank Leslie's Illustrated Newspaper*, Nov. 19, 1859, p. 383. Courtesy of the Library of Congress, Prints and Photographs Division, LC-USZ62–137591.

to denounce the antislavery firebrand's actions. The *New York Times* called the raid an "insane undertaking," while the *New-York Tribune* reported that "the whole affair seems the work of a madman." Even radical abolitionists like Garrison registered their disapproval. Harpers Ferry, he wrote in the *Liberator* on October 21, was "a misguided, wild, and apparently insane, though disinterested and well-intended effort." When Higginson voiced support for Brown in Worcester four days later, he was, in short, paddling against the current.[78]

Soon his more prominent Transcendentalist counterparts lent a hand. In late October and early November, Thoreau celebrated Brown before large audiences in Concord, Boston, and Worcester. "No man in America has ever stood up so persistently and effectively for the dignity of human nature, knowing himself for a man, and the equal of any and all governments," he claimed. Thoreau's eloquent address, which was reprinted in a number of New England newspapers, stood in stark contrast to the hostile reception that the Harpers Ferry raid had garnered in the press thus far.[79] Even more influential was the endorsement of Thoreau's neighbor, Emerson, arguably the most popular lecturer in antebellum America. Brown was "the rarest of heroes[,] a pure idealist, with no by-ends of his own," wrote Emerson in his journal. On November 8, he delivered a lecture titled "Courage" before Parker's large congregation at Boston Music Hall. Brown, said Emerson in a talk that was covered by newspapers across the country, was a "new saint ... who, if he shall suffer, will make the gallows glorious like the cross."[80]

Although Emerson's comparison of Brown to Jesus generated some controversy, his strident support for the militant abolitionist, when combined with that of his fellow Transcendentalists, helped shift the tide of northern opinion in the Harpers Ferry revolutionary's direction. Highlighting the impact of Emerson and Thoreau's recent talks, Sanborn wrote on November 14, "the feeling of sympathy with Brown is spreading fast over all the North, and will grow stronger if he is hanged." By the time Brown was executed, a good portion of the northern public counted

---

[78] *New York Times*, Oct. 20, 1859; *New-York Tribune*, Oct. 19, 1859; *Liberator*, Oct. 21, 1859.

[79] Henry David Thoreau, "A Plea for Captain John Brown," in *Echoes of Harper's Ferry*, ed. James Redpath (Boston: Thayer and Eldridge, 1860), 30; Reynolds, *John Brown, Abolitionist*, 344–347.

[80] Emerson, Journal, [Oct. 18–Dec. 2, 1859], in *JMN*, 14: 334; Reynolds, *John Brown, Abolitionist*, 365–367; Gougeon, *Virtues Hero*, 240–249; Petrulionis, *To Set This World Right*, 136–139; Janet Kemper Beck, *Creating the John Brown Legend: Emerson, Thoreau, Douglass, Child, and Higginson in Defense of the Raid on Harpers Ferry* (Jefferson, NC: McFarland, 2009), 117–123; *Liberator*, Nov. 18, 1859.

him a noble martyr. Church bells tolled from Boston to Chicago and even one-time critics such as Garrison declared themselves sympathetic to Brown's insurrectionary goals.[81]

Meanwhile, Higginson's New Romantic allies sounded in from across the Atlantic. Although Douglass had declined to join the raid at Harpers Ferry and fled abroad in its aftermath, he too defended Brown vigorously. In the November 1859 edition of *Douglass' Monthly*, the black editor insisted that "posterity will owe everlasting thanks to John Brown for lifting up once more to the gaze of a nation grown fat and flabby on the garbage of lust and oppression, a true standard of heroic philanthropy."[82] Stowe, who was on her third tour of Europe, placed the Harpers Ferry raid in an international context in a New Year's Day letter to the *Independent*. "John Brown is a witness slain in the great cause which is shaking Hungary, Austria, Italy, France; and his death will be mightier for that cause than even his success. The cross is the way to the throne," she wrote. Finally, Parker, whose failing health had led him to seek convalescence in the Caribbean and then Europe, commented on Brown's execution in a lengthy letter he sent from Rome in November. "Let the American State hang his body, and the American Church damn his soul; still ... the universal justice of the Infinitely Perfect God will take him welcome home," he held. "The road to heaven is as short from the gallows as from the throne; perhaps, also, as easy."[83]

South of the Mason-Dixon line, of course, this outpouring of support for Brown and his seditious raid was too much. The *Baltimore Sun* declared it "preposterous" for the South "to live under a Government, the majority of whose subjects or citizens regard John Brown as a martyr and a Christian hero, rather than a murderer and robber." The *Richmond Enquirer* was more to the point: "The Harper's Ferry invasion has advanced the cause of Disunion more than any other event that has happened since the formation of the Government."[84] Just one year later, South Carolina led a Deep South parade out of the Union. Lincoln's

---

[81] Franklin Sanborn to TP, Nov. 14, 1859, Franklin Benjamin Sanborn Papers, Concord Free Public Library, Concord, MA; *Liberator*, Dec.16, 1859; Harold K. Bush, "Emerson, John Brown, and 'Doing the Word': The Enactment of Political Religion at Harpers Ferry, 1859," in *Emerson Dilemma*, 208–210.

[82] *Douglass' Monthly*, Nov. 1859, p. 1.

[83] *Independent*, Feb. 16, 1860; TP to Francis Jackson, Nov. 24, 1859, in *LCTP*, 2: 178.

[84] *Baltimore Sun*, Nov. 28, 1859, quoted in Villard, *John Brown*, 568; *Richmond Enquirer*, Oct. 25, 1859, quoted in Oates, *To Purge This Land with Blood*, 323.

election was the most proximate cause of this disunionist procession, but secessionists' words testify to the lingering role Harpers Ferry played in the southern imagination. Brown intended "to light up the fires of a servile insurrection, and to give your dwellings to the torch of the incendiary, and your wives and children to the knives of assassins," Mississippian Fulton Anderson told the Virginia Secession Convention in early 1861. His "daring outrage on your soil" was "the necessary and logical result of the principles, boldly and recklessly advanced by the sectional party ... which is now about to be inaugurated into power." Despite Lincoln's disavowal of Brown's methods, suggested Anderson, the president had been elected by a northern public seemingly sympathetic to the violent destruction of the southern way of life. A Lincoln administration, in sum, spelled more Harpers Ferry raids to come.[85]

In a strange twist of fate, then, Brown's botched attack – at least as recast by Higginson and fellow romantic reformers – had helped deliver the very homeopathic dose to the American body politic Higginson had long desired. As the New Romantic wrote to Brown's family in early November, "*He has failed in his original effort only to succeed in greater result. The utmost good he could have done by success does not equal the good destined to follow this failure.*"[86] In search of something to speed the United States toward disunion and civil war, Higginson realized, he could not have asked for a better remedy than John Brown's raid.

The Culmination of the Training of a Life

In late December 1860, just days after South Carolina voted unanimously to leave the Union, Higginson wrote his mother that he was finally approaching "the mode of life" that he desired.[87] Having given up his Free Church pulpit in early 1858, he had, over the last few years, become a regular contributor to the *Atlantic Monthly*. After nearly a decade of militant antislavery activity, punctuated by moments of physical confrontation with proslavery forces, Higginson spent most of 1859, 1860, and 1861 acting the intellectual rather than the revolutionary. In a sense, the *Atlantic Monthly* promised him a much larger congregation to which

[85] Fulton Anderson, quoted in Charles B. Dew, *Apostles of Disunion: Southern Secession Commissioners and the Causes of the Civil War* (Charlottesville: University of Virginia Press, 2001), 62.
[86] TWH to "Dear Friends" [children of John Brown], Nov. 10, 1859, HUNT.
[87] TWH to Louisa Higginson, Dec. 23, 1860, TWHP, HL.

to preach, with forty thousand subscribers and as many as a hundred thousand readers.[88]

Yet the fundamental themes to which Higginson returned often in his *Atlantic Monthly* essays reveal that a life of the mind, at this point, was not for him. His body culture articles, for one, collectively argued that confining oneself to intellectual pursuits was both unwarranted and unhealthy. Likewise, his slave rebellion narratives, which had been inspired by the Harpers Ferry raid, highlighted his persistent engagement with the looming war over slavery.[89]

Truth be told, Higginson was itching for a fight. He had voted for Abraham Lincoln because he thought the Republican would move the country closer to abolition. But Higginson did not think the new president should work to end slavery gradually or even peaceably. While many Americans strove to avert bloodshed during the secession winter, he insisted that "there is more danger in compromise than in war." Accordingly, he spent his time drilling, studying military tactics, and fantasizing about leading a brigade into battle against slaveholders. Working out regularly at his local gymnasium, he cheered the fact that several dozen Worcester men had begun training at a local military school. And Higginson took pride in his role as "commander-in-chief" of a security detail that protected Wendell Phillips from anti-abolitionist mobs in Boston.[90]

When war finally arrived in April 1861, the New Romantic was ecstatic. The Confederacy had bombarded Fort Sumter, one of the few federal installations in the Deep South still controlled by the United States, into submission. In response, Lincoln issued a call for 75,000 militiamen to put down the insurrection. Worcester's citizens, like many across the North, responded with élan. "To-night we have more than enthusiasm," announced Higginson to the large crowd that gathered at City Hall in

[88] TWH to WP, Mar. 16, 1858, TWHP, HL; TWH to TP, Mar. 16, 1858, HUNT; Edelstein, *Strange Enthusiasm*, 204–205; Leonard Brill, "Thomas Wentworth Higginson and the *Atlantic Monthly*" (PhD diss., University of Minnesota, 1968), 27. On the early days of the *Atlantic Monthly*, see Ellery Sedgwick, *The Atlantic Monthly, 1857–1909: Yankee Humanism at High Tide and Ebb* (Amherst: University of Massachusetts Press, 1994) and James C. Austin, *Fields of the Atlantic Monthly: Letters to an Editor, 1861–1870* (San Marino, CA: Huntington Library Publications, 1953).

[89] TWH to James Russell Lowell, Oct. 23, 1859, TWHP, HL.

[90] TWH to Louisa Higginson, Feb. 8, 1861, TWHP, HL; TWH, *Cheerful Yesterdays*, 240–245; James M. McPherson, *The Struggle for Equality: Abolitionists and the Negro in the Civil War and Reconstruction* (Princeton, NJ: Princeton University Press, 1964), 23; Edelstein, *Strange Enthusiasm*, 241–245; TWH to Louisa Higginson, Apr. 5, 1861 and Jan. 21, 1861, TWHP, HL (quotation Jan. 21).

Worcester on April 16. "We have unanimity." As Higginson wrote his mother the day after the rally, "South Carolina has divided the Union & united the North." At the Disunion Convention four years earlier, he had predicted civil war to the horror of many in the audience. But now, Higginson noted, many of those same people "are saying the same."[91] The northern public was at last catching up to him.

Towns and villages from Maine to Missouri held rallies. In New York City, long a hotbed of southern sympathizers, a crowd of more than one hundred thousand voiced support for the Union at the largest public gathering in the republic's history. Even those who tended to view patriotic outbursts as unseemly started pledging themselves to the Union. Having once burned the Constitution in front of an inverted American flag, Garrison watched approvingly as the Stars and Stripes were raised on a high flagpole in front of the *Liberator*'s office.[92]

Higginson brimmed with confidence about northern prospects for success. Not only were his fellow citizens coming together like never before, the Union also had sizeable advantages in terms of manpower, industrial production, and financial resources.[93] Higginson pointed to less obvious factors as well. Unlike most in the South and many in the North, he thought that the martial capacities of Union men outstripped their Confederate counterparts. Four days after Fort Sumter fell, Higginson publicly lauded the marksmanship of northern hunters. "The rifle shooting of Maine and New York forests is probably not surpassed on this continent," maintained Higginson.[94] And Bleeding Kansas had confirmed in his mind that northerners were stronger and braver as well as better shots. Northern superiority had turned the territorial conflict into a "succession of steeplechases," he bragged, with "Missouri, Virginia and South Carolina invariably disappearing over one prairie-swell, precisely as the Sharp's rifles of the [free-state] emigrants appeared on the verge of the next."[95]

Despite his confidence, Higginson's first instinct once the war commenced was that the nation's capital was in jeopardy. So, he approached

[91] *Worcester Daily Spy*, Apr. 17, 1861; TWH to Louisa Higginson, Apr. 17, 1861, TWHP, HL.

[92] McPherson, *Battle Cry of Freedom*, 274–275; Goodheart, *1861*, 187–188; Russell McClintock, *Lincoln and the Decision for War: The Northern Response to Secession* (Chapel Hill: University of North Carolina Press, 2008), 260–263; Mayer, *All on Fire*, 518; Fredrickson, *Inner Civil War*, 65–66.

[93] TWH to Louisa Higginson, Apr. 23, 1861, TWHP, HL.

[94] *Worcester Daily Spy*, Apr. 18, 1861.

[95] TWH, "The Ordeal by Battle," *Atlantic Monthly* 8 (July 1861): 92.

Massachusetts Governor John Andrew for "a sum from his contingent fund," to raise a small company and go "with them into the mountains of Virginia, there to kindle a back fire of alarm and draw any rebel force away from Washington."[96] Eighteen months after helping John Brown invade Virginia, Higginson hoped Brown's son, John Brown Jr., would lead another such venture. "I want at least to get the *name* John Brown rumored on the border," he told his mother. Although this scheme gained some support from Andrew as well as Boston bankers, it never came to fruition. As Higginson would later explain, "the rapid progress of events strengthened the government enough to make any such irregular proceeding quite undesirable."[97]

When Higginson was offered a commission in more regular proceedings, however, he demurred. Later he claimed that he had doubts about his qualifications, but most of his other statements – and actions – speak to the contrary. His reluctance had more to do with his wife's chronic illnesses and his wariness about the war's politics. "It was wholly uncertain whether the government would take the anti-slavery attitude," wrote Higginson, "without which a military commission would have been for me intolerable, since I might have been ordered to deliver up fugitive slaves to their masters, – as had already happened to several officers." Higginson's radical politics, in other words, softened his martial enthusiasm, at least for a time. He continued to ready himself personally – drilling, fencing, and shooting – while waiting for the government's position regarding the slavery question to become clear.[98]

As the Union and the Confederacy rushed that summer to get on a war footing, Higginson publicly complained about the U.S. government's unwillingness "to avow itself anti-slavery, in the sense in which the South is pro-slavery. We conscientiously strain at gnats of Constitutional clauses, while they gulp down whole camels of treason." But Higginson proved reluctant to translate his disappointment with government policies into calls for revolution. Indeed, the man who had once bragged that he had "been trying for ten years to get the opportunity to commit treason" took to chastising fellow abolitionists for similar statements during the Civil War.[99]

[96] TWH, *Cheerful Yesterdays*, 246.
[97] TWH to Louisa Higginson, Apr. 23, 1861; TWH, notes on interview with Gov. Curtin, Apr. 29, 1861, HBSCL; TWH, *Cheerful Yesterdays*, 246.
[98] TWH, *Cheerful Yesterdays*, 247–248 (quotation 247).
[99] TWH, "The Ordeal of Battle," 93; *Proceedings of the Disunion Convention*, 30.

The next year, for example, Higginson wrote a curt letter to Wendell Phillips, who was reported to have suggested that a revolution led by an American Cromwell might be necessary. "I cannot overstate the earnestness with which I dissent from the opinion attributed to you at the Music Hall," he warned, "as to the need of a Cromwell, in certain contingencies, to disperse Congress." Such a move, Higginson believed, "is to surrender all logical ground between ourselves and the guillotine." He had no qualms about fighting "on the *defensive* for liberty even against the government," but insisted that attempting to overthrow it using force "even in the interests of liberty," is to move toward "slavery." After reading Phillips's address in the *Liberator* two days later, Higginson seemed pleased to learn that his colleague had not, in fact, made such an "unguarded" suggestion. The Worcester abolitionist agreed with Phillips that "poorly planned republican institutions are better than the despotism of the sword."[100]

What explains Higginson's newfound commitment to the American government? First, despite his militancy, he shared his fellow New Romantics' basic faith in the liberal tradition. Second, by mid-1861, Higginson had determined that whatever the Lincoln administration's stated war aims, armed conflict with the Confederacy would destroy slavery. If the Union won quickly, then the secessionists will be proven "feeble" and their "social system must go down" for "no one ever spares a beaten bully." If, however, "the war is protracted by slavery's proving strong, then the ultimate military emancipation of slaves, to a considerable extent, is inevitable." In either case, Higginson maintained in the *Atlantic Monthly*, "It is impossible to blink the fact that Slavery is the root of the rebellion; and so War is proving itself an Abolitionist, whoever else is." What is more, if the struggle dragged on, he forecasted that the enslaved would play a lead role in their emancipation. "The rising of the slaves, in case of continued war," he concluded, "is a mere destiny."[101]

And destiny appeared to be arriving quickly. Slaves had been running behind Union lines at any opportunity since the first days of the war. Following their lead, Congress in August 1861 passed the First Confiscation Act, which authorized the seizure of all property, including slaves, that was used to assist the rebellion. Not long after, Secretary of

---

[100] TWH to Wendell Phillips, July 9, 1862 and TWH to Wendell Phillips, July 11, 1862, TWHP, HL; *Liberator*, July 11, 1862; James Brewer Stewart, *Wendell Phillips: Liberty's Hero* (Baton Rouge: Louisiana State University Press, 1986), 239–240.
[101] TWH to Louisa Higginson, May 30, 1861, TWHP, HL; TWH, "Ordeal by Battle," 94.

War Simon Cameron instructed Union General Benjamin Butler that even those slaves who ran away from loyal masters should be received "into the service of the United States," for the duration of the war. Higginson judged these developments "the greatest step in advance taken by our gov't since its formation." "Now," he wrote his mother, the Civil War was "a war of emancipation."[102]

Convinced that abolitionists had to take a lead role in this fight for freedom, he started organizing a Massachusetts regiment in late 1861.[103] Although this regiment was disbanded as part of a statewide cessation of recruiting, Higginson recruited a second the following summer. But before he could take the Fifty-first Massachusetts Regiment into the field, the New Romantic received an offer that "seemed the culmination of the training of a life." In October 1862, Brigadier-General Rufus Saxton wrote from his headquarters in the South Carolina Sea Islands to ask Higginson to take command of the First Regiment of South Carolina Volunteers, the Union's original black regiment. This invitation "fell like a bombshell." Initially, Higginson worried that the "experiment" would not be "tried in earnest" – that the First South Carolina Volunteers would not be a true regiment but rather "a mere plantation-guard or a day-school in uniform." A short visit to South Carolina, however, convinced him that the opportunity was real. Shortly thereafter, a northern-bound steamer carried the new colonel's resignation from the Fifty-first.[104]

Corporal Robert Sutton and the Reconstruction of the American Body Politic

Two months after taking command of the First South Carolina Volunteers, Higginson led approximately 100 men on a late-night expedition in search

---

[102] Simon Cameron to Benjamin Butler, in *The Destruction of Slavery*, ser. 1, vol. 1 of *Freedom: A Documentary History of Emancipation, 1861–1867*, ed. Ira Berlin, et al. (New York: Cambridge University Press, 1985), 74; McPherson, *Struggle for Equality*, 72; McPherson, *Battle Cry of Freedom*, 355; Oakes, *Freedom National*, 84–105; TWH to Louisa Higginson, Aug. 13, 1861, TWHP, HL.

[103] TWH to Wendell Phillips, Oct. 12, 1861, TWHP, HL; TWH to Louisa Higginson, Nov. 1, 1861, TWHP, HL; TWH to Salmon Brown, Nov. 1, 1861, HUNT.

[104] TWH, Scattered Notes, TWHP, HL; TWH, *Army Life in a Black Regiment and Other Writings* (1869; repr., New York: Penguin Books, 1997), 2. Although black regiments from Louisiana and Kansas were officially mustered into the Union Army earlier than the First South Carolina Volunteers, Higginson's new command included soldiers who had been recruited in May 1862, well before any troops who served in Louisiana or Kansas. Thus, he fairly concluded that his unit, although organized initially without official authorization, was the first black Union regiment. TWH, "The First Black

of lumber. The real leader of the expedition, however, was Corporal Robert Sutton, a local freedman who, though "not yet grounded even in the spelling-book," boasted a "systematic intellect" and "modes of thought" that were "strong, lucid, and accurate." As a slave, Sutton had helped build a lumber path near the St. Mary's River, on the border of Georgia and Florida. Higginson hoped to use the corporal's knowledge of the area to sneak up on a Confederate cavalry camp to achieve "the thing really desirable": to get his men "under fire as soon as possible, and to teach them, by a few small successes, the application of what they had learned in camp."[105] The colonel was more interested in cultivating Robert Suttons than in gathering wood.

That evening the element of surprise belonged to the "secesh." A group of Confederates sprung on Higginson's advanced guard, forcing them to discharge their rifles and the rest of his men to take cover in tall grass by the side of the path. Fire was exchanged between the mounted rebels and the Volunteers for perhaps ten minutes, perhaps an hour, Higginson could not tell. Eight of his men were wounded or worse in this brief battle, while the Confederates had a dozen casualties.

Higginson attached immense importance to this encounter, which was later "baptized" the Battle of the Hundred Pines by his deputies. "To me personally the event was of the greatest value," maintained the colonel, because "it had given us all an opportunity to test each other, and our abstract surmises were changed into positive knowledge." His men had stood their ground and repelled the Confederate opponents, proving that black men had every bit the fighting prowess of their white counterparts. The martial valor emphasized in his slave rebellion narratives had been confirmed.[106]

Higginson's decision to focus on Sutton in his 1865 *Atlantic Monthly* article, "Up the St. Mary's," underscores the symbolic importance he attached to his corporal. Robert Sutton was both the embodiment of black achievement and the representation of black potential. Take Higginson's description of a meeting between Sutton and his former plantation mistress, Mrs. A. After the colonel introduced the corporal to Mrs. A, a look of "unutterable indignation ... came over the face of [his] hostess, as she

---

Soldiers," in *Army Life in a Black Regiment*, Appendix B, 211–215; Ash, *Firebrand of Liberty*, 35.

[105] TWH, "Up the St. Mary's," *Atlantic Monthly* 15 (Apr. 1865): 422, 425.

[106] TWH, "Up the St. Mary's," 427, 431; *The War of the Rebellion: A Compilation of the Official Records of the Union and Confederate Armies* (Washington, DC: Government Printing Office, 1880–1901) Series 1, 14: 195.

slowly recognized him." Mrs. A blurted out, "*we* called him Bob." The scene – a slave mistress being confronted by her former property, now dressed in the uniform of the conquering army – was "a group for a painter," Higginson wrote.

This dramatic encounter between master and slave, roles suddenly reversed, pointed to the conflict's potential to transform the future of American race relations, if not the nation itself. "The whole drama of the war seemed to reverse itself in an instant and my tall, well-dressed, imposing, philosophic Corporal dropped down the immeasurable depth into mere plantation 'Bob' again," he wrote. Yet, Higginson was quick to add, the backsliding was "in [his] imagination" rather than in the "personage himself." Indeed, the very corporeality of Corporal Sutton – his dignified self-presentation – demonstrated the progress freedmen could make by fighting in the war. The body, it seems, was not just the tool for physical resistance for Higginson but also the tablet on which progress would be written.[107]

This recurring emphasis on progress, however, had an unseemly underbelly, which emerged in his private writing during the war. As much as Higginson's *Atlantic Monthly* slave rebellion narratives steered clear of the murky waters of romantic racialism, his Civil War letters and journal were soaked in them. The Volunteers, he wrote the month after he arrived in the Sea Islands, "seem the world's perpetual children, docile & gay & loveable." Higginson thought they displayed irrational attachment to their leaders, were unable to master their emotions, and tended to be "cruel to animals," reminding him of "children pulling off flies legs, in a sort of pitiless untaught experimental way." "The extremes of jollity & sobriety being greater with them," he contended, they drilled sedately, "but the moment they are dismissed from drill every tongue is loosed & every ivory tooth is visible."[108] His soldiers' seeming immaturity reinforced a paternalistic bent that Higginson had displayed since his earliest days in uniform. "I like to go round the tents of an evening & hear them purring," the colonel wrote, "& know that they are happy, and happier for seeing me pass."[109]

---

[107] TWH, "Up the St Mary's," 432. When Higginson first wrote of this incident in his war journal, he attached less meaning to it, commenting, "it was all very dreamlike & funny beyond description." TWH, Journal, Feb. 4, 1863, in *CWJ*, 95.

[108] TWH, Journal, Dec. 16, 1862, Jan. 12, 1863, Nov. 27, 1862, in *CWJ*, 67, 85, 48.

[109] TWH to Louisa Higginson, Sept. 26, 1862, in *CWJ*, 235; TWH, Journal, June 27, 1863, in *CWJ*, 155.

Beyond such noxious stereotypes, Higginson also could not get skin color off his mind. References to skin color, such as "grimy," "dusky," and "inky" saturate his personal writings from the war.[110] Higginson also exhibited a fascination with his black soldiers' bodies. "They look magnificently often, to my gymnasium trained eye," he wrote. "& I always like to see them bathing."[111]

At times, Higginson even imagined that he was becoming black himself. "If I don't come home jet black you must be very grateful," he wrote his mother shortly after arriving in South Carolina. When he led his black troops at dress parade, Higginson felt so much a part of the regiment that it took "the line of white officers" coming forward "as the parade dismissed" to remind him that his "own face is not black as a coal."[112] On the surface, this momentary confusion of racial identity evokes blackface minstrelsy, the most popular entertainment form of the period. Like the white performers who painted their face with burnt cork and mocked African Americans on stage, Higginson seemed to enjoy the tantalizing possibilities of pretending to be a racial other. But to conflate Higginson's mental masquerade with minstrelsy would be a mistake. In spite of its complex combination of attraction and revulsion for black culture, blackface minstrelsy aimed to exploit – and in the process reinforce – widespread assumptions of African American inferiority. Higginson's moments of imaginative passing were something altogether different. They reflected, first and foremost, his desire to achieve the sympathetic identification that he and his fellow New Romantics believed lay at the heart of sentimentalism. As Adam Smith argued in *The Theory of Moral Sentiments*, the best way to understand the pain of another was to imagine oneself in the other's situation – to "enter as it were into his body." By imagining himself as black, the white colonel might, if only for a second, better understand the experiences of his men.[113]

---

[110] TWH, Journal, May 8, 1863, Sept. 12, 1863, in *CWJ*, 144, 167; TWH to James T. Fields, n.d., in *CWJ*, 249.

[111] TWH, Journal, Jan. 13, 1863, in *CWJ*, 87; Christopher Looby, "'As Thoroughly as the Most Faithful Philanthropist Could Desire': Erotics of Race in Higginson's *Army Life in a Black Regiment*" in *Race and the Subject of Masculinities*, ed. Harry Stecopoulos and Michael Uebel (Durham, NC: Duke University Press, 1997), 71–115.

[112] TWH to Louisa Higginson, Nov. 28, 1862, in *CWJ*, 248; TWH, Journal, Nov. 27, 1862, in *CWJ*, 47.

[113] Eric Lott, *Love and Theft: Blackface Minstrelsy and the American Working Class* (New York: Oxford University Press, 1993); William J. Mahar, *Behind the Burnt Cork Mask: Early Blackface Minstrelsy and Antebellum American Culture* (Urbana: University of Illinois Press, 1999); Smith, *Theory of Moral Sentiments*, 9.

Higginson's thinking on race, in other words, was anything but clear cut. Like the rest of the New Romantics, he did not believe racial difference was written in stone. Comparing southern freedmen and women to Portuguese peasants he had observed on the island of Fayal, he suggested that environment was really the determining characteristic when it came to those he deemed uncivilized. "A peasantry is a peasantry I suppose," he wrote in his journal, "black or white, slave or free; it has certain characteristics."[114] Ever the patronizing paternalist, Higginson hoped to assist his "boys," as he repeatedly called them, to follow in the footsteps of their "father." And on this score he thought he was succeeding. As his soldiers became more disciplined, better organized, and more sophisticated, they were all but whitewashed to him. Thus, even though he enjoyed toying with the idea of becoming black, the colonel placed greater emphasis on helping his black soldiers turn white.[115]

In the end, Higginson's paternalism left him of two minds about the progress displayed by the Volunteers. He was pleased by their development, but the transformation they were undergoing was not without problems. As he put it, "In every way I see the gradual change in them, sometimes with a sigh as parents watch their children growing up & miss the droll speeches & the confiding ignorance of childhood."[116] More often than not, though, Higginson's reflections on the strides made by his men were positive. In fact, he was so convinced of the success of his regiment that, by the first anniversary of his command, he began to suspect that the "great experiment" had lost its luster. Happy to be outside the public gaze, Higginson worried that his men, "in more perfect condition than ever before," were losing their motivation.[117]

Swimming Alone

Higginson's concern about waning enthusiasm among his men also reflected his own disappointment with military life, which did not live up to his lofty expectations. He regularly complained of the tedious nature of a military command. "So far as love of adventure goes," he wrote just months after he arrived in South Carolina, "it must yield less & less enjoyment as one goes up." Higginson was jealous of the possibilities a

---

[114] TWH, Journal, Dec. 1, 1862, in *CWJ*, 54.
[115] TWH, Journal, Feb. 20, 1863, Mar. 28, 1863, Mar. 7, 1864, in *CWJ*, 105, 119, 203.
[116] TWH, Journal, Feb. 11, 1864, in *CWJ*, 192.
[117] TWH, Journal, Nov. 28, 1863, in *CWJ*, 176–77.

private had to "run many risks" and "go out by night on scouts." Even the company chaplain, "who comes & goes at all hours, like a wild man, galloping on lean horse, wearing a pistol in each side of his belt & a rifle on his shoulder" seemed to play a more exciting role. Higginson, by contrast, felt overburdened by clerical duties, complaining that "the great drawback of these Southern col'd regt's will always be the severe burden of writing they throw on officers." He later lamented that his army experience "had been, after all, one mainly of outpost and guerrilla duty," noting that he "shared in none of the greater campaigns of the war."[118] Fighting may have transformed his men – and indeed the nation – but it had no such effect on the colonel himself.

Shortly after leaving his command in 1864, Higginson waxed misty about the tantalizing opportunities that seemed ever out of reach. "Every grove in that blue distance appears enchanted ground," he wrote, "and yonder loitering gray-back, leading his horse to water in the farthest distance, makes one thrill with a desire to hail him, to shoot at him, to capture him, to do anything to bridge this inexorable dumb space that lies between." Yet a colonel, Higginson explained, has little if any opportunity to hail, shoot, or capture. Nevertheless, what he admitted was a "boyish" impulse could not be entirely suppressed, and so Higginson decided one night to go out on a scouting mission alone – or so he would have his readers believe. Slipping naked into the shallow waters of the river near his camp was an exhilarating experience, he suggested, for "all the excitements of war are quadrupled by darkness."[119] This surreal episode – whether real or, more likely, imagined – did little to end Higginson's ennui.

Although Higginson never tasted "the tonic of war," he did put his stamp on the conflict in two important – and often overlooked – campaigns.[120] The first was the invasion of Jacksonville, Florida, in 1863. Higginson had set out in March with almost one thousand men – most of whom were former slaves – to capture the southern town. He thought Jacksonville could be the first in "a chain of ... posts" up and down the southeastern seaboard not unlike the Appalachian Mountain maroon "fastnesses" conceptualized by John Brown. Utilizing his black soldiers'

---

[118] TWH, Journal, Mar. 16, 1863, May 10, 1863, in *CWJ*, 111, 143; TWH, *Cheerful Yesterdays*, 267.

[119] TWH, "A Night in the Water," *Atlantic Monthly* 14 (Oct. 1864): 393–395 (quotations 393, 394).

[120] TWH, quoted in Edelstein, *Strange Enthusiasm*, 245.

firsthand knowledge of the region, Higginson hoped to establish a series of "advanced" positions, which would disrupt local slave economies, liberate the thousands of slaves who lived in the region, and, perhaps most critically, add new black recruits for the Union cause. Like the abolitionist martyr, he believed his raid would strike fear in the heart of the white South. And just as Brown had touted the "natural forts" and "good hiding-places" to be found in the Appalachians, Higginson highlighted Jacksonville's proximity to the Okefenokee Swamp, which made it "infinitely more defensible" than the South Carolina Sea Islands.[121]

Without firing a shot, Higginson's men steamed up the St. John's River, taking control of Jacksonville. They secured the town's defenses and sent out expeditionary forces to liberate slaves of local plantations. Less than a month after taking Jacksonville, however, Higginson was ordered to abandon the city. Frustrated by a directive that was never fully explained to him, the colonel and his men quickly returned to South Carolina. Although Higginson's regiment helped to liberate almost one thousand slaves that summer, they never managed to establish a permanent mainland outpost.[122]

Still, like the Harpers Ferry raid three and a half years earlier, the Jacksonville campaign bore fruit out of failure. Its early success helped to convert white Union soldiers, and white northerners more generally, to the cause of enlisting African Americans. The raid also provided bait for black recruiters, who pointed to the mission as evidence that black soldiers would, indeed, be given the opportunity to fight. Finally, as historian Stephen Ash has recently argued, the campaign, though short-lived, may have convinced the War Department to take up black recruitment in earnest. Lincoln had at last embraced the enlistment and arming of black men in his Emancipation Proclamation, yet three months later recruitment was proceeding slowly, with only eight total regiments in active duty. Not long after the news of the Jacksonville expedition made its way to Washington, however, Secretary of War Edwin Stanton ordered the full-scale enlistment that would put 180,000 black men in blue by the end of the war. Higginson, for his part, believed that his mission

[121] TWH to Rufus Saxton, Feb. 1, 1863, in *The War of the Rebellion: A Compilation of the Official Records of the Union and Confederate Armies* (Washington, DC: Government Printing Office, 1885), Series 1, 14: 198; TWH, *Cheerful Yesterdays*, 221; TWH, Journal, Feb. 15, 1863, in *CWJ*, 102; TWH, *Army Life in a Black Regiment*, 75–77, 195; FD, *Life and Times*, 340–341; Ash, *Firebrand of Liberty*, 70, 73, 84–86.

[122] TWH, Journal, Mar. 24, 1863, Mar. 30, 1863, in *CWJ*, 117–123; Ash, *Firebrand of Liberty*, 109, 166–181, 196.

had made the difference. In May 1863, he recounted a story that he had heard from a fellow officer in his journal. "Secretary Chase told him the Cabinet at Washington kept their whole action in regard to enlisting colored troops *waiting* to hear from us in Florida, & when the capture of Jacksonville was known, the whole question was regarded as settled," wrote Higginson. "This is, I think, the best expression of the importance of our action that has yet occurred."[123]

Higginson's New Romantic colleagues Douglass and Delany aspired to lead similar incursions in the years that followed. In the summer of 1864, Lincoln invited Douglass to the White House to discuss his frustrations over the fact that more than a year after he announced his final Emancipation Proclamation most of the Confederate enslaved remained behind enemy lines. Douglass suggested that Confederate masters were likely keeping news of the proclamation from their slaves. Perhaps, replied the president, Douglass could organize "a band of scouts, composed of colored men," who would venture behind Confederate lines carrying "the news of emancipation, and urg[ing] the slaves to come within our boundaries." The Rochester abolitionist agreed to this proposal, which struck him as similar to "the original plan" of his old friend John Brown, but Lincoln never followed up on the offer.[124] Six months later, Lincoln chose Douglass's former partner Delany to lead a remarkably similar venture. As we saw in Chapter 4, Delany met with the president in early 1865 to propose a plan to lead a black army into the heart of the Confederacy. Shortly thereafter, he was given a major's commission and ordered to report to South Carolina to serve under Higginson's old commander, Rufus Saxton. Had the war not come to a close two months later, Major Delany might have had his chance to follow in the path blazed by Colonel Higginson and Captain Brown.[125]

Higginson also joined Douglass and Delany in the long campaign to ensure that black soldiers received equal pay. When the Union first began recruiting African American soldiers in late 1862, Stanton had promised that they would "receive the same pay and rations as are allowed by law to volunteers in the service." In accordance with this directive, Higginson's

---

[123] Ash, *Firebrand of Liberty*, 200–202, 211–213; TWH, Journal, May 25, 1863, in *CWJ*, 145.

[124] FD, *Life and Times*, 435; FD to Abraham Lincoln, Aug. 29, 1864, in *LWFD*, 3: 405–406; Oakes, *Radical and the Republican*, 229–233; Levine, *Martin Delany, Frederick Douglass*, 220–221.

[125] Rollin, *Life and Public Services*, 168–175; Ullman, *Martin R. Delany*, 294–307.

men were initially paid the same salary as white soldiers, ranging from thirteen dollars for privates to twenty-one dollars for sergeants.[126]

The War Department announced an abrupt change of policy in June 1863. Stanton's original directive, according to the interpretation of Solicitor William Whiting, was inconsistent with the Militia Act of July 17, 1862, which stipulated that black military recruits should be paid ten dollars a month, minus three dollars for clothing. Despite the fact that the Militia Act was drafted to recruit black laborers for the Union army, rather than soldiers, Whiting directed the payment of all African Americans in uniform be reduced accordingly. An affront to all black soldiers, the move was especially galling in regiments like the First South Carolina Volunteers, which had been formed with promises of equal pay. Higginson reported that the pay cut led to "visible demoralization" among his Sea Island soldiers. With few means of formal protest, most of the Volunteers, like African American soldiers more generally, refused to accept any salaries until full pay was restored.[127]

Higginson lobbied against this new policy with vigor. He wrote letters to the War Department, leading politicians, and major newspapers like the *New-York Tribune*. He even petitioned Congress. The federal government, the colonel maintained, was in breach of its contract with the men who fought for its survival. Former slaves could not hope to participate in a free labor world, he maintained, if "any employer, following the example of the United States Government, may make with him a written agreement, receive his services, and then withhold the wages."[128]

Abolitionists, fellow white officers of black units, and key Republicans joined the chorus of outrage. Douglass and Delany temporarily halted their recruitment efforts to protest unequal treatment of black soldiers. Douglass even raised the issue with the president directly in an 1863 visit to the White House. Although Lincoln made no promises that he would remedy the situation, Douglass left the White House with hope. As he

---

[126] Edwin Stanton to Rufus Saxton, Aug. 25, 1862, quoted in Noah Andre Trudeau, *Like Men of War: Black Troops in the Civil War, 1862–1865* (Boston: Little, Brown, and Co., 1998), 91; Joseph T. Glatthaar, *Forged in Battle: The Civil War Alliance of Black Soldiers and White Officers* (New York: Free Press, 1990), 169–170.

[127] Glatthaar, *Forged in Battle*, 170–172; Edelstein, *Strange Enthusiasm*, 293; TWH, *Army Life in a Black Regiment*, 174.

[128] TWH to William P. Fessenden, Feb. 13, 1864, Thomas Wentworth Higginson Letters, New York Historical Society, New York, New York; TWH, "Regular and Volunteer Officers," *Atlantic Monthly* 14 (Sept. 1864): 356; TWH to the Editor of the *New-York Tribune*, Aug. 12, 1864, in *Army Life in a Black Regiment*, 225.

later wrote, the president believed that unequal pay was "a necessary concession to smooth the way to their employment at all as soldiers, but that ultimately they would receive the same."[129]

In typical fashion, Lincoln proved prophetic. By mid-1864, the efforts of Higginson, Douglass, and their many allies began to bear fruit. First, Congress voted to equalize pay for all soldiers from January 1, 1864, while adding that back pay was owed to any soldiers who were free on April 19, 1861. This stipulation – which denied the former slaves in the First South Carolina Volunteers the pay they were owed for service before 1864 – was modified the following year. In March 1865, Congress approved full back pay for all African American soldiers who had enlisted under the promise of equal remuneration.[130]

By this point, Higginson's army career was over. He had been wounded in the summer of 1863 while leading an expedition up the South Edisto River in South Carolina. Grazed by a bullet or shell, Higginson recovered on a twenty-day furlough to Worcester after a brief hospital stay. He was back in South Carolina by August, but two months later he was diagnosed with malaria. Ill for most of the winter, Higginson took a six-month furlough in the spring of 1864, although he had no intention of returning to active duty. "I have never regained my health since I was wounded last summer," he explained to Wendell Phillips that July, "& though I am slowly gaining now ... I am about to resign." Ironically, while Higginson had been spurred into battle by visions of the revitalizing influence of warfare, injury and illness undid him. His body let him down.[131]

Higginson left South Carolina in May 1864 for his new home in Newport, Rhode Island, the coastal resort to which his wife had recently relocated. Soon the war would seem a distant memory. "That I was in it myself seems the dreamiest thing of all" he wrote on April 9, 1865, the day Lee surrendered to Grant at Appomattox Court House. "I cannot put my head upon it in the least, and if some one convinced me, in five minutes, some morning, that I never was there at all, it seems as if it wd.

[129] Glatthaar, *Forged in Battle*, 172–173; Trudeau, *Like Men of War*, 252–254; Rollin, *Life and Public Service*, 151–154; Leon F. Litwack, *Been in the Storm So Long: The Aftermath of Slavery* (New York: Knopf, 1979), 80–81; Blight, *Frederick Douglass' Civil War*, 167–169; Oakes, *Radical and the Republican*, 210–217; FD, *Life and Times*, 423.

[130] Glatthaar, *Forged in Battle*, 174–175; Trudeau, *Like Men of War*, 254–255.

[131] Edelstein, *Strange Enthusiasm*, 289–290; TWH to Wendell Phillips, July 11, 1864, TWHP, HL.

all drop quietly out of my life, & I shld read my own letters & think they were some one's else."[132]

If an ethereal memory, Higginson's experiences in the Department of the South proved weighty enough for the New Romantic to put them to good use after the war. Drawing on his wartime journal, notes, and letters, he became an ardent essayist and public lecturer in the late 1860s. For a few years, he kept up a dizzying pace; in 1867 he published an essay nearly every month. Higginson collected a number of these pieces in his 1869 book, *Army Life in a Black Regiment*.[133]

Part personal memoir and part ethnographic notebook, *Army Life* sought to capture not just Higginson's wartime experiences but also the behaviors, songs, and speech patterns of the Sea Island freedpeople. Chapters like "Negro Spirituals" revealed the ways in which romanticism continued to shape Higginson's mind despite his disillusionment with his own command. Above and beyond "direct experiences," he confessed at the start of the chapter, the war brought "many a strange fulfillment of dreams of other days." Service in the Department of the South afforded Higginson the opportunity to follow in the footsteps of Walter Scott, who had sought to capture and preserve the vernacular culture of borderland Scotland. "The present writer had been a faithful student of the Scottish ballads and had always envied Sir Walter the delight of tracing them out amid their own heather, and of writing them down piecemeal from the lips of aged crones," wrote Higginson. The Sea Islands were "a kindred world of unwritten songs," where a people every bit "as simple and indigenous as the Border Minstrelsy" produced "plaintive" and "essentially poetic" spirituals. Like Scott, Higginson romanticized this seemingly primitive and authentic culture, which he described in horticultural terms. "I could now gather on their own soil these strange plants, which I had before seen as in museums alone," he wrote of black spirituals he heard in the Sea Islands. In another chapter he concluded that his black soldiers' "philosophizing is often the highest form of mysticism," adding that "our dear surgeon declares that they are all natural transcendentalists."[134]

Despite his ongoing engagement with black culture, Higginson's efforts on behalf of the freedmen dwindled after the war. As he explained in a

[132] TWH to Anna Higginson, Apr. 9, 1865, TWHP, HL.
[133] Cambridge Public Library, *A Bibliography of Thomas Wentworth Higginson* (Cambridge, MA, 1906), 13–14.
[134] TWH, *Army Life in a Black Regiment*, 149, 41; Jon Cruz, *Culture on the Margins: The Black Spiritual and the Rise of American Cultural Interpretation* (Princeton, NJ: Princeton University Press, 1999), 146–147.

letter to his sisters, "I do not want to give any more years of my life exclusively to those people now, as much as I am attached to them." Instead, the New Romantic wrote to Emerson that his "naturally happy temperament can turn to old pursuits again – with only occasional impulses of longing for the field." He returned to literary pursuits with a renewed "appetite ... lured by the joy of expression itself."[135] No longer ignited by the fire to crush the Slave Power, by the urge to free both the enslaved and himself, by the enthusiasms of war, Higginson would find shelter in the pleasure of writing.

In the spring of 1862, Thomas Wentworth Higginson had published a "Letter to a Young Contributor" in the *Atlantic Monthly*. Among the most frequent contributors to the fledgling journal, he proffered basic guidelines to aspiring writers. Three-fourths of the way through the essay, however, Higginson departed from his careful exposition of the role a young writer might play in the American literary scene to warn potential contributors not to be carried away with enthusiasm for war. "It is not needful here to decide which is intrinsically the better thing," he insisted, "a column of a newspaper or a column of attack ... each is noble, if nobly done, though posterity seems to remember literature the longest." Higginson later attributed these words of warning not to indecision about military life but rather to the frustration of trying to organize a regiment of volunteers in the war's first year. Still, his "Letter to a Young Contributor" betrays a wariness about wartime enlistment that is difficult to reconcile with Higginson's optimism about physical culture, desire to balance thought with action, and faith in the regenerative effects of violence.[136]

On one level, this ambiguity should not surprise us. After all, each of the New Romantics we have explored in this book struggled to square disparate, at times contradictory, elements in their thinking. Notwithstanding their soaring rhetoric and perfectionist striving, our *dramatis personae* displayed a degree of ambivalence not typically associated with antebellum reformers. Nowhere was this uncertainty more profound – or vexing – than on the question of how to defeat slavery.

---

[135] TWH to Mary and Susan Louisa Higginson, Oct. 9, 1865, TWHP, HL; TWH to Ralph Waldo Emerson, July 6, 1864, HUNT.

[136] TWH, "Letter to a Young Contributor," *Atlantic Monthly* 9 (Apr. 1862): 409; TWH, *Cheerful Yesterdays*, 248.

Like many opponents of slavery, the New Romantics wrestled with a variety of strategic responses in the years leading up to the Civil War. Could the peculiar institution be eradicated through an appeal to hearts and minds? What about political agitation? Or black emigration abroad? Over the course of the 1850s, many romantic reformers lost hope in these nonviolent solutions, turning increasingly instead to armed confrontation with the Slave Power. But, as we have seen, doubts about the efficacy of antislavery violence lingered. And none of the New Romantics traded their pen for a sword. None, that is, but Higginson.

While the antislavery colonel was not immune to bouts of ambiguity and spells of indecision, he adopted a resistant response to slavery more enthusiastically than did his peers. He also crafted a more fully developed theory of antislavery violence than the rest of the New Romantics. Drawing not only on higher law doctrine and martial heroism but also on romantic ideas about nature and self-culture, Higginson posited resistant abolitionism as *the* solution to the nation's problems as well as his own. What is more, he repeatedly proved ready to put his militant philosophy into action. Thus, Higginson's advice to aspiring *Atlantic Monthly* writers was remarkable. But it was also prescient.

After all, Higginson got his taste of war and he found it wanting. He had entered the fray inspired by visions of martial glory, only to learn that it was not the electrifying experience he had imagined when writing his physical culture and slave rebellion essays. And once fighting slaveholders stopped paying personal dividends, it no longer seemed worth all the effort.

Nevertheless, as historian Leslie Butler has recently written, the Civil War remained "the defining event" in Higginson's life in the decades that followed. As he saw it, the First South Carolina Volunteers had "solved the problem of the nation, so far as the arming of the blacks was concerned." "I have done my share," he wrote Wendell Phillips in 1864. Many of his fellow Americans would likely have agreed with these sentiments. For, as emancipation unfolded over the course of the war, it became clear that few reformers had done more to destroy slavery than Higginson and his fellow New Romantics.[137]

---

[137] Butler, *Critical Americans*, 4; TWH to Wendell Phillips, July 11, 1864.

Conclusion

Emancipation Day, 1863

As dawn broke across a cloudless sky over the South Carolina Sea Islands, Charlotte Forten, a black Pennsylvania missionary who had come south to teach local freedpeople, set out for Camp Saxton. After a short ride on an old carriage pulled by "a remarkably slow horse," she boarded the ship *Flora* for the trip up the Beaufort River to Port Royal Island. A band entertained the white and black passengers on the warm winter morning as they steamed toward the headquarters of the First South Carolina Volunteers. By midday, a crowd of thousands – comprising not only teachers like Forten but also Union soldiers, northern ministers, and ex-slaves – had gathered in the largest live-oak grove Forten had ever seen. Located on what had once been the Smith plantation, just a few miles outside of Beaufort, Camp Saxton was, according to Thomas D. Howard, another northern missionary teaching in the Sea Islands, "ideal for the occasion."[1]

Why had they come? It was the first day of 1863, yes, but more importantly, the day that Abraham Lincoln's Emancipation Proclamation was scheduled to take effect. It was, in other words, the moment in which Sea Island bondspeople – indeed, nearly all of the more than 3 million slaves who resided in rebellious southern states – were to be officially

[1] Harriet Ware, letter, Jan. 1, 1863, in *Letters from Port Royal Written at the Time of the Civil War*, ed. Elizabeth Ware Pearson (Boston: W. B. Clarke, 1906), 128; Charlotte L. Forten Grimké, Journal Three, Jan. 1, 1863, in *The Journals of Charlotte Forten Grimké*, ed. Brenda Stevenson (New York, Oxford University Press, 1988), 428; Ash, *Firebrand of Liberty*, 13; Reminiscences of Thomas Dwight Howard, in "Charles Howard's Family Domestic History," 103, #3256-z, Southern Historical Collection, University of North Carolina at Chapel Hill, Chapel Hill, NC.

declared "thenceforward, and forever free."[2] Lincoln's proclamation, to be fair, did little to change the lives of the enslaved who labored behind Confederate lines, at least in the short term. Yet, as many Lincoln critics overlooked then and afterwards, the proclamation also applied to tens of thousands of slaves living in Union-occupied portions of Arkansas, Florida, Mississippi, North Carolina, and the South Carolina Sea Islands. While most – if not all – of these men, women, and children had been liberated over the first two years of the war, the Emancipation Proclamation stamped their newfound status with the presidential imprimatur.[3]

At Camp Saxton, then, the first day of January signaled a definitive end to a barbarous institution that had thrived in the region since the seventeenth century. "When some future Bancroft or Motley writes with philosophic brain and poet's hand the story of the Great Civil War," wrote Thomas Wentworth Higginson, "he will find the transition to a new era in our nation's history to have been fitly marked by one festal day, – that of the announcement of the President's Proclamation, upon Port-Royal Island, on the first of January, 1863."[4]

The Transcendentalist colonel presided over the ceremony from his perch on a newly erected platform at the center of a grove. It was a remarkable scene, he recalled a year later: "The moss-hung trees, with their hundred-feet diameter of shade; the eager faces of women and children in the foreground; the many-colored headdresses; the upraised hands; the neat uniforms of the soldiers; the outer row of mounted officers and ladies; and beyond all the blue river, with its swift, free tide." Such a tableau, unthinkable a few years earlier, suggested both radical change and difficult work ahead. Sitting next to Higginson on the platform were a dozen Union officers, musicians, and dignitaries, mostly white. They stared out

---

[2] Abraham Lincoln, "Preliminary Emancipation Proclamation," Sept. 22, 1862, in the *Collected Works of Abraham Lincoln* (New Brunswick, NJ: Rutgers University Press, 1953), 5: 434.

[3] While some historians have argued that Lincoln's proclamation immediately freed tens of thousands of slaves in non-exempt Union-occupied regions like the Sea Islands, James Oakes makes a compelling case that federal legislation and War Department policy had already liberated bondspeople living in those areas. Eric Foner, *Forever Free: The Story of Emancipation and Reconstruction* (New York: Knopf, 2005), 50; Foner, *Fiery Trial*, 243; Louis P. Masur, *Lincoln's Hundred Days: The Emancipation Proclamation and the War of the Union* (Cambridge, MA: Belknap Press of Harvard University Press, 2012), 281; William C. Harris, "After the Emancipation Proclamation: Lincoln's Role in Ending Slavery," *North and South* 5 (Dec. 2001): 48; Harris, *Lincoln's Last Months* (Cambridge, MA: Belknap Press of Harvard University Press, 2004), 126; Oakes, *Freedom National*, 129–144, 192–255; James Oakes, e-mail to author, Mar. 5, 2013.

[4] TWH, "Regular and Volunteer Officers," 356–357.

at a sea of black faces, many of whom were now Union soldiers. These simple arrangements were a stark reminder that even emancipation celebrations could not escape the racial hierarchy of the day.[5]

The program began just before noon with a short musical selection, a prayer, and then a recitation of the preliminary Emancipation Proclamation – the final version was not sent out until later that day – by a local planter who had freed his slaves a quarter century earlier. On paper, Lincoln's proclamation may have had, in historian Richard Hofstadter's famous description, "all the moral grandeur of a bill of lading," but when read aloud at to the crowd at Camp Saxton – who repeatedly interrupted the recitation with loud cheers – it was plenty powerful.[6]

The real emotional chord that day, however, was struck by the freedpeople themselves, when, midway through the program, they broke out in an impromptu rendition of "My country 'tis of thee." Just as Higginson formally accepted regimental colors – a silk American flag and a regimental banner made of a lightweight wool fabric called bunting – from New York minister Mansfield French, "there suddenly arose, close beside the platform, a strong but rather cracked & elderly male voice, into which two women's voices immediately blended, singing if by an impulse that can no more be quenched than the morning note of the song sparrow." Soon hundreds of voices joined in. The singing eventually spread to the white officers and missionaries seated behind Higginson on the platform, before the colonel curtly commanded, "Leave it to them."[7]

By the end of the song, sobbing men and women erupted in applause. Dr. Seth Rogers, surgeon for the Volunteers, wrote that the freedmen and women "sang it so touchingly that everyone was thrilled beyond

---

[5] *Frank Leslie's Newspaper*, Jan. 24, 1863; *Liberator*, Jan. 16, 1863. On emancipation celebrations, see Mitch Kachun, *Festivals of Freedom: Memory and the Meaning of African American Emancipation Celebrations, 1808–1915* (Amherst: University of Massachusetts Press, 2003) and Kathleen Ann Clark, *Defining Moments: African American Commemoration & Political Culture in the South, 1863–1913* (Chapel Hill: University of North Carolina Press, 2005).

[6] *New-York Tribune*, Jan. 14, 1863; *New York Times*, Jan. 9, 1863; TWH, Journal, Jan. 1, 1863, in *CWJ*, 76; Thomas D. Howard to the *Christian Inquirer*, Jan. 2, 1863, in the *Christian Inquirer*, Jan. 17, 1863; Ash, *Firebrand of Liberty*, 22–28; Richard Hofstadter, *The American Political Tradition and the Men Who Made It* (New York: Vintage, 1989), 169. Although Hofstadter used these words to describe the final Emancipation Proclamation, he surely would have applied them to the equally legalistic preliminary proclamation.

[7] Laura M. Towne, *Letters and Diaries of Laura M. Towne, Written from the Sea Islands of South Carolina, 1862–1864*, ed. Rupert S. Holland (Cambridge, MA: Riverside Press, 1912), 98; TWH, Journal, Jan. 1, 1863, in *CWJ*, 76–77; Ware, letter, 130.

measure," while Charlotte Forten thought "it was a touching and beautiful incident." Higginson was more effusive. "I never saw anything so electric; it made all other words cheap," he observed. "Art could not have dreamed of a tribute to the day of jubilee that should be so affecting; history will not believe it." It was "the key note to the whole day."[8]

Just one day earlier, Higginson had wondered whether locals even cared about Emancipation Day. "They know that those in this Department are nominally free already," he noted, "and also they know that this freedom has yet to be established on any firm basis." The ceremony at Camp Saxton, however, put an end to such doubts. "Just think of it," Higginson wrote that evening, "the first day they had ever had a country, the first flag they had ever seen which promised anything to their people, – & here while others stood in silence, waiting for my stupid words these simple souls burst out in their lay, as if they were squatting by their own hearths at home."[9]

The spontaneity of the moment seemed to inspire the New Romantic, who offered lengthy off-the-cuff remarks. "I have for six weeks listened to the songs of these people," he told the crowd, songs that more often than not evoked "sadness and despair." Never before had Higginson heard them utter this hopeful hymn. "How could they sing it before to-day? Was it their country? Was it to them a land of liberty? But now, with this flag unfurled, 'the day of jubilee has come,'" he proclaimed. Higginson then called the regiment's color guard, Sergeant Prince Rivers and Corporal Robert Sutton, to the front of the stage. After presenting the Stars and Stripes to Rivers, Higginson reminded his sergeant that it was his solemn duty to defend the flag with his life. "Do you understand?" asked the colonel. Rivers said yes. Next Higginson presented the bunting flag to Sutton and ceded the platform to his men.[10]

Rivers, a freedman whom Higginson compared to Haitian rebel Toussaint Louverture, spoke first. He repeated his pledge that "he would die before surrendering" the flag, adding that "he wanted to show it to all the old masters." Corporal Sutton focused his remarks on the emancipations that had yet to come. Not a single person here, he told the assembled

---

[8] *New-York Tribune*, Jan. 14, 1863; Seth Rogers, "War Letters of Dr. Seth Rogers, 1862–3," *Proceedings of the Massachusetts Historical Society* 43 (Feb. 1910): 340; Grimké, Journal Three, Jan. 1, 1863, in the *Journals of Charlotte Forten Grimké*, 430; TWH, Journal, Jan. 1, 1863, in *CWJ*, 77, 76.

[9] TWH, Journal, Dec. 31, 1862, TWH, Journal, Jan. 1, 1863, in *CWJ*, 75, 77.

[10] TWH, quoted in Howard to the *Christian Inquirer*, Jan. 2, 1863, in the *Christian Inquirer*, Jan. 17, 1863; Ware, letter, 130–131 (quotation 131).

FIGURE C.1. Emancipation Day celebration, Camp Saxton, South Carolina, Jan. 1, 1863. Sergeant Prince Rivers of the First South Carolina Volunteers addresses the enthusiastic crowd.
Source: *Frank Leslie's Illustrated Newspaper*, Jan. 24, 1863, p. 276. Courtesy of the Library of Congress, Prints and Photographs Division, LC-USZ62–88808.

freedpeople, "but had sister, brother, or some relation among the rebels still." The ex-slave then insisted that "he could not rest satisfied while so many of their kindred were left in chains," before urging the Volunteers to "*show their flag to Jefferson Davis in Richmond.*" The audience showered both soldiers with shouts of approval (Figure C.1).[11]

The program continued with another hour's worth of speeches and songs, before the large crowd retired to crude tables to enjoy a feast of barbecued oxen, hard bread, and molasses-sweetened water. Finally, in a fitting coda to the day's events, the Volunteers demonstrated their new-found freedom in an expertly executed dress parade, their bright red trousers – which Higginson hated – the only reminder that the former slaves

[11] TWH, Journal, Jan. 13, 1863, in *CWJ*, 88; Mansfield French to S. P. Chase, Jan. 2, [1863], in *The Salmon P. Chase Papers, Volume 3: Correspondence, 1858-March 1863*, ed. John Niven (Kent, Ohio: Kent State University Press, 1996), 352; *New-York Tribune*, Jan. 14, 1863. The French letter is misdated January 2, 1862.

were any different from the hundreds of thousands of white Americans who wore Union blue.[12]

By four o'clock, the crowd began to make its way home from Camp Saxton. Some left on foot, while others boarded the *Flora*, which headed north toward St. Helenaville, and the *Boston*, which sailed south for Hilton Head. Music filled the air as the black men and women, leaving "their grove of gladness," in Howard's apt phrase, once again broke into song. "The singing," he wrote, "seemed to come from free hearts."[13]

Higginson's New England friends and colleagues, including Garrison, Stowe, and Emerson, also rang in Emancipation Day with song. In their case, however, they marked the occasion indoors, within the elegant confines of the Boston Music Hall. Having once hosted Parker's Twenty-Eighth Congregational Society, the Music Hall, on New Year's Day, 1863, was the site for a Grand Jubilee Concert. The event featured the music of Beethoven, Handel, and Mendelssohn, with all proceeds going to a freedpeople's education fund. Like Higginson, the concert promoters envisioned Emancipation Day as "the complement of the 4th of July, 1776."[14]

Three thousand people turned out for the afternoon performance, which one observer deemed as "brilliant" as its audience. As was the case in South Carolina, the day's most memorable moments were not part of the formal program. First, as the large audience took their seats, concert organizers announced that Emerson would open the proceedings with a poem that he had written for the occasion. John Sullivan Dwight had asked the Transcendentalist to write something for the Music Hall performance a few weeks earlier. Who better to punctuate this confluence of art and reform than the Sage of Concord he thought?[15]

Dwight had a point. Emerson, who years ago had shaken off his reluctance about lending his pen to the cause of the slave, had been thinking a great deal about Lincoln's Emancipation Proclamation. "Great is the virtue of the Proclamation," he confided in his journal not long after

---

[12] *New-York Tribune*, Jan. 14, 1863; *New York Times*, Jan. 9, 1863; TWH, Journal, Jan. 1, 1863, in *CWJ*, 78; Ware, letter, 133; TWH, *Army Life in a Black Regiment*, 6.

[13] Ash, *Firebrand of Liberty*, 27; Howard to the *Christian Inquirer*, Jan. 2, 1863, in the *Christian Inquirer*, Jan. 17, 1863.

[14] *Liberator*, Dec. 26, 1862; TWH, "Regular and Volunteer Officers," 357; *Liberator*, Jan. 9, 1863.

[15] "Letter from Boston," Jan. 5, 1863, in the *Christian Examiner*, Jan. 17, 1863; Dwight, "The Jubilee Concert," *Dwight's Journal of Music* 22 (Jan. 10, 1863): 326; Gougeon, *Virtue's Hero*, 291; Kenneth W. Cameron, "The First Appearance of Emerson's 'Boston Hymn,'" *ESQ: A Journal of the American Renaissance* 22 (1st qt. 1961): 97–101.

the president first announced the measure in September. "It works when men are sleeping, when the Army goes into winter quarters, when generals are treacherous or imbecile." In November, he published a short essay in the *Atlantic Monthly* that celebrated the proclamation as a once-in-a-century "poetic act." Accordingly, Emerson agreed to write a poem for the Grand Jubilee Concert, though in typical fashion he asked that his name be left off the program in case he did not finish in time.[16]

Emerson surely had in mind his late friend Theodore Parker as he began to read his "Boston Hymn" at the Music Hall. Earlier that day, he had spoken to the Parker Fraternity, which had stopped meeting regularly at the large venue after the popular minister's death.[17] Now, Emerson offered a poem that echoed many of the themes his fellow Transcendentalist had touched on time and again in that very space. Parker, recall, rooted his romantic approach to the problem of slavery in the eternal struggle between the Idea of Freedom and the Slave Power, the superiority of God's higher law, and the progressive course of history. In similar fashion, Emerson's hymn, which opened with God speaking to the audience's Puritan forbearers, posited a world divided between "fishers and choppers and ploughmen," on the one hand, and kings and tyrants, on the other. Like Parker, Emerson suggested that the Lord is on the side of the "wretch and slave," while imploring his listeners to follow God's law, making his angel of freedom "your king." Then, turning his attention more directly to the cause of the day, Emerson proclaimed that emancipation was, in fact, divine will. God commands:

> To-day unbind the captive
> So only are ye unbound;
> Lift up a people from the dust,
> Trump of their rescue, sound!

[16] Emerson, quoted in Masur, *Lincoln's Hundred Days*, 175; Emerson, "The President's Proclamation," *Atlantic Monthly* 10 (Nov. 1862): 638–640; Dwight, "The Jubilee Concert," 327.

[17] George Willis Cooke, *John Sullivan Dwight, Brook-Farmer, Editor, and Critic of Music: A Biography*, (Boston: Small, Maynard, and Co., 1898), 190–192; *Sixty-Sixth Annual Report of the Executive Committee of the Benevolent Fraternity of the Churches in the City of Boston* (Boston: L. H. Lane, 1900), 44. Although Cooke has Emerson delivering the Parker Fraternity lecture on Emancipation Day, his pocket diary for 1863 only mentions the Music Hall recital. Ralph Waldo Emerson, *The Letters of Ralph Waldo Emerson*, ed. Eleanor M. Tilton (New York: Columbia University Press, 1994), 9: 88n92.

Five years after Parker intoned in the Music Hall that "slavery must go down," Emerson, standing in the same spot, welcomed the institution's end.[18]

The august audience at the Music Hall, which included not only poets such as John G. Whittier and Henry Wadsworth Longfellow but also historian Francis Parkman and Oliver Wendell Holmes Sr., applauded enthusiastically when Emerson finished. Dwight judged the poem, which was soon published in his journal as well as the *Atlantic Monthly*, "a hymn of Liberty and Justice, wild and strong." Later that evening, Emerson reprised his performance at the home of Secret Six member George Luther Stearns, where he joined Julia Ward Howe, Bronson Alcott, Moncure Conway, and Wendell Phillips for an unveiling of a marble bust of John Brown.[19]

While Emerson no doubt thought about Theodore Parker as he read his "Boston Hymn" at the Music Hall, the Grand Jubilee audience appears to have had another New Romantic on its collective mind. Although she had no official role in the proceedings, Harriet Beecher Stowe became the focal point not long after word of the president's final proclamation arrived in the hall. This announcement was, to be sure, a tremendous relief to the audience, which feared a last-minute change of heart by the president. Stowe herself had even traveled that fall to Washington to ascertain whether emancipation would, in fact, become a reality. After meeting with numerous politicians and officials, including Lincoln himself, the novelist concluded that abolitionists had nothing to fear. "It seems to be the opinion here that the president will stand up to his Proclamation," she wrote from the capital in late November. "I have noted the thing as a glorious expectancy."[20]

Many of her fellow concertgoers, however, were not convinced that New Year's Day would be so glorious after all. At least, that is, until intermission, when a gentleman on the floor stood and announced that Lincoln's final proclamation was "coming over the wires." The crowd immediately erupted in "a storm of enthusiasm ... such as was never before seen from such an audience in that place," according to the *Liberator*. When a second man yelled, "The Proclamation is said to be all that was

---

[18] Emerson, "Boston Hymn," in his *Poems* (Boston: Houghton Mifflin, 1918), 201–203; TP, "Effect of Slavery," 336.

[19] *Liberator*, Jan. 9, 1863; *Boston Daily Advertiser*, Jan. 2, 1863; Indagator to *Christian Inquirer*, Jan. 5, 1863, in *Christian Inquirer*, Jan. 17, 1863; Dwight, "The Jubilee Concert," 327; Gougeon, *Virtue's Hero*, 292; Benjamin Quarles, *Lincoln and the Negro*, 144.

[20] Carl Sandburg, *Abraham Lincoln: The War Years, Volume Two* (New York: Harcourt, Brace and Co., 1939), 10; HBS to James T. Fields, Nov. 27, 1862, quoted in Hedrick, *Harriet Beecher Stowe*, 305.

expected or desired," three cheers were offered up for Lincoln, then three more, and three more after that. Garrison, who sat in the gallery, was recognized in a similar fashion, though his name elicited a few hisses, too.[21] Eventually, the crowd settled on a less divisive figure, who likewise sat in the gallery. Spotting the author of *Uncle Tom's Cabin*, they began waving handkerchiefs and chanting, "Mrs. Stowe! Mrs. Stowe! Mrs. Stowe!" As the cries got louder, Stowe – "her face all aglow with pleasure and excitement" – stood, moved closer to the rail, and bowed, wiping the tears from her eyes. Whether or not Lincoln ever credited Stowe with starting the Civil War, the Music Hall crowd certainly believed that she had helped bring on this day of emancipation.[22]

As far as we know, Stowe made no formal remarks at the Grand Jubilee Concert. In the final months of 1862, however, she had penned an essay that laid bare what the day meant to her. Defending the antislavery course charted by Lincoln and the Republicans in Congress to reformers in Great Britain, Stowe called the Emancipation Proclamation "the great, decisive measure of the war." Critics misrepresent Lincoln, she argued, when they suggest that his message was, "Be loyal, and you shall keep your slaves; rebel, and they shall be free." On the contrary, the Emancipation Proclamation must be interpreted in light of the abolishment of slavery in the District of Columbia and the western territories – developments that refashioned the very Union Lincoln sought to restore. "The President's Proclamation simply means this," held Stowe, "Come in, and emancipate peaceably with compensation; stay out, and I emancipate, nor will I protect you from the consequences."[23]

While Boston's liberal elite honored Stowe in the Music Hall, a more diverse set of reformers marked the occasion just a couple blocks away. Organized by the Union Progressive Association, a black club led by William C. Nell, the all-day meeting at Tremont Temple attracted thousands of black and white reformers, including Nell, Lewis Hayden, Leonard Grimes, Samuel May Jr., John S. Rock, William Wells Brown, and James Freeman Clarke. Matching the size and enthusiasm of the

[21] *Liberator*, Jan. 9, 1863; Mayer, *All on Fire*, 545–547; Wendell Phillips Garrison and Francis Jackson Garrison, *William Lloyd Garrison, 1805–1879: The Story of His Life Told By His Children* (Boston: Houghton, Mifflin, 1899), 4: 69–70.

[22] Wilson, *Crusader in Crinoline*, 486–487; Charles Edward Stowe and Lyman Beecher Stowe, *Harriett Beecher Stowe*, 211; Hedrick, *Harriet Beecher Stowe*, 306; Reynolds, *Mightier than the Sword*, ix–x.

[23] Hedrick, *Harriet Beecher Stowe*, 303–306; HBS, "Reply to 'the Affectionate and Christian Address,'" 129–130.

gatherings at Camp Saxton and in the Music Hall, the Tremont Temple meeting lasted much longer. And once again, a New Romantic was prominently featured. In this case, it was Frederick Douglass, who twice addressed the Temple crowd and then spoke again into the early morning at Grimes's Twelfth Baptist Church.[24]

Since Lincoln's election, Douglass had been as loud a critic of the president as had any abolitionist. But when Lincoln announced his preliminary Emancipation Proclamation, Douglass quickly became among its most enthusiastic cheerleaders. "We shout for joy that we live to record this righteous decree," he wrote in the October edition of *Douglass' Monthly*. Although well aware that "all written rules for the Government of the army and navy and people" would remain "'paper orders' ... were they not backed up by force," the Rochester abolitionist was confident that Lincoln intended to put the full weight of the Union behind the decree.[25]

Like Stowe, Douglass believed the president would not reconsider his proclamation. Thus, his first Tremont Temple speech, which he offered hours before the final proclamation came over the wire, bespoke measured optimism. Douglass began by expressing "his pleasure at the near prospect of the abolition of slavery." After years of suffering in darkness, he "saw a bright light" in the future. If Emancipation Day would not immediately bring "the abolition of the curse" of slavery, it was "the beginning of the end."[26]

When the news of Lincoln's final proclamation arrived at the Tremont Temple, the audience, just like their Music Hall counterparts, exploded in a "wild and grand" scene. Some shouted with joy and threw their hats and bonnets in the air, others sobbed tears of relief. "The effect was electric," reported the *Christian Inquirer*. Three cheers were given for Lincoln and, according to Douglass, "almost everybody else." The celebration lasted until midnight, when much of the crowd decamped to Twelfth Baptist Church, where they continued nearly until dawn. "It was one of

[24] *Liberator*, Dec. 26, 1862; *Liberator*, Jan. 16, 1863; *Boston Daily Advertiser*, Jan. 2, 1863; Kantrowitz, *More Than Freedom*, 338; FD, *Life and Times*, 427–428; FD, "Emancipation and the Dawn of Light: An Address Delivered in Boston, Massachusetts, on 1 January 1863," in *FDP*, 3: 546.

[25] FD, "Emancipation Proclaimed," in *LWFD*, 3: 273; FD, "The Slaveholders' Rebellion. A speech delivered on the 4th day of July, 1862, at Himrods Corners, Yates Co., N.Y.," in *LWFD*, 3: 258.

[26] Oakes, *Radical and the Republican*, 200–202; FD, "Emancipation and the Dawn of Light," 547.

the most affecting and thrilling occasions I ever witnessed, and a worthy celebration of the first step on the part of the nation in its departure from the thralldom of ages," wrote Douglass.[27]

The only New Romantic who, as far as we know, did not play a central role – either in spirit or person – in an Emancipation Day celebration is Martin Robison Delany. Still committed to African emigration at the start of 1863, Delany may have not been willing to publicly express his enthusiasm for Lincoln's proclamation. Whatever the case, the black reformer's respect for the president, according to biographer Frances Rollin, matched that of his colleagues. In the early stages of the war, Delany detected "in the course then being pursued by Mr. Lincoln, a logical conclusion, and which, if not at first intended, would ultimately result in accomplishing the desires of the friends of freedom – emancipation to the slaves of the South, and the freedmen's rights as an inevitable consequence." And, as we have seen, Lincoln's decision to begin enlisting and arming black Americans – which he announced in his final Emancipation Proclamation – led Delany to trade black emigration for Union recruitment in a matter of months.[28]

Emancipation Day, in sum, was the high watermark of the New Romantics' influence and power. They took center stage at freedom celebrations from Boston to the South Carolina Sea Islands and, in the years before and after that New Year's Day, they enjoyed private sittings with the president. The fame and impact of Higginson and Stowe, Douglass and Delany, would never be greater.

New Romantic ideas were also ascendant on Emancipation Day. Lincoln's proclamation of freedom, to be sure, was a victory for every activist who had labored to end slavery in America, not to mention millions of bondspeople. As historian Manisha Sinha has written, Lincoln "had come to abolitionist ground." But these second-generation romantic reformers could take special satisfaction at the dawn of 1863. After all,

---

[27] *Liberator*, Jan. 16, 1863; *Christian Inquirer*, Jan. 17, 1863; FD, "The Proclamation and a Negro Army: An Address Delivered in New York, New York, on 6 February 1863," in *FDP*, 3: 568; Masur, *Lincoln's Hundred Days*, 208–209; FD, *Life and Times*, 427–430 (quotation 430).

[28] Rollin, *Life and Public Services*, 137. One biographer suggests that Delany was lecturing in Chicago when Lincoln issued the final proclamation, but I have neither been able to verify this claim, nor to locate any information about whether he participated in Emancipation Day celebrations there. Ullman, *Martin R. Delany*, 282.

their distinctive approach to the problem of slavery had become – in effect – national policy.[29]

With a simple stroke of the pen, Lincoln had committed the United States to immediate emancipation for the majority of the nation's slaves. That the proclamation made no mention of protecting the legal and financial interests of slaveholders, nor of gradually introducing emancipation, thrilled immediatists of all stripes. Even Garrison, who had recently dismissed Lincoln as "a man ... without moral vision," called the final proclamation "a great historic event, sublime in its magnitude, momentous and beneficent in its far-reaching consequences, and eminently just and right alike to the oppressor and the oppressed."[30]

Other components of the Emancipation Proclamation, however, spoke more directly to the ideas of second-generation romantic reformers than those of their Garrisonian predecessors. The New Romantics, for one, better accommodated their perfectionist impulses to the realities of democratic institutions and practices. They urged American politicians to turn the federal government into an abolitionist instrument, even as the sectional crisis seemed to undermine that possibility. While Garrison dramatically burned the Constitution, Douglass sought to salvage the document's latent antislavery message. Once the war came, the New Romantics pushed Lincoln and his fellow Republicans in Congress to recognize that the only way to preserve the Union was to end slavery. "The circumstances of this eventful hour," insisted Douglass in early 1862, "make the cause of the slaves and the cause of the country identical."[31]

Even the disparate response of the New Romantics and Garrisonian perfectionists to the final proclamation is telling. Both sets of romantic reformers were disappointed by the document's shortcomings, particularly the exclusion of slaves who lived in the border states and many Confederate areas under Union control. But in the short term they responded quite differently. Less than two weeks after Emancipation Day, for instance, the American Anti-Slavery Society's executive committee held a special meeting in which they issued a series of unanimously adopted resolutions that underscored what Lincoln failed to accomplished. The president has been "derelict to his duty in exempting any part of the

---

[29] Manisha Sinha, "Allies for Emancipation? Lincoln and Black Abolitionists," in *Our Lincoln: New Perspectives on Lincoln and His World*, ed. Eric Foner (New York: Norton, 2008), 185.

[30] Garrison, quoted in Masur, *Lincoln's Hundred Days*, 191; *Liberator*, Jan. 2, 1863.

[31] FD, "The Black Man's Future in the Southern States: An Address Delivered in Boston Massachusetts, on 5 February 1862," in *FDP*, 3: 494.

Slave States, or any portion of the slave population," they insisted. The Garrisonian organization expressed "general joy" for the Emancipation Proclamation, but then betrayed its political tin ear by adding that "to attempt to keep a million of slaves in their chains, while essaying to liberate other millions in a similar condition, is to present a revolting spectacle to the civilized world."[32]

In contrast, the New Romantics saw the glass half full. When Douglass explored Lincoln's final Emancipation Proclamation in great detail in early February, he did not linger on the flaws that he believed were "more seeming than real." Instead, the Rochester abolitionist told a crowd at Cooper Union in New York City that the president had produced an "amazing approximation toward the sacred truth of human liberty." Invoking Theodore Parker's theories of romantic intuition, he continued, "All the space between man's mind and God's mind, says Parker, is crowded with truths that wait to be discovered and organized into law for the better government of society." Lincoln's proclamation was no mere accommodation, but rather "a grand moral necessity." For all its imperfections, it had a touch of the divine. "I believe in the millennium," Douglass declared, "and hail this Proclamation, though wrung out under the goading lash of a stern military necessity, as one reason of the hope that is in me." Thus, he concluded that the Emancipation Proclamation "may be called the greatest event of our nation's history, if not the greatest event of the century."[33]

If the moral foundations of the Emancipation Proclamation rewarded the New Romantics' faith in American democracy, then its most radical provision – the commitment to recruit and arm black men – seemed to come directly out of the militant playbook of Higginson, Delany, Parker, and Douglass. The president had been quietly tiptoeing toward this decision for months. But on New Year's Day – with the whole world watching – Lincoln publicly committed the nation to enlist its black population to fight against white southerners.

Such a dramatic policy change, unsurprisingly, sparked furious debate in Congress in the weeks that followed. After Thaddeus Stevens proposed a bill authorizing Lincoln to recruit 150,000 troops on January 12, 1863, Democrats unleashed a stream of racist invective. Some insisted

[32] *Liberator*, Jan. 16, 1863.
[33] FD, "Proclamation and a Negro Army," 563, 551–552, 549. Three decades earlier, Parker wrote that "all the space between the finite and the Infinite Soul is full of truth; why not open the heart and welcome the light of truth?" TP to Convers Francis, March [1839], in *LCTP*, 1: 121.

that African Americans were too cowardly to fight, others that they were too barbaric to fight effectively. Republicans in Congress responded that blacks' long history of military service undercut these racist assumptions, as did the military contributions made by runaways in Virginia, Missouri, and the Sea Islands of South Carolina in the first two years of the war. "To what place and condition are they to be returned?" asked Massachusetts congressman Benjamin Thomas. "Of course not to slavery," he answered. "No man who has ever served under our flag, whether for a day or for an hour, can be made again a slave."[34]

The New Romantics must have been thrilled finally to hear arguments, which they had been making for the past fifteen years, served up on the floor of the House. Since the early 1850s, in one fashion or another, each of them had touted the virtues of martial heroism. The New Romantics cataloged examples of black men's fighting spirit and capacity in the United States and abroad, penning fictional accounts of black revolutionaries when history's ink well went dry. Turning time and again to Byron's ode to self-emancipation, Higginson, Delany, and Douglass insisted that black resistance was essential both to the destruction of slavery and to the salvation of the enslaved themselves. Just weeks after Benjamin Thomas said that military service foreclosed any chance that a man might be returned to slavery in congressional debates, in fact, Higginson privately made much the same point in his journal. "The better soldiers they become the more they are spoiled for slaves," he wrote of the Volunteers from his Camp Saxton quarters. "I see that the latest rule proposed in the rebel Congress is to sell by auction all slaves taken in arms – but no rational man would buy them; they know too much."[35]

Years later, Higginson reflected on the profound influence that William Lloyd Garrison and his early supporters had had on his own generation of romantic reformers. "The Garrisonians were generally non-resistants, but those who believed in the physical rescue of fugitive slaves were nevertheless their pupils," he wrote. "The Garrisonians eschewed voting, but many who voted drew strength from them. The Garrisonians took little part in raising troops for the war, but the tradition of their eloquence did much to impel the army." Higginson's generous tribute reflected his debt to Garrison, whom he deemed "the original force" in the abolitionist movement.[36] It also highlights a crucial – and often overlooked – fact

---

[34] Masur, *Lincoln's First Hundred Days*, 219–238; Foner, *Fiery Trial*, 249–258; *Congressional Globe*, 37 Cong., 3 sess., 652.
[35] TWH, Journal, [February 1863], in *CWJ*, 106.
[36] TWH, "Two Antislavery Leaders," *International Review* 9 (Aug. 1880): 145.

about the latter stages of the antislavery movement that was so dramatically on display on Emancipation Day: Higginson and his fellow New Romantics had, starting in the 1850s, taken the abolitionist baton from their Garrisonian forerunners. Even Garrison himself implicitly admitted as much when he visited Charleston, South Carolina, the cradle of American slavery, in the final days of the war. According to Delany's eyewitness account, the Bostonian editor told a group of freedpeople, "I have always advocated non-resistance; but this much I say to you, *Come what will never do you submit again to slavery! Do anything; die first! But don't submit again to them – never again be slaves.*" It was fitting that the New Romantic who had preached resistance the longest was there to hear these words.[37]

In the end, Lincoln's final Emancipation Proclamation enlisted the United States in a campaign for which Delany and company had been fighting for more than a decade. Four years earlier, the New Romantics had supported and encouraged John Brown as he made war on slavery. Now, the rest of the country seemed to be catching up. "Good old John Brown was a madman at Harper's Ferry," Douglass told a cheering Cooper Union crowd in February 1863. "Two years pass away, and the nation is as mad as he. Every General and every soldier that now goes in good faith to Old Virginia, goes there for the very purpose that sent honest John Brown to Harper's Ferry."[38]

With the United States government now a part of their army, the New Romantics sought to return the favor. In the coming months, Colonel Higginson led the Volunteers in a successful invasion of Florida, proving Lincoln's gamble on black soldiers worthwhile and likely prompting the War Department to double-down on that bet. Meanwhile, Douglass and Delany took the lead in the recruitment of blacks across the North, helping to enlist thousands of free blacks in the Union army. Among Douglass's first recruits for the soon-to-be-famous Massachusetts Fifty-fourth Regiment were his sons Charles and Lewis. They were soon joined by one of Delany's sons, Touissant L'Ouverture Delany. Though excluded from such military service by the era's gender norms, Stowe participated by familial proxy through her brother James, who, like Higginson, commanded a black regiment.[39]

---

[37] Rollin, *Life and Public Service*, 195–196.
[38] FD, "Proclamation and a Negro Army," 553.
[39] Blight, *Frederick Douglass' Civil War*, 158; Sterling, *Making of an Afro-American*, 232; Hedrick, *Harriet Beecher Stowe*, 305.

While helping to fill the Massachusetts Fifty-fourth, Douglass made clear how much had changed in America since Harpers Ferry. "Can you ask for a more inviting, ennobling and soul enlarging work, than that of making one of the glorious Band who shall carry Liberty to your enslaved people?" he asked *Douglass' Monthly* readers in April 1863.[40] Byron could not have put the question any better.

[40] FD, "Why Should a Colored Man Enlist?," in *LWFD*, 3: 343–344.

Epilogue

The Reconstruction of Romantic Reform

The Civil War was a watershed moment for the New Romantics. It marked not only their highest degree of cultural authority but also the dawn of a new era for them – and for the nation. In the decades that followed the revolutionary conflict, Higginson, Douglass, Delany, and Stowe, like so many Americans, revisited and revised their most cherished beliefs and fundamental commitments. In the process, they reconstructed romantic reform in often surprising ways.

After the Civil War, Harriet Beecher Stowe continued to write. But rarely did the work that that poured forth from her pen – whether fiction or non-fiction, children's story or biblical treatise – touch directly on the topic that had consumed so much of her time and energy in the years before the conflict. This is not to say that Stowe was entirely indifferent to the plight of the nation's 4 million ex-slaves. In early 1866, she published a short story in which an antislavery character accurately predicted the racial strife that would plague the South over the next decade. Later that year, Stowe scolded her brother Henry for publicly backing Andrew Johnson's mild restoration policies.[1]

At the same time, however, she publicly broke with fellow abolitionists – including all of the other surviving New Romantics – on key issues like black suffrage and land reform. If black voting is forced on the white South, she insisted, "I do not see how any one in their senses can expect

---

[1] HBS, "The Chimney Corner for 1866: Being a Family-Talk on Reconstruction," *Atlantic Monthly* 17 (Jan. 1866): 88–100; HBS to [Henry Ward Beecher], Oct. 8, 1866, BFP, SML; Hedrick, *Harriet Beecher Stowe*, 326.

anything less than an immediate war of the races."[2] Although the novelist
counted herself a Republican, she had little time for its radical members'
ambitious designs to remake the South. Instead, she emphasized sympathy, charity, education, and forgiveness. Stowe even founded a short-lived
school for southern children – both black and white – after moving to
Jacksonville, Florida, in 1867.[3]

By the early 1870s, however, Stowe was more interested in luring
northern snowbirds to follow her to Florida than in assisting or edu-
cating former slaves. In a series of letters first published in her brother
Henry's *Christian Union* and later collected together in a book called
Palmetto-Leaves, the novelist advertised her new home as a warm and
inviting place. The St. John's River – the artery that Higginson and his
Volunteers had followed into the heart of the Confederacy – was now a
"grand water-highway through some of the most beautiful portions of
Florida," carrying "tourists, safely seated at ease on the decks of steam-
ers." In a period marred by white vigilante violence across the region,
Stowe served up an idyllic vision of southern race relations "for the benefit of those who may want to take up land in Florida." Former masters
and former slaves lived peaceably side by side, with the latter still laboring faithfully for the former in exchange for aid, advice, and now salaries
to boot.[4]

Stowe's most significant departure from her pre-war stance on race
relations emerges in the final chapter of *Palmetto-Leaves*. "Who shall do
the work for us?" asked the transplanted Yankee. Her answer: the freedman of the South, "the natural laborer of tropical regions." Black workers,
she insisted, do not shrink from toiling under the scorching summer sun
like their white counterparts. "If any thing," they work "more actively,
more cheerfully, than during the cooler months. The sun awakes all their
vigor and all their boundless jollity."[5] In *Uncle Tom's Cabin*, Stowe had
deployed romantic racialism to humanize the enslaved, thereby exposing the immorality and brutality of the institution of slavery. Twenty

2 HBS to the Duchess of Argyll, Feb. 19, 1866, in *SLL*, 27. Privately, Stowe approved of
   black enfranchisement. Gossett, *Uncle Tom's Cabin and American Culture*, 335–336.
3 HBS to [Henry Ward Beecher], Oct. 8, 1866; HBS, *Men of Our Times; or Leading Patriots
   of the Day* (Hartford, CT: Hartford Publishing Co., 1868), 567; Alex L. Murray, "Harriet
   Beecher Stowe on Racial Segregation in the Schools," *American Quarterly* 12 (Winter
   1960): 518–519; *SSL*, 343; Reynolds, *Mightier than the Sword*, 172–173.
4 HBS, *Palmetto-Leaves* (Boston: James R. Osgood, 1873), 247, 230–231; Edward J. Blum,
   Reforging the White Republic: Race, Religion, and American Nationalism, 1865–1898
   (Baton Rouge: Louisiana State University Press, 2007), 100–101.
5 HBS, *Palmetto-Leaves*, 279, 283, 280.

years later, Stowe put racial assumptions about black character to an altogether different use. African Americans' innate simplicity, piety, and cheerful nature, she believed, were a bulwark against discontent among the South's laboring class.

This harmonious vision of southern race relations reflected the author's sense of how much had changed since the Civil War. At a lavish garden birthday party that Houghton Mifflin threw for the novelist in 1882, for instance, Stowe urged a crowd of leading New England reformers and literati not to lose sight of the great victories that had been won over the last thirty years:

> If any of you have doubt ... about this world, ... just remember that this great sorrow of slavery has gone, gone by forever. I see it every day at the South. I walk about there and see the lowly cabins. I see these people growing richer and richer. I see men very happy in their lowly lot.... They are not perfect, but have their faults.... [T]hey do know how to enjoy themselves – a great deal more than you do.[6]

Uncle Tom's suffering, it seems, had died with the institution of slavery.

One cannot help but wonder what the guests at Stowe's birthday party made of this treacly tea. Had Frederick Douglass been able to attend, he certainly would have found her words difficult to stomach. But her fellow New Romantic sent a letter of regret, as did a host of others, including Higginson. At least one invitee who was unable to make it, Joel Chandler Harris, surely would have enjoyed what Stowe was serving up that afternoon.[7] After all, her rosy picture of postbellum race relations dovetailed neatly with the romanticized vision of southern life in Harris's wildly successful *Uncle Remus: His Songs and His Sayings.* Featuring nostalgic conversations between an avuncular ex-slave and a young white boy, Harris's 1880 collection was among the most popular examples of the plantation school of literature that emerged in the late nineteenth century. Along with Virginian Thomas Nelson Page and a host of imitators, Georgia-born Harris used the tropes of sentimental fiction to recast the Old South as a place of moonlight-and-magnolia romance and loving bonds between master and slave. And Harris, for his part, believed he was following a trail that Stowe had blazed. "I owe a great deal, in one way or another, to the author of Uncle Tom's Cabin," he told Stowe in 1882.

---

[6] HBS, quoted in "The Birthday Garden Party to Harriet Beecher Stowe," *Atlantic Monthly Supplement* 50 (Aug. 1882): 10; Gossett, *Uncle Tom's Cabin and American Culture*, 337.

[7] "Birthday Garden Party," 12–13, 16.

Harris counted Stowe's novel a "wonderful defense of slavery as it existed in the South," arguing that "all the worthy and beautiful characters in her book ... are the products of the system" she purported to condemn.[8]

Although Harris's against-the-grain reading of *Uncle Tom's Cabin* too easily dismisses the novel's abolitionist message, it nonetheless reveals how sentimental appeals and romantic racialist assumptions could be put to conservative ends. So, too, do the stage depictions of *Uncle Tom's Cabin* that proliferated after the Civil War. While some of the Tom shows were true to the novel's antislavery heart, many others joined the swelling chorus of Lost Cause apologists and plantation school writers by portraying slaves as happy-go-lucky figures who spent their days singing, dancing, and faithfully serving their kind masters. Tom was turned into an elderly, passive version of Stowe's original character, while Topsy supplied "low comedy" with ridiculous songs and vulgar antics. Meanwhile, broadsides for Tom plays represented its black characters as dehumanized and grotesque figures, and advertised shows featuring "18 Georgia Plantation shouters" and the "Original Whangdoodle Pickaninny Band ON THE OLD PLANTATION!"[9]

In the wake of the Civil War, then, the nation's most influential antislavery novelist came to sound like an Old South apologist, while stage renditions of her most famous story offered up demeaning caricatures that evoked the worst features of blackface minstrelsy. And Stowe was not alone. In the decades after the conflict, Higginson and Delany also found common ground with the planter class.

One year before Stowe's garden party, for instance, Colonel Higginson headed back down to South Carolina for the unveiling of a monument to commemorate the Revolutionary War Battle of Cowpens. As he addressed the crowd that had gathered in Spartanburg on a May afternoon, Higginson's thoughts wandered from America's war for independence to what he called "a later strife, now happily passed by." Twenty years after the shelling of Fort Sumter, Higginson hoped that the North

---

[8] Blight, *Race and Reunion*, 225–229; Grace Elizabeth Hale, *Making Whiteness: The Culture of Segregation in the South, 1890–1940* (New York: Pantheon Books, 1998), 52–59; Gossett, *Uncle Tom's Cabin in American Culture*, 349; Joel Chandler Harris to HBS, June 20, 1882, in "Birthday Garden Party," 13; Harris, *Uncle Remus: His Songs and His Sayings; The Folk-Lore of the Old Plantation* (New York: D. Appleton, 1881), 4; Harris, "The Negro as the South Sees Him," *Saturday Evening Post* **176** (Jan. 2, 1904): 1.

[9] Reynolds, *Mightier than the Sword*, 177–183; Anne E. Marshall, "The 1906 *Uncle Tom's Cabin* Law and the Politics of Race and Memory in Early-Twentieth-Century Kentucky," *Journal of the Civil War Era* **1** (Sept. 2011): 368–393; Gossett, *Uncle Tom's Cabin and American Culture*, 339, 379–380 (quotation 379).

and South might focus on healing "the terrible wounds of the later contest," facing "side by side the new social problems of the new age." Each side had sinned and Americans needed to, in modern parlance, put the blame game behind them.[10]

Higginson's Cowpens speech reflected the reconciliationist vision of Civil War memory that took hold, north and south, by the 1880s. Tales of intersectional romances between southern belles and Yankee soldiers – whether real life or imagined – became increasingly popular in newspapers and magazines. Meanwhile, a new tone emerged at the cemeteries where Americans had annually gathered to commemorate the victims of the war since it ended. Early on, Decoration Day ceremonies assumed a partisan cast. Unionists emphasized the sacrifices made to keep the nation together and end the scourge of slavery, while ex-Confederates forged the Lost Cause tradition, which honored Confederate valor while disassociating the war from the institution of slavery. A decade after the war, however, northerners and southerners began marking Decoration Day together. Stressing the shared bravery of the combatants, Union and Confederate, and downplaying the issue of slavery, these ceremonies transformed the ritual into a form of sectional reconciliation.[11]

In 1904, Higginson offered a Decoration Day address that again fit squarely within this reconciliationist vein. This time he spoke to a largely northern crowd of students and veterans at Harvard's Memorial Hall, a building built to honor students who had given their lives for the Union. The New Romantic thought the time had come for his alma mater to acknowledge the bravery of its Confederate veterans too. He looked forward to a day "when the names of other Harvard graduates who fought equally well against us ... find their place beside those already inscribed

---

[10] TWH, "Address of Thomas Wentworth Higginson, at the Celebration of the Battle of Cowpens at Spartanburg, S.C., May 11, 1881," Bound Pamphlets, Vol. 1, TWHP, HL.

[11] Nina Silber, *The Romance of Reunion: Northerners and the South, 1865–1900* (Chapel Hill: University of North Carolina Press, 1993), 39–86; Blight, *Race and Reunion*, 64–97, 313; Gaines M. Foster, *Ghost of the Confederacy: Defeat, the Lost Cause, and the Emergence of the New South, 1865–1913* (New York: Oxford University Press, 1987), 66. For studies arguing that Civil War reconciliation was never complete, see William Blair, *Cities of the Dead: Contesting the Memory of the Civil War in the South, 1865–1914* (Chapel Hill: University of North Carolina Press, 2003); John R. Neff, *Honoring the Civil War Dead: Commemoration and the Problem of Reconciliation* (Lawrence: University Press of Kansas, 2005); M. Keith Harris, "Slavery, Emancipation, and Veterans of the Union Cause: Commemorating Freedom in the Era of Reconciliation, 1885–1915," *Civil War History* 53 (Sept. 2007): 264–290; and Caroline E. Janney, *Remembering the Civil War: Reunion and the Limits of Reconciliation* (Chapel Hill: University of North Carolina Press, 2013).

in this hall." The nearly eighty-year-old Higginson also went out of his way to insist that southerners had fought for a cause worthy of respect. "We now see that they were not separated by a mere quarrel, not yet by an institution, even that of slavery, but by two principles of government on which men might honestly differ in opinion – the difference between state rights and the sovereignty of the nation." A half-century earlier, Higginson had yoked martial heroism to the antislavery mission, touting the exploits of revolutionaries like Nat Turner and Denmark Vesey. Now, he refashioned this romantic ideal into a balm for healing and forgetting.[12]

Higginson had not always been so sympathetic toward sectional reconciliation, nor so willing to disassociate the Civil War from its fundamental cause. In the fall of 1865, he had denounced Andrew Johnson's restoration plan as too lenient. Higginson was also a forceful proponent of black voting rights and southern land reform in the early years of Reconstruction.[13]

Eventually, however, the Transcendentalist became disenchanted with the Republican-led effort to remake the South. He even publicly praised Rutherford B. Hayes's controversial decision to bring Reconstruction to a quick conclusion after the Bargain of 1877 – in which Democrats agreed behind closed doors to allow Hayes to assume the presidency in exchange for the removal of federal troops from the Louisiana and South Carolina statehouses. Having once gone to war to secure the freedom of black Americans, Higginson, by this point, was preaching peace, however hollow. "There is one thing more important than the immediate welfare of the colored people of South Carolina and Louisiana," he wrote, "and that is, to maintain the right of each State in the Union to manage its own local affairs in its own way, well or badly, so long as the peace is kept and the Constitution obeyed."[14]

---

[12] TWH, *Address on Decoration Day in Sanders Theatre, Harvard Memorial Hall, May 30, 1904*, in author's possession; W. Scott Poole, "Memory and the Abolitionist Heritage: Thomas Wentworth Higginson and the Uncertain Meaning of the Civil War," *Civil War History* 51 (June 2005): 202–217.

[13] *New-York Tribune*, Nov. 24, 1869; Edelstein, *Strange Enthusiasm*, 299–300; McPherson, *Struggle for Equality*, 337–338, 411; James M. McPherson, *The Abolitionist Legacy: From Reconstruction to the NAACP* (Princeton, NJ: Princeton University Press, 1975), 56–58.

[14] Edelstein, *Strange Enthusiasm*, 330–335; McPherson, *Abolitionist Legacy*, 81–82, 89–91; Butler, *Critical Americans*, 200–201; TWH, *Cheerful Yesterdays*, 350–351; *New-York Tribune*, May 16, 1876; TWH, "Miss Forten on the Southern Question," *Woman's Journal*, Dec. 30, 1876, reprinted in *WTH*, 124–1267; TWH, "Letter to the Editor," *New-York Tribune*, Apr. 28, 1877, in *WTH*, 128–129 (quotation 129).

By the 1880s, Higginson had moved on to a new social cause: good government. Worried that government malfeasance posed a greater threat to the nation than an unreconstructed South, Higginson split from the Republican Party. He even ran for Congress as a Democrat on a platform of civil service reform and tariff reduction in 1888.[15]

This move led to a dustup with longtime friend and colleague Douglass. "While I have a warm and grateful appreciation of the valuable services rendered by Colonel Higginson in the old fugitive slave times, and would gladly vote for him as Colonel Higginson the abolitionist," wrote Douglass in a public letter, "no power could ever make me give him a vote as a Democrat." The black reformer judged his white counterpart's defection from the Republican Party as a betrayal not only of "that political organization, but to the cause of liberty itself." Higginson responded sharply to Douglass's critique in a late October speech in Lexington. "My good friend, Fred Douglass, who began his life by running away from a slaveowner, seems to have now convinced himself that he is a slaveowner, and every one who differs from him must be brought back," he declared. Several local newspapers rallied to the former minister's side after this speech, but his clunky comparison no doubt cost the Democratic candidate votes in Boston's black community and he lost the election.[16]

This defeat stung, but it also left Higginson free to return to the literary and cultural pursuits that he deemed more important at this stage in his life. Before the war, Higginson had tried to solve the Emersonian dilemma – how to reconcile self-culture and social reform – by waging war against slavery. But now, with slavery gone, it no longer seemed so easy to combine self-culture and social reform. Higginson no longer "crave[d] action," as he once put it, nor did he still think that literary pursuits should take a back seat to political and social engagement.[17] Quite the opposite, he argued in his seminal 1867 essay "A Plea for Culture" that educated citizens like him had become too focused on "public life." This minister-*cum*-essayist-*cum*-militant abolitionist concluded that Americans were asking themselves to wear too many hats.[18]

---

[15] Edelstein, *Strange Enthusiasm*, 368–377; *New York Times*, Sept. 26, 1888.
[16] FD to B. R. Wilson, Oct. 13, 1888, in the *Washington Post*, Oct. 19, 1888; *Washington Post*, Oct. 19, 1888; *Cambridge Chronicle*, Oct. 27, 1888; *Boston Herald*, Oct. 16, 1888, in the *New York Times*, Oct. 21, 1888; *Boston Daily Globe*, Oct. 18, 1888; *Boston Daily Globe*, Oct. 24, 1888; *Boston Daily Globe*, Nov. 4, 1888; Edelstein, *Strange Enthusiasm*, 378–381.
[17] TWH, quoted in Mary T. Higginson, *Thomas Wentworth Higginson*, 69.
[18] TWH, "A Plea for Culture," *Atlantic Monthly* 19 (Jan. 1867): 34.

Recasting his perfectionist impulse, Higginson planned to spend his twilight years – decades, as it turned out – on intellectual exploration, artistic expression, and scientific discovery. He started working on his first novel, publishing essays on literature, religion, and culture, and attending meetings of the Radical Club, a group of Boston-area elite who gathered to discuss religious and literary topics. The New Romantic, in short, became a genteel man of letters.

This new preoccupation with high culture was not, to be fair, as effete or elitist as some twentieth-century critics have suggested. Higginson did not think that intellectuals and artists should retreat into rarified "dens of culture," but rather spread knowledge and insight as widely as possible. Joining with a small circle of liberal reformers that included Charles Eliot Norton, James Russell Lowell, and George William Curtis, the New Romantic hoped "to saturate the mass with culture, and give a career to genius when it comes." To this end, Higginson wrote more than a hundred articles and editorials for newspapers and periodicals, ranging from highbrow journals such as the *Nation* and the *Atlantic Monthly* to popular women's magazines like *Harper's Bazaar*, as well as some twenty histories, biographies, and books of essays.[19]

Still, when it came to social issues, Higginson was a far cry from his antebellum self. Once the most radical man in John Brown's ear, he had become, by the turn of the twentieth century, a champion of Booker T. Washington's accommodationist platform. Although Higginson never went as far as Stowe in terms of embracing a rosy vision of postwar southern race relations, he even reached out to plantation school author Thomas Nelson Page. "I constantly urge my colored friends to be peaceful & hopeful and leave the future to settle matters for itself under the influence of higher education all round," Higginson wrote Page in 1905.[20] Having called one year earlier for Union and Confederate veterans to bury the hatchet at Harvard, he made a similar gesture of reconciliation to an author who idealized the social institution Higginson had done so much to destroy.

Fellow New Romantic Martin Robison Delany, who followed Higginson to the South Carolina Sea Islands, likewise supported radical

[19] Edelstein, *Strange Enthusiasm*, 308–318, 336–337, 374; Butler, *Critical Americans*, 128–131, 262–268 (quotation 130); TWH, "A Plea for Culture," 35–37 (quotation 36).
[20] Edelstein, *Strange Enthusiasm*, 381–392; TWH, in the *Boston Evening Transcript*, Mar. 10, 1899, reprinted as "Southern Barbarity" in *WTH*, 136–137; TWH to Thomas Nelson Page, May 3, 1905, Box 5, Thomas Nelson Page Papers, David M. Rubenstein Rare Book and Manuscript Library, Duke University, Durham, NC.

Reconstruction just after the Civil War only to embrace a more chastened approach to reform later on. Appointed sub-assistant commissioner of the Freedmen's Bureau in Beaufort as the war ended, Delany spent the next three years promoting economic uplift among local freedpeople through federal land distribution and what he called "a domestic triple alliance" of northern capitalists, southern white landowners, and black laborers. By working together and splitting the profits, Delany believed that these three groups could rejuvenate the southern economy and put the region's slave past behind it.[21]

Politically, the black major staked out more moderate positions than many fellow reformers. He watched approvingly as Sea Island freedmen flooded the polls in 1868 and his displays of black pride continued to unsettle his critics. The *Charleston News and Courier*, for instance, reported that he delivered an 1871 Emancipation Day address in "his usual black-man-better-than-any-other-man style."[22] Yet Delany also worried that many of the newly enfranchised citizens were not prepared for their new role in the body politic and he harbored even greater concerns about whether African Americans were "*ready*" or "*qualified*" to serve in high political office.[23]

Delany eventually lost faith in the Republican Party and its Reconstruction efforts in South Carolina, where he had settled. Like Higginson a decade later, the black major gave up on the idea that the party could be reformed from within and, instead, joined his longtime adversaries in the name of "good government." In 1874, he ran for lieutenant-governor of South Carolina on the Independent Republican ticket, which was supported by most of the state's white conservatives. Well aware that this was a controversial position – especially for a "John Brown Abolitionist," as he called himself before one Charleston crowd – Delany nonetheless held that the state's black citizenry needed to put old party conflicts behind them.[24]

[21] Ullman, *Martin R. Delany*, 366–370; MRD, "Prospects of the Freedmen of Hilton Head," *New South*, [1865], in Rollin, *Life and Public Services*, 230–242; MRD to the *New South*, Dec. 7, 1865, in Rollin, *Life and Public Services*, 242.

[22] Rollin, *Life and Public Services*, 279; Sterling, *Making of an Afro-American*, 277; MRD, *University Pamphlets*, 415; *Charleston News and Courier*, Jan. 3, 1871.

[23] MRD to Henry Highland Garnet, July 27, 1867, in the *New-York Tribune*, Aug. 6, 1867, in *MDR*, 410; *New York Times*, Aug. 21, 1867; MRD to the *Christian Recorder*, Sept. 27, 1867, in the *Christian Recorder*, Oct. 12, 1867; *Charleston Daily Republican*, June 24, 1870.

[24] *Charleston News and Courier*, Sept. 22, 1874; Ullman, *Martin R. Delany*, 449–455; *Charleston News and Courier*, Oct. 2, 3, 7, 16, 1874.

The New Romantic lost the 1874 election, but his drift away from
Radical Republicanism continued unabated. Delany indicted the
Republican Party for "every species of infamy, however atrocious, private and public, bare faced and in open daylight," maintaining that it was
up to South Carolina blacks to obliterate "this disgrace by the clearing of
our State Government of the pests who have heretofore held the rule in
their power."[25] To that end, Delany endorsed the Democratic gubernato-
rial candidate, Wade Hampton III, against incumbent Republican Daniel
H. Chamberlain, in the 1876 election. Scion of a wealthy planter family
and a Confederate war hero, Hampton ran a campaign that promised
to stamp out corruption. Reaching out to black citizens, he pledged to
uphold the Thirteenth, Fourteenth, and Fifteenth Amendments and put
an end to white vigilante violence. Delany took him at his word. Evoking
his decision to abandon emigration and join the U.S. army a decade earlier, Delany declared Reconstruction a failure and himself a Democratic
convert.[26]

Despite Hampton's public pleas for peace, many of his supporters –
especially the red-flannel clad rifle club members known as the Red Shirts
– intimidated, harassed, and sometimes violently assaulted Republican
candidates and black voters across the state that summer and fall. The
1876 campaign ended with both Republicans and Democrats claiming
victory in the races for governor and control of the General Assembly.
Each party quickly assembled their own legislature in Columbia and
the U.S. army was the only force preventing blood in the streets. After
President Hayes ordered the removal of federal troops from the state-
house in Columbia the following spring, Democrats took control of the
General Assembly and Hampton assumed the governorship. Governor
Hampton repaid Delany for his support by appointing him to the office
of trial justice in Charleston, but the Democratic honeymoon did not
last long. Before the decade's end, Hampton left for the U.S. Senate and
Delany was out of a job.[27]

---

[25] *Charleston Independent*, Aug. 21, 1875, quoted in Ullman, *Martin R. Delany*,
462–463.
[26] Sterling, *Making of an Afro-American*, 310; *Charleston News and Courier*, Sept. 27,
1876. On Hampton, see Robert K. Ackerman, *Wade Hampton III* (Columbia: University
of South Carolina Press, 2007).
[27] Michael M. Fitzgerald, *Splendid Failure: Postwar Reconstruction in the American South*
(Chicago: Ivan R. Dee, 2007), 204–207; Eric Foner, *Reconstruction: America's Unfinished
Revolution, 1863–1877* (New York: Harper & Row, 1988), 575–582; Ullman, *Martin R.
Delany*, 497–498; Adeleke, *Without Regard to Race*, 165–166.

By this point, he was dreaming again of Africa. As states across the South began dismantling the vestiges of Reconstruction in the late 1870s, many southern blacks had started looking for a new home. Twenty thousand Exodusters left for the western United States in the last two years of the decade. Others looked east. Delany became a member of the board of directors of the Liberian Exodus Joint Stock Steamship Company, which, in response to the menial position blacks were being asked to play in the region, raised money to support black migration to Africa. The New Romantic helped secure land in Liberia and raise money to purchase the steamship *Azor*, which set sail from Charleston with more than two hundred passengers in March 1878. Ultimately, however, the Exodus Company struggled with funding and, despite Delany's efforts as head of the Committee on Finance, it was forced to sell the *Azor* at a huge loss.[28]

The born-again emigrationist did not give up hope on getting to Africa. In 1880, Delany twice wrote to the secretary of the American Colonization Society about his recent efforts to secure a federal job, one that would pay him enough money to eventually move his family to Africa, which he referred to as "the field of my destined labor." Frederick Douglass had secured a position as marshal of the District Columbia, Delany explained, would not a similar role – say, the doorkeeper of the U.S. Senate – be available for him? Apparently not, as Delany spent the next few years trying in vain to acquire a federal appointment.[29]

Amid his campaign to find a job, Delany attended a banquet in honor of Douglass in Washington, DC. It took place on January 1, 1883 – the twentieth anniversary of Emancipation Day – and attracted the nation's leading black citizens, including former U.S. senator Blanche K. Bruce, and congressmen Robert Smalls and John R. Lynch. After speeches by Bruce and Douglass, distinguished guests exchanged a series of toasts – forty-one in all. Salutes went up for Douglass, Garrison, and Stowe as well as the black author, the black soldier, Howard University, and many

---

[28] Heather Cox Richardson, *West from Appomattox: The Reconstruction of America After the Civil War* (New Haven, CT: Yale University Press, 2007), 225; *The Liberian Exodus: First Voyage of the Azor. Liberia a Delightful Country. Climate, Soil, and Productions. Character of the People in Liberia; and How They Live. Full Information of the Exodus Movement* (Charleston, SC: W. J. Oliver's Print, 1978), 8; Bernard E. Powers Jr., *Black Charlestonians: A Social History, 1822–1885* (Fayetteville: University of Arkansas Press, 1994), 258; Sterling, *Making of an Afro-American*, 319–322.

[29] Miller, *Search for a Black Nationality*, 265–266; *MDR*, 459–462 (quotation 461); MRD to William Coppinger, Dec. 18, 1880, in *MDR*, 484–485.

other subjects. Still dreaming of Africa, Delany predictably toasted "the Republic of Liberia." He never made it back to the continent, however, dying in Xenia, Ohio, two years later.[30]

Like Higginson and Stowe, Delany struggled to find an ideological home in postwar America. If ambivalence about how to solve the problem of slavery plagued these romantic reformers in the decade before the Civil War, then ambivalence about what role they should play in the emancipation and Reconstruction processes – or even if they should play a role at all – dogged them in its aftermath. Douglass, in comparison, was the picture of consistency in this period. As his fellow New Romantics bounced back and forth between different positions on Reconstruction, the Republican Party, and southern race relations, Douglass tirelessly advocated for former slaves and the party that had helped emancipate them. Perhaps this had something to do with the fact that Douglass, alone, had once been a slave. Emancipation had freed white abolitionists like Stowe and Higginson to follow different pursuits, despite their lingering sympathy for ex-slaves. In the meantime, free black Delany, though a strong advocate for South Carolina freedpeople through the late 1860s, eventually fell prey to his elitist inclinations and allied himself not with emancipated slaves but rather their former masters. Not so for Douglass, who kept the interests of the nation's millions of freedpeople at the forefront of his mind.

Douglass hounded Republican congressmen to back radical measures, like black suffrage and land reform. When early Reconstruction accomplishments – the Civil Rights Bill, the Freedmen's Bureau Bill, and the Fourteenth Amendment – did not meet the challenges that ex-Confederates mounted south of the Mason-Dixon Line, he became a forceful proponent for a thoroughgoing reconstruction of the South. In 1869, Douglass outlined a plan in which Congress would buy southern land that could be sold cheaply to ex-slaves. Years later, the New Romantic counted the failure to put this plan – or a similar one – into action as the central failure of Reconstruction.[31]

If land reform was Reconstruction's great defeat to Douglass, then black suffrage was the era's great triumph in his mind. "You did not expect to see it; I did not expect to see it; no man living did expect to live to see

---

[30] *Washington Bee*, Jan. 6, 1883; *New York Globe*, Jan. 6, 1883; Blight, *Race and Reunion*, 301–303; Ullman, *Martin R. Delany*, 515.

[31] FD, *Life and Times*, 466–476, 482–483, 613; Blight, *Frederick Douglass' Civil War*, 190–194, 200–202.

this day," he told an Albany crowd in April 1870. But see it they did: "The black man is free, the black man is a citizen, the black men is enfranchised, and this by the organic law of the land." Two decades earlier, Douglass had put his faith in the antislavery potential of the Constitution. Now, with the Reconstruction Amendments, the Constitution he had imagined had become a reality.[32]

The Fifteenth Amendment reinforced Douglass's commitment to the Republican Party. In the 1850s, he had moved easily between political coalitions, backing parties ranging from the Free Soil Party to the Radical Abolitionist Party in different moments. No more. As he announced in October 1870 at a meeting of the New York Republican Association, "I am a Republican, a radical Republican, a Black Republican, a Republican dyed in the wool, and for one I want the Republican party to live as long as I do." This longtime proponent of perfectionist self-help and the virtues of self-made men began placing greater weight on party identity. "Men are important," he opined, "but parties are incomparably more important." And the Republican Party was the only thing that stood "between the Negro and murder."[33] Thus, Douglass wrote in 1871, "I had better put a pistol to my head and blow my brains out, than to lend myself in any wise to the destruction or defeat of the Republican party." Even as the nation retreated from Reconstruction a decade later – developments for which many young blacks blamed his party – Douglass did not lose faith in the Republicans.[34]

For his party allegiance, Douglass would be amply rewarded. He was appointed secretary to a federal commission sent to Santo Domingo (today the Dominican Republic) to investigate the possibility of annexing the republic and later served as marshal of the District of Columbia. This highly visible office required Senate approval, and so the former slave became the first black man to earn congressional confirmation for a federal office. Four years later, when President James Garfield turned the role of marshal over to a personal friend, Douglass was chosen as the District of Columbia's recorder of deeds. In 1899, he was appointed U.S.

[32] McFeeley, *Frederick Douglass*, 272; FD, "At Last, At Last, The Black Man Has a Future: An Address Delivered in Albany, New York, on 22 April 1870," in *FDP*, 4: 266.

[33] FD, "I Speak to You as an American Citizen: An Address Delivered in Washington, D.C., on 15 October 1870," in *FDP*, 4: 275; FD, "Great Bodies Move Slowly: An Address Delivered in New York, New York, on 25 October 1880," in *FDP*, 4: 582; FD, quoted in *LWFD*, 4: 72.

[34] FD to C. M. Clay, July 26, 1871, in *LWFD*, 4: 252; McFeeley, *Frederick Douglass*, 314–317; FD to Private Dalzell, Oct. 3, 1883, in the *New York Times*, Oct. 6, 1883.

minister to Haiti, a post he occupied for two years before leaving public service for good.[35]

As a Republican Party insider and operative, Douglass found himself fighting rearguard actions against former allies on several fronts, perhaps none as important as Civil War memory. In the decades after the conflict, ex-Confederates like Jubal Early did their best to glorify the Old South by promoting their Lost Cause interpretation of the war. And, as we have seen, they occasionally got help from unlikely sources, including Higginson. Douglass, by contrast, became a leading proponent of what historian David Blight calls "the emancipationist vision" of Civil War memory, which emphasized that slavery's central role in the conflict must not be forgotten.[36]

Douglass's commemorative addresses took direct aim at the sentiments that were served up across the South – and eventually the nation – at such events. Watching Confederate heroes like Robert E. Lee and Stonewall Jackson memorialized from the lectern, in print, and soon in stone, he could not help but question the nation's values. Lost Cause apologists, lamented Douglass, threw justifications for the Civil War out by the handful, hoping that one would stick. They said the war was a fight for independence, or liberty, or the right of self-governance, but, he was quick to point out, the South had enjoyed all of these things since the dawn of the republic. Instead, Douglass repeatedly reminded his listeners that the Confederacy went to war to defend one thing: the institution of slavery. Lost Cause proponents must not be allowed to whitewash the peculiar institution, or to minimize its connection to the Civil War, argued Douglass. "There was a right side and a wrong side in the late war, which no sentiment ought to cause us to forget," he insisted, "and while to-day we should have malice toward none, and charity toward all, it is no part of our duty to confound right with wrong, or loyalty with treason."[37]

Douglass was particularly dismayed by northern complicity in the Blue-Gray reconciliations of the late nineteenth century. "I do not hold, as some of our patriotic fellow-citizens just now seem, in their all-bounding charity to hold, that forgetfulness of the past is the absolute duty of

[35] McFeeley, *Frederick Douglass*, 276–293, 306, 334–335; FD, *Life and Times* (1892), 644–646; Stauffer, *Giants*, 310.

[36] Blight, *Race and Reunion*, 78–84, 2 (quotation 2).

[37] Blight, *Frederick Douglass' Civil War*, 222–233; FD, "We Must Not Abandon the Observance of Decoration Day," in *FDP*, 5: 49, 46–47; FD, "There Was a Right Side in the Late War," in *FDP*, 4: 481, 486, 489–491 (quotation 491).

the present and the sum of all human virtues," he confessed. Most disheartening of all were the olive branches offered by longtime allies like Higginson. The last decade has been a time "of reaction and darkness," he told a fellow reformer in 1892. "The air has been filled with reconciliations between those who fought for freedom and those who have fought for slavery." Douglass lamented that reunion between North and South has served to "morally obscur[e] the difference between right and wrong." It is not hard to imagine what Douglass would have said had he survived to hear Higginson's 1904 Decoration Day address at Harvard.[38]

Although Douglass did not hesitate to speak out against Lost Cause propaganda and the culture of reconciliation, he embraced a more measured approach to reform in the postbellum era. Once a John Brown abolitionist, in Delany's fine phrase, Douglass downplayed his early militancy and, more often than not, publicly renounced violence as an avenue for social change. In 1880 he called Republicans who voted Democratic traitors "to the cause of liberty" who deserved to drown at sea. But Douglass quickly – and explicitly – reminded his audience that he was not "for using any violence."[39] Two years later, he omitted a line pledging to support slave insurrection when feasible from a letter he reproduced in his third autobiography. Even after one of the great political disappointments of the late nineteenth century – the Supreme Court's 1883 ruling that the Civil Rights Act of 1875 was unconstitutional – Douglass urged prudence. For all of his fury over the decision, the black reformer told a large Washington, DC, audience, the Supreme Court decision must not be used to undermine the nation's faith in its public servants. "We should never forget, that, whatever may be the incidental mistakes or misconduct of rulers, government is better than anarchy, and patient reform is better than violent revolution," said Douglass, who, it is worth remembering, still occupied a federal office.[40]

In this way, Douglass was not so different from his fellow New Romantics, all of whom trimmed their sails in the postbellum era. As close a thing to a political insider as was possible for a black American in

[38] FD, "Thoughts and Recollections of the Anti-Slavery Conflict," n.d., p. 1, FDP, LOC, http://memory.loc.gov/cgi-bin/ampage?collId=mfd&fileName=30/30004/30004page. db&recNum=0&itemLink=/ammem/doughtml/dougFolder5.html&linkText=7; FD to Marshall Pierce, Feb. 18, 1892, Frederick Douglass Papers, MSRC.

[39] FD, "Great Bodies Move Slowly," 583.

[40] FD, letter, Oct. 31, 1859, in the *New York Herald*, Nov. 4, 1859; FD, *Life and Times*, 381; Stauffer, *Giants*, 31; FD, in "This Decision Has Humbled the Nation: An Address Delivered in Washington, D.C., on 22 October 1883," in *FDP*, 5: 113.

the nineteenth century, he tempered his language, his methods, even some
of his demands. But, as Douglass insisted at a surprise birthday party held
at the Bethel Literary Society in Washington, DC, in 1889, he remained
at heart a perfectionist. "During nearly fifty years of my life I have been
an unflinching, unflagging and uncompromising advocate and defender
of the oppressed," he said. "When the slave was a slave I demanded his
emancipation, and when he was free, I demanded his perfect freedom –
all the safeguards of freedom. In whatever else I may have failed, in this
I have not failed." Douglass died six years later, not long after advising a
young black student who came to visit him to follow one course of action
in life: "Agitate! Agitate! Agitate!" Unsurprisingly, this was precisely the
course of action prescribed by Higginson in a pamphlet a half-century earlier. Urging Worcester men to support the Free Democratic Party in 1852,
the Transcendentalist minister concluded, "Agitate, agitate, agitate."[41]

Romantic reform, in the end, did not die with the Civil War, as some scholars have suggested.[42] Yet, as was the case for so many boys in blue and
gray, that great conflict and its aftermath fundamentally altered the character of reform in the United States. After four bloody years of fighting –
which left hundreds of thousands of Americans dead, and millions more
injured in one way or another – perfectionist striving seemed naïve and
outmoded. Likewise, the abolition of slavery and the rise of a major political party that was willing to work, at least for a time, to secure social and
political rights for former slaves indicated that immediatism, too, was a
dated approach in postwar America. Appeals to resist manmade statutes
in the name of God's higher law gave way to amending the Constitution
and patiently working through the political system. Boundlessness, to use
John Higham's formulation, gave way to consolidation.[43]

Meanwhile, with the ascendance of Republican rule in the
Reconstruction South, violent resistance to political authority became
almost exclusively the provenance of ex-Confederates and other proponents of redemption and white rule. Although romanticism was nothing
new to the antebellum South, it was embraced with particular fervor by
Lost Cause mythmakers. Eventually, these southern writers, historians,
veterans, and propagandists joined with northern counterparts – even
abolitionists like Higginson and Stowe – to turn romantic ideas and

[41] FD, quoted in *LWFD*, 4: 113, 149; Stauffer, *Giants*, 314; TWH, "To the Young Men of
    Worcester County, 1852," Bound Pamphlets, Vol. 2, TWHP, HL.
[42] Fredrickson, *Inner Civil War*, 216; Menand, *Metaphysical Club*, x.
[43] Higham, "From Boundlessness to Consolidation," 158.

tropes into a regressive force in America. Once tools of liberation, romantic racialism and martial heroism became weapons of sectional reconciliation and black oppression.

It would be a mistake, however, to end this story on such a dispiriting note. After all, a frank acknowledgement of the shortcomings and failures of the New Romantics and their ideas during and after Reconstruction cannot efface all that they had done up to that point. Douglass, Delany, Higginson, Stowe, and Parker played a central role in the most important social movement of their day, if not any other. They helped bring on – and shape – a war that freed millions of people and ended a brutal institution that had dogged the nation since its founding. In his remarks on the twentieth anniversary of Emancipation Day in 1883, Douglass captured the magnitude of these accomplishments better than anyone else:

Until this day, twenty years ago, there was a vast incubus on the breast of the American people, which baffled all the wisdom of American statesmanship. Slavery, the sum of all villanies, like a vulture was gnawing at the heart of the Republic; until this day there stretched away behind us an awful chasm of darkness and despair more than two centuries…. We do well to commemorate this day. It was the first gray streak of morning after a long and troubled night of all abounding horrors.[44]

There would be more darkness to come. But Douglass could take comfort in the fact that he and his colleagues had helped to inaugurate that first streak of dawn. In the process, the New Romantics also pioneered a reform sensibility that inspired activists during the second Reconstruction a century later. While Martin Luther King Jr. paraphrased Theodore Parker by reminding audiences in the 1950s and 1960s that "the arc of the moral universe is long but it bends toward justice," civil rights leaders such as Julian Bond, Stanley Wise, and Stokely Carmichael cited Douglass's words and actions. It is little wonder that when the black fraternity Alpha Phi Alpha announced its commitment to Black Power in August 1966 it followed in the footsteps of Douglass, Delany, and Higginson by invoking Byron's romantic catechism that "to be free themselves must strike the blow."[45]

---

[44] FD, "Freedom Has Brought Duties: An Address Delivered in Washington, D.C., on 1 January 1883," in *FDP*, 5: 56–57.

[45] Martin Luther King Jr., quoted in Cohen, *Arc of the Moral Universe*, 17; Taylor Branch, *At Cannan's Edge: American in the King Years, 1965–1968* (New York: Simon & Schuster, 2006), 456, 608, 612; Alpha Phi Alpha statement, Aug. 1966, quoted in Mary L. Dudziak, *Exporting American Dreams: Thurgood Marshall's African Journey* (Princeton, NJ: Princeton University Press, 2008), 135.

Index

Page locators followed by "n" indicate footnotes. Those followed by "f" indicate illustrations.

CPSIA information can be obtained
at www.ICGtesting.com
Printed in the USA
LVHW03s0322080818
586338LV00001B/231/P